PENGUIN BOOKS

THE PENGUIN BOOK OF FOOD AND DRINK

Paul Levy was born in Lexington, Kentucky. He writes on the arts for the *Wall Street Journal*, and on food and wine for *You* magazine in the *Mail on Sunday*. He is a Fellow of the Royal Society of Literature and his collection of writings, *Out to Lunch*, was published by Penguin in 1988. He lives in Oxfordshire with his wife and two daughters.

The Penguin Book of
Food and Drink

Edited by Paul Levy

PENGUIN BOOKS

PENGUIN BOOKS

Published by the Penguin Group
Penguin Books Ltd, 27 Wrights Lane, London W8 5TZ, England
Penguin Books USA Inc., 375 Hudson Street, New York, New York 10014, USA
Penguin Books Australia Ltd, Ringwood, Victoria, Australia
Penguin Books Canada Ltd, 10 Alcorn Avenue, Toronto, Ontario, Canada M4V 3B2
Penguin Books (NZ) Ltd, 182–190 Wairau Road, Auckland 10, New Zealand

Penguin Books Ltd, Registered Offices: Harmondsworth, Middlesex, England

This selection first published by Viking 1996
Published in Penguin Books 1997
3 5 7 9 10 8 6 4

Introduction and selection copyright © Paul Levy, 1996
The acknowledgements on pages 372–4 constitute an extension of this copyright page
All rights reserved

Illustrations copyright © Laura Stoddart, 1996

The moral right of the author has been asserted

Printed in England by Clays Ltd, St Ives plc

CONTENTS

INTRODUCTION

Although this volume can be seen as an attempt to establish the canon of a subject that has yet to achieve recognition, it is also a completely personal choice of writing about or to do with food and drink. It could not be otherwise, especially as there are several excellent anthologies available that cover the rest of the obvious ground. Jane Austen, Dickens, Thackeray and even Virginia Woolf are well catered for; so are Shakespeare and Tolstoy, Athenaeus, Juvenal and Petronius. It is now the work of a moment to look up even a half-familiar quotation about apples, omelettes, wine or greed, to find what Proust liked best about Françoise's cooking or the Reverend Sydney Smith's rhyming prescription for dressing a salad. There is no excuse for producing yet another book that is the literary equivalent of spoonsful of jam.

Instead, I have set myself the task of compiling a collection that is mostly meat. Everything in this book is here to provide the curious or interested reader with something substantial to read. Sometimes this means an entire essay, sometimes an edited version of a preface to a classic cookbook, and sometimes part of a historical or scientific text. I have not paid much attention to the conventions of literary form or genre, I'm afraid, and have even included a particularly fine book review. But what I have tried to do is to make every selection complete and self-sufficient. This is meant to be an anthology of good prose writing about food and drink, with as much emphasis upon the quality of the writing as the nature of the subject; so I have taken the position that the extracts need to be long enough to be aesthetically satisfying as well as informative or virtuous in some other way.

No recipes have been included, except when to omit them would do violence to the text or when, as I would argue in the case of Norman Douglas and Jane Grigson, the recipes are themselves literary. Pieces with obvious consumerist intent have been excluded as well. It is very rare for an article meant to help the consumer buy an item of food or of kitchen equipment not to date quickly, or to be of more than passing interest. The consequences of this for most contemporary wine journalism are manifest, and explain why there is hardly any in this collection. It is one of the good features of food and wine journalism of our era that it is addressed to the consumer, but the gain to purse and palate is a loss to letters.

I have realized, I think since I began my own (second) career as a food and wine writer in the late 1970s, that there is a gulf between this kind of writing and cookbook writing. The readers (normally would-be users) of recipes are large in number, and cookbooks regularly figure on the bestseller lists. However, in the greater scheme of things, cooking is a minority interest, at least compared to the potential audience of people who are interested in food and drink. This larger group, which is neither predominantly male nor female, theoretically consists of everyone who has enough money to pay for their meat and mead, and who has the leisure to read – in effect, though by no means the entire population of any country, the advertiser's dream target audience.

It was the realization of this by Ann Barr, then of *Harper's & Queen*, and by Suzanne Lowry, my first editor on the *Observer*, and her successors, that made it possible for me to become one of the rare men to be employed in a field then dominated by women, and to be one of the few to write about food rather than to present recipes.

This had been done before, often and well, as I hope the present volume proves. But the demands of the press shifted at some time after the Second World War, perhaps as late as the 1960s, and editors began to want recipes and still more recipes. It came as a shock to me to read, in 1984, the pieces in Elizabeth David's collection of her journalism, *An Omelette and a Glass of Wine*. Most of these had been written in the 1950s and 1960s. People of my generation knew her only from her books. I had not been aware that she was an excellent food journalist, though frequently a cross and complaining one (there was plenty to be cross and to complain about in Britain). I had been a student in America in these years, and never read her pieces about the white truffles of Alba or Mme Barattero, not even when I wrote essays on both these topics myself. The lack of acknowledgement I believe annoyed her; but essays were out of fashion, recipe writing was the currency, and Britain's greatest food writer (with some competition for that title from Jane Grigson) was deprived of her just desserts.

For most of her own middle years, Elizabeth David was regarded and treated as a compiler of recipes that didn't always work, and which required ingredients that weren't always available. The injustice of this was palpable to those who knew her journalism; and it cannot be stressed too strongly that she made an enormous and all too seldom recognized contribution to Britain's post-war recovery. Food rationing did not end until the mid-1950s; lemons were scarce, olive oil, aubergines and courgettes unobtainable. But Elizabeth David's books and recipes gave heart to the middle classes, reminding them that just across the Channel was a land where the lemon trees still blossomed.

Despite the United States having had its own wartime rationing, America's food writers were never condemned to labour exclusively at the recipe coalface. I don't think M. F. K. Fisher ever went out of fashion or out of print, though recipes were not her forte. She was writing in a tradition that went back at least to Lucius Beebe at the turn of the century. Besides the fact that she was a great writer, whose words showed her to be a lover of the gifts and pleasures of the senses, one reason for her success was that *The New Yorker* published much of her writing, as it did that of Joseph Wechsberg, A. J. Liebling, Ludwig Bemelmans and probably some other writers that I don't know about. *The New Yorker* was the repository for the Golden Age of gastronomic journalism. What might occasion some wonder is that this Golden Age was only the (historical) day before yesterday.

I do not apologize for the large number of American writers represented in this volume: they were the heirs and keepers of this particular literary tradition. The single contributions here from French and Italian writers are, strangely, in proportion to the importance of this current in their nations' literatures, if you except fiction. Though the subjects of this anthology range over the whole world of food, there are only these two pieces not originally written in English. I read a good deal of current French food writing, and even began to translate some of the pieces myself. In the end I decided that some just didn't have the vigour of what was available in English, while the rest wasn't amenable to being filleted for an anthology.

By contrast, the single Chinese contribution I have included is insufficient to represent the large corpus of Chinese writing about food, stemming from the Confucianist tradition of considering food to be an important aspect of civilization. The piece reprinted here was written in English; lamentably little has been translated, and those of us who have no Chinese mostly know about this tradition from footnotes in the scholarly works of those who do read the language.

It will not escape the alert reader's attention that everything in this book is a product of our own century. As we are almost at the end of it, I don't think that should come as a surprise, for the literary tradition in question was mostly the creation of this century. I am sad that I have found so little to reprint on the subject of drink, especially wine. I plead in mitigation that in my reading I have found writing about food more likely to interest the common reader, and more likely to endure the test of time, than wine writing.

There are reasons for this. First, wine writing tends by its nature to be technical, which does not enchant many readers. Second, wine writing suffers (as does food writing, but to a smaller extent) from the fact that, for the moment at least, we have a meagre vocabulary with which to describe tastes and smells.

The 'terms of art' are limited to a few taste words, such as 'sour', 'sweet', 'savoury', 'bitter', 'salty', 'sharp', 'acid'; a few olfactory, such as 'smoky', 'flowery', 'acrid'; and a few texture, 'smooth', 'rough', 'soft', and 'harsh'. Otherwise, we have to describe tastes and smells by analogy. That is how the blackcurrants got into the claret, the cherries and raspberries into the red burgundy, the pepper into the wine of the northern Rhône, and the goose-berries into the white wines of the Loire.

As never ceases to amaze people of common sense, very few wines actually taste or smell of grapes. The extraordinary thing is that there should be general agreement about the analogies ('descriptors' in winespeak); for example, that it is desirable that meursault should be both nutty and buttery. At least the taste of wine is amenable to analysis. Food can be even trickier. It is an often-made and important philosophical observation that the taste of raspberries can be alluded to but not defined or analysed in any satis-factory fashion; we can say the fruit is sweet and acid at the same time, but in saying that you haven't captured anything distinctive or very interesting about the taste of raspberries. We can refer to the taste or fragrance of raspberries, and expect to be under-stood; but we can't say how or why. Note that the traffic is one-way: it is help-ful to find fruit in the wine, the raspberry note in the burgundy; but we can't claim to find the taste of red burgundy in a dish of raspberries.

In fact many activities that we consider to be 'art' rely on analogy for their verbal description. Try describing the human singing voice without resorting to analogy. There is a limited lexicon of specific words and phrases – chest voice, head voice, tessitura, range, register, timbre, and so on – and even some of these apply over a wider domain than vocal performance. Baritones, if they are lucky, have 'dark' or 'warm' voices, and so do some mezzo-sopranos. Tenors can seldom lay claim to either of these adjectives, and vanilla ice cream never.

Paradoxically, the use of analogy in writing about wine and food has, I think, a more rational justification than in writing about music, at least. The science of taste and smell is now advanced enough to allow the identification of some of the chemical compounds, esters, aldehydes and others, which are identified with particular smells and tastes; recently developed techniques of analysis can demonstrate the presence of such compounds in food and wine that tasters say (or complain) taste or smell of, for example, banana, pineapple and bubble gum. Precision is therefore possible when talking about beaujolais, though per-haps not yet when the critic describes the quality of voice of the dramatic soprano who sings Brünnhilde. The vocabulary available to writers about food and drink may be small, but it seems to be increasingly precise. That is surely why it is possible to write so pleasingly and well about food, although with such a narrow and specific stock of words. The mystery still remains – why food writing is generally superior to writing about wine.

There is much to be learned from the works collected in these pages. I increased my knowledge not just of food and drink, but also of geography, language and history while spending several leisurely years reading the candidates for inclusion. However, knowledge is incidental to the real point, which is pleasure. Nourishing the mind is as important as is nutrition to the body, but when reading the pieces in this book, I hope we shall all, finally, be elegant voluptuaries.

The spinach principle has not been applied here. I have put nothing in this book because I thought it was good for you – or for me. In making my selection I have not been influenced by a wish to take the book in a particular direction or to give it some kind of shape or balance. Everything has been chosen on merit alone, although, obviously, I have some prejudices. As a failed philosopher and lapsed academic I like reading rigorously argued texts, so I have included some pieces that may raise an unscientific eyebrow or two. I have also thought it proper to include some work by writers who most definitely do not have any professional relationship with eitner food or drink. The reader would not wish to have been deprived of the pieces by S. J. Perelman, Nelson Algren, or George Orwell, Norman Douglas and Elias Canetti, on the grounds that they were not full-time food writers.

We all know that the pleasures of food, drink and sex are intimately related, and I have done my best to include plenty of demonstrations of this truth. I wish I had been able to include arias like the one in praise of salami by the librettist Karl Friberth from Haydn's *L'Incontro Improvviso*, if only because of my own passion for opera. I'd also like to have included the food-laden lyrics of many blues songs but, ultimately, I decided not to – partly because of the difficulties of establishing correct texts. Recordings exist, but transcripts are impossible to come by, and because the songs are invariably in dialect, they are difficult to transcribe accurately. Reluctantly, I decided to omit lyrics as well as fiction, on grounds of space. They are, I concluded with some sadness, the stuff of another book.

Such riches are there that I am sure it would be possible to make another such compilation with no overlap at all. The late Cyril Ray used to make an anthology of food and wine writing as often as once a year, so it would be foolish to claim that any collection could be definitive. In putting together mine, I have been well aware that my choice is necessarily one man's, but I have tried to keep a serious purpose in mind – to show that there is a distinguished strand of literature, at least in the English language, which takes food and drink as its subject. So strong is this tradition, especially in America, that it really deserves the attention of the academic as well as of the general reader. This volume can be seen as a first attempt to establish the literary importance of such work. I hope knowledgeable readers will agree that the *maîtres* are included in the present book, although I will not dispute that there are also many *petits-maîtres*.

Such is the strength of the American tradition that I have decided to devote the first part of this book to the New World. The first two pieces in the collection demonstrate one great aspect of the American tradition: humour. Both Calvin Trillin's essay and S. J. Perelman's parody of Raymond Chandler are funny; but we can also admire the charm of Ludwig Bemelmans's character sketches, of Joseph Wechsberg's near-profiles and of A. J. Liebling's full-blown portraits of his dining companions. Wit is an essential quality of the American strain of food writing, equally manifest in the emotion-recalling prose of M. F. K. Fisher, in the fact-packed paragraphs of Waverley Root, in the elegance of Richard Olney's writing and of Barbara Kafka's, and taking a sardonic turn in Charles Perry's night-of-the-living-dead account of the invariably fatal condiments of the medieval Middle East.

The best of today's American food writers are the heirs to this great tradition, though they no longer have access to *The New Yorker*, once the house journal of the writers who established the canon of American food writing. In magazines ranging from *Natural History* and *Vogue* to their own self-published newsletters, Raymond Sokolov (Liebling's biographer), Jeffrey Steingarten, Edward Behr, Colman Andrews and John Thorne are clearly writing with the grain, not against it.

All these writers show another trait common to the current generation of American food writers – they are not afraid of science. This is another American virtue. Liebling, for example, was a great sports writer, and could describe the blows landed and parried in a boxing match with both precision and poetry. He was also capable of writing many thousands of words about the zoological identity of the *rascasse*, the fish considered essential to the making of bouillabaisse.

Raymond Sokolov and Jeffrey Steingarten show the same enthusiasm for analysis, and the penchant for detail exemplified by the encyclopedic appetite of Waverley Root. Curiosity seems to be the motive spring for some of the finest American food writing, from those three writers through Margaret Visser to John Thorne and Edward Behr. Even Charles Perry, who also writes about rock music, began his dark exploration of sinister comestibles because he was genuinely puzzled by references he had come across. This proceeds from a different impulse than that which drives the writing of M. F. K. Fisher,

Joseph Wechsberg, Samuel Chamberlain or Ludwig Bemelmans, who want to explain or describe people, situations or even a particular meal or dish.

One bit of special pleading is in order. There were many essays I could have chosen from the pen of James Villas. The piece on Pearl Byrd Foster is here because this wonderfully eccentric lady became a friend of mine, too, in her later years, and I reprint this as a tribute to her powerful personality as well as to Mr Villas's amusing style.

The extracts from Sidney Mintz and Harold McGee make a smooth transition to the second part of the book. They show that you can write elegantly about aspects other than the romance of food and drink, and that writing about food, which does not merely allude to the scientific and anthropological, but actually is a work of science or anthropology, can give pleasure, too. Their transatlantic counterpart might be said to be Alan Davidson, who is guru to scholar foodies all over the world. Mr Davidson, the world's leading culinary expert on fish, sometime British Ambassador to Laos, and the editor of the forthcoming *Oxford Companion to Food*, the most important work of reference on the subject ever undertaken, shows in his piece on funeral cookbooks that he is in no danger of allowing his scholarship to overwhelm his sense of fun.

Dorothy Hartley was, until her death, the senior food writer in Britain. I doubt if she thought of herself in this light, for despite the importance of *Food in England*, she regarded herself as an historian of England, not of food. Alan Davidson, Elizabeth David, Jane Grigson and Patience Gray formed the next generation. Jane Grigson was a prodigiously learned and talented writer, who shared her catholic interests with her husband, the poet, critic and naturalist Geoffrey Grigson. She began her career as a translator, and was always conscious that she was interested in literature long before food became her *métier*. Still, I think Jane Grigson's meticulous and practical recipes actually had more to do with the present improvement in the British standard of cooking than did Elizabeth David's.

Patience Gray was the first women's-page editor of the *Observer*; in 1957 she was working as a researcher at the Royal College of Art when she and Primrose Boyd wrote a bestselling cookbook, *Plats du Jour*. Her great period as a food writer, though, came when she threw over her London life and moved to a succession of Mediterranean homes, at the latest of which, in Apulia, she manages without a supply of electricity. She was rediscovered as a food writer by Alan Davidson, when he was running his small publishing firm, Prospect Books, and she became his first and only bestseller.

Jane Grigson often said to me that no one who was any good as a food writer ever set out to be one. Claudia Roden, the great-great-granddaughter of the last Chief Rabbi of the Ottoman Empire, was an art student in post-Suez Crisis exile from her native Egypt when, like Jane Grigson, she was encouraged to write about food by Elizabeth David. She has the distinction of being one of those writers who has introduced a whole new cuisine to the world. In her case, this does not mean only the English-speaking world, for Claudia Roden's nostalgia-born book of Middle Eastern recipes is the standard work on the subject, even in the Middle East itself.

Several of the writers here, especially the younger ones, have made their names as critics – Fay Maschler and Jonathan Meades are at present the best-known restaurant critics in Britain. The pieces I have chosen by them are not restaurant criticism, however. I have tended to avoid this genre – although there is plenty about restaurants in these pages – because when such criticism is occasioned by a particular meal, in specific circumstances with no abstract point to be made, it tends to be consumerist and ephemeral. Quentin Crewe deserves a special word in this regard. Like the others, his piece reprinted here is not restaurant criticism. But he was a pioneer of the category, for he was the first critic, in Britain at least, to review other aspects of the eating-out experience besides the food and wine. It is because of his column in *Queen* in the 1960s that today's critic routinely tells his reader whether an eating place has pink tablecloths and whether the chairs are comfortable, what the other guests are wearing, and whether they are allowed to ruin your meal by chattering on their mobile phones.

The editing has, for the most part, preserved the spelling of the original, which accounts for the inconsistencies that will be noticed by the alert reader.

Thanks to Philip Abrams, Roy Shipperbottom, Julian Barnes, David Plante, Angela Mason, Margaret Leibenstein and Barbara Kafka for calling some tasty titbits to my attention, and to other friends who did me the same service; to Nach Waxman for supplying me with some very exotic titles indeed; to the staff of the London Library for pointing me to the appropriate places in the stacks, which allowed me to make some strange discoveries; to Jessica Isaacs and Iain Burnside, who shared with me their research for their own 'gastronomic edition' of BBC Radio 3's *Voices*, and thereby saved me hours of labour; to Marianne Charles and to Ann Wilson for their help.

My wife, Penelope, did almost all the considerable research necessary to find some of the bizarre and fugitive pieces reprinted here, as well as showing her usual flair and imagination in calling to my attention quite a few things I'd never come across before. My daughter Tatyana assisted, importantly, at the copying machine. This book is for them and for Georgia.

PART ONE

THE NEW WORLD

CALVIN TRILLIN

Spaghetti Carbonara Day

I have been campaigning to have the national Thanksgiving dish changed from turkey to spaghetti carbonara. In a complicated way, it all has to do with my wife, Alice. There came a time when Alice began to refer to a certain sort of people I have corresponded with over the years – the sort of people who are particularly intense about, say, seeking out the best burrito in East Los Angeles – as 'food crazies'. She spoke of them as bad company. She even spoke, I regret to say, as if I might be in danger of becoming a food crazy myself. I knew I had to do something. What I decided to do was launch a campaign to have the national Thanksgiving dish changed from turkey to spaghetti carbonara.

At one time, Alice had displayed a certain sympathy for my approach to eating. Maybe 'understanding' would be a better word. When I began traveling around the country in the line of duty some years ago, she understood that if I didn't devote a certain amount of my time to searching out something decent to eat I would find myself having dinner in those motel restaurants that all buy ingredients from the same Styrofoam outlet or in that universal Chamber of Commerce favorite that I began referring to as La Maison de la Casa House, Continental Cuisine. That is not a fate to wish on a husband simply because he may have an irritating habit or two – insignificant ones, really, like a tendency to eat from the serving bowl late in the meal.

When did it all begin to change? The signs, I now realize, were there almost from the start. Why, I should have asked myself, do dinner-table conversations at our house so often turn to the perils of gluttony? Why had Alice continued to preach the benefits of limiting our family to three meals a day even after I presented incontrovertible scientific evidence that entire herds of cattle owe their health to steady grazing? Why, in planning a trip to Sicily, would Alice seem so insistent on staying in towns that have world-renowned ruins, whether those towns are known for their pasta con sarde or not? Looking back, I realize that I shouldn't have been so surprised on that dark and rainy night – we had just arrived in a strange town after a long trip, and I was inspecting the Yellow Pages in the hope of happening upon some clue as to where a legitimate purveyor of barbecue might be found – when Alice uttered those dreaded words: 'Why don't we just eat in the hotel?'

Naturally, I tried to put everything in context. Around that time, I happened to read in the *Dallas Morning News* that a Frenchman who goes by the name of Monsieur Mangetout had been hired to entertain at a Dallas waterbed show and had done so by eating several cocktail glasses, a few dozen razor blades, and about a third of a queen-size waterbed, including the pine footboard with brass brackets.

'Now that is excessive,' I said to Alice. 'The article says that he once consumed fifteen pounds of bicycle in twelve days, and he's negotiating with Japan to eat a helicopter.'

The point I was trying to make to Alice – who, I must say, was not really keeping up her end of the conversation – was that compared to somebody like M. Mangetout (who, I hasten to admit, is obviously on one extreme), I am someone of moderate appetite. When M. Mangetout talks about eating junk, after all, he is not talking about those packages of roasted sweetcorn kernels from Cedar Rapids that I love. He is talking about eating junk. Just as an example, I have never eaten so much as a pound of bicycle. Although Alice may criticize me for always showing my appreciation of the hostess's cooking by having a second helping – to be perfectly honest, what she criticizes me for is showing my appreciation of the hostess's cooking by having a third helping – I can see myself acting with considerable restraint at a dinner party at which the main course is, say, queen-size waterbed ('No thank you. It was delicious, but I couldn't eat another bite'), even though I might risk spending a sleepless night from worry over the hostess's feelings or from the effects of the first helping.

The comparison I drew between me and M. Mangetout did not impress Alice. I began to see that the problem was not context but point of view. Seen from the right point of view, for instance, someone who seems intent on obtaining a fair sampling of foodstuffs wherever he happens to be is engaged in serious research – not research done for the purpose of, say, probing for soft spots in the New England fast-food taco market, but the sort of pure research that in more cultivated times was often done by educated gentlemen interested in knowledge for its own sake – and the appropriate way to comment on such research would not be with phrases like 'You're making an absolute pig of yourself.'

What better way to demonstrate one's seriousness than to start a campaign to change the national Thanksgiving dish from turkey to spaghetti carbonara? Alice would see some serious historical research going on, right under her own roof. Our daughters might be convinced that my interest in food is far too complicated to be summed up with the phrase 'Daddy likes to pig out.' They are always being told that an informed citizenry is the cornerstone of democracy, after all, so they could appreciate the value of informing the citizenry that the appropriate Thanksgiving dish is spaghetti carbonara. The adventure inherent in such a campaign might even stir their souls sufficiently to free them from what I regard as a crippling dependence on canned tuna fish.

It does not require much historical research to uncover the fact that nobody knows if the Pilgrims really ate turkey at the first Thanksgiving dinner. The only thing we know for sure about what the Pilgrims ate is that it couldn't have tasted very good. Even today, well-brought-up English girls are taught by their mothers to boil all veggies for at least a month and a half, just in case one of the dinner guests turns up without his teeth. Alice and I did have a fine meal of allegedly English food in New York once, at the home of a friend named Jane Garmey – it included dishes with those quaint names the English give food in lieu of seasoning, like Aunt Becky's Kneecap – but I suspected that Jane had simply given real food English names, the way someone might fit out a Rumanian with a regimental blazer and call him Nigel. I liked the meal well enough to refrain from making any of the remarks about English cooking that I often find myself making when in the presence of our cousins across the sea ('It's certainly unfair to say that the English lack both a cuisine and a sense of humor: their cooking is a joke in itself'), but I can't get over the suspicion that hidden away somewhere in the Garmey household is a French cookbook that has a recipe for something called *La Rotule de Tante Becky*.

It would also not require much digging to discover that Christopher Columbus, the man who may have brought linguine with clam sauce to this continent, was from Genoa, and obviously would have sooner acknowledged that the world was shaped like an isosceles triangle than to have eaten the sort of things that English Puritans ate. Righting an ancient wrong against Columbus, a great man who certainly did not come all this way only to have a city in Ohio named after him, would be a serious historical contribution. Also, I happen to love spaghetti carbonara.

I realize that these days someone attempting to impress his own wife and children with his seriousness might be considered about as quaint as Aunt Becky's kneecap. Where we live, in New York City, just having a wife and children is considered a bit quaint. I sometimes think that some day we might be put on the Grayline Tour of Greenwich Village as a nuclear family. As I imagine it, the tour bus pulls up to the curb in front of our house, after the usual stops have been made at Washington Square Arch and Aaron Burr's stable and Edna St Vincent Millay's brownstone and Stephen Crane's rent-controlled floor-through. As the tourists file out, a fat lady in the back of the bus says, 'How about the hippies? I want to see the hippies.' Instead, they see us – an American family. Mommy and Daddy and their two children are having dinner. Mommy asks Abigail what she did in school all day, and Abigail describes a math problem that Daddy doesn't understand. Mommy is helping Sarah cut her meat. Mommy is telling Abigail to sit up straight. Daddy is telling Sarah that if she doesn't stop playing with her meat he will arrange to have her sent to a foster home. Mommy is discussing the perils of gluttony. Daddy is being manipulated by Abigail and Sarah, who want a cat. Mommy says Daddy hates cats. Daddy says it's not that he hates cats – Daddy doesn't want to teach Abigail and Sarah prejudice – but simply that he has never met a cat he liked. Mommy is helping Daddy cut his meat. After a while, the tourists seem to grow restless. The sight did seem unique at first, but it has begun to remind them of reruns of the old 'Ozzie and Harriet' show. The tour guide, discerning their mood, leads them out the door. The fat lady says, 'Now can we see the hippies?'

The tourists might assume that such a family celebrates Thanksgiving every year with a traditional meal at that same dinner table. Not so. When it comes to national holidays, there is a quiet war for hearts and minds going on in our family – it is fought over Halloween and Christmas – and Thanksgiving has tended to get overlooked as territory that is not hotly contested by either side. Halloween is my holiday. For days before Halloween, people who telephone me have to be told by Alice, 'He's in the basement making sure that the witch piñata is still in good enough shape to hang out the window' or, 'He's upstairs trying to decide whether the ax-murderer's mask goes better with his Panama or his Stewart Granger bush hat.' I'm always in town for Halloween. Even if I didn't happen to enjoy walking in the Village Halloween parade in my ax-murderer's mask, I would feel it my duty to be there because of the long-established role of a father in passing on important cultural traditions to the next generation. Alice's attitude toward Halloween, I regret to say, borders on the blasé. By the time Halloween comes, Alice is already thinking about Christmas, a holiday whose modern celebration always makes me wonder whether December might be a nice month to spend in Saudi Arabia. As a result, we engage in one of those quiet struggles common to marriages of mixed cultural emphasis. If I were not in town to press my case on Halloween, I sometimes think my girls might find themselves spending October 31 trimming a Christmas tree – pausing now and then to hand out tiny 'Joyeux Noël' wreaths to the visiting trick-or-treaters.

Being a kind of demilitarized zone, Thanksgiving has often been celebrated away from home. It was at other people's Thanksgiving tables that I first began to articulate my spaghetti carbonara campaign – although, since we were usually served turkey, I naturally did not mention that the campaign had been inspired partly by my belief that turkey is basically something college dormitories use to punish students for hanging around on Sunday. I did bring up some esthetic advantages of replacing turkey with spaghetti carbonara – the fact, for instance, that the President would not be photographed every year receiving a large platter of spaghetti carbonara from the Eastern Association of Spaghetti Carbonara Growers. (As King Vittorio Emmanuel may have said to his Chancellor of the Exchequer, spaghetti doesn't grow on trees.) I spoke of my interest in seeing what those masters of the floatmaker's art at Macy's might come up with as a 300-square-foot depiction of a plate of spaghetti carbonara. I reminded everyone how refreshing it would be to hear sports announcers call some annual tussle the Spaghetti Carbonara Day Classic.

I even had a ready answer to the occasional turkey fancier at those meals who would insist that spaghetti carbonara was almost certainly not what our forebears ate at the first Thanksgiving dinner. As it happens, one of the things I give thanks for every year is that those people in the Plymouth Colony were not my forebears. Who wants forebears who put people in the stocks for playing the harpsichord on the Sabbath or having an innocent little game of pinch and giggle? In fact, ever since it became fashionable to dwell on the atrocities committed throughout American history – ever since, that is, we entered what the intellectuals call the Era of Year-Round Yom Kippur – I have been more and more grateful that none of my forebears got near this place before 1906. When it comes to slavery and massacring Indians and the slaughter of the American buffalo and even the assorted scandals of the Spanish-American War, my family's hands are clean. It used to be that an American who wanted to put on airs made claims about how long his family has been here. Now the only people left for our family to envy are the immigrants who arrived in the last decade or so. They don't even have to feel guilty about the Vietnam War.

Finally, there came a year when nobody invited us to Thanksgiving dinner. Alice's theory was that the word had got around town that I always made a pest out of myself berating the hostess for serving turkey instead of spaghetti carbonara – although I pointed out that even if a hostess had taken some offense at the mention of my campaign, she must have forgotten all about it in the glow of hearing me ask for thirds on stuffing. Abigail and Sarah, I'm happy to say, did not believe that our lack of invitations had anything at all to do with my insistence on bringing the spaghetti carbonara issue to the attention of the American people at any appropriate opportunity. They seemed to believe that it might have had something to do with my tendency to spill cranberry sauce on my tie.

*

However it came about, I was delighted at the opportunity we had been given to practice what I had been preaching – to sit down to a Thanksgiving dinner of spaghetti carbonara. In the long run, I saw it as an opportunity to inspire our daughters to seek the truth and test frontiers and engage in pure research and never settle for eating in the hotel. In the short run, I saw it as an opportunity to persuade Sarah to taste spaghetti carbonara. Sarah does not taste casually. Abigail has expanded her repertoire to the point of joining us in the ritual lobster supper we always have in Maine on the way to Nova Scotia, where we live in the summer, but Sarah celebrates that occasion each year with a tuna fish sandwich. ('The tuna fish here is excellent,' she always says.) If Sarah is finally persuaded to try something new, she usually cuts off the sort of portion I have come to think of as a micro-bite, chews on it tentatively, swallows it, and says, 'It's OK, but I'm not crazy about it.'

Confident that our family was about to break new ground, I began preparations for Thanksgiving. I did some research on what ingredients would be needed for the main course. I prepared for any questions the girls might have about our forebears:

'Was Uncle Benny responsible for the First World War just because he was already in St Joe then?' Abigail might ask.

'Not directly,' I would say. 'He didn't have his citizenship.'

'Is it really true that your grandparents got mixed up about American holidays when they first got to Kansas City, and used to have a big turkey dinner on the Fourth of July and shoot fireworks off in Swope Park on Thanksgiving?' Sarah might ask.

'At least they had nothing to do with snookering the Indians out of Massachusetts,' I would be able to say. 'Be thankful for that.'

Naturally, the entire family went over to Raffetto's pasta store on Houston Street to see the spaghetti cut. I got the cheese at Joe's Dairy, on Sullivan, a place that would have made Columbus feel right at home – there are plenty of Genoese on Sullivan; no Pilgrims – and then headed for the pork store on Carmine Street for the bacon and ham. Alice made the spaghetti carbonara. It was perfection. I love spaghetti carbonara. Sarah, a devotee of spaghetti with tomato sauce, said, 'I'm not crazy about it,' but she said it in a nice, celebratory kind of way. After a few forkfuls, we paused to give thanks that we weren't eating turkey. Then, I began to tell the children the story of the first Thanksgiving:

In England, a long time ago, there were people called Pilgrims who were very strict about making sure everyone observed the Sabbath and cooked food without any flavor and that sort of thing, and they decided to go to America, where they could enjoy Freedom to Nag. The other people in England said, 'Glad to see the back of them.' In America, the Pilgrims tried farming, but they couldn't get much done because they were always putting their best farmers in the stocks for crimes like Suspicion of Cheerfulness. The Indians took pity on the Pilgrims, and helped them with their farming, even though the Indians thought the Pilgrims were about as much fun as teenage circumcision. The Pilgrims were so grateful that at the end of their first year in America they invited the Indians over for a Thanksgiving meal. The Indians, having had some experience with Pilgrim cuisine during the year, took the precaution of taking along one dish of their own. They brought a dish that their ancestors had learned many generations before from none other than Christopher Columbus, who was known to the Indians as 'the big Italian fellow'. The dish was spaghetti carbonara – made with pancetta bacon and fontina and the best imported prosciutto. The Pilgrims hated it. They said it was 'heretically tasty' and 'the work of the devil' and 'the sort of thing foreigners eat'. The Indians were so disgusted that on the way back to their village after dinner one of them made a remark about the Pilgrims that was repeated down through the years and unfortunately caused confusion among historians about the first Thanksgiving meal. He said, 'What a bunch of turkeys!'

As is traditional after a Thanksgiving family meal, I was content. I considered the campaign a success even if no other family converted. Everything seemed possible. I could see the possibility of doing pure research (not 'pigging out') around the country in the company of like-minded researchers (not 'food crazies'). I could see the possibility of inspiring Sarah to try dishes far more exotic than spaghetti carbonara. I could see the possibility of Alice's thinking that someone given to serious inquiry might have a third helping out of an honest curiosity about whether it could taste even better than the second. I had a third helping of spaghetti carbonara.

1983

S. J. PERELMAN

Farewell, My Lovely Appetizer

Add Smorgasbits to your ought-to-know department, the newest of the three Betty Lee products. What in the world! Just small mouth-size pieces of herring and of pinkish tones. We crossed our heart and promised not to tell the secret of their tinting.

> Clementine Paddleford's food column in the *Herald Tribune*

The 'Hush-Hush' Blouse. We're very hush-hush about his name, but the celebrated shirtmaker who did it for us is famous on two continents for blouses with details like those deep yoke folds, the wonderful shoulder pads, the shirtband bow!

> Russeks advertisement in the *New York Times*

I came down the sixth-floor corridor of the Arbogast Building, past the World Wide Noodle Corporation, Zwinger & Rumsey, Accountants, and the Ace Secretarial Service, Mimeographing Our Specialty. The legend on the ground-glass panel next door said, 'Atlas Detective Agency, Noonan & Driscoll', but Snapper Driscoll had retired two years before with a .38 slug between the shoulders, donated by a snowbird in Tacoma, and I owned what goodwill the firm had. I let myself into the crummy anteroom we kept to impress clients, growled good morning at Birdie Claflin.

'Well, you certainly look like something the cat dragged in,' she said. She had a quick tongue. She also had eyes like dusty lapis lazuli, taffy hair, and a figure that did things to me. I kicked open the bottom drawer of her desk, let two inches of rye trickle down my craw, kissed Birdie square on her lush, red mouth, and set fire to a cigarette.

'I could go for you, sugar,' I said slowly. Her face was veiled, watchful. I stared at her ears, liking the way they were joined to her head. There was something complete about them; you knew they were put there for keeps. When you're a private eye, you want things to stay put.

'Any customers?'

'A woman by the name of Sigrid Bjornsterne said she'd be back. A looker.'

'Swede?'

'She'd like you to think so.'

I nodded toward the inner office to indicate that I was going in there, and went in there. I lay down on the davenport, took off my shoes, and bought myself a shot from the bottle I kept underneath. Four minutes later, an ash-blonde with eyes the color of unset opals, in a Nettie Rosenstein basic black dress and a baum-marten stole, burst in. Her bosom was heaving and it looked even better that way. With a gasp she circled the desk, hunting for some place to hide, and then, spotting the wardrobe where I keep a change of bourbon, ran into it. I got up and wandered out into the anteroom. Birdie was deep in a crossword puzzle.

'See anyone come in here?'

'Nope.' There was a thoughtful line between her brows. 'Say, what's a five-letter word meaning "trouble"?'

'Swede,' I told her, and went back inside. I waited the length of time it would take a small, not very bright, boy to recite *Ozymandias*, and, inching carefully along the wall, took a quick gander out the window. A thin galoot with stoop-ing shoulders was being very busy reading a paper outside the Gristede store two blocks away. He hadn't been there an hour ago, but then, of course, neither had I. He wore a size seven dove-colored hat from Browning King, a tan Wilson Brothers shirt with pale-blue stripes, a J. Press foulard with a mixed red-and-white figure, dark-blue Interwoven socks, and an unshined pair of oxblood London Character shoes. I let a cigarette burn down between my fingers until it made a small red mark, and then I opened the wardrobe.

'Hi,' the blonde said lazily. 'You Mike Noonan?' I made a noise that could have been 'Yes', and waited. She yawned. I thought things over, decided to play it safe. I yawned. She yawned back, then settling into a corner of the wardrobe, went to sleep. I let another cigarette burn down until it made a second red mark beside the first one, and then I woke her up. She sank into a chair, crossing a pair of gams that tightened my throat as I peered under the desk at them.

'Mr Noonan,' she said, 'you – you've got to help me.'

'My few friends call me Mike,' I said pleasantly.

'Mike.' She rolled the syllable on her tongue. 'I don't believe I've ever heard that name before. Irish?'

'Enough to know the difference between a gossoon and a bassoon.'

'What *is* the difference?' she asked. I dummied up; I figured I wasn't giving anything away for free. Her eyes narrowed. I shifted my two hundred pounds slightly, lazily set fire to a finger, and watched it burn down. I could see she was admiring the interplay of muscles in my shoulders. There wasn't any extra fat on Mike Noonan, but I wasn't telling *her* that. I was playing it safe until I knew where we stood.

When she spoke again, it came with a rush. 'Mr Noonan, he thinks I'm try-ing to poison him. But I swear the herring was pink – I took it out of the jar myself. If I could only find out how they tinted it. I offered them money, but they wouldn't tell.'

'Suppose you take it from the beginning,' I suggested.

She drew a deep breath. 'You've heard of the golden spintria of Hadrian?' I shook my head. 'It's a tremendously valuable coin believed to have been given by the Emperor Hadrian to one of his proconsuls, Caius Vitellius. It dis-appeared about 150 AD, and eventually passed into the possession of Hucbald the Fat. After the sack of Adrianople by the Turks, it was loaned by a man named Shapiro to the court physician, or hakim, of Abdul Mahmoud. Then it dropped out of sight for nearly five hundred years, until last August, when a dealer in secondhand books named Lloyd Thursday sold it to my husband.'

'And now it's gone again,' I finished.

'No,' she said. 'At least, it was lying on the dresser when I left, an hour ago.' I leaned back, pretending to fumble a carbon out of the desk, and studied her legs again. This was going to be a lot more intricate than I had thought. Her voice got huskier. 'Last night I brought home a jar of Smorgasbits for Walter's dinner. You know them?'

'Small mouth-size pieces of herring and of pinkish tones, aren't they?'

Her eyes darkened, lightened, got darker again. 'How did you know?'

'I haven't been a private op nine years for nothing, sister. Go on.'

'I – I knew right away something was wrong when Walter screamed and upset his plate. I tried to tell him the herring was supposed to be pink, but he carried on like a madman. He's been suspicious of me since – well, ever since I made him take out that life insurance.'

'What was the face amount of the policy?'

'A hundred thousand. But it carried a triple-indemnity clause in case he died by sea food. Mr Noonan – Mike –' her tone caressed me – 'I've got to win back his confidence. You could find out how they tinted that herring.'

'What's in it for me?'

'Anything you want.' The words were a whisper. I leaned over, poked open her handbag, counted off five grand.

'This'll hold me for a while,' I said. 'If I need any more, I'll beat my spoon on the high chair.' She got up. 'Oh, while I think of it, how does this golden spintria of yours tie in with the herring?'

'It doesn't,' she said calmly. 'I just threw it in for glamour.' She trailed past me in a cloud of scent that retailed at ninety rugs the ounce. I caught her wrist, pulled her up to me.

'I go for girls named Sigrid with opal eyes,' I said.

'Where'd you learn my name?'

'I haven't been a private snoop twelve years for nothing, sister.'

'It was nine last time.'

'It seemed like twelve till you came along.' I held the clinch until a faint wisp of smoke curled out of her ears, pushed her through the door. Then I slipped a pint of rye into my stomach and a heater into my kick and went looking for a bookdealer named Lloyd Thursday. I knew he had no connection with the herring caper, but in my business you don't overlook anything.

The thin galoot outside Gristede's had taken a powder when I got there; that meant we were no longer playing girls' rules. I hired a hack to Wanamaker's, cut over to Third, walked up toward Fourteenth. At Twelfth a mink-faced jasper made up as a street cleaner tailed me for a block, drifted into a dairy restaurant. At Thirteenth somebody dropped a sour tomato out of a third-story window, missing me by inches. I doubled back to Wanamaker's, hopped a bus up Fifth to Madison Square, and switched to a cab down Fourth, where the second-hand bookshops elbow each other like dirty urchins.

A flabby hombre in a Joe Carbondale rope-knit sweater, whose jowl could have used a shave, quit giggling over *The Heptameron* long enough to tell me he was Lloyd Thursday. His shoebutton eyes became opaque when I asked to see any first editions or incunabula relative to the *Clupea harengus*, or common herring.

'You got the wrong pitch, copper,' he snarled. 'That stuff is hotter than Pee Wee Russell's clarinet.'

'Maybe a sawbuck'll smarten you up,' I said. I folded one to the size of a postage stamp, scratched my chin with it. 'There's five yards around for anyone who knows why those Smorgasbits of Sigrid Bjornsterne's happened to be pink.' His eyes got crafty.

'I might talk for a grand.'

'Start dealing.' He motioned toward the back. I took a step forward. A second later a Roman candle exploded inside my head and I went away from there. When I came to, I was on the floor with a lump on my sconce the size of a lapwing's egg and big Terry Tremaine of Homicide was bending over me.

'Someone sapped me,' I said thickly. 'His name was —'

'Webster,' grunted Terry. He held up a dog-eared copy of Merriam's Unabridged. 'You tripped on a loose board and this fell off a shelf on your think tank.'

'Yeah?' I said skeptically. 'Then where's Thursday?' He pointed to the fat man lying across a pile of erotica. 'He passed out cold when he saw you cave.' I covered up, let Terry figure it any way he wanted. I wasn't telling him what cards I held. I was playing it safe until I knew all the angles.

In a seedy pharmacy off Astor Place, a stale Armenian whose name might have been Vulgarian but wasn't dressed my head and started asking questions. I put my knee in his groin and he lost interest. Jerking my head toward the coffee urn, I spent a nickel and the next forty minutes doing some heavy thinking. Then I holed up in a phone booth and dialed a clerk I knew called Little Farvel in a delicatessen store on Amsterdam Avenue. It took a while to get the dope I wanted because the connection was bad and Little Farvel had been dead two years, but we Noonans don't let go easily.

By the time I worked back to the Arbogast Building, via the Weehawken ferry and the George Washington Bridge to cover my tracks, all the pieces were in place. Or so I thought up to the point she came out of the wardrobe holding me between the sights of her ice-blue automatic.

'Reach for the stratosphere, gumshoe.' Sigrid Bjornsterne's voice was colder than Horace Greeley and Little Farvel put together, but her clothes were plenty calorific. She wore a forest-green suit of Hockanum woolens, a Knox Wayfarer, and baby crocodile pumps. It was her blouse, though, that made tiny red hairs stand up on my knuckles. Its deep yoke folds, shoulder pads, and shirtband bow could only have been designed by some master craftsman, some Cézanne of the shears.

'Well, Nosy Parker,' she sneered, 'so you found out how they tinted the herring.'

'Sure – grenadine,' I said easily. 'You knew it all along. And you planned to add a few grains of oxylbutane-cheriphosphate, which turns the same shade of pink in solution, to your husband's portion, knowing it wouldn't show in the post-mortem. Then you'd collect the three hundred *G*'s and join Harry Pestalozzi in Nogales till the heat died down. But you didn't count on me.'

'You?' Mockery nicked her full-throated laugh. 'What are you going to do about it?'

'This.' I snaked the rug out from under her and she went down in a swirl of silken ankles. The bullet whined by me into the ceiling as I vaulted over the desk, pinioned her against the wardrobe.

'Mike.' Suddenly all the hatred had drained away and her body yielded to mine. 'Don't turn me in. You cared for me – once.'

'It's no good, Sigrid. You'd only double-time me again.'

'Try me.'

'OK. The shirtmaker who designed your blouse – what's his name?' A shudder of fear went over her; she averted her head. 'He's famous on two continents. Come on Sigrid, they're your dice.'

'I won't tell you. I can't. It's a secret between this – this department store and me.'

'They wouldn't be loyal to you. They'd sell you out fast enough.'

'Oh, Mike, you mustn't. You don't know what you're asking.'

'For the last time.'

'Oh, sweetheart, don't you see?' Her eyes were tragic pools, a cenotaph to lost illusions. 'I've got so little. Don't take that away from me. I – I'd never be able to hold up my head in Russeks again.'

'Well, if that's the way you want to play it . . .' There was silence in the room, broken only by Sigrid's choked sob. Then, with a strangely empty feeling, I uncradled the phone and dialed Spring 7-3100.

For an hour after they took her away, I sat alone in the taupe-colored dusk, watching lights come on and a woman in the hotel opposite adjusting a garter. Then I treated my tonsils to five fingers of firewater, jammed on my hat, and made for the anteroom. Birdie was still scowling over her crossword puzzle. She looked up crookedly at me.

'Need me any more tonight?'

'No.' I dropped a grand or two in her lap. 'Here, buy yourself some stardust.'

'Thanks, I've got my quota.' For the first time I caught a shadow of pain behind her eyes. 'Mike, would – would you tell me something?'

'As long as it isn't clean,' I flipped to conceal my bitterness.

'What's an eight-letter word meaning "sentimental"?'

'Flatfoot, darling,' I said, and went out into the rain.

Late 1940s

RAY SOKOLOV

One Man's Meat is Another's Person

Of all the taboos in Western society, the prohibition against the eating of human flesh is the most widely obeyed. Thousands among us kill someone every year. Incest is not common, yet it occurs – and enriches the fantasy life of many an analysand. But cannibalism is an infraction of the social order that very few have risked.

Like all forbidden fruits, nevertheless, cannibalism fascinates us. Ever since Columbus first discovered it among the Caribs (who were called *canibales*, whence the name), it has inspired an entire literature of speculation and raised a dark question in the minds of people too civilized to feel anything but repulsion at the idea of bolting human steaks but unable to keep from wondering in untrammeled moments what they taste like.

Explorers, probably translating a Fijian phrase, reported that the stuff was known to its fanciers in the Pacific as 'long pig'. This never seemed more than a dubious description of the savor of our muscular Christian selves. The enigma basically remained until late 1972. Survivors of a Uruguayan plane crash in the Andes, who were cut off from the outside world for weeks, in desperation ate fellow passengers killed in the accident. After their rescue, the survivors told Piers Paul Read – who set down their story in the current best-seller *Alive* – that after cooking the meat briefly (they tried it first raw), 'the slight browning of the flesh gave it an immeasurably better flavor – softer than beef but with much the same taste'.

That is the kind of testimony one can believe, especially from Uruguayans, who know their beef. It is also good news that humans taste good: alternatives to soyburgers are always welcome, and we can at last exonerate cannibal societies of the charge of unrefined savagery. Instead, they were gastronomes.

I anticipate the retort that the anthropophagic banquets of Fiji and Papua and the Amazon began with the butchery of neighboring tribes. But who are we, with our kill ratios and My Lais, to question the civility of, say, Tupinambá warriors? To begin with, they captured prisoners live, led them back through the great forest of the Amazon, and then allowed them to live for months in virtual freedom until the final blood rite. Prisoners were given wives, and thus shared their genes with the victorious village before they gave up their bodies in a ceremonial war game that they were doomed to lose. The quartered body, according to an eyewitness account, was barbecued. Women and children rushed to drink the blood. Mothers smeared their nipples with it so that their babies could taste it. Delicacies, wrote anthropologist Alfred Métraux, such as fingers and the grease around the liver and heart, were given to distinguished guests.

Ethnographers have advanced several theories to explain such full-blown bloodthirstiness. Some say that meat hunger caused it, a craving brought on by poor, monotonous diets of manioc or sago. This won't entirely wash. Contiguous tribes with equally drab and deficient diets did not practice cannibalism. And the Tupinambás, who had plenty of nonhuman protein in their diet, ate slain enemies primarily as a form of revenge.

Other experts point to the ritual content of most cannibal acts. For the Tupinambás, the ceremony associated with cannibalism was so important that after cannibalism was effectively outlawed, the ritual continued to be performed on skeletons exhumed for the purpose. In the northwestern Amazon area, Cubco warriors' wives ate the penis of a dead victim to promote fertility. And several endocannibalistic societies recycled the souls of their own villagers by drinking the ashes of naturally deceased relatives dissolved in corn beer or a banana drink.

Endocannibalism – whether practiced by primitives or by Uruguayan rugby players – is less shocking than exocannibalism because it does not normally include murder. But the simple act of consuming human flesh, even when enshrined in ritual, is obnoxious to most people (although excusable *in extremis*). It seems to arise from a fundamental sense of solidarity with one's species. Even higher primates do not (with rare and ambiguous exceptions) eat each other. It may be that exocannibalism results from a narrow system of taxonomy that limits the nonedible 'species' group to the kinship group and defines unrelated human outsiders as fair game. Clearly, no all-encompassing principle of human brotherhood informed the daily life of the Tupinambás.

The real difference between us and the Tupinambás, however, is that we are more adept at making our cannibalistic acts and impulses into metaphor or else hiding them from view. We certainly enjoy the fruits of warfare, not in the form of flesh, but as territory, wealth, or influence. Moreover, Christianity's most fundamental ritual, the Eucharist, is symbolic endocannibalism; the consumption of the body and blood of 'Our Father's Son'. Orthodoxy denies that communion is only symbolic eating and claims that the sacramental wine and wafer do actually transsubstantiate into Christ's flesh and blood in the mouths of the faithful. True cannibals are less 'civilized' only in degree.

The best ethnographic information, as a matter of fact, shows that cannibalism was not practiced by men at a low level of subsistence but rather arose after the invention of agriculture and the intensification of warfare that followed it.

In our society, we have moved beyond the agricultural-tribal stage, into something we are pleased to call advanced civilization. From this lofty vantage, we shudder at the 'bestial' conditions from which we have risen. We instill the fear of cannibalism in our children with tales of 'Jack and the Beanstalk' and 'Hansel and Gretel'. Adult squeamishness extends to include both cannibalism and the eating of nonhuman flesh. For Americans particularly, food that still looks like the animal it came from is often cause for (irrational) disgust. Whole fish, live lobsters, sides of beef on hooks all inspire distaste in people who will blithely eat a slab of steak (it is no longer recognizably lopped from a steer, but the national meat hunger supports giant abattoirs in which wholesale slaughter takes place). Unfortunately, organ meats cannot be so easily disguised. Brains look, almost inevitably, like brains. The sight of those convoluted lobes forces us to admit that we are about to dine on mammal. And so we prefer less obvious cuts. Unlike the Tupinambás, we hide from our killing.

1975

High Torte

After a day or so, the body adjusts to high altitude, and we can begin to walk through a normal life without headaches, nausea, and a pounding heart. Cooking, however, remains a problem. Low air pressure complicates nearly all the processes of the kitchen. It slows down boiling and speeds up deep frying. It throws sugar cookery out of kilter, and it turns the baking of breads and cakes into a fiendishly unpredictable affair.

The alpine poltergeists begin to meddle with our meals as soon as we rise 2,500 feet above sea level. Significant trouble settles in at 5,000 feet, approximately the elevation of Denver. And by the time we reach Leadville, Colorado, the nation's highest city (elevation 10,190), or Leadville's tiny neighbor, Climax, at 11,300 feet probably the loftiest settlement in the country, we have attained a height where it is all but impossible to cook beans in the conventional manner, where bread rises too quickly, and where a poached egg is an achievement.

Of all the pesky changes brought on by thin air, the most unsettling for sea-level natives is the lower boiling point of water. For most of us, 212°F is one of the basic benchmarks of life. It is certainly a crucial factor in cooking because it acts as an upper limit, a foolproof temperature ceiling for anything we might choose to cook in water. You simply can't heat water higher than 212° (unless you put it under artificial pressure). Above that limit, it turns to steam, bubbles away. At sea level, that is.

But, as the air pressure falls at significantly high altitudes, water will turn to vapor more easily. There is less air pushing down on the surface of the water, and so it can bubble up and away with less of a push from beneath, for example, at a lower temperature. This means that boiling will occur sooner, but that the boiling point – that crucial heat ceiling – will be proportionally lower. At 5,000 feet, water boils at 202.6°. At 10,000, the hottest it will get is 194°. At 14,000, water boils away in furious, giant bubbles at only 187.3°.

Consequently, when you put food into this 'cool' boiling water, it cooks much more slowly than you might have expected. Bubbles or not, the heat is simply not there.

I tested this proposition last fall on the trail leading up Mount Whitney at the lower right-hand corner of the Sierra Nevada in eastern California. At approximately 12,000 feet, it took slightly more than six minutes to produce a 'three-minute' egg. The white took that long to turn opaque. It was delicious, nonetheless. The egg had been purchased the day before when very fresh in Shoshone, California, near Death Valley, where it takes just *under* three minutes to soft-boil eggs at 280 feet below sea level. But the altitude on the Whitney Trail had turned my stomach and taken away my appetite for eggs or anything else.

Even after fourteen hours of supine acclimatization in a small orange and blue tent bought for $10 at a bankruptcy sale, I was still slightly nauseated. But my body had adjusted enough to the air so that I was able to lace my boots and consider with some confidence the final stage of my assault on the highest peak in the contiguous United States. Whitney rises 14,495 feet. My job: bake a cake at the top.

I will spare you a step-by-step account of my heroic ascent over the last five miles of snow-covered trail, which zigzags skyward in a great, jagged bowl and then rounds a corner to the mountain's back slope, where, smack, the previously hidden entirety of the Sierra hits your glare-strained eyes. Stretching hugely away below are trees, peaks, valleys, and flashing monocle lakes.

Getting there is no great feat. Hundreds of Boy Scouts and sedentary marmot-lovers climb Whitney every summer. Baking a cake at fourteen and a half thousand feet, however, is a real accomplishment. Indeed, it may never have been attempted before, because altitude interferes more severely with cakes than it does with anything else in cookery. Even at relatively low elevations, trouble sets in. At a mere 3,000 feet, *The Joy of Cooking* warns us, cake doughs will begin to suffer 'pixie-like variation that often defies general rules'.

If you were to mix up a standard white cake dough and bake it in the usual way in your oven in Denver or Laramie, it would come out flat and dry. The dryness is caused by the low humidity of the mountain atmosphere, while the flatness is a result of the thin air, which defeats the best efforts of baking powder, beaten eggs, shortening, and sugar to hold air in the cake and keep it light.

Baking powder is a chemical raising agent in which an acid and an alkaline substance react, in the presence of moisture, to emit carbon dioxide. This gas forms small bubbles in a normal cake dough. The heat of baking then 'sets' the cells formed in the dough by the bubbles. (Modern baking powders are double acting; they begin to act in cold dough, but they do not do most of their work until they are subjected to heat. This permits us to mix up a batter, then wait a while before using it.)

High altitude plays havoc with this chemistry. The gas has less air pressure to work against, so it works too well. The batter puffs up and bubbles as if it were boiling. Then the gas escapes before the cells have set and the cake collapses. Other factors also contribute to the density of cakes at high altitude. Sugar, in excess, produces a coarse, crumbly texture. Beaten eggs are a source of unwanted air. Butter and other shortenings also cause problems in air retention.

In other words, if we are to bake cake at high altitude, we must significantly alter the delicate balance of a batter designed for use at sea level. And, indeed, if you look at most cookbooks' baking sections, they present you with various rules of thumb for alpine cakemaking. A typical set of such instructions might direct you to reduce the baking powder in a conventional recipe by ⅛ to ¼ teaspoon per 1,000 feet of rise above sea level. It would also advise decreasing the sugar by ½ tablespoon per 1,000 feet, and the shortening by ½ teaspoon. Conversely, you will sometimes be told to add extra flour, say one tablespoon per cup in the original recipe, and extra liquid, a tablespoon for every additional 2,500 feet of altitude above 5,000 feet.

I do not present these adjustments as established principles. No one does, because different recipes turn out differently. Or, to speak frankly, no one really knows precisely how to adapt a specific recipe for high altitude without trial and error. Normal cooking, it appears, is in many ways a sea-level phenomenon, a trick that works in one environment and not in others.

Prospectors and mountain climbers, for instance, long ago learned that above 10,000 feet they had to use pressure cookers to cook beans and other foods that require long boiling even at the high temperatures practicable at sea level. Similarly, at alpine altitudes, the standard adjustments for cakes approach a practical limit. If you continue to reduce the baking soda by decrements of ⅛ teaspoon per 1,000 feet, you eventually reach a point at which you must, following the rule, eliminate baking soda altogether from the recipe. For example, the 2 teaspoons of baking soda called for in *The Joy of Cooking*'s recipe for gold layer cake would have to be omitted in any version of the dessert prepared above 16,000 feet. This is, of course, a technical possibility only in Alaska, the Himalayas, and a few other extreme environments where cake baking is not, perhaps, essential. I mention it only to emphasize the specialized nature of cakes and the ingenious balance of natural forces they represent.

At any rate, my own bid for a place in the *Guinness Book of World Records* as history's highest baker met with fair success. Cooked for about forty-five minutes in an Optimus Mini-oven (an aluminum torus sold in camping equipment outlets) over a butane burner's medium-high flame, this white cake emerged very much a cake. It was not the puffy, convex ring one might have ideally wished for, but neither was it concave and unacceptably dense.

Unfortunately, I did not remain at the summit long enough to develop a normal appetite, so for an assessment of the cake's taste, I had to depend on the opinion of the others present who devoured it before I had a chance to ice it. I had intended to do so because icing is essential for keeping cakes moist for any length of time in the dry air at high elevations.

If I had stayed longer, I might also have verified certain other textbook nostrums about cooking in the upper reaches. As things stand, I am willing to take it on faith that above 2,500 feet, it is a good idea to compensate for dryness by covering prepared foods with aluminum foil and by using slightly less flour or more liquid in bread doughs (and watching carefully so that the more rapid action of yeast does not take you by surprise). I am also ready to believe that pressure cookers require an extra pound of pressure for every 2,000 feet above sea level and an increase of 5 per cent in cooking time for every 1,000 feet above the first 2,000. And I will not hesitate, when next in Leadville, to add extra liquid to pancake batter or to consult a table of high-altitude temperature equivalents before attempting to cook sugar for candy or icing. All the usual stages, from soft ball to hard crack, occur sooner (at lower heats) the higher you go.

Finally, I take pleasure in advising the fast-food moguls that when they set up shop atop Pike's Peak, they will have the devil's own time serving crisp French fries. Even at relatively modest altitudes, the recommended frying temperature has to be reduced to about 355°, from the normal 375°, because the boiling point of the internal water in the potatoes is lower. Without lowering the fat temperature, you get external browning well before the inside has cooked. Presumably, at high enough altitudes, correcting for this anomaly will force French-fry vendors to lower their fat temperature to a point so low that it will seep into the potatoes and leave them as limp and greasy as some I once ate in a low dive in Austin, Texas. But that's another story for another time, when we have come down to earth.

1976

NELSON ALGREN

Festivals in the Fields

'We shuk an' bresh'd the dry corn silks offen our cloes an' went inter the house
. . . In the middel o' the long tabel thet tuk up the senter o' the room stud a
roasted shote thet look'd mos'es nateral es life, wi' a yer o' corn in its mouth
an' a ring o' tumblers full o' biled custard wi' littel dabs o' red jell on top a surlin'
roun' it. An' piled on over' whars' on the outside o' this 'ere wus ven'zon an'
wile turkey an' jole an' cabbage an' pumpkin butter an' cowcumber pickles an'
biskits an' smokin' hot corn aigy bred an' stacks o' all kins' o' pies an' cakes
know'd ter pi'neers an' a small o' fride ham an' coffee a purvadin' thet putt on
the cap sheef an' made us ten times hongrier'n ever.'

The French were the first, and the quickest, to learn the wilderness ways
from the Indian hunters who fished the secret rivers of that lost and secret
wilderness: the Huron and Illiniwek, the Pottawattomi and Fox. Their arrows
in the aspen leaves first taught the French, then all the races that followed. Till
the teaching was no longer by arrow but by the peacepipe and the banquet
board. By the ripening maize and the harvest festival.

To the Indian, the ripening of the corn marked the beginning of the new
year and the end of the old. Among many tribes, at this time of year no tribe
member would eat of or even handle any part of the harvest until the Festival
of First Fruits had been conducted. This was a forerunner of the white man's
husking bees and harvest homes.

Other tribes, before going on the warpath, avoided all meat. But the Kansas
Indians in preparing for war conducted a feast in the chief's hut, of which the
principal dish was roast dog. This was a custom in the tradition of homeo-
pathic magic common to all peoples of the globe in all stages of civilization,
the theory being that an animal capable, as the dog was supposed to be, of
letting himself be destroyed in defense of his master must necessarily inspire
an equal courage in the eater. Upon a similar assumption, the Sioux reduced to
powder the hearts of valiant enemies, hoping thus to appropriate the dead
man's gallantry. Or, when through eating, wiped his hands on his feet to lend
them speed.

In the old French time the voyageurs sat at roast-dog feasts, clothed as colorfully as the blue-feathered braves themselves. They wore shirts and waist-coats of cotton, blue cloth or deer-skin trousers, and blue-beaded moccasins of bright Indian weave. In winter they wore long woolen coats with blue hoods attached which in wet weather or cold were drawn up over the head. And the head was commonly covered with a blue cotton handkerchief folded as a turban.

They learned not only to hunt and dress like the Indian but to eat like him. Marquette pronounced the wild oats or the *folles avoines* of as delicate a flavor as French-cooked rice. The precooked fish and buffalo meat served him by the Peoria Indians on the banks of the Mississippi he found both strengthening and palatable, and sagamité, mortar-pounded cornmeal flavored with berries and fried in bear grease, he pronounced delicious.

LaSalle's men ate heartily of a bear-meat feast tendered them by the Peorias. The Illiniwek fed Henri de Tonti of the best they had, though there came a time when he was reduced to digging with his one good hand the wild onions on the banks of the Chicago River.

A food custom peculiar to the Sioux was that of the Virgin Feast, a banquet conducted to resolve the truth or falsity of tribal scandal. When such scandal, concerning a young woman of the tribe, reached the ears of the girl's mother, the mother commanded the daughter to cook rice and to invite the other maidens of the tribe to partake of it. These young women would appear with the crimson circle of virginity painted on each cheek, seat themselves in a semi-circle, and each be served a bowl of rice. Then a circular boulder painted red was placed about ten feet distant and a knife plunged into the ground before it. The young men of the band then stood about with deadpan expressions, watching the maidens eat. If none of the youths spoke and the meal was

finished without interruption, the maiden was vindicated and the gossip halted. But if one of the bucks had his doubts, he stepped forward, seized the girl by the hand, pulled her out of the ring, and made his charges point-blank. She had the right of swearing, by the circular stone and the plunged blade, to her innocence: this went a considerable distance toward vindication but was not considered conclusive. If her accuser persisted, an altercation ensued, upon which final tribal sentiment was formed.

The Sioux around St Paul adapted the French custom of making calls on New Year's Day and receiving cakes, wines, and kisses. The Indians called it the kissing day and were inclined to make their calls very early in the morning, braves and squaws presenting themselves together, receiving equal gifts and equal kisses from the St Paul householders.

On New Year's Eve it was the custom of the young men of the French colony around Cahokia, Illinois, to assemble dressed in masquerade costumes and each provided with a bucket, sack, basket, or other article for the carrying of solid or liquid provisions. About nine o'clock in the evening they started on the rounds of the homes, singing 'La Guignolée' and receiving sugar, coffee, lard, candles, flour, maple syrup, ratafia, eggs, meat, and poultry. If a householder who was able to give refused, he commonly had his chicken house stripped clean.

And six days later, on the evening of the feast of Epiphany, the maidens of the town were invited by the youths to bake pancakes. The supplies gathered on New Year's Eve were then brought out to provide the feast.

On such holidays the French, both of Minnesota and of Illinois, fed the local Indians on anything and everything they had handy. But especially in southern Illinois on *galettes sauvages* or *croquecignolles*. These were two varieties of doughnuts, both made of the same ingredients but the latter being large, oblong in shape, and slit several times all the way through beginning about an inch from each end, with alternate sections raised. They were familiarly called tangled breeches. The *galettes sauvages* were about half the size of the *croquecignolles* and slit through three times. Sections were not raised, the slits taking the place of the hole in the common present-day doughnut.

The French also fashioned a tart called *pâté marraine* or Godmother's tart. For this, dough was rolled as in preparing pie crust and cut out in the form and size of a big plate. One kind of fruit was placed on half of the shaped dough, and the other side of the dough was punctured, as in ordinary fruit pies. This side was then folded over the fruit and the edges crimped to keep juice from escaping. Such tarts were given the godchildren upon visits to the godparents' home as something especially for godchildren.

Among other dishes which the Indian learned to eat from the hospitable French were crêpes, or pancakes, and brioche, a coffee cake. For this, an exceptionally rich dough was used, but only moderately sweet. It was usually shaped in rings, snails, or braids and covered with nuts or fruits. It was made up with butter instead of with the usual vegetable shortening. This was a breakfast bread served with strong black coffee . . .

The French in all parts of the Middle West have had a penchant for bouillon parties, from the first settlements down to the present. At such occasions as card parties, eaten with crackers or bread, bouillon still replaces coffee in southern Illinois among the French.

Another old French custom of the same area still lends an added zest to holiday suppers by using in the bouillon chickens stolen by one member of the community from another. To invite a neighbor to dine on his own fowl is considered a social grace, to be caught prowling in the henhouse is something else.

The French still make a stew in southern Illinois, cooked all day over a slow fire, called potpourri and reported to be more savory than American stew, its essence being its treatment by such spices as thyme and bay leaf.

It was a Frenchman, too, who was instrumental in originating burgoo, a stew still popular in the Lincoln country and western Kentucky. His name was Gus Jaubert, and he was associated with the Confederate raider John Hunt Morgan. On an occasion when Morgan had conducted a successful supply raid, Jaubert was commissioned to cook the spoils. Into a five hundred-gallon kettle used for making gunpowder he threw beans, chickens, potatoes, corn, cabbage, tomatoes, and everything else he could find. The result was neither a soup nor a stew but possessed the best qualities of both. And has since been a favorite in the Kentucky country on occasions when a large crowd of people is to be fed. But Morgan County in Illinois is today, appropriately enough, the country's biggest burgoo county. It is also common enough in Jersey, Greene, and Macoupin Counties.

In these counties, a harvest-home festival today requires that all foods served be raised within county bounds. After the supper, the dancing begins – square dancing to the mountain tunes that came to the Illinois country long ago:

> Oh I want none of your weevily wheat,
> I want none of your barley,
> I'll take some flour and a half an hour
> And bake a cake for Charley.

After the dancing and eating are done, the leftover food is packed in bushel baskets for distribution among the poor. There have been harvest-home suppers downstate when enough was left over to fill sixty-five such baskets.

Late 1930s

LUCIUS BEEBE

Eatalls and Tosspots

The history of gastronomy, the legend of gourmandism in Boston, was inaugurated the day that Julien evolved his soup. The precise date of this event can only be left to conjecture, but it was either three or four years before the end of the eighteenth century.

Scrodded codfish, brown bread, baked kidney beans and Cotuit oysters are, naturally enough, universally and reverently associated with the tradition of Boston table fare. They are characteristic, indigenous dishes to the region, deriving from its setting, the tastes of its inhabitants and the genius produced by their early necessities and resources. It comes as a surprise, however, to learn that such an essentially Gallic contriving should have as its source, *fons et origo*, within the precincts of Yankee Congress Street as that arrangement through whose agency Julien became known to fame. Consommé, somehow, is not as patently a Down East derivative as, say, quahogs or salt-rising bread.

Jean Baptiste Gilbert Payplat *dit* Julien came to town in 1794, a refugee from the Paris terror. He had at his disposal, it appears from the records, the sum of $6,000, and with this he undertook to introduce to an as yet strictly home-faring Boston an authentic French restaurant. Up till then people had eaten in public at cook-shops and taverns, but Julien's 'Restorator', as he called his enterprise, set diners out by the ears with its Parisian elegance of fare, its new and foreign dishes and their cachet of fashionable smartness. His modest frame establishment at the corner of Congress Street and Milk became the resort of the town. The Restorator thrived. Gustatory symphonies were prepared to the accompaniment of a leitmotiv of clattering dishes and tinkling crystal. Hogsheads of fine Claret washed down firkins of Strasbourg *foie-gras*. Crêpes a l'orange came into ambrosial being over flaming spirit-lamps. Truffles from Périgord appeared to ornament galantines of grouse and cold sides of Restigouche salmon. The proprietors of the Hat and Helmet and the Green Dragon waxed vainly apoplectic.

And then one day Julien created a new consommé and fame and fortune hovered over the tureen of its birth. Overnight Jean Baptiste Gilbert Payplat became the toast of gastronomes, a veritable prince of soups. The recipe for Julien flew out of town with a hundred galloping stagecoaches, and from far and wide eatalls and epicures converged on Congress Street in hungry hundreds.

Rumors of this gastronomic Klondike reached Hartford and the most distinguished gourmet of all time simultaneously. Claude Anthelme Brillat-Savarin, whose *Physiology of Taste* was a few years later to become a classic of good living, was on a wild turkey shoot. He hung up his fowling piece and engaged passage on the first stage to Boston. The Field of the Cloth of Gold palls beside the meeting of those two mighty monarchs of the saucepan.

In return for the boon of a new consommé, Brillat-Savarin taught Julien the secret of cheese fondue, and the proprietor of the Restorator found that in inventing one new dish he had acquired two. Cheese fondue, a sort of lineal antecedent of our own rarebit of Wales, became the favorite late-supper dish of Boston, and when Brillat-Savarin went back to New York on his way home Julien sent him a fine roe deer which, the father of transcendental gastronomy records, was vastly appreciated at a party he gave on the eve of his sailing. No reigning sovereigns could have exchanged more princely tokens of their mutual esteem.

When Julien died his wife inherited the property and the recipe for the consommé and held forth at the old stand a decade before she sold it to Frederick Rouillard. This estimable boniface, unlettered, perhaps, in the subtleties of Continental cuisine, ran the Restorator as a chop-house, as the following verses, penned by an anonymous patron, survive to indicate:

Julien's Restorator

I knew by the glow that so rosily shone
Upon Frederick's cheeks, that he lives on good cheer;
And I said, 'If there's steaks to be had in the town,
The man who loves venison should look for them here.'

'Twas two; and the dinners were smoking around,
The cits hastened home at the savory smell,
And so still was the street that I heard not a sound
But the barkeeper ringing the Coffee House bell.

'And here in the cosy "Old Club",' I exclaimed,
With a steak that was tender and Frederick's best wine,
While under my platter a spirit blaze flamed,
'How long could I sit and how well could I dine!'

By the side of my venison a tumbler of beer
Or a bottle of sherry how pleasant to see,
And to know that I dined on the best of the deer,
That never was dearer to any than me!

The Restorator, apparently, like other taverns and ordinaries of the time, held with the old custom of naming its various apartments and dining-rooms, and the Old Club must have been one of these.

Julien's was torn down in 1824 after three decades of service, but the name was evidently too valuable a one to be allowed to perish, as is attested by an insertion in the *Boston Advertiser* in 1831 which informs the public that at the Julien House in Congress Street 'Gentlemen and ladies from the country who are in pursuit of board and pleasant situation will be most thankfully received.'

Until the third decade of the century the various taverns, ordinaries and stage-coach inns of Boston were sufficient, both in numbers and appointments, to accommodate the transient travel of the city, but in 1828 it appeared that there was a real need for more spacious and impressive facilities for the entertainment of visitors, especially of distinguished foreigners, who were flocking to town in ever-increasing numbers. To meet this need a group of public-minded citizens pooled their resources to build, in the Tremont House, the earliest first-class hotel in America.

The inaugural dinner of this establishment, the distinguished guests at which included Daniel Webster and Edward Everett, was indicative of the manner in which meals were served in public restaurants at this period.

The waiters [wrote a contemporary] filed into the upper end of the room where the landlord, Dwight Boyden, stood with a long white apron around him, and carving knife and fork in hand; and at the sound of a bell one seized upon a quantity of plates, another knives, a third forks, a fourth a lot of large soup spoons, and a fifth the smaller spoons. At the second sound of the bell they moved into line, and at the third marched with sedate steps behind the chairs of the guests, and simultaneously the bearers of plates, knives, forks and spoons, with a flourish of the hand, placed the various articles upon the table before the guests, and then gracefully stepped back into line ready to carry out their orders. In the meantime, the landlord was carving.

Such was the ritual of the host's dinner, a ritual which obtained until the first à la carte bills of fare made this pleasant regimentation of service a thing of the past. The Tremont House was for many years the wonder and glory of American hotel-keepers who came from far and wide to study its crystal chandeliers, Turkey carpets, French ormolu clocks, its free New Year's Day dinners to all guests and its innovation of free slippers provided for guests while their jack-boots were being cleaned and returned to the long row of gleaming footgear in the front office. It was the Boston residence of celebrities including Charles Dickens, President Van Buren, the Prince de Joinville, Edwin Forrest, Daniel Webster, William C. Macready and President Tyler.

Boston's next great hotel, constructed during the fabulous forties some score of years later, was the Revere House, then considered a palatial caravanserai, which in its time sheltered Jenny Lind, the Prince of Wales, the Grand Duke Alexis, the Emperor Dom Pedro and General Grant. A tattered railroad guide of the fifties in the possession of the writer recommends that voyagers who have safely survived the perils of the train brigade trip from New York by the Long Island and New London ferry route may with confidence put up at the then new Adams House, the American House, the Revere House, the Tremont House or the United States Hotel.

It was Harvey D. Parker, however, who made modern history in the Boston world of hotels. Parker House rolls were to bear his name and renown throughout the world. Parker's Hotel was to become a Boston institution almost as representative of the town as the proverbial codfish, whose image hangs in the State House, and second only in fame to the Athenaeum, the *Transcript* and the uncontrolled passion of authentic Bostonians for attending funerals.

Mr Parker, whose seaman's beard, innocent of mustaches, and sturdily handsome profile you can still see hung in the up-to-the-minute Parker House of today, came to Boston from Paris, Maine, and served his apprenticeship as coachman for a lady of circumstance living in Watertown. His cockaded topper bravely set over one ear, his top-booted feet planted firmly against the dash of a lurching coach which swayed in a seagoing manner over the roads on cantilever springs, young Parker drove her on shopping trips into the city at frequent intervals, and it was his custom to lunch in a modest Court Square restaurant kept by one John E. Hunt.

Whether it was because he found the orders short and indulged that almost universal hanker to be proprietor, some day, of an establishment in which one has received a fancied slight, or because he saw a more secure and affluent future as boniface than as groom must be a matter for conjecture, but in any event, in 1832, he bought Hunt out for the sum of $432, and some notion of the shrewdness of the trading involved may derive from the circumstance that items as small as a ten-cent lemon squeezer were listed in the bill of sale.

Parker's restaurant, in the conduct of which he interested as steward John F. Mills, prospered because of the perfection of its service. The Jacks and Pats and Timothys who were its waiters practiced all the little attentive touches long since bequeathed to a Gallic race of Henris and Marios in the restaurants of the land. The Tremont Restaurant fairly coined money.

In 1854 Parker bought the old John Mico house, hung a simple shingle with the word 'Parker's' over the busy sidewalk, and set out to test an idea he had harbored in the back of his head for some time: namely that perhaps hotel patrons might like their meals at other than specified hours. Heretofore, even amid the almost Babylonish elegances of the Tremont House, meals had been served at fixed hours, and he who was late went without. The American plan, as it is to this day known, and continuous dining-room service came into immediately popular being at Parker's.

Subsequent additions to the original Mico house carried the School Street façade of Parker's to the corner of Tremont Street, opposite King's Chapel, and almost as far down the hill as to be opposite the stone and iron gates of City Hall. Parts of its exterior suggested a Georgian mansion, others the Chateau of Chambord. Its corridors, as most Bostonians recall, resembled gas-lit catacombs carpeted in Turkey red and full of improbable angles, turns and levels. The chances were heavily against a late diner's ever getting to his own apartment, even if the lift deposited him in its approximate vicinage, and one gay old dog used to recall that he slept more frequently in linen closets than in his own bed. Its lobby, with its black and white marble floor and mahogany-fitted desks and offices, was one of the sights of the town, and the writer's father was fond of recalling how, as a boy in the sixties, he used to be brought to Parker's for the heavenly experience of seeing the famous wall-paper, gay as it was with steeple chases, departing coaches and huntsmen galloping across the rolling and perpetual countryside of its pattern.

What the Brown Palace was to Denver, the Planters to Saint Louis, the Saint Charles to New Orleans, Brown's to London and the Windsor to Montreal, the Parker House, as it became formally known after the death in 1884 of Mr Parker, was to all New England. It was the meeting place of countrymen, with chin-whiskers and carpet bags, of the sort known as Silas on every comedy stage in the land, of mutton-chopped bankers over from New York in George Pullman's new plush and maple walnut palace cars, of white-top-hatted sports who matched their trotters of a Sunday afternoon on the 'Mile Ground' as the stretch of Commonwealth Avenue was known that lay beyond Cottage Farm Bridge. The whiskered and Tattersall waistcoated blades of Harvard arrived and departed, refreshed, on the hourly horse-cars to Cambridge that stopped at the little waiting-room on the corner of Bosworth Street. State Street merchants had their first Scotch grouse of the season, washed down with Perrier Jouet extra sec in its sober dining-rooms. Drummers, literateurs, the unspeakable Mr Dickens who returned America's gracious hospitality with a vulgarian's churlishness, *bon viveurs*, all the world of travelers for a third of a century made their rendezvous there.

It was as the meeting place of The Saturday Club that Parker's inspired Dr Holmes to his well-known lines:

> Turn half-way round, and let your look survey
> The white façade that gleams across the way, –
> The many windowed building, tall and wide,
> The palace-inn that shows its northern side
> In grateful shadow when the sunbeams beat
> The granite wall in summer's scorching heat.
> This is the place; whether its name you spell
> Tavern or caravanserai or hotel.
> Such guests! What famous names its record boasts,
> Whose owners wander in a mob of ghosts.

For many years Parker's bar-room made more than $100,000 annual clear profit, and now that common sense has again been incorporated into the Constitution it is possible that the new Parker House may approximate this handsome source of legitimate revenue. Heaven knows the place was dismal enough during the great dry spell, and the writer recalls the horror registered on the face of a waiter captain when, in a private dining-room, a bucket of ice was commanded for the cooling of a couple bottles of wine at a dinner for a prospective bridegroom.

The Parker House roll was, of course, the most famous of the contributions to the tradition of gastronomy in School Street, but other things, especially game, were notable as specialties of the house. The following menu, that of a private dinner given in an era of less Spartan table fare than is currently fashionable, gives a fair index of what a Bostonian of the seventies might expect at Parker's when he had, with anticipatory forethought, unbuttoned his Albert watch chain and smoothed his napkin into the folds of his white linen vest.

Château Yquem Grand Vin
Little Neck Clams
Yriarte Pâle
Clear Green Turtle aux Quenelles   Pôtage à la Reine
Schloss Johannesberger
Soft Shell Crabs, Sauce Tartare
Spanish Mackerel à la Maitre d'Hôtel
Pommery and Gréno 'Sec'
Filets of beef à la Triano
Green Goose Purée of Chestnuts
Sweetbreads à la Toulouse   Broiled Fresh Mushrooms
Supreme of Chicken aux Truffles
Pâté de foie gras à la Bellevue
Roman Punch
Château Mouton Rothschild
Upland Plover   Doe Birds
Parisienne Soufflé   Opera Biscuit
Chantilly Cream   Petits Charlotte
Roquefort and Camembert   Olives, ripe and green
Hamburg Grapes   Apricots, Cherries
Strawberries   French Fruit
Ice Cream Sherbet
Pousse Café
Café Noir
Cognac 1811
Liqueurs

These casual snacks would not, of course, have been considered anything suitable for a formal occasion. The terrapin, saddle of mutton, canvasback, mongrel goose, grouse and other essentials of true dining were omitted altogether, but the bill will indicate what was esteemed proper for a small supper tendered to an eminent barrister on the occasion of a notable legal triumph. The rapid whirring sound audible in the direction of the Granary burying ground is doubtless the Puritan father who watered his family's soup lest they should enjoy it overmuch, turning over in his grave.

No account of the annals of dining in Boston would be complete without mention of the old Bell in Hand, of Jake Wirth's immortal resort of beer and song and of Billy Park's, beloved of Harvard students, but space compels us to Winter Place.

The brass sign on either side of the door reads Locke-Ober's Winter Place Wine Rooms, and it is here that an entire school of Boston eatalls and tosspots of enduring fame for more than half a century have resorted. For here, in a narrow alley, scarcely a long stone's throw from Brimstone Corner, is a true shrine of the culinary art in its robuster moods, and like pious incense the savors of its service drift through the open windows into the tranquil evening of the city around it, complemented by an amiable leitmotif of laughter and clinking crystal.

Early in the eighties Louis Ober hung out his bush in Winter Place. Eben Jordan, the great merchant, ate there and drank deep and was pleased, and his patronage brought a prosperity to the taverner. Twenty years later Frank Locke, a rival boniface, established a similar place of business next door, and the substantial citizens of the community found it agreeable to drink a whisky sling at Locke's before having a Medford rum at Ober's, where the food was admittedly superior. Sometimes these potations were retroactive in effect and the doors between the establishments were kept in a state of abrupt oscillation by customers hurrying from sling to rum and, conversely, from rum to sling. On such occasions the food consumption was practically negligible, but everyone agreed that Locke's and Ober's were essential one to the other, and in 1894 the party wall between them was torn down with what amounted to a public demonstration. The two taverns were merged as Locke-Ober's Winter Place Wine Rooms and the brass sign in the alley still announces this cheerful circumstance.

Prosperity has always been associated with Winter Place tavern, as it is commonly known. Even during the years of the great drought, when its bar was dedicated to oysters alone, the bright youth and chivalry of Harvard thronged its tables and were careful of the disposition of their feet so as not to disturb the bottles under their chairs. The long carved mahogany bar with its French mirrors, imported from San Domingo at great expense and installed with public rejoicing, the steam dishes of the free lunch with their intricate system of chains and counterweights for lifting the covers, the magnificent bar-room nude at the end of the room with a crystal goblet in her hand and vine leaves in her hair, all are symbolic of physical well-being dating from the days when the burgesses in frock coats and top hats lined the bar and invented the Ward Eight.

The invention of this arrangement was unquestionably the high point in the history of Winter Place. The precise details of the epochal event, together with the name of the pioneer in bar-craft of its first designer, are shrouded in the mists of antiquity, but word of the phenomenon spread rapidly and it was shortly after this that Locke and Ober jointly participated in a ceremony which consisted of throwing the key to the front door into Boston harbor. The Ward Eight is a sort of whisky sling based on ancient Bourbon and served in a highball glass. Compared with it a bolt of lightning is a very mild form of stimulant. The tinkle of ice in the glasses appropriate to this toddy became louder than the traffic in Temple Place hard by, and if the secret of its composition had not become generally known it is probable that excursion trains from all over New England would have converged upon the common goal of Boston filled with thirsty enthusiasts. Locke and Ober, as a result, got rich.

The increased patronage of the house called for a revision of the menu, and Emil Camus, who succeeded to the property when Locke and Ober took the Ward Eight with them to the Elysian Fields, and Nick Stuhl, the manager, designed a bill of fare which became famous for its fish and game, sweetbreads Eugenie, lobster Savannah, monumental filets of beef and distinguished cellarage full of hocks. Theodore Roosevelt invariably patronized it when in Boston. Thomas Lawson, between moments of frenzied finance, projected his urbane personality and inevitable gardenia upon its festive scene. Thomas Bailey Aldrich and Henry Cabot Lodge were members of a regular patronage and Enrico Caruso could hardly be dragged away when it was curtain time at the opera house up in Huntington Avenue. As a matter of fact, Louis H. Mudgett, oldtime manager of the opera house, used to detail a special agent who was to cut off the great man's supply of edibles when it was becoming apparent that if he consumed one more entrée he might have convulsions on the stage in the midst of *Aida.*

Nor has the passing of time dissolved in any appreciable degree the flavor of authenticity which pervades this substantial ordinary. The man who has fared there on Cotuits and grilled Scotch grouse complemented by a bottle of Rudesheimer Oberfeld of that greatest of years, 1921, the whole served by Charlie, dean of waiters, has dined indeed. By custom the older patrons of the establishment who are dining alone are seated together at a long common table. There H.T.P. of the *Transcript* was for many years the arbiter of its conversation. Professor John Livingston Lowes of Harvard has been no stranger to its board, and at one time a mysterious undergraduate organization known as the Michael Mullins Chowder and Marching Society put in a not too reticent appearance, arriving in horse-drawn herdics and, for the earlier part of the evening at least, immaculately attired in silk hats and tailcoats. Neither chowder nor marching gave its members very much concern.

Only masculine persons are permitted in the restaurant proper or at the oyster bar presided over by the ingratiating Jacimo, but there are *cabinets particuliers* upstairs, upholstered in the crimson satin of tradition, dating from the period when drinking champagne from the slipper of a dancing lady was considered the very smartest, if slightly daring form. Under its florid and ornate electroliers Winter Place has seen much of Boston history. For more than half a century it has dispensed sound food and mellow liquors and it is possessed of the worn quality, the patina of useful age which only time and good cheer and the passage of stout eaters and happy drinkers can impart.

It will be apparent, perhaps, from the foregoing memoranda on the most important of the arts devised for human comfort and delight that neither as a Puritan community nor as a latter-day Tyre of the Western World was Boston an undernourished citadel of lean fare or languishing trenchermen. And private entertainment was not accustomed to lag behind that at public functions if one is to judge by the catalogue of the fare set before the guests of William Gallagher a century or so ago with all its lavishness and occasionally frightening Gallicisms intact.

BILL OF FARE

CENTENNIAL DINNER

Exchange Coffee House, September 17, 1930

Mock Turtle Soup	Perdrix au Chou
Boiled Bass	Dindons a la Gallentine
Baked Cod Fish	Fricandeau aux Tomata
Auguille a la Tartare	Lobster Curried
Boiled Hams	Roast Beef
Boiled Corned Beef	Roast Leg of Mutton
Boiled Tongues	Roast Mongrel Geese
Boiled Legs of Mutton	Roast Tame Ducks
Boiled Turkey, Oyster Sauce	Roast Chicken
Beef Alamode	Roast Larded Wild Pigeons
Beef Bouille	Roast Partridges
Chicken a la Suprème	Roast Wild Ducks
Vol au vent au Huitres	Roast Wild Gray and Black
Vol au vent de Volaille	Roast Woodcocks
Vol au vent a la St Lambert	Roast Plovers
Vol au vent Wild Pigeons	Roast Quails
Poulettes a la Conti	Roast Snipes
Puddings, Pies, Custards	Turks Caps, Ice Creams, etc.

Dessert

Nor has the passage of time diminished the capacity of the town's gourmets, who celebrated the first year of repeal and the arrival of André Simon, President of the Wine and Food Society of England, with libations whose echoes must have reached even to the vault on the Common where Master Julien dreams of vanished triumphs. At the dinner accorded him in a private home on Beacon Hill, M. Simon was able subsequently to recall that with the hors d'œuvres was served a very old Madeira, a Cossart Gordon's 1826 Rainwater; a Batard Montrachet with the soup; a century-old pale Sherry with the fish; a hock with the entrée; Burgundies of three distinguished years ranging from a Clos de Vougeot '87 to a Grand Chambertin '15, with the roast (a Mallard duck per guest); a sweet hock with the soufflé; and then, said M. Simon, the real drinking started.

Coffee was supplemented with six brandies; two kinds of Armagnac, two Charentes and two Cognacs of 1820 and 1848, respectively. After these came a couple of bottles of wonderful old Medford rum, described by the celebrated diner-out as 'a steel fist in a velvet glove', and finally a very rare old Bourbon and a hundred-year-old Rye out of the cellar of the host's grandfather. M. Simon later told newspaper reporters he did not expect to meet such hospitality elsewhere on his grand tour of the United States.

An amusing sidelight on the Puritan cast of thought which has animated the Boston licensing authorities down to the present day is the requirement that the entire interior of taverns must be visible from the street. By this device it was hoped citizens would be shamed from standing up to bars and drinking in full view of the populace. But the result has, happily, been the reverse, and strollers, until then quite unconscious of their need, have viewed the happy topers through the window and dashed inside to get themselves in similar case.

Warmed by the genial fires of third-proof rum, Boston has always been a town of eatalls, but it required Julien and Brillat-Savarin to make it a city of gourmets. And the coot stew at Haussman's in Avery Street, like the inimitable cream cheese and bar-le-duc dear to old gentlemen at teatime in the lounge of Clark's Hotel next to the Adams House, are as much a part of the Boston legend as the elusive accent of its inhabitants, the First Corps Cadets, or the tradition of John L. Sullivan, the strong boy of Roxbury and the wonder and glory of an entire generation of sporting Americans.

1935

JAMES VILLAS

The Inimitable Mrs Foster

You arrive at the front door of Mr & Mrs Foster's Place in proper attire, having been informed while making a reservation on the phone that it's jacket and tie for the gentlemen. You've also been told politely by that soft Virginia voice not to be late and not to have much for lunch. You knock just as you would at a private home, the locked door opens, and there stands the elegant Pearl Byrd Foster swathed in dark Ultrasuede and hardly the image of one who's been cooking since noon. The place is minuscule; the décor would be described as austere were it not for the exquisite flower arrangements. No menu, no fancy china or flatware, a limited but intelligent wine list, no nonsense. You're here to see Mrs Foster and taste her American food, and, like the others waiting to be served, you know this is serious business.

To suggest that Mr & Mrs Foster's Place has become an institution in New York City is not hyperbole, and to insinuate that Pearl Byrd Foster is a veritable anachronism in this graceless age of submediocrity is a triumph of understatement. Professional gastronomes and journalists show up repeatedly on East 81st Street in hopes of discovering the secrets of Pearl's duck pâté, hot lemon soup, and snow cream. Such luminaries as Robert Redford, Walter Cronkite, Ethel Merman, and Malcolm Forbes consider the restaurant a haven where great food can be enjoyed in much the same manner as at home. As for myself, I've come to cherish this place as a sort of culinary shrine, just as I've come to cherish my close friendship with Pearl more than that with anyone else in the profession. The truth is that, whether the subject be the Biblical origins of carob, the gustatory merits of mutton, the medicinal qualities of garlic, the intricate seasoning of pâtés, or the boning of a gigantic goose, she is an encyclopedia of knowledge. Most food enthusiasts flock to their vast culinary libraries when in need of inspiration and information; I pick up the phone and call Pearl Byrd Foster.

'Exactly who is Mrs Foster and what is she really like?' are the questions asked most by those who visit the restaurant, watch her ring the small silver bell that preludes the description of her famous soups and desserts, and listen to her informal table discourses on food and wine punctuated throughout by her very southern 'Honey' this and 'Darling' that. Well, I suppose I could go into biographical detail about how, as a child, she crossed the Oklahoma prairie in a covered wagon, foraged for wild persimmons and Jerusalem artichokes (which she crunched raw), cultivated her own quarter-acre of tomatoes, and, by the age of twelve, was creating and preparing dishes for the family meals; or how she played the New York stage before meeting her late husband; or why she turned over the opportunity to be the first passenger to fly the Atlantic to a girl named Amelia Earhart ('I was frightened, let's face it, and she was brave'); or why she used to meet her celebrated cousin, Admiral Richard E. Byrd, under the clock at the Biltmore ('Don't forget, honey, I'm a Byrd on both sides of the family'). Over the years her pink cloche hats and smart white turbans contributed much to the orchidaceous July transatlantic sailings of the *France* and *QE 2*, and Pearl still boards the magnificent Cunarder each year bearing such staples as almonds, carob powder, and raw sugar as precautions against the possibility that she might be asked by Chef Bainbridge or somebody in England or France to prepare her carob almond torte. Summers in Europe find her rambling about the kitchen of some Scottish castle, talking food with Waverley Root in Paris, learning to skin eels in Brussels, grilling *loup au fenouil* at an apartment in southern France, observing the subtleties of pasta making at the Gritti Palace in Venice, or savoring the glories of Alsatian cuisine at her beloved Auberge de l'Ill in Illhaeusern. When there's something new to learn about food, no place is too distant for Pearl.

'Oh, darling, why must you go on about those aspects of my life?' she's forever chiding. And indeed the only topic that really sustains Pearl's interest at any given time is the dish or the formal dinner on which she currently happens to be working. Most customers are content enough just to hear her discuss the luscious creations served on a regular basis as part of the six-course, fixed-price dinner: tiny chicken livers in Madeira; a wedge of feathery quiche (the recipe for which even I have never managed to obtain); a choice of homemade soups (Virginia peanut, hot lemon, mushroom consommé, cold apple) with fresh corn sticks 'for dunking'; such main courses (ordered in advance on the phone) as Crustacean Broil, Bourbon Beef and Oyster Pot, and Boned Duck with Apple and Wild Rice; and, for dessert, Pecan Pie, Carob Cheesecake, Snow Cream, or Frosty Lime Pie.

But Pearl's inventive mind is eternally in search of new flavors, different textures, and new combinations that might contribute to her lifelong campaign to elevate the spirit of American cookery from the banal to the sublime. When someone sent her a case of California walnuts, she set out to create both a new paté that had crunch and a plantation molasses-and-walnut pie; when a twelve-pound country ham arrived from an admirer in Kentucky, she first tested it in her jambalaya, found the cured flavor too assertive, then incorporated it successfully into Texas wheat puffs; and no sooner had she received a freshly killed goose from Long Island than she devised an apple, prune, and walnut stuffing for the goose, which was served with port gravy. Yogurt pie enriched with pure clover honey, Brussels sprouts sautéed with peanuts, squash soup spiked with apple, shrimp-and-corn chowder, boned roast chicken with curried chutney glaze, potato salad with hot Creole mustard, lemon soufflé pudding – Pearl's creations go on and on, year after year, and after begging so long for recipes, friends and customers of Pearl wait patiently for her forthcoming cookbook.

No one who knows Pearl can be unaware of her short temper in the face of phoniness and pretension, and nothing incurs her wrath faster than any suggestion that Paul Bocuse, Michel Guérard, and other famous French chefs have brought about a radical change in the food world by insisting that the freshest ingredients be prepared in the simplest manner possible. 'Baloney!' she retorts. 'I've personally done the Lyon markets with Bocuse – at a date, that is, when he actually shopped himself – and what I saw him doing was no different from what I've been doing for decades. No doubt Paul is a very fine chef during those increasingly rare moments he's actually in the kitchen, but as for creating a new approach to food and cooking, well, it's just not so. Darling, if you want to see a couple of truly serious cooks in France who share many of my own views, either make your way into Paul Haeberlin's kitchen at the Auberge de l'Ill or visit Richard Olney at his villa near Toulon.'

Unlike the many other chefs of whom she doesn't exactly approve, Pearl *does* do her rounds of the markets every single working day of the week, and she *does* stay in her kitchen from exactly twelve noon till the last order is served late in the evening. Having picked up a few kiwi fruit (and Pearl was using 'New Zealand gooseberries' years before other eastern chefs even heard of the fruit), salad greens and fresh vegetables, dairy products from a health-food store, perhaps an especially handsome chicken or slab of calf's liver, and heaven knows what other items intended for heaven knows what dishes to be either tested or served that evening, she prepares herself for deliveries of meat and seafood in much the same way Henri Soulé used to await his caviar merchants at Le Pavillon. 'Honey, those lobsters had better be kicking!' I once heard her say to a terrified delivery boy, 'and if there's one whiff of odor to that lump crabmeat, you'll be making a trip back here within the hour.' 'You see, honey,' she continued, turning to me while grabbing for a tin of crabmeat, 'the question you must always ask is "How fresh is fresh?" Sure, they'll tell you that the shrimp and pompano are fresh, but what I want to know is how long did it take that shrimp to arrive in New York from the Carolinas, and how long did it sit there on ice before reaching my front door? You just never know, not till you smell it and check the texture.'

Although a lady of a certain age (a subject one would be well advised not to pursue in her presence), Pearl is generally viewed as a cyclone of energy, deter-mination, and self-confidence, the type of dynamic individual who has tremen-dous faith in her own instincts and abilities and little respect for those who don't strive to realize their full potential. If some might accuse her of *amour-propre* when it comes to the way she enjoys talking about her food, it's only because they don't quite understand her overall sense of mission and her pro-found devotion to the art of cooking and eating well. 'My taste buds are alive and I have a lot of energy,' she once wrote me from France. 'My vitality seems endless, and my desire to learn is so deep it burns inside me. Change my style of American food at the Place? No, no, a thousand times no! But I must learn more about French foods – the uses of butter and fats, the fascinating ways of preparing vegetables, the different cuts of meat, the sauces.' People who mis-take this almost childlike enthusiasm and dedication for egoism had best, indeed, stay clear of Pearl Byrd Foster.

Over the years I must have exchanged with Pearl hundreds of notes, letters, and spur-of-the-moment memos resulting from our mutual obsession with the gustatory experience (as well as our mutual loathing of the telephone), but I treasure none of her astute communications more than the one she was once forced to write during a typical night of insomnia. Scrawled, as always, on sheets of personalized Tiffany stationery, the rambling missive not only sums up much of her gastronomic philosophy but also identifies her, like M. F. K. Fisher, as a female Brillat-Savarin of the twentieth century. I doubt that Pearl will mind my sharing a few timeless random examples:

– 'Purity and simplicity: the keys to great cooking.'

– 'Food must be beautiful in the cooking pan, on the serving platter, and on the dinner plate. This is a big order, but an important one.'

– 'Nature's own earthy ingredients are mouth-watering, and the flavors must be maintained by not overcooking.'

– 'Clear consommé should be a must at any great dinner.'

– 'Plates should be spare – never overloaded.'

– 'Fullness and richness of flavor must not be lost in a blanket of sauce.'

– 'When invited to a dinner, punctuality is the loftiest virtue.'

– 'With food there must always be a rhythm of design. Color effects a delight to the eye. Harmony is the key.'

– 'Like life, food must not become routine. There are many things to do just ahead in a full life. So with food – many new experiences of taste. So one must work with great zest coupled with the desire for achievement. And there must be a bit of glory about it all.'

Postscript

Pearl Foster always said that when her time came to leave this earth she prayed she'd 'drop' while working in her kitchen. Her wish was not granted in full, but sure enough, the afternoon she was stricken with her first stroke and I rushed over to 'the Place', where she and her small staff had been preparing for the evening meal, I noticed that she had been boning a duck. Although she was unable to continue cooking and the famous little restaurant on East 81st Street was thus forced to close, Pearl, with typical fight and determination, lived just long enough to complete her remarkable cookbook, *Classic American Cooking*, published in 1983. She was eighty-three when she died – I think.

Quite often, people get perturbed at the way I severely criticize many of today's young American superstar chefs: their lack of training and experience, their arrogance, their much-too-frequent absence from the working kitchen, their claims to be 'revolutionizing' American food. Well, believe me, Pearl Byrd Foster, along with other legends like James Beard, was demonstrating true culinary innovation twenty years before most of these kids were even born; all would be wise to study her legacy. Pearl had it all: a strong sense of discipline and responsibility to her public, a devotion to basics, an insatiable craving for greater knowledge, and, God knows, a distinct style not only in the dishes she created but in everything she did.

1978

A Few Choice Words about the Manhattan

Not meaning to invoke the wrath of my many highly regarded fellow tipplers, I don't hesitate one second to say that when it comes to real cocktail pedigree in America, the so-called mysterious and ever-popular Martini – not to mention hundreds of other alcoholic concoctions – simply is not and never has been in the same class with the Manhattan. Over the decades, the virtues of the Martini have been extolled by celebrated novelists, songwriters, and veteran boozers around the world, but what tribute has been paid to that wondrous, subtle, classic mixture of whiskey, sweet vermouth, and Angostura bitters that for serious connoisseurs still symbolizes both the ultimate in sophisticated drinking and the very spirit of the great city that shares its name?

I mean, let's face it: After all is said about what does and does not constitute a great Martini, it's still a pretty crass drink that involves little more than straight gin or (heaven forbid) vodka that is *flavored* with dry vermouth, stirred or shaken with any form of ice, and served straight up or on the rocks in almost any glass with an olive, lemon peel, stuffed onion, or who knows what else. By contrast, a properly made Manhattan represents the height of the mixologist's art. The whiskey must be fine Bourbon or blended American, the vermouth must be the best sweet Italian, the bitters must be Angostura, and the proportions must be measured exactly, chilled quickly but thoroughly with large ice cubes to prevent dilution, and poured through a strainer over a stemmed maraschino cherry into a chilled 4- to 6-ounce stemmed cocktail glass. The result is a beautiful amber drink that is at once complex but discreet, potent but mellow, short-lived but eminently satisfying. Contrary to what some might have you believe, devoted Martini fanciers still slug down their silver bullets day and night: at lunch, in the office, after work in bars, throughout a meal, and whenever a situation calls for getting smashed. Urbane Manhattan aficionados, on the other hand, make a veritable ritual of their cocktail, rarely indulging anytime except right before dinner, never exceeding more than two drinks, and generally respecting the object of their bibulous passion as the genteel but powerful aristocrat that it is.

For years enthusiasts have believed that the Manhattan was created in 1874 by a bartender at New York's Manhattan Club especially for a banquet given by Lady Randolph Churchill (mother of Sir Winston) to celebrate the election

of Governor Samuel J. Tilden. Well, after having been put in touch with Carol Truax, a prolific octogenarian food writer who states in one of her twenty-seven cookbooks that none other than her father, Supreme Court Judge Charles Henry Truax, came up with the drink when he was president of the Manhattan Club around 1890, I'm now ready to dispute the long-time theory. 'It's true that the old Manhattan Club on lower Fifth Avenue was originally the home of Jenny Jerome (Lady Churchill),' said Miss Truax, 'but she really had nothing to do with the invention of the cocktail. What really happened was that my father, who was very fat, would stop his carriage at the club every day on his way home from court and drink a few Martinis (two at a time, since they were two for a quarter!). When the doctor told him he absolutely had to cut out the Martinis if he hoped to lose weight, he swiftly dropped by the club, told the bartender they had to come up with a new cocktail, and the Manhattan was born – named after the club. Of course, when he later returned to his physician, heavier than ever, and told about the delicious substitution for Martinis he'd come up with, the doctor roared, "But that's even worse!"'

If memory serves, I sipped my first Manhattan cocktail at the ripe age of twelve, the same year I first crossed to Europe in a majestic superliner and the year I was confirmed in the Holy Episcopal Church of America. The location was the now legendary bar at the Hotel Astor in New York, and the occasion was an early-evening rendezvous my father and I had with my sartorial-minded Swedish uncle to determine which items should be included in my wardrobe during a planned shopping spree the next day at Brooks Brothers.

'Two Manhattans,' my father directed as the distinguished gray-headed bartender arranged three napkins on the oak, 'and a Coke for the boy.'

Of course for years back home I'd watched my father go through the ceremony of mixing his colorful drink each evening before dinner, and it had always been a special treat when he would let me pluck the rye-flavored cherry from the glass. But not till that night in New York, not till I had reached adolescence, was I finally allowed to take a sip of the mysterious potion. I'm sure if I had been of age he wouldn't have hesitated a moment to order three Manhattans. Given the antiquated restrictions of our forever overprotective drinking laws, however, he simply pushed my Coke aside, moved his stemmed glass in front of me, and said, 'Here, son, see how you like this.'

Suffice it that since that epiphanic evening the Manhattan cocktail has remained my steadfast companion through years of grueling education, joy, heartbreak, success, failure, and, needless to say, gustatory hedonism. The ice-cold libation I still share today with my father must, by his orders, be composed of exactly 2½ ounces of blended American whiskey, 1 ounce of Martini & Rossi sweet vermouth, 'less than a dash' of Angostura bitters, and a maraschino cherry, and must be strained into a 4-ounce stemmed cocktail glass. An estimated two to three hundred bartenders, maîtres d'hôtel, restaurant captains, waiters, hoteliers, and friends around the globe know automatically when I arrive on the scene that a Bourbon Manhattan is in order – and preferably a single bolt made with 2½ ounces of bonded whiskey, 1½ ounces of Cinzano red, a quick dash of Angostura, and a fat stemmed cherry, and served in a chilled stemmed 6-ounce cocktail glass. Unfortunately, a perfect Manhattan (and by 'perfect' I'm by no means referring to the abomination by that name that includes a shot of *dry* vermouth) is as rare in a bar or restaurant these days as 100-proof sipping Bourbon, so much so that the absurd and shoddy practice in some places of not stocking maraschino cherries in order to protect unwary customers from Red Dye No. 2 has even forced me to carry my own cherries at all times in a special pocket vial. While experts like the bartenders at The Four Seasons in New York or a couple of old vets at the Drake Hotel in Chicago still care enough to ask not only which brand of whiskey and vermouth you like but also the proportions you prefer, what you run up against more often than not are amateurs who do little more than slosh unmeasured cheap whiskey and domestic vermouth with shaved ice in a shaker, pour the diluted sacrilege into an unchilled glass, and ask the ridiculous question: 'A cherry or lemon twist?'

Exactly which proportions of ingredients constitute the perfect Manhattan does depend on personal taste and can only be determined after considerable experimentation. Years ago I insisted on 3 ounces of Bourbon to 1 ounce of vermouth with a full dash of bitters, but today I prefer a more subdued drink with less whiskey and bitters and can usually tell whether the formula is correct just by looking at the cocktail. The main things to remember, whatever blend you finally decide upon, are to stick with it till age or taste buds or whatever coaxes you to reconsider, and, when ordering a Manhattan in public, demand that the bartender measure the drink according to your exact specifications. Furthermore, if a bartender or restaurant captain informs you that the establishment does not have proper cocktail glasses (why in all French restaurants must they serve cocktails in those impossible sherry glasses?), Angostura bitters, or maraschino cherries, order a glass of ale or walk out.

In this rather anemic present-day society, when the very trendy but rather silly practice of slugging down glasses of cheap white wine has virtually stifled the civilized art of drinking a well-made cocktail before dinner, I must say I often find it consoling and revealing the way innocents always stare at my Manhattan in wonderment, comment on its beauty, ask what it tastes like, and eventually have to take a sip. Without exception they smile, their eyes light up, and, with an almost evil sense of fulfillment, I am reassured once again that this mellow prince of cocktails will not only survive an era of spurious values but will continue for generations to nourish the souls of those with both style and substance.

THE ORIGINAL MANHATTAN COCKTAIL

This is the original Manhattan formula created around 1890 by Supreme Court Judge Charles Henry Truax when he was president of New York's Manhattan Club.

> *2 ounces rye (blended American) or Bourbon whiskey*
> *1 ounce sweet Italian vermouth*
> *Dash of Angostura bitters*
> *A stemmed maraschino cherry*

Combine the whiskey, vermouth and bitters in a mixing glass or pitcher, add 2 or 3 ice cubes, stir quickly till well chilled, and strain into a 4-ounce stemmed cocktail glass. Add the cherry.

Postscript

I don't remember when, where, or exactly why I composed this unpublished encomium to my beloved Manhattan cocktail, but I can reconfirm that each statement expressed here remains as alive as ever. There was a very tense and trying period not long ago when, after the doctor insisted I cut out Bourbon Manhattans to help reduce an alarming triglyceride count, I switched to the Negroni as a regular cocktail. The experiment was a dismal failure, and I'm happy to report that once again virtually no major dinner is undertaken without my noble and potent companion as a prelude.

1988

LUDWIG BEMELMANS

Art at the Hôtel Splendide

'From now on,' lisped Monsieur Victor, as if he were pinning on me the Grand Cross of the Legion of Honor, 'you will be a waiter.'

It was about a year after I had gone to work at the Splendide as Mespoulets' bus boy and only a month or two after I had been promoted to commis. A commis feels more self-satisfied than a bus boy and has a better life all around, but to become a waiter is to make a really worthwhile progress.

The cause of my promotion was a waiters' mutiny. On a rainy afternoon several of the waiters had suddenly thrown down their napkins and aprons and walked out. One had punched the chief bus boy in the nose and another had upset a tray filled with Spode demitasse cups. They wanted ten dollars a week instead of six; they wanted to do away with certain penalties that were imposed on them, such as a fine of fifty cents for using a serving napkin to clean an ashtray; and they wanted a full day off instead of having to come back on their free day to serve dinner, which was the custom at the Splendide, as at most other New York hotels. The good waiters did not go on strike. A few idealists spoke too loudly and got fired, and a lot of bad waiters, who had mediocre stations, left.

After my promotion I was stationed at the far end of the room, on the 'undesirables' balcony, and my two tables were next to Mespoulets'.

It rained all that first day and all the next, and there were no guests on the bad balcony. With nothing to do, Mespoulets and I stood and looked at the ceiling, talked, or sat on overturned linen baskets out in the pantry and yawned. I drew some pictures on my order pad – small sketches of a pantryman, a row of glasses, a stack of silver trays, a bus boy counting napkins. Mespoulets had a rubber band which, with two fingers of each hand, he stretched into various geometric shapes. He was impressed by my drawings.

The second night the dining room was half full, but not a single guest sat at our tables. Mespoulets pulled at my serving napkin and whispered, 'If I were you, if I had your talent, that is what I would do,' and then he waved his napkin toward the center of the room.

There a small group of the best guests of the Splendide sat at dinner. He waved his napkin at Table No. 18, where a man was sitting with a very beauti-ful woman. Mespoulets explained to me that this gentleman was a famous cartoonist, that he drew pictures of a big and a little man. The big man always hit the little man on the head. In this simple fashion the creator of those two figures made a lot of money.

We left our tables to go down and look at him. While I stood off to one side, Mespoulets circled around the table and cleaned the cartoonist's ashtray so that he could see whether or not the lady's jewelry was genuine. 'Yes, that's what I would do if I had your talent. Why do you want to be an actor? It's almost as bad as being a waiter,' he said when we returned to our station. We walked down again later on. This time Mespoulets spoke to the waiter who served Table No. 18, a Frenchman named Herriot, and asked what kind of guest the cartoonist was. Was he liberal?

'*Ah,*' said Herriot, '*c'ui là? Ah, oui alors! C'est un très bon client, extrêmement généreux. C'est un gentleman par excellence.*' And in English he added, 'He's A-1, that one. If only they were all like him! Never looks at the bill, never complains – and so full of jokes! It is a pleasure to serve him. *C'est un chic type.*'

After the famous cartoonist got his change, Herriot stood by waiting for the tip, and Mespoulets cruised around the table. Herriot quickly snatched up the tip; both waiters examined it, and then Mespoulets climbed back to the balcony. '*Magnifique,*' he said to me. 'You are an idiot if you do not become a cartoonist. I am an old man – I have sixty years. All my children are dead, all except my daughter Mélanie, and for me it is too late for anything. I will always be a waiter. But you – you are young, you are a boy, you have talent. We shall see what can be done with it.'

Mespoulets investigated the famous cartoonist as if he were going to make him a loan or marry his daughter off to him. He interviewed chambermaids, telephone operators and room waiters. 'I hear the same thing from the rest of the hotel,' he reported on the third rainy day. 'He lives here at the hotel, he has a suite, he is married to a countess, he owns a Rolls-Royce. He gives wonder-ful parties, eats grouse out of season, drinks vintage champagne at ten in the morning. He spends half the year in Paris and has a place in the south of France. When the accounting department is stuck with a charge they've for-gotten to put on somebody's bill they just put it on his. He never looks at them.'

'Break it up, break it up. Sh-h-h. Quiet,' said Monsieur Maxim, the maître d'hôtel on our station. Mespoulets and I retired to the pantry, where we could talk more freely.

'It's a very agreeable life, this cartoonist life,' Mespoulets continued, stretch-ing his rubber band. 'I would never counsel you to be an actor or an artist-painter. But a cartoonist – that is different. Think what fun you can have. All you do is think of amusing things, make pictures with pen and ink, have a big man hit a little man on the head, and write a few words over it. And I know you can do this easily. You are made for it.'

That afternoon, between luncheon and dinner, we went out to find a place where cartooning was taught. As we marched along Madison Avenue, Mespoulets noticed a man walking in front of us. He had flat feet and he walked painfully, like a skier going uphill.

Mespoulets said 'Pst,' and the man turned around. They recognized each other and promptly said, '*Ah, bonjour.*'

'You see?' Mespoulets said to me when we had turned into a side street. 'A waiter. A dog. Call "Pst," click your tongue, snap your fingers, and they turn around even when they are out for a walk and say, "Yes sir, no sir, *bonjour, Monsieur-dame.*" Trained poodles! For God's sakes, don't stay a waiter! If you can't be a cartoonist, be a streetcleaner, a dishwasher, anything. But don't be an actor or a waiter. It's the most awful occupation in the world. The abuse I have taken, the long hours, the smoke and dust in my lungs and eyes, and the complaints – *ah, c'est la barbe, ce métier.* My boy, profit by my experience. Take it very seriously, this cartooning.'

For months one does not meet anybody on the street with his neck in an aluminum-and-leather collar such as is worn in cases of ambulatory cervical fractures, and then in a single day one sees three of them. Or one hears Mount Chimborazo mentioned five times. This day was a flat-foot day. Mespoulets, like the waiter we met on Madison Avenue, had flat feet. And so did the teacher in the Andrea del Sarto Art Academy. Before this man had finished interviewing me, Mespoulets whispered in my ear, 'Looks and talks like a waiter. Let's get out of here.'

On our way back to the hotel we bought a book on cartooning, a drawing board, pens and a penholder, and several soft pencils. On the first page of the book we read that before one could cartoon or make caricatures, one must be able to draw a face – a man, a woman – from nature. That was very simple, said Mespoulets. We had lots of time and the Splendide was filled with models. Two days later he bought another book on art and we visited the Metropolitan Museum. We bought all the newspapers that had comic strips. And the next week Mespoulets looked around and everywhere among the guests he saw funny people. He continued to read to me from the book on how to become a cartoonist.

The book said keep a number of sharpened, very soft pencils handy for your work. I did, and for a while I was almost the only waiter who had a pencil when a guest asked for one. 'And remember,' said the book, 'you can never be expert in caricaturing people unless you shake off the fear of drawing people.' I tried to shake off the fear. 'Most people like to have their own pictures drawn,'

Mespoulets read solemnly. 'Regular-featured people should be avoided, as they are too simple to draw. Your attention should be concentrated on the faces with unique features.'

The most 'unique' faces at the Splendide belonged to Monsieur and Madame Lawrance Potter Dreyspool. Madame Dreyspool was very rich; her husband was not. He traveled with her as a sort of companion-butler, pulling her chair, helping her to get up, carrying books, flasks, dog leashes, small purchases and opera glasses. He was also like the attendant at a sideshow, for Madame was a monstrosity and everyone stared at her. They were both very fat, but she was enormous. It was said that she got her clothes from a couturier specializing in costumes for women who were *enceinte*, and that to pull everything in shape and get into her dresses she had to lie down on the floor. She was fond of light pastel-colored fabrics and her ensembles had the colors of pigeons, hyacinths and boudoir upholstery. Her coat covered her shoes and a wide fur piece her neck, and even in the middle of winter she wore immense garden hats that were as elaborate as wedding cakes.

Monsieur and Madame Dreyspool were the terror of maîtres d'hôtel all over the world. Wherever they stayed they had the table nearest the entrance to the dining room. This table was reserved for them at the Splendide in New York, at Claridge's in London, at the Ritz in Paris, and in various restaurants on the luxurious boats on which they crossed. Like the first snowflakes, Monsieur and Madame Dreyspool always appeared in the Splendide at the beginning of the season. They left for Palm Beach at the first sign of its end.

Their entrance into the dining room was spectacular. First Madame waddled in, then Monsieur with a Pekingese, one of the few dogs allowed in the main dining room. Madame answered with one painful nod Monsieur Victor's deep bow, climbed up the two steps to the balcony on the right, where their table was, and elaborately sat down. Everyone in society knew them and nodded, coming in and going out. Monsieur and Madame thanked them briefly from the throne. They never spoke to each other and they never smiled.

Monsieur Dreyspool had consoled himself with whisky so many years that his face was purple. The gossip in the couriers' dining room, where the valets and maids and chauffeurs ate, was that he also consoled himself with Susanne, Madame's personal maid. He did not seem so fat when he was alone, but when he and Madame were sitting together at their table on the good balcony, they looked like two old toads on a lily leaf.

The maître d'hôtel who took care of them was a Belgian and had come from the Hôtel de Londres in Antwerp. He never took his eyes off their table and raced to it whenever Monsieur Dreyspool turned his head. Monsieur and Madame were waited upon by a patient old Italian waiter named Giuseppe.

Because he never lost his temper and never made mistakes, he got all the terrible guests, most of whom paid him badly. Madame Dreyspool was not allowed any sugar. Her vegetables had to be cooked in a special fashion. A long letter of instruction about her various peculiarities hung in the offices of the chefs and maîtres d'hôtel of all the hotels she went to. It was mailed ahead to the various managers by Monsieur.

The exit of Monsieur and Madame Dreyspool was as festive as the entrance. When they were ready to leave, the maître d'hôtel pulled Monsieur's chair out. Monsieur pulled out Madame's chair. Madame produced the dog from her generous lap – it had slept there under a fold of the tablecloth while she ate – and gave the dog to Monsieur, who placed it on the carpet. Then the maître d'hôtel, taking steps as small as Madame's, escorted her out, walking on her left side and talking to her solicitously, his face close to hers. Monsieur followed about six feet behind, with a big Belinda Fancy Tales cigar between his teeth, his hands in his pockets and the leash of the dog slipped over one wrist. From where Mespoulets and I stood on the bad balcony, she looked like several pieces of comfortable furniture piled together under a velvet cover and being slowly pushed along on little wheels.

Mespoulets was convinced that Madame Dreyspool was the very best possible model for me to begin drawing. The book said not to be afraid. 'Take a piece of paper,' it said, 'draw a line down the center, divide this line, and draw another from left to right so that the paper is divided into four equal parts.' I took an old menu and stood on the good balcony between a screen and a marble column. It was possible there to observe and sketch Madame Dreyspool unnoticed. I divided the back of the menu into four equal parts. Once I started to draw, I saw that Madame's left half-face extended farther out from the nose than her right and that one eye was always half closed. When someone she knew came in, the eyelid went up over the rim of the pupil in greeting and the corners of the lips gave a short upward jump and then sank down again into a steady mask of disgust.

Monsieur and Madame were easy to draw; they hardly moved. They sat and stared – stared, ate, stared, stirred their coffee. Only their eyes moved, when Giuseppe brought the cheese or the pastry tray. Quickly, shiftily, they glanced over it, as one looks at something distasteful or dubious. Always the same side-ways glance at the check, at Giuseppe when he took the tip, at the Belgian maître d'hôtel, and at Monsieur Victor as they left.

I took my sketches back to Mespoulets, who had been studying the book on art in the linen closet. 'It shows effort and talent,' he said. 'It is not very good, but it is not bad. It is too stiff – looks too much like pigs, and while there is much pig at that table, it is marvelously complicated pig.' He considered the book a moment and then slapped it shut. 'I think,' he said, 'I understand the gist of art without reading any more of this. Try and be free of the helping lines. Tomorrow, when they come again, think of the kidney trouble, of the thousand pâtés and sauces they have eaten. Imagine those knees, the knees of Madame under the table – they must be so fat that faces are on each knee, two faces, one on each knee, laughing and frowning as she walks along. All that must be in the portrait. And the ankles that spill over her shoes – this must be evident in your drawing of her face.'

Monsieur and Madame came again the next day, and I stood under a palm and drew them on the back of another menu. Mespoulets came and watched me, broke a roll in half and kneaded the soft part of the bread into an eraser. 'Much better,' he said. 'Try and try again. Don't give up. Remember the thousand fat sauces, the ankles. The eyes already are wonderful. Go ahead.'

He went back to his station and soon after I heard 'Tsk, tsk, tsk, tsk!' over my shoulder. It was the Belgian maître d'hôtel and he was terror-stricken. He took the menu out of my hand and disappeared with it.

When I came to work the next noon I was told to report to the office of Monsieur Victor. I went to Monsieur Victor's desk. Slowly, precisely, without looking up from his list of reservations, he said, 'Ah, the *Wunderkind*.' Then, in the manner in which he discharged people, he continued, 'You are a talented young man. If I were you, I would most certainly become an artist. I think you should give all your time to it.' He looked up, lifted the top of his desk and took out the portrait of Monsieur and Madame Lawrance Potter Dreyspool. 'As your first client, I would like to order four of these from you,' he said. 'Nicely done, like this one, but on good paper. If possible with some color – green and blue and purple. And don't forget Monsieur's nose – the strawberry effect, the little blue veins – or the bags under the eyes. That will be very nice. A souvenir for my colleagues in London, Paris, Nice, and one for the maître d'hôtel on the *Mauretania*. You can have the rest of the day off to start on them.'

1934

No Trouble at all

The world is full of maîtres d'hôtel, many of whom are able, well-informed men. But only one in a hundred thousand is blessed with that rarest, most priceless of qualities so generously evident in Gabriel, the Maître of the Cocofinger Palace Hotel in New York.

We see this peculiar talent in the profile below, behind the ear, under 'Detail and Executive Ability'. It is the faculty of 'Anticipation', an astral clairvoyance with which to sense catastrophe, anywhere in the wide realm of his authority. Not only to feel it ahead, but to prepare for it and minimize the effect thereof.

One more look at the graph, and it is evident to anyone why, with such talents, Gabriel has come up, up, up, from the position of third piccolo at the humble King Wenceslaus in Przemysl, through the pantries and over the red carpets of Madame Sacher's, the Negresco, Shepheard's, the Meurice, Claridge's, up to the golden doors of the restaurant of the hotel of hotels – the Cocofinger Palace Hotel in New York.

Gabriel smokes Dimitrinos, he has ten dozen shirts, Lobb makes his boots, he is driven in a Minerva, thinks in French, his hats come from Habig in Vienna, and both Noel Coward and Cole Porter have asked him who builds his fine tailcoats.

To his many subordinates, he speaks through his assistant, one Hector de Malherbes, who at one time worked for Max Reinhardt. (This tempera-

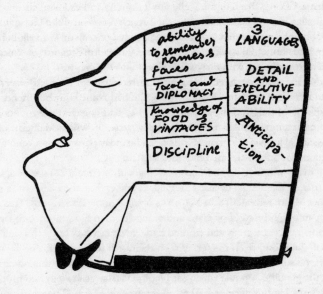

After Bemelmans

mental aesthetic experience has fitted Malherbes most admirably for his present position.) Between the Maître and Malherbes is perfect, wordless understanding.

Never was proof positive of Gabriel's great talents and of the mute felicity of Malherbes more clearly demonstrated than on the night and day of February the twenty-fifth, 1937.

On that Thursday at three-fifteen in the afternoon, when the last luncheon guest had left, Gabriel leaned on his desk with its seven drawers, one for each day of the week, and nodded gently to Malherbes. Malherbes bent down to the drawer *Jeudi* – because it was Thursday – and took from it a salmon-colored folder with a sulphur label, on which was written, 'Birthday Party, February 25, 1937, Mrs George Washington Kelly.'

Gabriel carried the folder up to his room; Malherbes bowed and left. In his room, Gabriel took off his fine tailcoat, which was rounded from much bowing, hung it up, sat on his bed and carefully unfolded the bills that five-, ten- and one-dollar patrons had pressed into his hand. He added them up and entered into a little crimson book, 'February 25, *Déjeuner*, $56'. Then he took off his boots, leaned back into the pillows, stretched his toes in the sheer, black Sulka silk socks, and opened the salmon-colored folder.

Madame George Washington Kelly was a difficult and exacting client.

The Italian waiters called her *bestia*, the French *canaille* and the Germans *die alte Sau*. She had a desperate countenance, partly concealed by a veil; behind this, her face shone the color of indigo. Her skin had the texture of volcanic rock seen from the air, with dirty snow swept into the crevices.

She dressed with complete immunity to fashion, except for the Beaux Arts Ball. On the night of that elaborate *affaire*, she had come with her friend, the 'Spirit of the Midnight Sun', and together they had engaged the rooms and made the preliminary plans for this birthday party, of which Malherbes had said to Gabriel in *sotto voce* French, 'It is not a birthday party – it is a centennial celebration.' Gabriel had stared him into silence.

After many more visits and consultations with architects, stage designers and florists, Madame had decided to build, at one end of the ballroom, a rep-lica of her Miami retreat, O Sole Mio, in its original noble dimensions. This was to be set among hibiscus, poinciana and orange trees in bloom, surrounded by forty-foot royal palm trees and fronted by wide terraces. Cutting through the center of the room, from the terraces on the north to a magnificent flight of stairs on the south, ran the lagoon, filled with real water, and in this water was to float the genuine gondola which Mr George Washington Kelly had brought as a souvenir from Venice and taken all the way to Miami. The stairs on the north end rose to a balcony; from there, a birthday cake was to be carried down, placed on the gondola and rowed across to Sole Mio, where Mrs Kelly's own 'darkies' would bring it to her table to be cut.

The gondola was in Miami, also the royal palms, also the four white-haired Negroes, brothers named Morandus. The Fire Department had sent a captain to study the position of the hydrants and windows, to connect a pumping truck and fill the lagoon, which, it was estimated, would take fourteen hours.

To do all this properly, the complete entertaining facilities of the hotel had been rented for the three days preceding the party and for an additional two following it, to clear away the debris.

Since Monday morning, the house was filled with drafts from open doors and windows, tall ladders and empty smilax crates. Careless carpenters, careless stagehands, careless plumbers and florists ruined the peace and the carpets of the hotel with hammering, riveting and soldering together of the two-hundred-foot tank. Following on the heels of the plumbers came the painters, who painted the sides of the lagoon emerald green and a pattern of underwater scenery on its bottom. An eminent artist from Coral Gables supervised this.

The menu for this party was dictated by Madame herself, without benefit of Gabriel's advice. It was in the tradition of her entertainments and composed itself – at twelve dollars a cover for four hundred guests – of the following: Caviar aux Blinis, Borsch, Homard Sole Mio, Faisan Miami, Purée de Marrons, Pommes Soufflées, Salade Georges et Marthe, Bombe Washington, Café.

For the one thousand five hundred additional guests for supper, she had chosen an equally unfortunate repast. This, at five dollars a cover, consisted of Velouté Marthe aux Croûtons, Poussin en Cocotte Washington, Nouilles Polonaise, Petits Pois Parisienne, Bombe Sole Mio aux Fraises Cardinal, Gâteaux Georges, Café.

Breakfast was to be served from four o'clock on, at one dollar and fifty cents per person. Provision was also made for eighty musicians' suppers, suppers for chauffeurs, maids, the secretaries at the door, and the announcer and detectives, at one dollar per person.

Cocktails were to be served during the reception: a fantastic, violent drink of Madame's own invention, named 'High Diddle', the secret formula for which Madame fortunately gave to no one. Closely guarded, her trusty 'darkies' – the Morandi – were to mix this, bringing most of the ingredients themselves.

After Gabriel had read the papers and made several notes, he rose, looked into a mirror and took a loose smoking jacket from his closet. He slipped on a pair of white gloves and walked below. Malherbes was waiting for him. It was six o'clock.

Gabriel nodded, and his assistant followed him with a silver pencil and a morocco portfolio.

They walked through the kitchen, where the cooks fished red lobsters out of steaming casseroles and chopped them in half. From there they went on to the cellar. Here, men broke open cases of *cordon rouge* 1921, at eleven dollars a bottle, put them away in tubs and stood them on top of one another. From here, they walked up to the ballroom proper. The tables, seating eight guests each, were set to the left and right of the lagoon. Sole Mio was finished, and on the lower terraces in front of it – as indicated on the plan – was the crescent-shaped table, facing the room. Here, Monsieur and Madame George Washington Kelly and their son, George Washington Kelly, Jr, as well as their most intimate friends, were to sit.

Two painters were busy pouring and stirring fifty gallons of turquoise ink into the lagoon, to give it the precise color of the waters in Miami. The Coral Gables artist had left with them a sample of that shade on a piece of water-color paper, and, from time to time, they compared this and then added more ink. Up on the balcony of Sole Mio two electricians were focusing spotlights across the room, up to the magenta curtain on the other side.

From the street could be heard the last '*Poooommmph*', '*Puuuuuumph*', '*Poomph*' of the Fire Department pumping truck. The lagoon was filled.

Gabriel, walking into the hall, saw the last of twenty royal palms – in tubs, with their leaves carefully bandaged – being carried upstairs, and below from the street appeared the neck of the Venetian gondola.

The great Maître nodded to Malherbes. Malherbes ran down to the door and told the men, 'Watch out for the paint, you.' Later on, in the office, Malherbes made certain that a gondolier had been engaged. Yes, he had. He was to report at the ballroom in costume, with a knowledge of how to row a gondola and ability to sing '*O Sole Mio*'.

Gabriel went back to his room, lit a cigarette, and rested in his bath for half an hour. Then he dressed.

As on every evening, so now he received the dinner guests of the hotel at the door of the restaurant.

Madame George Washington Kelly's party over in the ballroom was in the able hands of his third assistant, Monsieur Rudi, a withered, one-time stable boy of Prince Esterházy.

At regular intervals a courier crossed from the ballroom and whispered to Malherbes, 'The guests are arriving.' Then again, 'The cocktails are being passed.' After this, 'The guests are entering the ballroom.' Then, 'Madame George Washington Kelly is very pleased,' and on to 'The guests are sitting down,' and 'The soup is being served.' These bulletins were translated into French by Malherbes and whispered on to Gabriel, who nodded.

Dinner was almost over in the restaurant when Gabriel went into a little side room, where, on a table behind a screen, a plain meal was prepared for him. It consisted of some cold pheasant, cut from the bones, field salad with lemon dressing, and a plain compote of black cherries cooked without sugar. In ice under the table was his favorite wine, an elegant, slim bottle of Steinberger Kabinett, Preussische Staatsdomäne, 1921

In the middle of his meal, before he had touched the great wine, Gabriel rose abruptly and quickly walked across the restaurant. Malherbes, who had eaten out in the second little room, swallowed quickly and followed him. Almost running, they crossed the entrance hall of the ballroom and went up the staircase, to the third palm.

Gabriel stopped and beside him, as always, stopped Hector de Malherbes. The dessert had just been served, the remnants of the Bombe Washington were being carried from the room by the waiters, and, as set forth in the sheet of instructions, the lights were lowered.

Two heralds sounded the *Aida* theme as a command to silence and attention.

The heavy magenta curtains sailed back, and high above the audience appeared the birthday cake. It was magnificent, of generous proportions, and truly beautiful. The masterpiece of Brillat Bonafou, *Chef Pâtissier* of the Cocofinger Palace Hotel, twice the winner of the Médaille d'Or de la Société Culinaire de Paris, Founder and President of the Institut des Chefs Pâtissiers de France. In weeks of patient, sensitive, loving labor, he had built a monument of sugar, tier upon tier, ten feet high, of raisin and almond cake. Of classic simplicity, yet covered with innumerable ornaments that depicted scenes from a happy sporting life. Up and down the sides of the cake, dozens of cherubim were busy carrying ribbons; these – Bordeaux and emerald – represented the racing colors of the G. W. K. stables.

But the most wonderful part of the wonderful cake was its top. There, complete in all details, stood a miniature replica of O Sole Mio, correct as to palms, orange trees, the lagoon, the gondola. Under the portico, an inch high, smiling, hand in hand, stood Monsieur and Madame George Washington Kelly – Madame with a bouquet of roses, Monsieur with his ever-present cigar, an Hoyo de Monterrey, at the end of which was a microscopic tuft of cotton.

That was, however, not all. Over the miniature Sole Mio hovered a brace of doves. In their beaks, most artfully held, were electric wires, so arranged that flashing on and off they spelled first 'George' and then 'Martha'. 'George' in green, 'Martha' in red. Five lady midgets, dressed as the Quintuplets, carried the cake downstairs in the light of the amber spotlights.

The Hawaiians played 'Happy Birthday to You, Happy Birthday to You'. Everyone sang, and all eyes were moist.

The gondolier started to punt down the lagoon to receive the cake.

At that moment, with all eyes upon them, one of the Quintuplets, Yvonne, stepped on an olive pit and turned her ankle. The cake trembled, swayed and fell into the lagoon, taking the midgets with it. '*Ffssssss-hss*' went the electric wires.

But where was Gabriel?

He stood under the royal palm and nodded quietly to Malherbes. Malherbes lifted one finger and looked up at the man with the spotlight.

The amber light left the lagoon and raced up the stairs. Out came the trumpeteers again and sounded the *Aida* theme, the curtain swung open once more, again the Hawaiians played 'Happy Birthday to You, Happy Birthday to You'.

As if the last dreadful minutes had never been on the watches of the world, there appeared to the unbelieving eyes of Monsieur and Madame George Washington Kelly and their guests and friends – THE CAKE again, unharmed, made with equal devotion, again the work of Brillat Bonafou, identically perfect and complete, with the scenes of the happy life, the cherubim, cigar and smoke, lagoon and gondola, doves, lights flashing the names in green and red, and carried on the shoulders of a new set of Quintuplets.

The miserable first set of midgets swam to the shore of the lagoon, scrambled out and tried to leave the ballroom in the shade of the tables.

Gabriel hissed '*Imbéciles!*' to Malherbes. Malherbes hissed '*Imbéciles!*' down to the midgets.

The new cake was rowed across, besung, carried to the table, cut and served. Not until then did the great maître d'hôtel leave the protecting shadow of the royal palm. Now he walked quietly, unseen, to his room, for, in spite of possessing every talent, and besides the gift of 'Anticipation', Gabriel was a very modest man.

1934

JOHN THORNE

Learning to Eat

I

A man who is rich in his adolescence is almost doomed to be a dilettante at table. This is not because all millionaires are stupid but because they are not impelled to experiment. In learning to eat, as in psychoanalysis, the customer, in order to profit, must be sensible of the cost.

A. J. Liebling, *Between Meals*

My first piece of cooking equipment was an 8-inch cast-iron frying pan. I was in a junk shop on Manhattan's Lower East Side, rooting around for two used chairs to bring back to my new apartment at East Ninth Street. I had moved in the day before and discovered I had inherited three pieces of furniture: a mattress, a vintage-model air conditioner the size of a refrigerator, and a table. The first two of these were to be reclaimed that morning by the former tenant's boyfriend. He didn't take the table, however, perhaps because it stood up only when propped against a wall.

I was sorry to see the mattress go because, wretched as it was, without it I was reduced to sleeping on the floor. But it was even more important to have a table. Using the floor as a bed is an inconvenience that most of us have suffered at least once, but using it as a table is to lose all touch with civilized life and, with it, all hope. The gift of a table, however, means the buying of a chair. I could afford that, and I hoped I could afford two of them. A second chair was a promise of company. I didn't know anyone in New York City right then, but I wanted to.

So I had come to this place where old chairs went to die. Eventually I found two whose demise had been misjudged by a year or so, and as the old proprietor was tying them together so that I could carry them back home, he asked me if I was moving into the neighborhood. I told him that I had just rented my first apartment and that these two chairs would be my first pieces of furniture. He nodded and, when he had finished with them, turned and rummaged through a huge pile of junk that was dumped across the table behind him. He emerged from it with the frying pan. It was a disgusting-looking object, crusted thickly all over – inside and out – with dust caked onto ancient grease. He held it out to me. 'With this,' he said, 'you'll never starve. It's a whole kitchen by itself. Take it.' As I hesitated, he thrust it forward and said, 'As a moving-in present. Yours for seventy-five cents.'

When I still stood there motionless, he set it down on the counter without rancor. 'Let me give you a little cooking lesson for free,' he said. 'This pan is a gem. You don't know why because you've never cooked anything. So, I'll tell you.' He leaned a little toward me over the counter and hissed, *'Because it's never been washed,* that's why. And it never should be washed. When you're done using it, throw in some salt and scrub it out with a crumpled piece of newspaper, a paper bag. No soap, no water – no stick.' I paid him, balanced it on the two chairs, and brought it home. I didn't believe him about the pan, but I knew he was right about one thing: I didn't know how to cook. The truth was, I hadn't yet even found out how to eat.

I lied when I told the junk dealer that this was my first apartment. I had already dropped out of college to share a place in New York City a year earlier, but that time was a lark. This time I had left college for good, committed to becoming a writer. I had arrived in Manhattan the day before at five in the morning, alone, with precious little money and too many expectations: in short, so far as this city was concerned, a rube.

I threw my luggage into a locker at the Port Authority Bus Terminal, picked up a copy of *The New York Times,* and went to an all-night cafeteria on Forty-second Street for steak and eggs. I left my tray at a vacant table to go back for some packets of sugar, and when I returned I found a vagrant polishing off my breakfast. Shaken, I went through the line again and sat somewhere else, spending the next two hours marking off places I thought I could afford. By 9 a.m. I was working my way through the list from East Fourteenth Street down.

The day was gray and bitter cold. Snowflakes floated in the air. The apartments were universally grim. I rejected them, one after another, with growing despair. In some the ends of each hallway were pitch black; in others there was a common toilet shared by the whole floor. The rooms reeked of unwashed bodies and stale food. The one I finally chose, on East Ninth Street between First Avenue and Avenue A, was on the top floor of a five-floor walkup. But the stairwell was brightly lit, the toilet had a closet to itself off the single (windowless) bedroom, and the two windows looked out onto a neatly kept back yard where a large sycamore grew, its bare branches reaching almost as high as the sill.

Thirty years now and I can still remember that apartment almost as if I had just stepped out of it, from the feel of the lock knob to the location of the electric sockets to the shape of the tub, the size of the closet, the pane of glass with a crack shot through it that popped out of its frame during a February blizzard. I can call back to the mind's eye that first long night spent carefully painting the living-room walls and ceiling a bone white, then scrubbing the floors and rubbing them with paste wax, to coax out of their scuffed wood a reluctant, soon-to-vanish sheen.

The smell of fresh paint barely overlaid a fainter, more pungent odor, the accumulated fear and loneliness and terrified excitement of those who had lived here before me. My immediate predecessor had simply vanished, leaving her possessions behind. Her boyfriend took what he wanted; the landlord told me to throw the rest out. She was young, or at least her clothing was; I packed it up in her battered fiberboard suitcase. But after a month of keeping it in the closet, I carried it down to the basement and abandoned it. It was too vivid a reminder of my own fear about what might happen to me.

New York is a brutal city, especially if you come there without friends, work, or money, and if your sense of self is buoyed by nothing but the flimsy dreams of youth. It isn't just the eruption of random, sudden violence – the electric iron flung during a family fight out of a third-floor window, the gunshot on the roof overhead – but the brutality of walls and moldings that have been painted over so many times that their outlines are swollen, shapeless . . . layer on layer of fresh hope that has eventually turned as grimy and black as those that lie beneath. The brutality of too much fragile experience crushed together.

I blocked off my windows with long drapes cut from a bolt of burlap dyed royal blue. When I woke in the morning, wrapped up in my living-room rug, the sun streamed in through the loose weave in the coarse-grained color of an early Technicolor movie. Although the room was dark and starkly empty, it was filled with flecks of blue-tinged light, as if it were a closed eyeball and I myself an overstimulated optic nerve.

I had come to New York to become a writer, but the story that was my life was washed out from under me by a violent torrent of sensation – inner impulse and outer stimuli. At my age, that story was my single subject. I was entirely flushed of words. The typewriter took a long slow fade; it was only after someone broke in and stole it that it reappeared in my consciousness, now an ironic symbol. I was a refugee whose forged passport had been stolen and, with it, the fantasy of escaping into a false, safe self. All my dreams at the time were of elevated trains shooting over chromatic cityscapes on roller-coaster trestles. In waking life that ride often left me breathless, but I found that it didn't take my appetite away. In fact, I was very, very hungry.

2

Outside my apartment – that large, shut eye – were Russians, Poles, Ukrainians. A Russian Orthodox church sat on a nearby corner and near it a genuine Russian bathhouse; the single display windows of assorted tiny import stores sported rugs with savage bears wandering in forests or pious religious motifs woven in Day-Glo hues on black backgrounds. Signs promised safe delivery of parcels to behind the Iron Curtain. In other windows had been propped cards that read 'Apartment to Let – Polish People Only'. This, a super explained, didn't mean me – who could pass as a kind of Pole – but blacks and also the Hispanics encroaching in from Avenues C and D.

It was, in fact, a neighborhood of old people. I did once see a crowd of fresh-faced, well-scrubbed Boy Scouts, a Polish-American troop (in ironed uniforms!) waiting for a bus to camp, but they probably accounted for every Slavic youth on the entire East Side. Mostly I encountered suspicious, wrinkled faces peering from behind chained doors, sagging bodies on withered legs shuffling up the steep flights of stairs in carpet slippers, dragging a shopping cart behind. Now and then I would pass an old woman, dressed entirely in black, down on her hands and knees, scrubbing the sidewalk with a brush and a pail of soapy water.

Once my presence became familiar to these people, I ceased to exist. Exciting no fear or interest, I was not worth seeing. I was the Invisible Man. I passed them on the sidewalk or in the hallway without remark; they barely glanced at me or answered a greeting when I edged past them on the stoop or waited next to them at a counter.

This intensified the dreamlike quality of my life. It also had another effect. Nothing among these puffy, dowdy women and crabby, withered men, these religious shops and churches, the cramped, furniture-stuffed, heavily curtained apartments, echoed back or reflected any part of the intense sexual excitement that my youth and this flood of sensation had sent rushing through my responsive but tightly reined-in flesh.

At the time, I didn't think of it as restrained. On the contrary, my brain reeled with sex. I read Jean Genet, Henry Miller, William Burroughs, Allen Ginsberg, Wilhelm Reich. I absorbed Fellini's ½, Kenneth Anger's *Scorpio Rising*, the then budding oeuvre of Andy Warhol's film factory. Even so, all this was in my head – the same head that had locked my body into what would prove to be a near-unbroachable shell. Looking back, I see I had already made a clear if unconscious choice by locating myself not in the permissive Village but on the Lower East Side, a repressed-seeming neighborhood where I would be kept safe from finding – or myself becoming – an object of desire.

At the age of twenty, however, desire is not that easy to avoid. With nothing else to do, I used up my free time walking the city. That first winter, every other Friday – payday – I would find myself walking west, into the Village, to browse the bookstores for a mystery or to see a movie, and end up discovering, once again, that I had somehow managed to brush up against it. My body charged with electric current, I would walk back home, stopping at the Night Owl Grocery on the corner of Tenth Street and First Avenue for a bag of potato chips. Back in my apartment, I would take these and my mystery and go straight to bed.

At the time about which I write, any pretensions I had regarding connoisseurship revolved around tobacco. My cooking, such as it was, came mostly out of cans. I was too intensely inhibited to directly focus on the pleasure of eating in the company of anyone, even myself. Now, lying under the covers, my mind absorbed in a book, I would eat through the bag of chips, producing – like the solitary sex that often followed after – a state of contented oblivion, a self-induced warmth that filled mind and body, wadding it as best as I could against the reality without.

Once let into my life, however, I found it hard to confine this kind of eating to the safety of my bed. As summer approached, I became more and more reluctant to return home. Nightfall came later, my rooms were hot and airless, and I began instead to head south, crossing Houston Street into Little Italy, Chinatown, and the Jewish neighborhoods by the Williamsburg Bridge. Here were places where I had already seen food being conspicuously enjoyed; here also were places where, if I had any change in my pocket, I could afford to eat.

Still, if desire urged me forward, repression, shyness, continued to hold me back. I became, at least at first, a gastronomic voyeur. I stared into shop windows. If the shop was large and crowded, I might let myself go in and browse, peering into the display cases, watching, still clinging to my invisibility, the interplay between counterman and customer. I would hover about the Essex Street Market, a block-sized building the city had erected years ago to get the pushcarts off the street, letting myself be swept in at one end and out the other, safe and unseen in crowds of every ethnicity and human hue, who pushed their way through the alleyways between the stands. These, often no more than planks on sawhorses, displayed hog maws, plantains, live turtles, rabbits, violent-colored unwrapped confections, blocks of halvah, vats of olives, and tubs of brine-cured onions, cucumbers, and chili peppers.

What little of this that I bought and ate had already been made eatable –

pickles, olives, cheese. Mostly I observed. A leg of beef was one thing, a plucked and eviscerated duck – complete with head, bill, and feet – another. I came from a place where appetite was diffident and picky and didn't want to know too much. It was a place where supermarkets trimmed meat into individual portions in the back and wrapped these in cellophane; where waiters brought out food only after it had already been chosen; where, that is, appetite was stimulated by packages, advertisements, menus – by words and pictures, not by the food itself.

Here, however, appetite was raw aggression, and those who meant to feed it did so on those terms. Not only were shop windows full of actual, unpackaged food, but on slow days shopmen stood in their doorways to urge your custom, street vendors saluted you as brazenly as beggars. So did their food. The air was full of appetizing smells: roasted chestnuts, hot peanuts, hot dogs. Good Humor men, with no scents to waft, jangled bells. Eateries, in competition, put on their own performances. Peppers, onions, and sausages fried in full view in a whole row of electric frying pans; huge gyros (which for years I believed to be legs from some Greek strain of supersheep) rotated on vertical skewers, sweating grease; and, of course, solemn pizzaioli flipped and spun large, twirling disks of dough with two clenched fists, as watchers gawked and they themselves stared coolly at nothing at all.

Working as a mail boy for fifty dollars a week, I shared with this crowd its hunger; I was alone in my shame of it. I could not imagine eating hugely, openly; the prickling of appetite was exciting until I reached out my hand to take . . . then it fled. There were times when I could have afforded a whole Sicilian pizza – the kind I coveted: rectangular, thickly crusted, heaped with cheese and sauce – but I could never bring myself to order more than a slice or two.

Even eating that made me self-conscious; I preferred to scoop it up and run. Eating while reading had been my introduction to gastronomic pleasure because the mind was too buried in words to notice what the mouth was up

to. Walking and eating, I now discovered, nearly replicated that experience. Paradoxically, eating made me feel less, not more, conspicuous out on the street; like taking out the dog, it was a reason to be there. Those who had previously looked straight through me now looked at what I was doing . . . and responded with a smile. *I* was still unseen – they looked at the eating, not at me – but the warmth inside me drew up a warmth outside as well. Unnoticed, between two warmths, I had found a way into another safe and private place.

Now on the prowl for such pleasure, I began to notice that this was the one form of sensuality my neighbors did explicitly encourage. Up and down First Avenue were food stores. The bakery windows were crammed with bread of every shape, flavor, and texture – plump, round loaves of pumpernickel; elongated, sleek-crusted loaves of rye; rough, heavy, chunky loaves of Polish 'corn' (made not with corn at all but coarse-ground rye); and glossy, brown-crusted, braided loaves of challah with a soft, yolk-yellow crumb. Pastry shops offered their own elaborate concoctions: split puffs oozing whipped cream, hazelnut tortes, Black Forest cakes, and fruit tarts sporting impossibly huge, glossy strawberries.

Pork butchers draped long links of sausage across their windows – German bratwurst, mettwurst, blood sausage. With them hung lengths of Polish *wiankowa* and kielbasa; red-faced, fatty hams and whole smoked loins were tucked into the corners. Thick blocks of sweet butter, hefty as cornerstones, sat on the counter of the dairy store. One tiny shop, no more than a door, tucked around a corner on Seventh Street, sold 'Farm Fresh Eggs – Thursdays Only'. Produce shops burst out onto the sidewalk, their bins overflowing with cabbages, carrots, cauliflowers, leafy greens beyond my capacity to identify or, in some instances, even imagine eating.

Furthermore, entering food stores to take food out, I learned I could linger and still retain that place within. A delicatessen on Houston Street sold potato knishes – large, bright yellow, pillowy squares, deep-fried in chicken fat – for a quarter each. I ate these, washed down with celery tonic, while leaning against the stand-up counter along the wall, watching countermen hand-slice paper-thin cuts of smoked salmon, while bakers, towels tied around their heads, brought out huge trays of bagels and bialys.* All around me, I was starting to see, was food that I could also bring home.

---

* A bialy is a bagel that got lost inside a Polish joke: its outside is crusty instead of glossy and the hole in the center doesn't make it all the way through. But, fresh from the oven, it is a delicacy unique to itself, crisp and chewy at once, the center dimple stuffed with translucent onion bits and (if wished) garlic. At the time, these were two for a quarter, and some weeks those two were all I could afford – or would want – for lunch.

In the Village, on the corner of MacDougal and Bleecker, a thickly musta-chioed Chilean sold empanadas out of a booth built from a packing crate. These came two ways (I think his only English was 'meat' and 'cheese'), fried fresh to order: he would plunge the chosen pastry into boiling oil and prod it with tongs until it was golden and crisp. I had just left the late-night double fea-ture at the Bleecker Street Cinema, and this hot pastry was my company on the long, dark walk home. I carried it gingerly until it was cool enough to eat. Even then, on a cold night, the first bite released a savory cloud of steam.

I am not, and never have been, a gourmet. I possess no curiosity about world-class restaurants, and while I am more drawn to the idea of exemplary foods – truffles, caviar, goose liver, rack of lamb – the fact that I have never tasted any of these except in the most adulterated form must mean that, finally, they are not all that important to me. It is character, not the tongue, that determines one's gustatory destiny, and that empanada was the key to mine.

I soon knew its physiognomy as well as I knew the contours of my own face. I was drawn to the immediate, enveloping comfort of fat: fried wontons or potatoes or onion rings or pieces of chicken or grilled sausage on a stick. More specifically, it was always something hot, salty, succulent, preferably compact enough to be eaten casually, quickly, standing up, on the go.

This, for better or worse, was to become my chosen form of gastronomic pleasure. Not for me the elegant, massive, public presence of a standing rib roast; I chose instead the single barbecued beef rib, which, with its rebarbative, greasy chunks of flesh, vein, and gristle, claims for its eater a kind of animal privacy. This is a form of enjoyment that, no matter the company, remains deeply solitary, totally absorbing, hurriedly done with, and, let it be said, at times edged with shame.

In New York City, where there was no sense of safety anywhere, I had now found two havens: reading and eating in bed, and walking and eating in the street. But supper remained a can of Campbell's cream of celery soup with a fistful of oyster crackers. Before I could learn to cook, I had to not only learn to eat, but learn to eat at home . . . and in some other place than bed.

1992

JOSEPH WECHSBERG

Provence without Garlic

. . . M. Raymond Thuilier was a jovial, mustachioed Frenchman who looked as if he'd just heard some good news about himself. He would have been fat for a middleweight champion, but he was rather trim for a chef. He wore a topcoat over his white chef's outfit and explained apologetically that he'd been about to prepare *déjeuner* and that there had been no time to dress. M. Thuilier, it seemed, was that *rara avis*, the owner of a well-known restaurant who actually did the cooking himself.

As soon as we left the old ramparts of Tarascon behind us, M. Thuilier stepped down on the gas. Soon we were going at eighty-five miles an hour.

'I used to drive much faster,' M. Thuilier said apologetically. 'But I'm getting old.'

We traversed the Provence at suicidal speed. I love the Provençal landscape with its soft colors and deep shadows, the permanent, silky glow in the air, and the omniscient memory of bold warriors and romantic troubadours, but there was no time for thoughtful appreciation. We stopped briefly in the small village of Maillane, where Frédéric Mistral, last of the great troubadours, lived and is buried.

'Pablo Casals came here last year to play Bach at Mistral's grave,' said M. Thuilier. 'It was Mistral's poetry that made me come here. I'm from Chambéry, in the Savoie, where my parents and my grandparents were hotel-keepers.'

The road began to ascend and the lovely countryside became rocky and wild. Presently the rocks grew into rocky hills and the hills became jagged mountains with grotesque patterns, like the eerie moonscapes in Arizona and New Mexico.

'Lots of fennel and thyme here,' M. Thuilier said. 'The air is too dry to keep our Camembert. They bring it up all *mûr* and within twenty-four hours it's as dry as bread crust.'

We reached the pass. The mountains were called Les Alpilles – 'the little Alps' – and below us were the bizarre formations of Val d'Enfer, the Valley of Hell, where, according to legend, Dante had found the inspiration for his

Inferno. Way up on the hilltop, built into the rocks so that it was hard to distin-
guish the houses from the rocks, was the centuries-old village of Les Baux.
Baux is a Ligurian word that means 'steep'; the mineral later called Bauxite was
first found here in 1822.

Back in the thirteenth century the township of Les Baux had boasted of
three thousand six hundred people, but now there were only fifty-six. All that
has remained of the glory of the lords and knights of Les Baux is their coat of
arms, which shows in the upper shield a cavalier with his bare sword and in the
lower a star with sixteen silver rays.

M. Thuilier turned the car off the road. Suddenly, as if the scenery had been
switched on a revolving stage, I found myself back in the twentieth century,
with its more advanced comforts. There was a swimming pool, a stately stone
house, a *patio fleuri* and a wide terrace with comfortable chairs, from where you
could look out over the mysterious Camargue country, the plains of the
Provence in the rear, and the bluish haze indicating the far-away Mediterranean.

'I fell in love with the place,' M. Thuilier said, with the quiet satisfaction of
an artist showing his life's work. 'There wasn't much here when I came up in
'46. A dilapidated, abandoned farmhouse. We had to rebuild the whole thing,
but we stuck to the Provençal style and to the old name. *Oustau* means "house"
in Provençal. We are not sure about the origin of the word *Baumanière*. It may
be the name of the family that built the house, in 1634. Or it may mean the
House of the Black Cave, or the House near the Rock with Easy Access. There
was a mill here and a sheep farm. The family of Mistral lived here for some
time. Mistral wrote: "*Di Baus farien ma capitado* – in Baux I'll make my capital."'

An affectionate young police dog rushed up to M. Thuilier and was introduced as Ajax. 'When we bought the place with Monsieur Moscolini, my
partner,' said M. Thuilier, 'we had trouble finding water. We drilled, and after a
few months we found enough to fill the pool.'

A few people were sitting in the patio and on the terrace, and from the
kitchen came the nervous sounds that always mount before mealtime like the
tide. M. Thuilier said there was no hurry; he didn't like to hurry; first he was
going to show me the house.

There are only ten guest rooms, but M. Thuilier knows the importance of
showers, bathrooms, fireplaces, telephones, good beds, and rough towels.
There were even screens on the windows. The floor had Renaissance tiles, and
above the entrance was a sun clock with an inscription:

> *A la Teulisso lou Teule*
> *Au Toulissaire lou Souleu.*

The vaulted dining-room was comfortable with its big fireplace, Gobelin-covered chairs, and flowers everywhere. Most people were eating outside, but I thought I would rather have lunch here.

M. Thuilier agreed. 'It's all right to have a picnic on the terrace – cold meat and cheese and salad – but you can't really appreciate the food outside, with the wind blowing dust on your plate and blossoms falling into your wineglass. I'm going to prepare your lunch. What do you like?'

I never tell a good chef what I like to eat; I eat what he likes to make for me. M. Thuilier was delighted. 'So many people come here and order,' he said. 'They don't give me a chance to show what I can do.'

Rodolphe, the headwaiter, was a relaxed young fellow who had worked in Paris and London and wanted to go to America. Did I think it was difficult to get to America and find a job if you knew your métier?

As we talked, a couple sat down at the table next to me, and Rodolphe turned toward them. The man was stiff and unsmiling and wore a small Swiss flag in his lapel. His wife was heavy-set and needed a shampoo. Rodolphe made suggestions. They have a printed menu but rarely bother to show it. There are three or four specialties at the most – not a long list of seventeen dishes, all as impersonal as so many cans of peaches.

'How about some warm hors-d'œuvres to start with?' said Rodolphe. 'Perhaps *cervelas truffé en brioche* or a *parfait de foie gras en croûte*?' Afterward he would recommend either the *gratin de langoustes* or the *filets de soles*, both specialties of the house. Then perhaps a *poulet* or an *entrecôte*?

The fat woman started to swallow in happy anticipation.

'*Filets de soles* for me and an *entrecôte*,' she said. You could almost hear her mouth watering.

'Wait!' her husband commanded. 'Waiter, how much are the *soles*?'

Rodolphe kept smiling. 'Five hundred and fifty francs, monsieur. A very fine dish, served with *sauce crevettes* and *quenelles* that have been *flambées à l'Armagnac*.'

'Too much. We'll have an *entrecôte* only.'

'Very well, monsieur. A nice *entrecôte*, with a *béarnaise* . . .' Rodolphe knew his métier.

Three red-faced, hungry-looking Dutchmen came in, shook hands with Rodolphe and with René, the *sommelier*, and ordered even before they sat down. They ordered everything that Rodolphe suggested and would have ordered more.

René brought a flat-bellied bottle, uncorked it with a quick turn of his wrist, and filled their glasses. He is a blond, easy-going fellow – everybody seems to be relaxed at the Baumanière – and told me that he was half Alsatian, half

Savoyard. René judged his clients by their faces. If he liked a client, he would do everything for him.

'Monsieur Thuilier is going to make you his *soles*,' he said, with amiable authority. 'I want you to try this *Muscat blanc des Alpilles*.'

He brought the bottle, tasted a little in his silver cup, and filled my glass, looking at me expectantly. The wine was light, agreeable, aromatic, like the air above the soil from which the wine came.

Réne laughed. '*Amusant, hein*? One wouldn't think that such a wine could come from this countryside. You must try our red Gigondas later. It comes from a place a few kilometers east of the Châteauneuf-du-Pape. A little lighter and less *brûlant*.'

It was a fine lunch. The *filets de soles* were poached in dry Cinzano and served with a *sauce crevettes*. Any cookbook tells you how to make shrimp butter, which is the important ingredient of *sauce crevettes* – 'pound shrimp remains, add their weight of butter, strain through a fine sieve' – but no book could possibly explain how M. Thuilier made his sauce.

Afterward I had a *pintadeau au porto*, with a sauce that was made of the juice of the guinea cock, with port wine and Madeira added. The mixture had been simmering on a low flame for hours. It was delicious.

M. Thuilier had his lunch at my table, a little cold meat and salad. He said he rarely ate a big meal; sometimes he didn't eat all day long. After tasting every dish in the kitchen he wasn't hungry.

'I have a small staff,' he said, 'an assistant, a *commis*, a *charcutier* who prepares the cold hors-d'œuvres, and a *pâtissier*. Good boys, all of them, but the trouble with the help is that they remember the difficult things and are apt to forget the simple ones. I keep telling the boys that they must never roast a chicken in a very hot oven, and only in its *own* fat. So first thing they turn on the fire and cover the *poulet* with butter. Wrong. The skin gets blisters and even the finest *poulet* from Bresse dries out inside. I put the chicken in, sprinkle it with its own juice, and when it gets gold-brown, I put a little butter on the legs. Thus the juice is kept inside and gently bloats up the chicken.'

M. Thuilier asked the waiter for a bottle of Vichy water and said: 'A cook shows how good he is when something goes wrong and he's got to show presence of mind. One of my friends in Morocco has a good Arab cook who can copy anything from a recipe but is not able to think for himself. He will lose his head when his *sauce béarnaise* curdles. Silly, what? Easiest thing in the world to make a good *béarnaise*.'

Sure, I said. As easy as it is for Jascha Heifetz to perform the Walton Concerto.

'He added hot water to the warm sauce. Of course, it got even worse.' M. Thuilier laughed, genuinely amused about such ignorance. 'The trick is to add tepid water when the *béarnaise* is cold, and to add cold water when the sauce is tepid. A simple chemical reaction. Did you know that if you serve *fonds d'artichaut* you have to peel the vegetable before you cook it?'

He had another glass of Vichy water. He drinks little wine, not more than half a bottle of champagne a month, and never hard liquor. He never smokes.

'Can't afford to hurt my palate. A chef is good only as long as his palate is reliable.'

Being isolated in the mountains, M. Thuilier has problems of logistics and supply. Everything has to be ordered and brought up. The chicken comes from Bresse, the *langouste* from Cap Finistère, the fish from the Mediterranean and from Lake of Annecy in the Haute-Savoie.

'The train leaves there at eight p.m. and gets here at eight in the morning,' said M. Thuilier. 'Of course, you've got to trust your fishmonger. I buy only the best and I must be sure that I get what I want. I had an argument last week. The fellow knows that I don't want my *rouget* [red mullet] larger than 180 or 200 grams. No *rouget* is worth anything when it's over 300 grams, *hein?*'

I couldn't help wondering what my 'gourmet' friends would say to *that*. They always talk about spices and dressings and sauces and soufflés and forget the basic things – the size of the red mullet, for instance.

'I had the mullets packed in ice and sent them back,' said M. Thuilier. 'The next time I'll throw them away and look for another dealer. You can't compromise on quality.'

M. Thuilier prepares the mullets *en papillottes*. 'You put them on vegetable parchment that is well soaked with olive oil. You place a laurel leaf on one side of the fish and a slice of slightly cured pork across the other. You close the paper at the ends like a paper bag and cook the fish in olive oil, for eighteen minutes. You open the paper bag only when you serve the fish. It is served with a sauce that is made like a *hollandaise*, except that you mash *filets d'anchois* into the butter before you let the butter melt.'

A petite brunette and a man came to our table and M. Thuilier introduced me to Mme and M. Moscolini, his partners.

'Léon is from Lyon,' said M. Thuilier. 'Oh, la la, the Lyonnais! They board the train at Lyon-Perrache station in great dignity, carrying that conservative paper *Le Noveliste*, but as soon as the train has passed the tunnel, they take out *La Vie parisienne*, which they had kept hidden under their coat.'

Mme Moscolini said the refrigerator would be out of order for four days. They were enlarging the kitchen for the second time since the end of the war. The Baumanière serves sixty luncheons and thirty-five dinners on weekdays; on Sundays there are as many as a hundred and twenty people. During the winter most guests are French, but in summertime there is a higher percentage of foreigners – British, Dutch, Swiss, Spaniards, and many Americans.

'Americans are beginning to know a great deal about good food,' M. Thuilier said. 'I hope in due time they will learn that the best dishes are simple dishes. My mother used to say: "*Il faut manger simplement et sainement*," simple food is healthy food. But simple dishes are often the most difficult to prepare. Take *purée des pommes de terre* [mashed potatoes]. The slightest mistake shows up. The potatoes must be steamed, not boiled. The purée must not be too liquid and not too firm. And it must not be allowed to wait. One of the most difficult feats of the *grande cuisine* is a good omelet. But the clients would stop coming here if we served them omelets. They want things that *sound* complicated, *rougets en papillottes au beurre d'anchois* or *caneton à l'orange*, a dish that has never been my favorite. In cooking, as in music, there should be harmony, and duck just doesn't harmonize with oranges. Sometimes we have to remake a dish three or four times until it is just right. Last week one of my assistants prepared a *gratin de langoustes*. The sauce was "short", too thick and not clear enough. The client might have been satisfied. I wasn't. I made him remake it three times. You cut down on your profits, but you can't run a good restaurant by keeping an eye on the cash register. Above all, you must never hurry. A few weeks ago a client told me he was in a hurry, could I serve him in twenty minutes? I said to him: "Of course I realize that you're in a hurry, monsieur, and I will serve you – a sandwich."'

'We work too hard here,' said M. Moscolini, who had been listening in gloomy silence. 'We should close one day of the week.'

'Difficult,' said M. Thuilier. 'Restaurants like Pic in Valence and Point in Vienne can afford to close once a week. There is always some other place near Route 7. But people make a detour to come up here and they would be stuck. Have you been at Point's Pyramide in Vienne lately? Ah, the great Fernand Point! We are old friends. We come from the same region and were both born in the same year, 1897. Last year we both got the Légion d'Honneur and Point gave a special dinner. Served us a whole pheasant, with head and feathers, but the body was made of *pâté de faisan*. Ah!'

There was a minute of reverent silence. Then we walked over to the cave to look at some vintages of Château Lafite, Château Gruaud-Larose, a 1928 Chambolle-Musigny, a 1929 Charmes-Chambertin. The small cellar has a fine assortment of Côtes du Rhône wines, Hermitage La Chapelle, and a '29 Châteauneuf-du-Pape. We started to talk about wines. M. Thuilier compared the Bordeaux to a *grande dame*, and the Burgundy to an 'exciting mistress'. René, the *sommelier*, remembered a Clos Vougeot '29 which –

I tiptoed away. The sun was setting. I walked up to the high plateau past a Roman chapel where, an old man told me, 'even the unbelieving feel the urge to kneel down'. I saw a dead city of broken walls, scattered rocks, and troglodyte dwellings, and the tenth-century castle, which Louis XIII had demolished in 1632, two years before the Baumanière was built.

When I came back, the lights were burning in the patio and there were candles on the dining-room tables. M. Thuilier was working again. I had a 'simple' dinner, a marvelous *gratin de langoustes* ('nothing to it,' said M. Thuilier, 'once you have the feel of the sauce') and a steak that M. Thuilier rubs with butter lightly before broiling it over a hot fire, and butters once more later so the juice will stay in.

Later that night, when I walked up to my room, the moon was bright and the rocks seemed to be strangely alive. I thought I was hearing the old Provençal battle cry of the lords of Les Baux; '*A l'hasard Bauthésard!*' but it was only the voice of René, downstairs in the patio, telling a guest of the wonderful bottle of Moët & Chandon 1906 which had been in perfect condition when he opened it forty-six years later.

1953

'Worth a Special Journey'

. . . From Paris we drove to Saulieu, a small town in Burgundy, by way of Fontainebleau and Auxerre, following the ancient Via Agrippina, or, as it is nowadays called, Route Nationale No. 6. An astonishing number of good restaurants is concentrated in this region: the Hôtel de Paris et de la Poste in Sens, in the Champagne; the Hostellerie de la Poste in Avallon; the Restaurant Aux Trois Faisans in Dijon; the Chapon Fin in the Beaujolais country.

We arrived in front of the Hôtel de la Côte-d'Or in Saulieu just in time to join the impressive array of automobiles with license plates from all over Europe. People who have been here once always come back.

After the refined luxury of many Paris restaurants, the rustic simplicity of the Hôtel de la Côte-d'Or was refreshing. The hotel was an inconspicuous two-story building with a large wood-paneled hall. The walls were covered with photographs of the owner, M. Alexandre Dumaine, a plump, mustachioed, heavy-set fellow in a white chef's outfit. Next to his likenesses hung the menus

he had created for some noted eaters. There was one given in honor of
Curnonsky, the 'Prince of Gastronomes', which read:

Crème de Faisan
Suprême de Brocheton
Feuilleté de Morilles
Jambon de Saulieu Rôti
Gigue de Chevreuil
Fromages
Crème Chocolat

Another menu featured M. Dumaine's *pot-au-feu aux quatre services* – beef,
chicken, ham, and tongue boiled *à la ficelle* (tied by a string), cooked in a bouillon
in a sealed vessel. This boiled symphony was preceded by cold chicken *gelée à
la Marsala*, and followed by *quenelles de brochet*, *salmis de bécasse*, and cheese.

One wall near the small bar was taken up by a big poster, which read:

CHER CLIENT

The quality of the products that we use and the care that we devote to
the preparation of our dishes assure you of a pleasant and classic meal
whenever you are here . . .

However, if you will notify us in advance, at least the day before, and
if you don't arrive too late, you can get, in accordance with the various
seasons, and according to your taste:

*un feuilleté léger de queues d'écrevisses, un pâté de brochet, une matelote d'anguille, une truite
au Chambertin, un bisque d'écrevisses, un crème Saint-Hubert, un jambon du pays aux
quatre purées, ou un millefeuille de jambon fourré au foie gras, un ris de veau Nantua, un
bœuf à la cuillère, un aspic de crêtes et de rognons de coq, un pâté de canard ou de gibier, un
lièvre à la royale, un porcelet rôti et farci de boudins blancs et noirs, une poularde des Ducs de
Bourgogne, un coq en pâté, un dindonneau Louis XIV ou*
l'Oreiller de la Belle-Aurore,

which is one of the most beautiful creations of the *grande cuisine Française*.

We went into the bright, comfortable dining-room. Trays with fruits and cheese
were standing around informally. On the printed menu it said: 'Give us 45 minutes for the preparation of our *poulardes de Bresse*.'

Mme Dumaine, the wife of the chef proprietor, came to take the order. She
is a slim, modest, friendly woman, with the serious mien of a schoolmarm.
When she talked about her husband's creations, her eyes lighted up. We ordered
two specialties, a *terrine de pâté maison* and a *gratin de médaillons de langouste Cardinal*,

which we shared. In a good French restaurant they don't mind if two people share several dishes; on the contrary, they consider it an expression of culinary interest.

Next we shared one of M. Dumaine's masterpieces, called *la poularde cuite à la vapeur d'un pot-au-feu*, which is M. Dumaine's version of 'creamed chicken'. It is neither poached, poëled, braised, roasted, cooked, nor grilled, but steamed – steamed in the aroma of a *pot-au-feu* inside a hermetically closed large earthenware vessel. The *pot-au-feu* (boiled beef with fresh vegetables) is kept simmering for three hours; then the chicken, with thin slices of truffles inserted between skin and breasts, is placed in a casserole on top of a tripod inside the vessel. For one hour it is left steaming in the aroma of the *pot-au-feu*, which slightly expands the truffled fowl. The result is miraculous, served with a cream sauce made of the fowl's liquor.

Afterward we tried another Dumaine specialty, *jambon de Saulieu à la crème gratiné*: thin slices of rosy ham, cooked in heavy cream, sprinkled with cheese, and baked. Shows you what you can do with ham, cream, and cheese, if you know how. There are other Dumaine delights. He makes *fonds d'artichaut*, with a *sauce d'écrevisses, gratiné*, which is a dream.

Dumaine, a native of Digoin, served his apprenticeship in Dijon and Vichy and at the Café de Paris, under the great chef Mourier. In the twenties he got sidetracked to North Africa, where he worked for the Compagnie Générale Transatlantique's Grands Hôtels des Circuits du Sahara, which at that time had a gastronomic reputation.

'Sometimes the supply truck wouldn't arrive and we were stuck with African mutton,' Madame said. 'They're still talking about the things my husband would make out of mutton.'

In 1931 the Dumaines bought the Hôtel de la Côte-d'Or and settled in Saulieu, where Monsieur feels securely surrounded by an abundance of supplies – fine meats and poultry, excellent cream, butter and cheese, and the wines of Burgundy. It's a chef's paradise. On the town square of Saulieu stands the monument of a cow, which, I suppose, gave only heavy cream.

M. Dumaine does all his work himself, with a few helpers in a small kitchen. He lives, talks, dreams cooking and, like all genuine artists, is never satisfied with his work.

'You must be absolutely sure of your technique,' he said to us when we'd managed to get him away from his kitchen for a while. 'People ask me how do I know that the steamed chicken will be right when we open the earthenware vessel. Well, it's my business to know that it will be right. It's mathematics and chemistry. You know the weight of the chicken, and the heat inside the vessel, don't you? The rest is up to you. If you open the vessel ten minutes early, the chicken will be underdone; if you wait ten minutes too long, it will fall apart.'

'A few years ago he was very sick,' his wife said. 'We worried a lot about him. Between attacks of delirium he would talk only of cooking. Once he said to me: "I think I know now how to make a good *coq au vin*." I said: "But you've made it for the past thirty years," and he said: "That was just practice!"'

Among the many cheeses was an excellent Château Double-Crème, one of the finest of France's two hundred and forty varieties of cheese. The wine card of the hotel looked like a list of stockmarket quotations, liberally sprinkled with such blue chips as Richebourg '34 and '29, Chambertin Clos de Bèze '29, many fine years of Romanée-Conti, back to 1926, and Château d'Yquem 1900 and 1892, at 6,000 francs. We drank the pleasant local wines, a Pouilly-Fuissé 'Le Clos' and a Morgan 1950, which cost 300 francs and blended admirably with the food. We left with a satisfied glow and the aftertaste of a pleasant meal. It was four p.m., and M. Dumaine was back in his kitchen, preparing a special dish for the Princess of Monaco who was coming through for dinner on her way to Paris.

1953

The Last Time I Saw Point

On a memorable day, in the fall of 1949, I made my first pilgrimage to Fernand Point's Restaurant de la Pyramide and met the greatest chef of our time. Six years later I had my last meal with him – a few weeks before he died.

I had been there many times. Once in a while I would make a long, uncomfortable trip across the Continent to spend a day with Fernand Point. Our friendship had long progressed beyond the realm of gastronomy. Point was a philosopher, tolerant and wise and witty, a man of compassion and understanding. He loved company. During the last years of his life he lived almost in seclusion in his pleasant home whose ground floor is taken up by the restaurant's kitchen and the dining rooms. He tried to give his customers the illusion that they were guests in a private, civilized home. He rarely ventured out of the house or of the city of Vienne but he was a man of acute perception and well aware of what was going on in the world. Until the very end he remained an amused observer of the follies of the human race. A meal in the company of this extraordinary man was a conversational and intellectual delight. Gastronomically, it was the event of a lifetime.

I remember it as if it were yesterday. The ninth of January, 1955. A cold, snowy day and, as it turned out, a very sad one for me. The plane trees in the garden, which all summer form a cathedral-like roof over the restaurant's outdoors dining room, were bare. So were the white tables underneath. There is something cold and sad about unset restaurant tables, as about a dark, empty theater. It was very quiet. The only sounds came from the small basin with running water near the kitchen entrance, where the live trout and crayfish were kept. On the hills beyond the railroad tracks overlooking the Rhône a blanket of snow covered the slopes and vineyards and olive groves.

Inside the house there was much warmth though – the warmth of cordial hospitality. From the large kitchen came the comforting clatter of casseroles, the sounds of voices and a mixture of tempting flavors. Crayfish butter? A sauce made with port wine? The buttery taste of a fine crust? The flavors created a pleasant sense of anticipation and of speculation. It was like leaning back in one's orchestra stall at the opera house, half listening to the vague sounds of the orchestra's tuning up shortly before the house lights dim. The oboe plays a familiar theme from the score. The horn player practices a difficult passage. You have an electrifying feeling that it's going to be a great night. You cannot explain it: a sense of tension seems to hover over the auditorium, a mysterious fluidum moves back and forth between audience and stage. The artists feel it even before the curtain has gone up. Tonight everybody will perform a little better than usual.

We sat in the small private room, next door to the large dining room, where Fernand Point always used to receive his friends. He no longer greeted the customers at their tables, as he'd done when I was there six years ago, but would remain in his room, sitting at the end of the table from where he could glance through a small, curtained, half-concealed window into the adjoining dining room. Some people had already started with their lunch. Once in a while Point would automatically look through the window to make sure that everything out there was all right. He had the perfect restaurateur's sixth sense; he always knew what was going on. Sometimes he would dispatch a waiter with a secret message to Vincent, his faithful maître d'hôtel. He might have noticed something that bothered his sense of perfection. In no time the shortcoming was corrected.

Sitting there in his comfortable armchair, Point looked every inch 'Le Roi', as his own peers, the great chefs, called him. He had lost some weight after a strict diet, and his long face looked sadder than before. The sadness remained in his melancholy eyes even while he told us a very funny story. There was something of the greatness and the tragic of a Shakespearean king about him, but the tragic was always blended with humor. He wore his flamboyant bow tie of black silk that made him look like a member of the cast of *La Bohème*. A magnum of champagne in a silver bucket stood on the table next to him. It belonged to him like the bow tie.

This was the hour of the day Point liked best, the hour before lunch. Champagne, companionship and good talk, while waiting for the great meal, the climax of the day. He always had friends at his table; I've often suspected that Fernand Point in his later years ran his restaurant mainly for the thinly veiled purpose of inviting his friends. He would have loved to invite all the customers as his guests. He was a grand seigneur who considered bills and ledgers distasteful appurtenances of our modern civilization.

That day the magnum contained a Cramant Blanc de Blancs, a pleasant, 'white' champagne made of the white Pinot grape, much lighter than the golden-hue champagne made from black grapes. Point told the waiter to fill our glasses but he didn't touch the champagne and drank Vittel water. He was a very sick man but also a very brave one.

There were many affectionate gifts and personal mementos in the small room. Drawings, paintings and small ceramics, gifts of the artists who had made them, among them a drawing by Jean Cocteau. Point's favorite was a picture which his daughter Marie-Josette had painted when she was seven years old. There was also a piece of Marie-Josette's first ski, an ornamental sugar bowl, a beautiful Swiss clock, a couple of small sculptures showing the Roman pyramid in the street outside after which the restaurant was named.

There were four of us for lunch that day. Mme Point, who was in and out of the room, greeting people at the door, giving orders, running the restaurant.

Docteur Couchoud, an old friend of the Points who wrote poetry; and I. Point was talking about the old house in Condrieu, the small fishing and wine-making village on the other side of the Rhône, which he'd bought a while ago and was now turning into his vision of Paradise. It would be a small, intimate version of the Pyramide, a sanctum where he would experiment with the wonders of *la grande cuisine* for his family and his closest friends. A small but perfectly furnished kitchen, that would have everything needed within reach, from the compact, small range to the built-in salamander. The kitchen would be the distilled essence of a lifetime's experience, a marvel of efficiency. He talked about the kitchen with enthusiasm and loving attention to detail, moving his large hands as he described the arrangement of the cooking utensils.

I had visited the house in Condrieu earlier that morning with Mme Point. A very old stone house that reminded me of a medieval castle with a terrace over-looking the slow, dark, eerie waters of the Rhône, a dining room under huge oak beams, and a cave deep below in the rocks, an ideal, natural wine cellar. Mado Point told me that Fernand was busily collecting candelabra, amphoras, pieces of old bronze for the house; but while she was talking, she seemed per-turbed, and her mind was elsewhere. She knew that her husband wasn't going to live long enough to move into his dream house in Condrieu.

Fernand was still talking about the house when Mme Point came into the small dining room. He must have seen the agony in her eyes, for suddenly he changed the subject and talked about his last trip to Paris, a few years ago, when a greedy cabdriver had taken one look at the fat uncle from the provinces as Point got into a taxi in Place Vendôme and wanted to be taken to the Madeleine. A fifteen-minute walk at the most. The taxi got there forty minutes later, after a scandalous detour by way of Montmartre, Etoile and the Champs Elysées. Point knew Paris well and enjoyed himself hugely, asking the expected questions (*'Dites-donc, mon vieux,* what do those *femmes* wear at the Folies Bergère?'*) When they arrived at last, he got out, paid the fare, gave the driver a large tip, and quietly told him how to get back quickly to the Place Vendôme.

'The silly expression on the face of the *type* was worth all the money,' Point said, still chuckling at the memory.

He was a master raconteur with a sure grasp of detail, a great mimic who performed the parts of both the driver and his victim, a somewhat huge ver-sion of Fernandel. We all laughed, even Madame Point – I'm sure now that was Fernand's reason for telling the story. The waiter assigned for the day to the table of the 'chef' – they still called Point 'chef' though he no longer worked in his kitchen – laughed so hard that he spilled a few drops of champagne while he filled my glass. At once, Point gave him a stern glance and pointed at the table top. The waiter quickly rubbed off the spots.

Point had designed our lunch 'after thorough consideration of the best things available at this time of the year'. I remember the menu well:

Terrine de Foie Gras Frais
Pâté de Chevreuil Chaud
Barquette de Moules
Saucisson de Campagne
Gratin de Queues d'Écrevisses
Le Canard à la façon du Docteur Couchoud
Les Fromages de Reblochon et de Saint-Marcellin
Gâteau Bonne Fête
Corbeille de Fruits

The hors d'oeuvres and the *gratin* were accompanied by an exquisite Meursault 1950, Cuvée des Hospices de Beaune. With the duck we had the *vin de la maison*, a pleasant, fruity, year-old Juliénas. The great bottle at the end, while the cheese was served, was a Château Ausone 1929, perfectly kept and perfectly served.

Escoffier might have considered this a very simple lunch. Carême wouldn't have dared suggest such an austere meal to Talleyrand. But Point's predecessors would certainly have agreed, if they had been with us, that it was a perfect meal from beginning to end, *'une petite merveille'* in its delicate balance and refined orchestration, with its masterful blend of flavors, tastes, colors.

The *terrine* of fresh goose liver was a beautiful composition, on which Point had worked for years; now, he said, he was 'almost' satisfied. The first hors d'oeuvre was followed by the traditional change of plates and silverware. The second hors d'oeuvre was a delicious, warm pâté of venison, a succulent composition served with a special sauce whose taste is still very much on my palate as I write this. Then came a *barquette de moules*: a fine, buttery crust shaped in the form of tiny boats, filled with mussels cooked in white wine, served in a pinkish sauce. It took you to the heavenly regions of gastronomical perfection, while the fourth and last hors d'oeuvre, a robust sausage made especially for Point by a trusted butcher in the vicinity, took you back down to earth. Point always explored the vicinity for new specialties; why shop in Lyons or Paris, he would say, when there were so many good things next door? He always regretted he didn't have his own vegetable garden and couldn't serve his guests the freshly plucked vegetables, the very first *primeurs* with their original taste still intact.

I've mentioned Point's *gratin de queues d'écrevisses* before. Of all his 'little wonders' this was the greatest. I wish a sample of this magnificent dish could be preserved in an epicurean time capsule to give future generations, perhaps brought up on vitamin pills, and on frozen, canned and dehydrated food, an idea of the gastronomic greatness of our time. Fernand Point didn't invent the *gratin* of crayfish tails, a classic creation of *la grande cuisine*, but he had perfected it for almost thirty years, until the ragout became a masterpiece of refined simplicity, the very essence of the flavor of crayfish and butter. It is a triumph of finesse and demonstrates Point's gastronomic philosophy, that the original flavors should be enhanced, not camouflaged, and that the perfect dish should appeal not only to our palate, but to all senses.

Point knew that we can no longer eat as the pantophagic guests of Talleyrand ate for whom Carême made his sumptuous banquets; we can't even eat as the lucky people ate at the Paris Ritz or the London Carlton when Escoffier was in charge there. Knowing that our eyes are always greedier than our stomachs, Point would try to please all our senses – eyes and ears, tastebuds and nostrils. His *barquette de moules* looked as if it had been painted by Renoir. The crayfish *gratin*, a lovely symphony in bright red, was a delight for eyes and palate. You enjoyed looking at it, inhaling its fragrance, and you would taste it as if it were a great wine. Compared to the gastronomic symphonies of Escoffier, the art of Fernand Point was more delicate, chamber-musical rather than orchestral; his finest dishes had almost a gastronomic intimacy, an exquisite texture. It was a risky art, for even the smallest mistake would at once become evident.

Point's crayfish *gratin* is now imitated by many able chefs but never equaled. It is still served in its original form only at the Pyramide, under the uncompromising guidance of Madame Point, and it is still as fine as it used to be when Fernand Point was alive. No greater homage can be paid to the great woman who keeps intact her husband's genius.

The discovery that *la grande cuisine* should please all our senses, and not merely satisfy our palate, remains the lasting achievement of Fernand Point. To him the lovely sound of a Baccarat glass was as important as the taste of the *gratin*. The touch of fresh linen, dried in full sunshine, was as essential as the bouquet of a fine old claret. The beautiful presentation of a dish was not a mere effect of showing off but a calculated effort to enhance the pleasure of the food. I once had a *blanquette de veau à l'ancienne* there, a delicious, 'old-fashioned' white veal ragout, which is never served to the customers at the Pyramide; most people go there once in a lifetime and wouldn't want to eat an omelet or a stew, no matter how good they are. The *blanquette* is a homely dish, except in the home of Point, where it arrived in a large rectangular silver container. When the waiter took off the cover with a flourish, there was a rhapsody in cream there, the beautiful bubbling sauce covering the vessel almost up to the rim, with the pieces of meat, small onions and mushrooms simmering in it – a feast for the eyes, for the nostrils, for the palate.

The next dish, roasted duck, had been done under the supervision of Fernand Point, who said he had 'amused himself' with a new variation in honor of his old friend Docteur Couchoud. It was purposely underdone and served with a dreamlike sauce. After we'd tasted it in rapt silence, Point asked us to identify the ingredients. He was as happy as a kid when no one guessed correctly. Mme Point, a great epicure in her own right – and, according to Point, a greater connoisseur of wines than he himself ever was – came close but she too missed one detail. It was an indescribable blend of the duck's liquor with port wine, truffles and cream. Toward the end Point had added a few drops of *Fine Champagne*, 'to give the sauce that supreme lift'.

Such a sauce cannot be described in prose. Fortunately there was a poet at the table. While we sipped the Château Ausone with a Saint-Marcellin, Point's favorite goat cheese, made in the nearby town of the same name, Docteur Couchoud composed a little poem about the sauce.

He read it beautifully but then he shrugged in frustration and turned toward Point. 'Such a meal cannot even be described in poetry,' he said. 'And certainly it couldn't be paid for in money. To give a customer a bill after this repast would be the wrong note after a beautiful symphony. No – there should be a top hat in the entrance hall, and when the guests are about to leave, they should place their offerings in the top hat, in grateful appreciation, as offerings were made to the gods in ancient times. The women should take off their rings and ear-rings, their bracelets and diamond pins. The men should leave their watches and wallets, their travel checks and letters of credit – everything they happen to have on them. Then the guests would bow three times toward this room and tiptoe away in silence, their hearts filled with gratitude.'

'Yes,' Fernand Point said, nodding several times in his musing way. 'And then someone would come from the outside and take away the top hat with everything in it.'

I never saw Fernand Point again. He died a few weeks later, only fifty-seven years old. His armchair in the small dining room is empty but his spirit is very much alive at the Pyramide. Everything is done exactly as it was when he was here. Every day Mado Point puts the red gladiolas which Fernand loved into the large vases but never on the tables. Fernand didn't permit flowers there because he felt their fragrance would detract from that of the food. The running-water basin in the garden is always well stocked. All day long men bring the finest supplies to the kitchen of the Pyramide where Paul Mercier, the great chef, carried on with dedication and perfection until he suddenly died in April 1962. Mercier, a master craftsman with a sure touch and a formidable temper, had worked under Fernand Point since the end of the war, and knew all the big and little secrets; even before the death of Point, Mercier was already in charge of the kitchen. But at the Pyramide tradition has a true meaning of responsibility. The artists recruited and trained by Mercier continue their work as though Point's genius and Mercier's mastership were still around. The wines which Point loved to collect as little boys collect postage stamps are impeccably kept and perfectly served by Louis Thomasi, one of the world's few authentic *sommeliers* who studied his art under Point and knows about the mysteries of the harmony between food and wine.

In the dining room the faithful Vincent keeps up the out-of-the-world *ambiance* of peace and tranquillity that surrounds every meal at the Pyramide, where time seems to stand still and no one is in a hurry. On nice summer days people eat on the tree-covered terrace where, I remember, Fernand Point was never quite happy. He used to say that gastronomy doesn't belong in the garden while he noticed a leaf from a tree dropping into somebody's *gratin de queues d'écrevisses*.

When a waiter spills a drop of champagne, he is quickly admonished by a stern glance from *la patronne*. In an art and métier that always remained a man's domain in France, Mme Point carries on with charm, knowledge and courage. There were those who said after her husband's death that no woman could do it. And there were others who said the Pyramide 'wasn't quite the same anymore'.

They all know better today. The consensus of erudite gastronomic opinion in France is that Mme Point has kept the Pyramide alive, intact and perfect as a memorial to her husband. She never compromised; there was no doubt in her mind that she would much rather let the restaurant go out of existence than let it go down. It was a heroic battle but Mado Point won.

Now she receives her friends in the small dining room where we used to sit with Fernand, and at the same time supervises the complex operation of the greatest restaurant this side of Heaven. She will be the first woman who made gastronomic history in France. In the kitchen they still remember how Fernand would come down at seven in the morning when the rest of the large house was still quiet. The 'chef' would sit down with the cooks at the long table, helping them with their chores, splitting string beans (the split beans are cooked more quickly and their flavor is better preserved), or plucking the tiny leaves of watercress. At the Pyramide they don't use watercress to garnish *le bifteck* but make a vegetable of the leaves that tastes like spinach, only much finer, more delicate. Sometimes Point would ask a connoisseur friend how he'd liked the 'very young spinach'. No connoisseur ever passed the test of the watercress leaves.

They still serve the 'very young spinach' there. Nothing at all has changed at the great restaurant. Wherever Fernand Point is, he must be very pleased with the way things are going at his Pyramide.

1962

Beloved Tempest

. . . Almost at once Dumaine said, 'You are hungry? That's good. Your menu has been prepared.'

Since he seemed to be in a benevolent mood, I asked timidly if I might join him in the kitchen before my lunch. He nodded, and said he would call me. Then he went out back to cut a rump steak for the family's lunch, and his wife volunteered to show me the cellar. She said her husband had walled up one section of it to conceal many bottles of precious wine shortly before the Wehrmacht entered Saulieu, on June 16, 1940. The Germans carried away two truckloads of wine from the hotel, but they never found the cache.

During the war, the hotel was open but the restaurant wasn't, because, much as Dumaine missed his beloved cooking, he didn't want to go in for the black-market buying that would have been necessary to keep operating. But many a Resistance fighter was secretly served a *bifteck* and *pommes frites* by the *grand chef* of the Hôtel de la Côte-d'Or. After the Germans left, the wall was removed, but a number of the fine wines it concealed are still there – all the great vintage years of La Romanée-Conti back to 1926, and an excellent selection of Chambolle-Musigny Les Amoureuses, Charmes-Chambertin, Clos de Vougeot, Romanée St-Vivant, Volnay Clos des Ducs, Vosne-Romanée Les Grands Suchots, Chambertin Clos de Bèze, and Vosne-Romanée Les Gaudichots.

There is a smaller but still impressive selection of Bordeaux wines; I saw Château d'Yquem '92 and '00, Château Haut-Brion '06, '28, and '29, Château Cheval-Blanc '24, and Château Ausone '16. Quite a few of the wines in the Dumaine cellar are held in reserve for favorite guests, and not listed on the restaurant's wine card.

'I always try to discourage strangers from ordering one of these irreplace-able bottles,' Mme Dumaine said. 'The other night, a party of Americans ordered a Romanée-Conti '29, which is listed at 95 francs. One lady put water in it. It was very, very sad, monsieur.'

1962

A. J. LIEBLING

Regional Cooking

All over the country pig snouts are a favorite regional dish with people who can afford nothing better. With the snouts a Bowery epicure can get soup, potatoes, two kinds of vegetables, stewed prunes, pudding, all the slightly shopworn bread he can eat and a bowl of coffee, for fifteen cents. That is a *diner de gala*, but the quality probably would not please you. The standard Bowery meal consists of four terrifying crullers and coffee, all for a nickel. Coffee is usually served in a porridge bowl.

Still, there are viands at which the Bowery palate revolts. I remember that toward the end of President Hoover's blessed reign, Mrs Gifford Pinchot suggested a five-and-a-half cent meal to sustain the depressed. It included cabbage rolls stuffed with salmon and rice, apple and orange salad, sticks of corn bread, breadsticks of whole wheat flour and spinach. I discussed this menu with a man named Minder who runs a Bowery restaurant. He said, 'It sounds lousy. I couldn't sell no crap like that.' Minder was a thinker. He wore a purple turtleneck sweater and khaki pants while he presided over his own place in the joint quality of maître d'hôtel and bouncer. He said that he thought a good many of the men on the Bowery had been driven from their homes by wives who prepared food like cabbage rolls stuffed with salmon and rice. Reluctant to go home to dinner, these men had taken to hanging around saloons, drinking on empty stomachs. Eventually they had hit the skids and been forced to abscond from the genteel communities where their wives still lingered, commiserated by their neighbors and continuing to copy recipes out of the *Ladies' Home Journal*.

The typical Bowery eating house is a long, high-ceilinged room with a plate-glass storewindow in front for all its light by day. There are long wooden tables varnished with gravy, which has been massaged into the grain of the wood in the course of years. Salt and pepper are in open dishes and the customers reach in with their hands. The average check is ten cents, and payment entitles the customer to sit up all night and keep out of the cold.

The Bowery restaurateur has his own problems.

'Sometimes my customers come in with one of those nickel shots under their belt,' Mr Minder says. 'They order some soup. The hot soup does not go good with the alky. When the hot soup gets in their stomach they drop right off the chair. Then we got to telephone for the ambulance. The telephone call adds to the overhead.'

It would be difficult to say which is the oldest school of cooking back where I came from – the Armenian or the Chinese. Both began when French cooking was a matter of a naked Gaul tearing a raw rabbit. I know an Armenian named Krikor Sousikian, who is 'cooker and treasurer' of a small restaurant called the Bosporus, and who was once the chef of Derdat Babayan, Abdul Hamid's jeweler, in Constantinople. I know Babayan's son, Levon, who lives in Paris and vouches for old Krikor. I once knew a New Yorker named Sam Johnson who claimed to be an illegitimate son of Abdul Hamid's, but I never believed him and it has nothing to do with cooking anyway. I just mention it to show what quaint characters we have back here.

The cook of a great jeweler occupied a peculiarly responsible position under Abdul Hamid because the Chief Eunuch bought the jewels for the harem. The only way to the Chief Eunuch's affection was through his stomach. Krikor cooked Derdat Babayan into a monopoly of the wedding present market, which was important because the Sultan took a new wife every year. At each wedding there were great gifts, not only to the bride, but to the guests and to the members of the harem who ranked her. Krikor's cooking had no personal importance to the Sultan, who ate nothing at all except eggs boiled in the shell and soup out of cans because he was afraid of being poisoned. Krikor says this. He learned his cooking from a man named Avedis Azdikian, who was the Escoffier of the Near East. I once asked Krikor Sousikian how many dishes were in Azdikian's repertoire.

'Ai! From patlijan, eggplant, he could make three million dishes. Patlijan karniyark. Patlijan moussaka. Patlijan dousme. Patlijan chaup kehab. Patlijan azyze – in the style beloved of the Sultan Aziz. Patlijan' –

'That's plenty!'

Sousikian paused meekly. 'In all there are three million.'

Krikor cooked his first state dinner at the age of twenty. It was the birthday of one of the jeweler's family.

'What did you serve?'

'Chirim, fish,' he said. 'Chirim in cream soup.' So it seems a bisque of shrimps was the first course. But the shrimps of the Sea of Marmora are to the shrimps of Fulton Street as the dome of St Sophia is to the Little Church Around the Corner, he explained. Everything tastes better in Constantinople.

'Then,' he said, 'was patlijan moussaka – eggplant stuffed with meat and tomatoes. Then bouillabaisse our style, fish stew from wonderful fish of Constantinople. Then kouzou guvej – lamb in casserole with leeks and peppers. Then mushrooms in pastry. Then' –

'What sort of wines?'

'Wait, wait, there is more eating to tell. Then, Russian salad. Then lokma – like fritters in honey. Then varti anoush, rose leaf jelly; then hanoum dour dahel, so sweet – dessert we call "the lady's lips" – and kaymak, heavy cream, on everything, and honey – ai! That was a dinner!'

'And the wines?'

'Champanya,' said Mr Sousikian, shortly, as if to ask 'and what should the Sultan's jeweler drink but champanya?'

'And after dinner,' he recalled, 'Derdat Babayan called upstairs and congratulated me and gave me gold.'

'Where is he now?'

'He is dead.'

'And what did he die from?'

'From over-eating.'

The greatest Chinese cook I ever met was named Henry Hong – at least the Chinese I knew told me he was the greatest cook, for I never ate any of his handiwork.

'North China cook not much,' said Henry Hong. 'Shanghai cook different, not much. Nobody China people beat Canton, Hankow. Nobody Canton, Hankow, beat me.

'When we see Eulopean eat steak,' he said, 'we think there go one half-civilize. He know he hungry; no know make utensil for cook, burn meat on piece fire.'

I thought him an arrogant fellow, like most experts on regional cooking.

NOT QUITE GONE ARE THE DAYS ...

Until the end of prohibition there were certain blocks in New York with virtually identical speakeasies in every house. The block I remember best was west of Eighth Avenue, in the Forties. The houses were all brownstone, and the speakeasies all had entrances under the stoops. They were not primarily stand-up-at-the-bar speakeasies, although practically every one had a small bar in the kitchen, where customers paused for a quick one on the way back from the men's room. They were restaurants with vaguely French table-d'hote dinners and Italian proprietors, and everybody you met knew one where the cooking was the real thing. 'The place doesn't look like much,' you would be told, 'but you ought to taste the food. Did you ever have crepes Suzette?' In those basements middle-class New Yorkers were taught that the ultimate in desserts was a pancake that burned with a wan flame. If you let yourself be persuaded to try a new place, you found yourself in a speakeasy exactly like the one three doors down the street, where you went habitually. The only difference would be that the proprietor was named Victor instead of Jean, or Emilio instead of Roberto. The proprietors in the block ran to names like these; never Frank, or Joe, or Al. That was Mulberry Street stuff – not chic. In almost all these places the dinner was a dollar and a half until 1930, when it got down to a dollar and a quarter. Then, in about 1932, it dropped to a dollar. Wine was a dollar and a half a bottle white or red, during the good days, and a dollar later. Some places charged sixty cents for a highball, the extra dime representing pure snobbishness.

Our crowd used to favor a place on this block called Aldo's. I do not remember why we started going there, but after a while it became a habit. Aldo Bulotti was in the Polyclinic Hospital with some vague ailment at the time of our first visits, and later he went back to Italy and died. His wife, a woman named Maria, ran the place while he was sick, and kept on running it after his death. She was four feet eleven inches tall and weighed a hundred and sixty pounds, and she had bobbed hair set in a series of abrupt permanent waves about half an inch apart. She was an agreeable woman. Mrs Bulotti had two children: a boy, eight, and a girl, five. She lived with them in Corona, out in Queens. She did not think a speakeasy was any place to raise children. An Italian doctor lived somewhere in the four stories above the basement, and twice, while we were going to Aldo's, he was deported for practicing medicine without a licence. He came back both times. The doctor had needle-pointed mustaches and a skin like old, yellowed paper. He ate dinner at Aldo's most nights and was always glad to join parties of other customers, especially if they included young women. He was a real doctor, graduated from the University of Naples, he once told me, but he had never learned much English and, besides, he was so old that his medical theory might have been considered obsolete. For these, and I suppose for other reasons, he was afraid to take the Medical Board examinations.

Aldo's was a small place, even for a speakeasy of that sort. Maria had one waiter and a cook. She kept the bar herself. She changed waiters often, but Bruno, the cook, seemed to be permanent. He was an Umbrian, very fair for an Italian, with a sharp, tired face. A widower, he got on very well with Maria. When you came into Aldo's, there was a hall leading from the door straight to the kitchen, and there were two small, connecting rooms that opened off the hall. In the front room were five tables, a disused fireplace, and a mirror, and in the room between that and the kitchen were three tables and a painting of a scene on Lake Como.

Along one wall of the kitchen was a bench, with a trellis over it, and across from that a bar. Also in the kitchen were two tables with checkered cloths, and some of the customers preferred to sit there, where they could talk to Maria and Bruno while they were eating. That way they could hear all about the customers in the front rooms, since Maria and Bruno carried on a running discussion of them, with the waiter joining in from time to time. The customers included a number of married women who liked to talk to strangers about their troubles, and a beautiful girl named Ruth, who told people she was a private secretary and was always busting into other people's parties. There were also several discreet couples who chose the smallest room when they could get a table there and argued in whispers until they began to feel good, when they would come out in the kitchen and join the other parties. Several of the steadiest customers came from Reuters, the British news agency. Reuters' office is over on the other side of town, but people used to migrate into those West Side blocks from everywhere to take their dinners. One of the Reuters men was impressive because of his habit of sitting all alone in the front room, staring at the curtained windows and drinking brandy and black coffee out of a tall glass. His name was Skerry. He was a very dignified gentleman with an Old World courtliness. Occasionally, after a good many mazagrans and brandies, he would poke his head into the kitchen before he left for the night and make a little speech to the people at the bar. 'By this means,' he would say, swaying gently, 'I disinfect myself from the American turmoil.' Then he would bow and go home. We always felt that he was doing all he could to uphold the traditions of the Empire, like the legendary Englishman in the Borneo outpost who dresses every night for dinner in order to keep from going native.

Maria made her wine at home in Corona out of California grapes. Some of the customers were allergic to the wine and fell on their heads, but others, thank God, could stand a lot of it. I think it was in these speakeasies that 'allergy' got started on its way to being a common word. Everybody, it seemed, was allergic to some particular kind of liquor. You never met a man in a speakeasy who was merely an incompetent drinker. He always said, 'I can drink any amount of Scotch or rye, but I'm allergic to brandy.' Or else, 'I can hold my hard liquor, but when I drink red wine, I never remember what happens.' One night a man named Jim, who Maria said was a very sweet gentleman except that he couldn't drink gin, was sitting in the kitchen with his wife. He was drinking gin. Pretty soon he threatened to tear his wife's clothes off. She said, 'Go ahead!' very scornfully, not thinking that he would do it, and he did tear them off, all but a brassiere. The outraged woman rushed from the kitchen into the front room, in search of privacy. It happened, however, that Skerry, the courtliest of the Reuters men, was sitting there alone, drinking and thinking. He turned his face to the wall. 'What a big surprise for Mr Skerry!' Bruno remarked when he told me about it the next evening. Maria lent the woman a coat and put her in a taxi, and Skerry soon after went back to England and got married. In time he will tell incredulous juniors this anecdote of his life in the United States under prohibition, and they will say, among themselves, that it's a bit thick – the old boy's in his dotage.

When repeal came, I didn't bother my head much about Aldo's. I happened to walk through the block a few weeks afterward, and I noticed that a dozen of the speakeasies had secured licences, hung out signs, and opened up, but that Maria hadn't. From then on I took it for granted that she had not been able to raise the fee, and had gone out of business. Then, about a month ago, I found myself in the old neighborhood and I got to thinking with some tenderness of Maria and Bruno, and I walked around to the house where Aldo's had been. The front of the place looked as dismal and taciturn as ever, with all the shades drawn in the barred basement windows. But I thought that the recurrent Italian physician might be living in the house, and that he might be able to tell me what had become of Mrs Bulotti. Perhaps she had opened a little café in a more prepossessing part of town, I thought, and it would be fun to visit her.

I therefore walked down the two steps from pavement level and rang the bell beside the basement grille. Maria herself came to the door. She was dazzled by the daylight, and peered out warily until I pressed my face against the bars. Then she grinned, and released the catch by pressing an electric button. It seemed to me that time in its flight turned backward to 1928. 'Come in the kitch', Mista Lieba,' she said. 'Maybe you like a drink. Bruno!' she yelled down the hall. 'Itsa Mista Lieba!' I followed her. The door to the front room was ajar, and I could see the familiar tables laid with their white cloths. Nothing in the kitchen had changed: the copper saucepans hanging above the range, the trellis with its artificial yellow vine leaves, the red-and-black lacquer bar, and on the liquor shelf the pink lamp made out of a French cordial bottle.

Bruno, in his white cap and apron, was slicing eggplant with a long knife, just as I remembered him in a previous gastronomic existence. Maria bought a drink of Courvoisier and smiled as I looked about me. 'Just the same as ever, eh?' she said. 'I got the whole house now. The Doctor, he'sa gone back to Italy for good. I got the children with me, living on the first floor. Dino is in the third year 'igh school. 'E's seventeen. Gilda, she's a freshman. She's fourteen. I rent out eight rooms on the other floors. Bruno and me, we do pretty good now.'

She has never really got out of the speakeasy business, she told me. Some of the old customers, like me, had taken her retirement for granted and gone off to licenced restaurants. She didn't see them any more. But a few, either from habit or because they liked personal attention while drinking, had continued to come. Now there were a good many new clients, introduced by the old ones. Some people have never got used to drinking in public restaurants, it seems. The atmosphere is too formal and grasping. Even in reformed speakeasies that have tried to retain the old spirit, the management takes a cold, impersonal attitude toward disorderly conduct. The owners, Maria says with scorn, are afraid that the Alcohol Board will revoke their licences.

If Maria had bought a licence, she said, she would have had to open her door to everybody. On that block, this would inevitably have meant invasion by uncouth types. 'Truckadriv'!' Maria said. 'They cannot mix with my people. My people would desert me. I gotta keep my place nice.'

It sounded reasonable to me. I asked her if she wasn't afraid of being arrested. Maria said that she was less worried now than she had been during prohibition. About half the places on the block had opened as saloons, she told me, and the rest operated as speakeasies. They all got along amicably. The saloon-keepers didn't want any more open drinking places on the block, and so, since they knew the speakeasy trade came from outside the neighborhood, they didn't complain about the speakeasies.

Even if there was a raid, possession of legitimately bottled liquor was no offence. If inspectors remarked on the quantity, Maria could say that the men who lived upstairs boarded with her and liked a drink with their meals. She never sold to strangers. Anyway, the mere circumstance that a stranger would want to buy a drink at a private house nowadays would suffice to warn the least wary proprietor. As she is not subject to licence regulations, Maria stays open until six o'clock in the morning, while legal bars close at four. This is a great convenience to some of her customers.

Naturally, the business is on a small scale, but expenses also are low. Repeal was such a blow to brownstone rental values that she leases the entire house for one hundred and twenty-five dollars a month. She used to pay one hundred and seventy-five dollars for the basement. The eight roomers, who pay four or five dollars a week each, furnish enough money for the rent for the whole building, including Maria's own living quarters. It is no longer necessary to invest money in liquor in large lots, or in tons of grapes for wine-making. She can buy whiskey by the bottle and wine by the gallon at the liquor store in the next block. At thirty-five cents a drink for whiskey and forty-five cents a pint for wine, there's a nice profit. The dinner is a dollar, and of course there's a profit in that. Maria waits on the tables herself now. It agrees with her, apparently, because her weight has gone up to two hundred pounds. She says that she averages about a dozen customers at dinner. There are generally one or two afternoon clients who want seclusion, and then there are usually a couple of drinkers who stay on after four in the morning. It all amounts to twenty or thirty dollars a day, and half of that is profit.

I stayed for dinner and we talked. Bruno likes it better than working as assistant chef in some Italian restaurant. When there are no customers, he plays dominoes with one of the roomers, or reads Italian sporting papers, which are brought to him by stewards on the *Rex* and the *Conte di Savoia*. He used to be in the merchant marine, and the place is not far from the piers, so he keeps up his acquaintance. Twice a week he goes to boxing shows.

Every so often, without any particular reason, an old patron will return to the house just as I did, Maria told me. It's like coming back to the scene of a crime, or one's childhood. Sometimes the oldsters even pay prohibition-time tabs. One of them, a week earlier, had paid her seventeen dollars which he had owed since 1932.

A woman came in and sat down at the table next to me in the kitchen. Maria introduced us; her name, as nearly as I could make out, was Mrs Buttercup. Soon we were all talking, as in the good days. Mrs Buttercup told me that she had a daughter twenty-one years old, to whom she had presented a Boston terrier for Christmas, but the daughter, just because she wanted to go to California, had returned the terrier to her, Mrs Buttercup, although she knew full well that the Buttercup apartment in London Terrace was no place for a dog. 'No sense of responsibility,' Mrs Buttercup said. She had an irritating way of repeating herself and she was not particularly handsome, but she had an archaic charm, like a Gibson girl. She drank Old-Fashioned cocktails throughout her meal. I found that when a client, especially a lady, is approaching the saturation point, Maria still dilutes the drinks, although of course she does not reduce the prices on the check, as that would arouse suspicion. The place soothed me. Bruno's chicken *en casserole* and his *cannelloni* were really rather good. After all, one needn't eat the crepes Suzette. Before I left, Maria told Mrs Buttercup and me about a woman in the front room the other night whose husband had got so angry at her drinking that he knocked out one of her front teeth. Then he had had to pay sixty dollars to have it put back, Maria said, because he couldn't stand her smile without it.

WHAT DO YOU EXPECT FOR $2.00?

There never were many people in the finest restaurant I ever discovered within the city limits (it was at one of New York's bathing beaches) and most of those there were seemed unwanted. Sometimes a party of four sunburned adults and maybe three children would sit around a table uneasily for half an hour, the men in shirtsleeves, the women in cotton dresses, and no waiter would come near them. Three or four waiters, old, acrid fellows, would be standing in the farthest corner of the vast room, talking and laughing bitterly, and looking over at the people at the table. The waiters wore black alpaca coats and round tin badges with numbers on them. Once we saw a man at a table grow angry and bang on the water carafe with a knife. There was only yellow, tepid water in the carafe. A waiter shuffled to his table from the far corner. He seemed to take an interminable time getting there, and the slup, slup of his broken old shoes on the floor sounded loud in that almost silent place. The man said something to him, and then the waiter said in a loud, contemptuous voice, 'We don't serve sandwiches or soft drinks here.' The party went out, the men looking ashamed, the women scolding their males for subjecting them to such embarrassment.

'Some of them turf-cutters,' our waiter said, flicking crumbs off our table with the end of his napkin. '"Turf-cutter" is a word we use for cheap Irish,' he said, knocking most of the crumbs into my girl's lap. He looked Irish himself. 'The Beach is full of them,' he said. 'Let them go down to the Limerick House.'

The restaurant must have been built shortly after the Columbian Exposition. It was an imitation of a cake-frosting exposition building, with seven senseless minarets on it. Most of the white paint had flaked off, or turned gray with age and sea air. The signs about specialties of the house were painted right on the building, in what had once been silver lettering, on what had once been a maroon ground. Evidently the lettering had not been changed since the restaurant was built. Most of the signs said, 'Rhode Island Clambake, $1.75', or 'Roast Chicken Dinner, $1.50'. In the state to which the Beach has declined, these are high prices. They must have been high forty years ago, too, but then the Beach was a fashionable resort, with a clientele of hot sports. It cost a dollar just to get there from Manhattan, in a steamboat. Now the most dashing attractions are a couple of tired carrousels and a few saloons that advertise in the Irish-American newspapers; but most of the people who come to the Beach do not patronize even them. They just change into their bathing suits under the boardwalk and go swimming, and when they come out, they eat at hot-dog stands. The swimming is good.

The floor of the restaurant sloped like a ship's deck in a big sea. Like all the older buildings at the Beach, it had been built without a foundation, and it had settled in the sand unevenly. The dish covers, the soup tureens, and the rest of the tableware had an antiquarian interest. Each piece bore the name of an old, vanished restaurant: Shanley's, Churchill's, or Jack's.

The restaurant was so obviously decadent and unprosperous that we had not ventured into it the first few times that we went to the Beach to swim. It was only after investigating the possibilities of the Greek lunchrooms, the Japanese waffle shops, and the saloons that we had dared that ghostly pavilion, deciding that we had nothing to lose. The food in the old restaurant had astonished us. The steamed clams were small, clean, and accompanied by a stiff sauce of butter with tarragon vinegar and curry powder blended into it. The chicken fricassee was not smothered in a white flour paste, but yellow and succulent. The three-and-a-half-dollar steak, for two, was perfect. As long as we ordered substantially, took cocktails before dinner, and drank plenty of beer with the meal, the waiters tolerated us.

One evening I ordered a 'combination' of steamed clams and a broiled lobster, with potatoes. It had seemed to me that included in this offering, on the menu, was a green salad. Having finished the lobster, I asked for this salad.

The waiter said, 'What do you expect for two dollars? A *gold* watch?'

It was this same waiter, however, who on another evening began to talk to me, almost without condescension. It is true he had been drinking.

'The place is a hundred years behind the times,' he said. 'It's a summer home for broken-down waiters.'

He put one hand on our table and leaned his weight on it.

'The cook is forty-nine million years old,' he said. 'Some day he'll fall into the clam chowder. At the end of every season the old man says to him, "I never want to see you no more. You're as dead as a doornail." And at the beginning of the next season he sends a taxicab for him. He used to cook at Burns's. The old man is in his second childhood. That's him setting up on the high stool by the bar. He ain't got no cash register, only an old wooden cash box. He sets there from ten o'clock in the morning until closing time, to see that no waiter gets away with a glass of beer.'

The waiter pointed his chin angrily toward the figure on the stool, diagonally across the room from us. The old gentleman was dressed in a black broadcloth suit, such as a conservative undertaker might wear in winter. The upper part of the vest looked very big for him, but his lower abdomen ballooned out like a spider's. On top of his head he balanced an old *Panama* hat, colored like a meerschaum pipe. Even from there we could see how badly he needed a shave.

'He's had that *Panama* hat for twenty years,' the waiter grumbled. 'Every spring he has it cleaned, and I think painted, and he brags to everybody he knows about it. "See," he says, "the *Panama* hat is good for another season." He's in his second childhood. But try to take a dime off him,' the waiter said, 'and he ain't in his second childhood no more. You can't do it.'

The old man came down off the stool, reluctantly, like a boy sliding into a too-cold swimming pool. He shuffled toward our end of the room, glaring suspiciously over the tops of his spectacles. He had a long, pointed nose. Fifteen feet from our table the old man stopped and stared at us for a minute. Then he turned and went away. Laboriously he climbed up on the stool.

'He was just coming over to see there wasn't too many customers in the place,' the waiter explained. 'The other night they was lined up two deep at the bar, for once, so he says to the bartender, "Come out from behind that bar, Joe, and take a walk around the block until they clear out of here." He don't like no customers. It's second childhood. Do you know what worries him the most? The fear that somebody would park at the curb here. He hates automobiles. So he puts a stepladder in front of the curb and a pot of green paint on top of it. So anybody that drives in will knock the ladder over and get paint on his car. "Oh, he-he-he," the old man laughs the last time that happens. "Look at the damn fool! Too bad he didn't get it on his clothes," the old man says.'

The dining room opens onto a terrace on a level with the sidewalk. We looked out and saw the ladder, with the paint pot perched on the top step.

Another waiter, even older than ours, who was pretty old himself, edged up to our man.

'I don't like to say nothing, Murph,' he said, 'but them people over at that table over there says they give you their order half an hour ago.'

'Tell them it's a two-mile walk to the kitchen and back,' said our waiter. The people, two men and two women, had been watching him right along, and knew he had not been to the kitchen. When they saw he was not going to do anything about it, they got up and left.

'Deaf as a post the old man is,' the waiter went on. 'You should hear him talk on the telephone with his sister that lives at the Plaza. "I'm fine," he yells as soon as he picks up the phone. He thinks she's asking him how he is. No matter what the hell she calls up to talk to him about, he just says, "I'm fine," and hangs up. But if you drop a dollar bill on the floor, he hears it hit.'

Perhaps the old man sensed that we were talking about him. Hesitantly, he got down off his stool again and walked over toward us, then stopped, irresolute, at the same point as before, and turned and went back.

'It's on account of him that the Beach is going to hell,' said our waiter. 'He owns all the property for a mile around and he won't put a coat of paint on a building. Last year four blocks of his stuff burnt up, the damned old tinder-boxes. "It don't do me no good anyway," he says. "I couldn't get no insurance on them." The papers says, "$500,000 Fire at the Beach," but he couldn't get five cents for them buildings.'

'Why does he keep the place open if he doesn't want any customers?' my girl asked.

'So he can lose money and take it off his income tax,' Murph told her. 'And now for God's sakes don't order no pie à la mode like the last time, for I have to walk down to one end of the old shack for the pie and then I have to walk to the other end to the icehouse for the ice cream. Before you can get an order together in this place, you got to get a letter from the Pope. And then before you can find a dish to serve it in, you got to go through all that heap of old tinware, like a junk shop.'

My girl meekly ordered watermelon, but Murph did not start to get it. He felt like talking.

'Before his wife died sixteen years ago, it wasn't so bad,' he said. 'Sometimes she would buy a round of drinks for the house. She was always soused. Twenty-four seasons I've worked here, God help me, and now it's too late to get fired. He'll die next winter surely.'

1938

A Good Appetite

The Proust *madeleine* phenomenon is now as firmly established in folklore as Newton's apple or Watt's steam kettle. The man ate a tea biscuit, the taste evoked memories, he wrote a book. This is capable of expression by the formula TMB, for Taste > Memory > Book. Some time ago, when I began to read a book called *The Food of France*, by Waverley Root, I had an inverse experience: BMT, for Book > Memory > Taste. Happily, the tastes that *The Food of France* re-created for me – small birds, stewed rabbit, stuffed tripe, Côte Rôtie, and Tavel – were more robust than that of the *madeleine*, which Larousse defines as 'a light cake made with sugar, flour, lemon juice, brandy, and eggs'. (The quantity of brandy in a *madeleine* would not furnish a gnat with an alcohol rub.) In the light of what Proust wrote with so mild a stimulus, it is the world's loss that he did not have a heartier appetite. On a dozen Gardiners Island oysters, a bowl of clam chowder, a peck of steamers, some bay scallops, three sautéed soft-shelled crabs, a few ears of fresh-picked corn, a thin swordfish steak of generous area, a pair of lobsters, and a Long Island duck, he might have written a masterpiece.

The primary requisite for writing well about food is a good appetite. Without this, it is impossible to accumulate, within the allotted span, enough experience of eating to have anything worth setting down. Each day brings only two

opportunities for field work, and they are not to be wasted minimizing the intake of cholesterol. They are indispensable, like a prizefighter's hours on the road. (I have read that the late French professional gourmand Maurice Curnonsky ate but one meal a day – dinner. But that was late in his life, and I have always suspected his attainments anyway; so many mediocre witticisms are attributed to him that he could not have had much time for eating.) A good appetite gives an eater room to turn around in. For example, a non-professional eater I know went to the Restaurant Pierre, in the Place Gaillon, a couple of years ago, his mind set on a sensibly light meal: a dozen, or possibly eighteen, oysters, and a thick chunk of steak topped with beef marrow, which M. Pierre calls a *Délice de la Villette* – the equivalent of a 'Stockyards' Delight.' But as he arrived, he heard M. Pierre say to his head-waiter, 'Here comes Monsieur L. Those two portions of *cassoulet* that are left – put them aside for him.' A *cassoulet* is a substantial dish, of a complexity precluding its discussion here. (Mr Root devotes three pages to the great controversy over what it should contain.) M. Pierre is the most amiable of restaurateurs, who prides himself on knowing in advance what his friends will like. A client of limited appetite would be obliged either to forgo his steak or to hurt M. Pierre's feelings. Monsieur L., however, was in no difficulty. He ate the two *cassoulets*, as was his normal practice; if he had consumed only one, his host would have feared that it wasn't up to standard. He then enjoyed his steak. The oysters offered no problem, since they present no bulk.

In the heroic age before the First World War, there were men and women who ate, in addition to a whacking lunch and a glorious dinner, a voluminous *souper* after the theater or the other amusements of the evening. I have known some of the survivors, octogenarians of unblemished appetite and unfailing good humor – spry, wry, and free of the ulcers that come from worrying about a balanced diet – but they have had no emulators in France since the doctors there discovered the existence of the human liver. From that time on, French life has been built to an increasing extent around that organ, and a niggling caution has replaced the old recklessness; the liver was the seat of the Maginot mentality. One of the last of the great around-the-clock gastronomes of France was Yves Mirande, a small, merry author of farces and musical-comedy books. In 1955, Mirande celebrated his eightieth birthday with a speech before the curtain of the Théâtre Antoine, in the management of which he was associated with Mme B., a protégée of his, forty years younger than himself. But the theater was only half of his life. In addition, M. Mirande was an unofficial director of a restaurant on the Rue Saint-Augustin, which he had founded for another protégée, also forty years younger than himself; this was Mme G., a Gasconne and a magnificent cook. In the restaurant on the Rue Saint-Augustin, M. Mirande would dazzle his juniors, French and American, by dispatching a lunch of raw Bayonne ham and fresh figs, a hot sausage in crust, spindles of filleted pike in a rich rose *sauce Nantua*, a leg of lamb larded with anchovies, artichokes on a pedestal of foie gras, and four or five kinds of cheese, with a good bottle of Bordeaux and one of champagne, after which he would call for the Armagnac and remind Madame to have ready for dinner the larks and ortolans she had promised him, with a few *langoustes* and a turbot – and, of course, a fine *civet* made from the *marcassin*, or young wild boar, that the lover of the leading lady in his current production had sent up from his estate in the Sologne. 'And while I think of it,' I once heard him say, 'we haven't had any woodcock for days, or truffles baked in the ashes, and the cellar is becoming a disgrace – no more '34s and hardly any '37s. Last week, I had to offer my publisher a bottle that was far too good for him, simply because there was nothing between the insulting and the superlative.'

M. Mirande had to his credit a hundred produced plays, including a number of great Paris hits, but he had just written his first book for print, so he said 'my publisher' in a special mock-impressive tone. 'An informal sketch for my definitive autobiography,' he would say of this production. The informal sketch, which I cherish, begins with the most important decision in Mirande's life. He was almost seventeen and living in the small Breton port of Lannion – his offstage family name was Le Querrec – when his father, a retired naval officer, said to him, 'It is time to decide your future career. Which will it be, the Navy or the Church?' No other choice was conceivable in Lannion. At dawn, Yves ran away to Paris.

There, he had read a thousand times, all the famous wits and cocottes fre-quented the tables in front of the Café Napolitain, on the Boulevard des

Capucines. He presented himself at the café at nine the next morning – late in the day for Lannion – and found that the place had not yet opened. Soon he became a newspaperman. It was a newspaper era as cynically animated as the corresponding period of the Bennett-Pulitzer-Hearst competition in New York, and in his second or third job he worked for a press lord who was as notional and niggardly as most press lords are; the publisher insisted that his reporters be well turned out, but did not pay them salaries that permitted cab fares when it rained. Mirande lived near the fashionable Montmartre cemetery and solved his rainy-day pants-crease problem by crashing funeral parties as they broke up and riding, gratis, in the carriages returning to the center of town. Early in his career, he became personal secretary to Clemenceau and then to Briand, but the gay theater attracted him more than politics, and he made the second great decision of his life after one of his political patrons had caused him to be appointed *sous-préfet* in a provincial city. A *sous-préfet* is the administrator of one of the districts into which each of the ninety *départements* of France is divided, and a young *sous-préfet* is often headed for a precocious rise to high positions of state. Mirande, attired in the magnificent uniform that was then de rigueur, went to his 'capital', spent one night there, and then ran off to Paris again to direct a one-act farce. Nevertheless, his connections with the serious world remained cordial. In the restaurant on the Rue Saint-Augustin, he introduced me to Colette, by that time a national glory of letters.

The regimen fabricated by Mirande's culinary protégée, Mme G., maintained him *en pleine forme*. When I first met him, in the restaurant, during the summer of the Liberation, he was a sprightly sixty-nine. In the spring of 1955, when we renewed a friendship that had begun in admiration of each other's appetite, he was as good as ever. On the occasion of our reunion, we began with a *truite au bleu* – a live trout simply done to death in hot water, like a Roman emperor in his bath. It was served up doused with enough melted butter to thrombose a regiment of Paul Dudley Whites, and accompanied, as was right, by an Alsatian wine – a Lacrimae Sanctae Odiliae, which once contributed slightly to my education. Long ago, when I was very young, I took out a woman in Strasbourg and, wishing to impress her with my knowledge of local customs, ordered a bottle of Ste Odile. I was making the same mistake as if I had taken out a girl in Boston and offered her baked beans. 'How quaint!' the woman in Strasbourg said. 'I haven't drunk that for years.' She excused herself to go to the telephone, and never came back.

After the trout, Mirande and I had two meat courses, since we could not decide in advance which we preferred. We had a magnificent *daube provençale*, because we were faithful to *la cuisine bourgeoise*, and then *pintadous* – young guinea hens, simply and tenderly roasted – with the first asparagus of the year, to show our fidelity to *la cuisine classique*. We had clarets with both courses – a Pétrus with the *daube*, a Cheval Blanc with the guineas. Mirande said that his doctor had dis-counseled Burgundies. It was the first time in our acquaintance that I had heard him admit he had a doctor, but I was reassured when he drank a bottle and a half of Krug after luncheon. We had three bottles between us – one to our loves, one to our countries, and one for symmetry, the last being on the house.

Mirande was a small, alert man with the face of a Celtic terrier – salient eye-brows and an upturned nose. He looked like an intelligent Lloyd George. That summer, in association with Mme B., his theatrical protégée, he planned to pro-duce a new play of Sartre's. His mind kept young by the theater of Mme B., his metabolism protected by the restaurant of Mme G., Mirande seemed fortified against all eventualities for at least another twenty years. Then, perhaps, he would have to recruit new protégées. The Sunday following our reunion, I encountered him at Longchamp, a racecourse where the restaurant does not face the horses, and diners can keep first things first. There he sat, radiant, sur-rounded by celebrities and champagne buckets, sending out a relay team of commissionaires to bet for him on the successive tips that the proprietors of stables were ravished to furnish him between races. He was the embodiment of a happy man. (I myself had a nice thing at 27-1.)

The first alteration in Mirande's fortunes affected me so directly that I did not at once sense its gravity for him. Six weeks later, I was again in Paris. (That year, I was shuttling frequently between there and London.) I was alone on the evening I arrived, and looked forward to a pleasant dinner at Mme G.'s, which was within two hundred metres of the hotel, in the Square Louvois, where I always stop. Madame's was more than a place to eat, although one ate superbly there. Arriving, I would have a bit of talk with the proprietress, then with the waitresses – Germaine and Lucienne – who had composed the original staff. Waiters had been added as the house prospered, but they were of less marked personality. Madame was a bosomy woman – voluble, tawny, with a big nose and lank black hair – who made one think of a Saracen. (The Saracens reached Gascony in the eighth century.) Her conversation was a chronicle of letters and the theater – as good as a subscription to *Figaro Littéraire*, but more advanced. It was somewhere between the avant-garde and the main body, but within hail-ing distance of both and enriched with the names of the great people who had been in recently – M. Cocteau, Gene Kelly, la Comtesse de Vogüé. It was always well to give an appearance of listening, lest she someday fail to save for you the last order of larks *en brochette* and bestow them on a more attentive customer. With Germaine and Lucienne, whom I had known when we were all younger, in 1939, the year of the *drôle de guerre*, flirtation was now perfunctory, but the *carte du jour* was still the serious topic – for example, how the fat Belgian industrialist from Tournai had reacted to the *caille vendangeuse*, or quail potted with fresh grapes. 'You know the man,' Germaine would say. 'If it isn't dazzling, he takes only two portions. But when he has three, then you can say to yourself . . .' She and Lucienne looked alike – compact little women, with high foreheads and cheekbones and solid, muscular legs, who walked like *chasseurs à pied*, a hundred and thirty steps to the minute. In 1939, and again in 1944, Germaine had been a brunette and Lucienne a blonde, but in 1955 Germaine had become a blonde, too, and I found it hard to tell them apart.

Among my fellow customers at Mme G.'s I was always likely to see some friend out of the past. It is a risk to make an engagement for an entire evening with somebody you haven't seen for years. This is particularly true in France now. The almost embarrassingly pro-American acquaintance of the Liberation may be by now a Communist Party-line hack; the idealistic young Resistance journalist may have become an editorial writer for the reactionary newspaper of a textile magnate. The Vichy apologist you met in Washington in 1941, who called de Gaulle a traitor and the creation of the British Intelligence Service, may now tell you that the General is the best thing ever, while the fellow you knew as a de Gaulle aide in London may now compare him to Sulla destroying the Roman Republic. As for the women, who is to say which of them has resisted the years? But in a good restaurant that all have frequented, you are likely to meet any of them again, for good restaurants are not so many nowadays that a Frenchman will permanently desert one – unless, of course, he is broke, and in that case it would depress you to learn of his misfortunes. If you happen to encounter your old friends when they are already established at their tables, you have the opportunity to greet them cordially and to size them up. If you still like them, you can make a further engagement.

On the ghastly evening I speak of – a beautiful one in June – I perceived no change in the undistinguished exterior of Mme G.'s restaurant. The name – something like Prospéria – was the same, and since the plate-glass windows were backed with scrim, it was impossible to see inside. Nor, indeed, did I notice any difference when I first entered. The bar, the tables, the banquettes covered with leatherette, the simple décor of mirrors and pink marble slabs were the same. The premises had been a business employees' bar-and-café before Mme G., succeeding a long string of obscure proprietors, made it illus- trious. She had changed the fare and the clientele but not the cadre. There are hundreds of identical fronts and interiors in Paris, turned out by some mass producer in the late twenties. I might have been warned by the fact that the room was empty, but it was only eight o'clock and still light outdoors. I had come unusually early because I was so hungry. A man whom I did not recognize came to meet me, rubbing his hands and hailing me as an old acquaintance. I thought he might be a waiter who had served me. (The waiters, as I have said, were not the marked personalities of the place.) He had me at a table before I sensed the trap.

'Madame goes well?' I asked politely.

'No, Madame is lightly ill,' he said, with what I now realize was a guilty air.

He presented me with a *carte du jour* written in the familiar purple ink on the familiar wide sheet of paper with the name and telephone number of the restaurant at the top. The content of the menu, however, had become Italianized, the spelling had deteriorated, and the prices had diminished to a point where it would be a miracle if the food continued distinguished.

'Madame still conducts the restaurant?' I asked sharply.

I could now see that he was a Piedmontese of the most evasive description. From rubbing his hands he had switched to twisting them.

'Not exactly,' he said, 'but we make the same cuisine.'

I could not descry anything in the smudged ink but misspelled noodles and unorthographical '*escaloppinis*'; Italians writing French by ear produce a regression to an unknown ancestor of both languages.

'Try us,' my man pleaded, and, like a fool, I did. I was hungry. Forty minutes later, I stamped out into the street as purple as an *aubergine* with rage. The minestrone had been cabbage scraps in greasy water. I had chosen *côtes d'agneau* as the safest item in the mediocre catalogue that the Prospéria's prospectus of bliss has turned into overnight. They had been cut from a tired Alpine billy goat and seared in machine oil, and the *haricots verts* with which they were served resembled decomposed whiskers from a theatrical-costume beard.

'The same cuisine?' I thundered as I flung my money on the falsified *addition* that I was too angry to verify. 'You take me for a jackass!'

I am sure that as soon as I turned my back the scoundrel nodded. The restaurant has changed hands at least once since then.

In the morning, I telephoned Mirande. He confirmed the disaster. Mme G., ill, had closed the restaurant. Worse, she had sold the lease and the good will, and had definitely retired.

'What is the matter with her?' I asked in a tone appropriate to fatal disease.

'I think it was trying to read Simone de Beauvoir,' he said. 'A syncope.'

Mme G. still lives, but Mirande is dead. When I met him in Paris the following November, his appearance gave no hint of decline. It was the season for his sable-lined overcoat *à l'imprésario*, and a hat that was a furry cross between a porkpie and a homburg. Since the restaurant on the Rue Saint-Augustin no longer existed, I had invited him to lunch with me at a very small place called the Gratin Dauphinois, on the Rue Chabanais, directly across from the building that once housed the most celebrated sporting house in Paris. The Rue Chabanais is a short street that runs from the Square Louvois to the Rue des Petits Champs – perhaps a hundred yards – but before the reform wave stimulated by a Municipal Councilor named Marthe Richard at the end of the Second World War, the name Chabanais had a cachet all its own. Mme Richard will go down in history as the Carry Nation of sex. Now the house is closed, and the premises are devoted to some low commercial purpose. The walls of the midget Gratin Dauphinois are hung with cartoons that have a nostalgic reference to the past glories of the street.

Mirande, when he arrived, crackled with jokes about the locale. He taunted me with being a criminal who haunts the scene of his misdeeds. The fare at the Gratin is robust, as it is in Dauphiné, but it did not daunt Mirande. The wine card, similarly, is limited to the strong, rough wines of Arbois and the like, with a couple of Burgundies for clients who want to show off. There are no clarets; the proprietor hasn't heard of them. There are, of course, a few champagnes, for wedding parties or anniversaries, so Mirande, with Burgundies discounseled by his doctor, decided on champagne throughout the meal. This was a *drôle* combination with the mountain food, but I had forgotten about the lack of claret when I invited him.

We ordered a couple of dozen *escargots en pots de chambre* to begin with. These are snails baked and served, for the client's convenience, in individual earthenware crocks, instead of being forced back into shells. The snail, of course, has to be taken out of his shell to be prepared for cooking. The shell he is forced back into may not be his own. There is thus not even a sentimental justification for his reincarceration. The frankness of the service *en pot* does not improve the preparation of the snail, nor does it detract from it, but it does facilitate and accelerate his consumption. (The notion that the shell proves the snail's authenticity, like the head left on a woodcock, is invalid, as even a suburban housewife knows nowadays; you can buy a tin of snail shells in a supermarket and fill them with a mixture of nutted cream cheese and chopped olives.)

Mirande finished his dozen first, meticulously swabbing out the garlicky butter in each *pot* with a bit of bread that was fitted to the bore of the crock as precisely as a bullet to a rifle barrel. Tearing bread like that takes practice. We had emptied the first bottle of champagne when he placed his right hand delicately on the point of his waistcoat farthest removed from his spinal column.

'Liebling,' he said, 'I am not well.'

It was like the moment when I first saw Joe Louis draped on the ropes. A great pity filled my heart. '*Maître*,' I said, 'I will take you home.'

The dismayed *patronne* waved to her husband in the kitchen (he could see her through the opening he pushed the dishes through) to suspend the preparation of the *gendarme de Morteau* – the great smoked sausage in its tough skin – that we had proposed to follow the snails with. ('Short and broad in shape, it is made of pure pork and . . . is likely to be accompanied . . . by hot potato salad.' Root, page 217.) We had decided to substitute for the *pommes à l'huile* the *gratin dauphinois* itself. ('Thinly sliced potatoes are moistened with boiled milk and beaten egg, seasoned with salt, pepper, and nutmeg, and mixed with grated cheese, of the Gruyère type. The potatoes are then put into an earthenware dish which has been rubbed with garlic and then buttered, spotted with little dabs of butter, and sprinkled with more grated cheese. It is then cooked slowly in not too hot an oven.' Root, page 228.) After that, we were going to have a fowl in cream with *morilles* – wild black mushrooms of the mountains. We abandoned all.

I led Mirande into the street and hailed a taxi.

'I am not well, Liebling,' he said. 'I grow old.'

He lived far from the restaurant, beyond the Place de l'Étoile, in the Paris of the successful. From time to time on our way, he would say, 'It is nothing. You must excuse me. I am not well.'

The apartment house in which he and Mme B. lived resembled one of the chic modern museums of the quarter, with entrance gained through a maze of garden patches sheathed in glass. Successive metal grilles swung open before us as I pushed buttons that Mirande indicated – in these modern palaces there are no visible flunkies – until we reached an elevator that smoothly shot us upward to his apartment, which was rather larger in area than the Square Louvois. The décor, with basalt columns and floors covered with the skin of jumbo Siberian tigers – a special strain force-fed to supply old-style movie stars – reminded me of the sets for *Belphégor*, a French serial of silent days that I enjoyed when I was a student at the Sorbonne in 1926. (It was, I think, about an ancient Egyptian high priest who came to life and set up bachelor quarters in Paris in the style of the Temple of Karnak.) Three or four maids rushed to relieve Mirande of his sable-lined coat, his hat, and his cane topped with the horn of an albino chamois. I helped him to a divan on which two Theda Baras could have defended their honor simultaneously against two villains of the silents without either couple's getting in the other's way. Most of the horizontal surfaces in the room were covered with sculpture and most of the vertical ones with large paintings. In pain though he was, Mirande called my attention to these works of art.

'All the sculptures are by Renoir,' he said. 'It was his hobby. And all the paintings are by Maillol. It was *his* hobby. If it were the other way around, I would be one of the richest chaps in France. Both men were my friends. But then, one doesn't give one's friends one's bread and butter. And, after all, it's less banal as it is.'

After a minute, he asked me to help him to his bedroom, which was in a wing of the apartment all his own. When we got there, one of the maids came in and took his shoes off.

'I am in good hands now, Liebling,' he said. 'Farewell until next time. It is nothing.'

I telephoned the next noon, and he said that his doctor, who was a fool, insisted that he was ill.

Again I left Paris, and when I returned, late the following January, I neglected Mirande. A Father William is a comforting companion for the middle-aged – he reminds you that the best is yet to be and that there's a dance in the old dame yet – but a sick old man is discouraging. My conscience stirred when I read in a gossip column in *France-Dimanche* that Toto Mirande was convalescing nicely and was devouring caviar at a great rate – with champagne, of course. (I had never thought of Mirande as Toto, which is baby slang for 'little kid', but from then on I never referred to him in any other way; I didn't want anybody to think I wasn't in the know.) So the next day I sent him a pound of fresh caviar from Kaspia, in the Place de la Madeleine. It was the kind of medication I approved of.

I received a note from Mirande by tube next morning, reproaching me for spoiling him. He was going better, he wrote, and would telephone in a day or two to make an appointment for a return bout. When he called, he said that the idiotic doctor would not yet permit him to go out to a restaurant, and he invited me, instead, to a family dinner at Mme B.'s. 'Only a few old friends, and not the cuisine I hope to give you at Maxim's next time,' he said. 'But one makes out.'

On the appointed evening, I arrived early – or on time, which amounts to the same thing – *chez* Mme B.; you take taxis when you can get them in Paris at the rush hours. The handsome quarter overlooking the Seine above the Trocadéro is so dull that when my taxi deposited me before my host's door, I had no inclination to stroll to kill time. It is like Park Avenue or the near North Side of Chicago. So I was the first or second guest to arrive, and Mme B.'s fourteen-year-old daughter, by a past marriage, received me in the Belphégor room, apologizing because her mother was still with Toto – she called him that. She need not have told me, for at that moment I heard Madame, who is famous for her determined voice, storming at an unmistakable someone: 'You go too far, Toto. It's disgusting. People all over Paris are kind enough to send you caviar, and because you call it monotonous, you throw it at the maid! If you think servants are easy to come by . . .'

When they entered the room a few minutes later, my old friend was all smiles. 'How did you know I adore caviar to such a point?' he asked me. But I was worried because of what I had heard; the Mirande I remembered would never have been irritated by the obligation to eat a few extra kilos of fresh caviar. The little girl, who hoped I had not heard, embraced Toto. 'Don't be angry with *Maman!*' she implored him.

My fellow guests included the youngish new wife of an old former Premier, who was unavoidably detained in Lille at a congress of the party he now headed; it mustered four deputies, of whom two formed a Left Wing and two a Right Wing. ('If they had elected a fifth at the last election, or if, by good luck, one had been defeated, they could afford the luxury of a Center,' Mirande told me in identifying the lady. '*C'est malheureux*, a party without a Center. It limits the possibilities of maneuver.') There was also an amiable couple in their advanced sixties or beginning seventies, of whom the husband was the grand manitou of Veuve Clicquot champagne. Mirande introduced them by their right name, which I forget, and during the rest of the evening addressed them as M. and Mme Clicquot. There was a forceful, black-haired man from the Midi, in the youth of middle age – square-shouldered, stocky, decisive, blatantly virile – who, I was told, managed Mme B.'s vinicultural enterprises in Provence. There were two guests of less decided individuality, whom I barely remember, and filling out the party were the young girl – shy, carefully unsophisticated and unadorned – Mme B., Mirande, and me. Mme B. had a strong triangular face on a strong triangular base – a strong chin, high cheekbones, and a wide, strong jaw, but full of stormy good nature. She was a woman who, if she had been a man, would have wanted to be called Honest John. She had a high color and an iron handgrip, and repeatedly affirmed that there was no affectation about her, that she was *sans façon*, that she called her shots as she saw them. 'I won't apologize,' she said to me. 'I know you're a great feeder, like Toto here, but I won't offer you the sort of menu he used to get in that restaurant you know of, where he ruined his plumbing. Oh, that woman! I used to be so jealous. I can offer only a simple home dinner.' And she waved us toward a marble table about twenty-two feet long. Unfortunately for me, she meant it. The dinner began with a kidney-and-mushroom mince served in a giant popover – the kind of thing you might get at a literary hotel in New York. The inner side of the pastry has the feeling of a baby's palm, in the true tearoom tradition.

'It is savory but healthy,' Madame said firmly, setting an example by taking a large second helping before starting the dish on its second round. Mirande regarded the untouched doughy fabric on his plate with diaphanously veiled horror, but he had an excuse in the state of his health. 'It's still a little rich for me, darling,' he murmured. The others, including me, delivered salvos of compliments. I do not squander my moral courage on minor crises. M. Clicquot said, 'Impossible to obtain anything like this *chez* Lapérouse!' Mme Clicquot said, 'Not even at the Tour d'Argent!'

'And what do you think of my little wine?' Mme B. asked M. Clicquot. 'I'm so anxious for your professional opinion – as a rival producer, you know.'

The wine was a thin *rosé* in an Art Nouveau bottle with a label that was a triumph of lithography; it had spires and monks and troubadours and blondes in wimples on it, and the name of the *cru* was spelled out in letters with Gothic curlicues and pennons. The name was something like Château Guillaume d'Aquitaine, *grand vin.*

'What a madly gay little wine, my dear!' M. Clicquot said, repressing, but not soon enough, a grimace of pain.

'One would say a Tavel of a good year,' I cried, 'if one were a complete bloody fool.' I did not say the second clause aloud.

My old friend looked at me with new respect. He was discovering in me a capacity for hypocrisy that he had never credited me with before.

The main course was a shoulder of mutton with white beans – the poor relation of a gigot, and an excellent dish in its way, when not too dry. This was.

For the second wine, the man from the Midi proudly produced a red, in a bottle without a label, which he offered to M. Clicquot with the air of a tomcat bringing a field mouse to its master's feet. 'Tell me what you think of this,' he said as he filled the champagne man's glass.

M. Clicquot – a veteran of such challenges, I could well imagine – held the glass against the light, dramatically inhaled the bouquet, and then drank, after a slight stiffening of the features that indicated to me that he knew what he was in for. Having emptied half the glass, he deliberated.

'It has a lovely color,' he said.

'But what is it? What is it?' the man from the Midi insisted.

'There are things about it that remind me of a Beaujolais,' M. Clicquot said (he must have meant that it was wet), 'but on the whole I should compare it to a Bordeaux' (without doubt unfavorably).

Mme B.'s agent was beside himself with triumph. 'Not one or the other!' he crowed. 'It's from the *domaine* – the Château Guillaume d'Aquitaine!'

The admirable M. Clicquot professed astonishment, and I, when I had emptied a glass, said that there would be a vast market for the wine in America if it could be properly presented. 'Unfortunately,' I said, 'the cost of advertising . . .' and I rolled my eyes skyward.

'Ah, yes,' Mme B. cried sadly. 'The cost of advertising!'

I caught Mirande looking at me again, and thought of the Pétrus and the

Cheval Blanc of our last meal together *chez* Mme G. He drank a glass of the red. After all, he wasn't going to die of thirst.

For dessert, we had a simple fruit tart with milk – just the thing for an invalid's stomach, although Mirande didn't eat it.

M. Clicquot retrieved the evening, oenologically, by producing two bottles of a wine 'impossible to find in the cellars of any restaurant in France' – Veuve Clicquot '19. There is at present a great to-do among wine merchants in France and the United States about young wines, and an accompanying tendency to cry down the 'legend' of the old. For that matter, hardware clerks, when you ask for a can opener with a wooden handle that is thick enough to give a grip and long enough for leverage, try to sell you complicated mechanical folderols. The motivation in both cases is the same – simple greed. To deal in wines of varied ages requires judgment, the sum of experience and flair. It involves the risk of money, because every lot of wine, like every human being, has a life span, and it is this that the good vintner must estimate. His object should be to sell his wine at its moment of maximum value – to the drinker as well as the merchant. The vintner who handles only young wines is like an insurance company that will write policies only on children; the unqualified dealer wants to risk nothing and at the same time to avoid tying up his money. The client misled by brochures warning him off clarets and champagnes that are over ten years old and assuring him that Beaujolais should be drunk green will miss the major pleasures of wine drinking. To deal wisely in wines and merely to sell them are things as different as being an expert in ancient coins and selling Indian-head pennies over a souvenir counter.

Despite these convictions of mine about wine, I should never have tried a thirty-seven-year-old champagne on the recommendation of a lesser authority than the blessed M. Clicquot. It is the oldest by far that I have ever drunk. (H. Warner Allen, in *The Wines of France*, published circa 1924, which is my personal wine bible, says, 'In the matter of age, champagne is a capricious wine. As a general rule, it has passed its best between fifteen and twenty, yet a bottle thirty years old may prove excellent, though all its fellows may be quite undrinkable.' He cites Saintsbury's note that 'a Perrier Jouet of 1857 was still majestical in 1884,' adding, 'And all wine-drinkers know of such amazing discoveries.' Mr Root, whose book is not a foolish panegyric of everything French, is hard on champagne, in my opinion. He falls into a critical error more common among writers less intelligent: he attacks it for not being something else. Because its excellences are not those of Burgundy or Bordeaux, he underrates the peculiar qualities it does not share with them, as one who would chide Dickens for not being Stendhal, or Marciano for not being Benny Leonard.)

The Veuve Clicquot '19 was tart without brashness – a refined but effective understatement of younger champagnes, which run too much to rhetoric, at best. Even so, the force was all there, to judge from the two glasses that were a shade more than my share. The wine still had a discreet *cordon* – the ring of bubbles that forms inside the glass – and it had developed the color known as 'partridge eye'. I have never seen a partridge's eye, because the bird, unlike woodcock, is served without the head, but the color the term indicates is that of serous blood or a maple leaf on the turn.

'How nice it was, life in 1919, eh, M. Clicquot?' Mirande said as he sipped his second glass.

After we had finished M. Clicquot's offering, we played a game called lying poker for table stakes, each player being allowed a capital of five hundred francs, not to be replenished under any circumstances. When Mme B. had won everybody's five hundred francs, the party broke up. Mirande promised me that he would be up and about soon, and would show me how men reveled in the heroic days of *la belle époque*, but I had a feeling that the bell was cracked.

I left Paris and came back to it seven times during the next year, but never saw him. Once, being in his quarter in the company of a remarkably pretty woman, I called him up, simply because I knew he would like to look at her, but he was too tired. I forget when I last talked to him on the telephone. During the next winter, while I was away in Egypt or Jordan or someplace where French papers don't circulate, he died, and I did not learn of it until I returned to Europe.

When Mirande first faltered, in the Rue Chabanais, I had failed to correlate cause and effect. I had even felt a certain selfish alarm. If eating well was beginning to affect Mirande at eighty, I thought, I had better begin taking in sail. After all, I was only thirty years his junior. But after the dinner at Mme B.'s, and in the light of subsequent reflection, I saw that what had undermined his constitution was Mme G.'s defection from the restaurant business. For years, he had been able to escape Mme B.'s solicitude for his health by lunching and dining in the restaurant of Mme G., the sight of whom Mme B. could not support. Entranced by Mme G.'s magnificent food, he had continued to live 'like a cock in a pie' – eating as well, and very nearly as much, as when he was thirty. The organs of the interior – never very intelligent, in spite of what the psychosomatic quacks say – received each day the amount of pleasure to which they were accustomed, and never marked the passage of time; it was the indispensable roadwork of the prizefighter. When Mme G., good soul, retired, moderation began its fatal inroads on his resistance. My old friend's appetite, insufficiently stimulated, started to loaf – the insidious result, no doubt, of the advice of the doctor whose existence he had revealed to me by that slip of the tongue about why he no longer drank Burgundy. Mirande commenced, perhaps, by omitting the fish course after the oysters, or the oysters before the fish, then began neglecting his cheeses and skipping the second bottle of wine on odd Wednesdays. What he called his pipes ('*ma tuyauterie*'), being insufficiently exercised, lost their tone, like the leg muscles of a retired champion. When, in his kindly effort to please me, he challenged the *escargots en pots de chambre*, he was like an old fighter who tries a comeback without training for it. That, however, was only the revelation of the rot that had already taken place. What always happens happened. The damage was done, but it could so easily have been averted had he been warned against the fatal trap of abstinence.

1959

Just Enough Money

If, as I was saying before I digressed, the first requisite for writing well about food is a good appetite, the second is to put in your apprenticeship as a feeder when you have enough money to pay the check but not enough to produce indifference to the size of the total. (I also meant to say, previously, that Waverley Root has a good appetite, but I never got around to it.) The optimum financial position for a serious apprentice feeder is to have funds in hand for three more days, with a reasonable, but not certain, prospect of reinforcements thereafter. The student at the Sorbonne waiting for his remittance, the newspaperman waiting for his salary, the free-lance writer waiting for a check that he has cause to believe is in the mail – all are favorably situated to learn. (It goes without saying that it is essential to be in France.) The man of appetite who will stint himself when he can see three days ahead has no vocation, and I dismiss from consideration, as manic, the fellow who will spend the lot on one great feast and then live on fried potatoes until his next increment; Tuaregs eat that way, but only because they never know when they are going to come by their next sheep. The clear-headed voracious man learns because he tries to compose his meals to obtain an appreciable quantity of pleasure from each. It is from this weighing of delights against their cost that the student eater (particularly if he is a student at the University of Paris) erects the scale of values that will serve him until he dies or has to reside in the Middle West for a long period. The scale is different for each eater, as it is for each writer.

Eating is highly subjective, and the man who accepts say-so in youth will wind up in bad and overtouted restaurants in middle age, ordering what the maître d'hôtel suggests. He will have been guided to them by food-snob publications, and he will fall into the habit of drinking too much before dinner to kill the taste of what he has been told he should like but doesn't. An illustration: For about six years, I kept hearing of a restaurant in the richest shire of Connecticut whose proprietor, a Frenchman, had been an assistant of a disciple of the great Escoffier. Report had it that in these wilds – inhabited only by executives of the highest grade, walking the woods like the King of Nemi until somebody came on from Winnetka to cut their throats – the restaurateur gave full vent to the creative flame. His clients took what he chose to give them. If they declined, they had to go down the pike to some joint where a steak cost only twelve dollars, and word would get around that they felt their crowns in danger – they had been detected economizing. I finally arranged to be smuggled out to the place disguised as a *Time-Life* Executive Vice-Publisher in Charge of Hosannas with the mission of entertaining the advertising manager of the Hebrew National Delicatessen Corporation. When we arrived, we found the Yale-blue vicuña rope up and the bar full of couples in the hundred-thousand-dollar bracket, dead drunk as they waited for tables; knowing that this would be no back-yard cookout, they had taken prophylactic anesthesia. But when I tasted the food, I perceived that they had been needlessly alarmed. The Frenchman, discouraged because for four years no customers had tasted what they were eating, had taken to bourbon-on-the-rocks. In a morose way, he had resigned himself to becoming dishonestly rich. The food was no better than Howard Johnson's, and the customers, had they not been paralyzed by the time they got to it, would have liked it as well. The *spécialité de la maison*, the unhappy *patron* said when I interrogated him, was jellied oysters dyed red, white, and blue. 'At least they are aware of that,' he said. 'The colors attract their attention.' There was an on-the-hour service of Brink's armored cars between his door and the night-deposit vault of a bank in New York, conveying the money that rolled into the *caisse*. The wheels, like a juggernaut's, rolled over his secret heart. His intention in the beginning had been noble, but he was a victim of the system.

The reference room where I pursued my own first earnest researches as a feeder without the crippling handicap of affluence was the Restaurant des Beaux-Arts, on the Rue Bonaparte, in 1926–27. I was a student, in a highly generalized way, at the Sorbonne, taking targets of opportunity for study. Eating soon developed into one of my major subjects. The franc was at twenty-six to the dollar, and the researcher, if he had only a certain sum – say, six francs – to spend, soon established for himself whether, for example, a half bottle of Tavel *supérieur*, at three and a half francs, and braised beef heart and yellow turnips, at two and a half, gave him more or less pleasure than a *contre-filet* of beef, at five francs, and a half bottle of *ordinaire*, at one franc. He might find that he liked the heart, with its strong, rich flavor and odd texture, nearly as well as the beef, and that since the Tavel was overwhelmingly better than the cheap wine, he had done well to order the first pair. Or he might find that he so much preferred the generous, sanguine *contre-filet* that he could accept the undistinguished *picrate* instead of the Tavel. As in a bridge tournament, the learner played duplicate hands, making the opposite choice of fare the next time the problem presented itself. (It was seldom as simple as my example, of course, because a meal usually included at least an hors d'oeuvre and a cheese, and there was a complexity of each to choose from. The arrival, in season, of fresh asparagus or venison further complicated matters. In the first case, the investigator had to decide what course to omit in order to fit the asparagus in, and, in the second, whether to forgo all else in order to afford venison.)

A rich man, faced with this simple sumptuary dilemma, would have ordered both the Tavel *and* the *contre-filet*. He would then never know whether he liked beef heart, or whether an *ordinaire* wouldn't do him as well as something better. (There are people to whom wine is merely an alcoholized sauce, although they may have sensitive palates for meat or pastries.) When one considers the millions of permutations of foods and wines to test, it is easy to see that life is too short for the formulation of dogma. Each eater can but establish a few general principles that are true only for him. Our hypothetical rich *client* might even have ordered a Pommard, because it was listed at a higher price than the Tavel, and because he was more likely to be acquainted with it. He would then never have learned that a good Tavel is better than a fair-to-middling Pommard – better than a fair-to-middling almost anything, in my opinion. In student restaurants, renowned wines like Pommard were apt to be mediocre specimens of their kind, since the customers could never have afforded the going prices of the best growths and years. A man who is rich in his adolescence is almost doomed to be a dilettante at table. This is not because all millionaires are stupid but because they are not impelled to experiment. In learning to eat, as in psychoanalysis, the customer, in order to profit, must be sensible of the cost.

There is small likelihood that a rich man will frequent modest restaurants even at the beginning of his gustatory career; he will patronize restaurants, sometimes good, where the prices are high and the repertory is limited to dishes for which it is conventionally permissible to charge high prices. From this list, he will order the dishes that in his limited experience he has already found agreeable. Later, when his habits are formed, he will distrust the originality that he has never been constrained to develop. A diet based chiefly on game birds and oysters becomes a habit as easily as a diet of jelly doughnuts and hamburgers. It is a better habit, of course, but restrictive just the same. Even in Paris, one can dine in the costly restaurants for years without learning that there are fish other than sole, turbot, salmon (in season), trout, and the Mediterranean *rouget* and *loup de mer*. The fresh herring or sardine *sauce moutarde*; the *colin froid mayonnaise*; the conger eel *en matelote*; the small fresh-water fish of the Seine and the Marne, fried crisp and served *en buisson*; the whiting *en colère* (his tail in his mouth, as if contorted with anger); and even the skate and the *dorade* – all these, except by special and infrequent invitation, are out of the swim. (It is a standing tourist joke to say that the fishermen on the quays of the Seine never catch anything, but in fact they often take home the makings of a nice fish fry, especially in winter. In my hotel on the Square Louvois, I had a room waiter – a Czech naturalized in France – who used to catch hundreds of *goujons* and *ablettes* on his days off. He once brought a shoe box of them to my room to prove that Seine fishing was not pure whimsy.) All the fish I have mentioned have their habitats in humbler restaurants, the only places where the aspirant eater can become familiar with their honest fishy tastes and the decisive modes of accommodation that suit them. Personally, I like tastes that know their own minds. The reason that people who detest fish often tolerate sole is that sole doesn't taste very much like fish, and even this degree of resemblance disappears when it is submerged in the kind of sauce that patrons of Piedmontese restaurants in London and New York think characteristically French. People with the same apathy toward decided flavor relish 'South African lobster' tails – frozen as long as the Siberian mammoth – because they don't taste lobstery. ('South African lobsters' are a kind of sea crayfish, or *langouste*, but that would be nothing against them if they were fresh.) They prefer processed cheese because it isn't cheesy, and synthetic vanilla extract because it isn't vanillary. They have made a triumph of the Delicious apple because it doesn't taste like an apple, and of the Golden Delicious because it doesn't taste like anything. In a related field, 'dry' (non-beery) beer and 'light' (non-Scotchlike) Scotch are more of the same. The standard of perfection for vodka (no color, no taste, no smell) was expounded to me long ago by the then Estonian consul-general in New York, and it accounts perfectly for the drink's rising popularity with those who like their alcohol in conjunction with the reassuring tastes of infancy – tomato juice, orange juice, chicken broth. It is the ideal intoxicant for the drinker who wants no reminder of how hurt Mother would be if she knew what he was doing.

The consistently rich man is also unlikely to make the acquaintance of meat dishes of robust taste – the hot *andouille* and *andouillette*, which are close-packed sausages of smoked tripe, and the *boudin*, or blood pudding, and all its relatives that figure in the pages of Rabelais and on the menus of the market restaurants. He will not meet the *civets*, or dark, winy stews of domestic rabbit and old turkey. A tough old turkey with plenty of character makes the best *civet*, and only in a *civet* is turkey good to eat. Young turkey, like young sheep, calf, spring chicken, and baby lobster, is a pale preliminary phase of its species. The pig, the pigeon, and the goat – as suckling, squab, and kid – are the only animals that are at their best to eat when immature. The first in later life becomes gross through indolence; the second and third grow muscular through overactivity. And the world of tripery is barred to the well-heeled, except for occasional exposure to an expurgated version of *tripes à la mode de Caen*. They have never seen *gras-double* (tripe cooked with vegetables, principally onions) or *pieds et paquets* (sheep's tripe and calves' feet with salt pork). In his book, Waverley Root dismisses tripe, but he is no plutocrat; his rejection is deliberate, after fair trial. Still, his insensibility to its charms seems to me odd in a New Englander, as he is by origin. Fried pickled honeycomb tripe used to be the most agreeable feature of a winter breakfast in New Hampshire, and Fall River, Root's home town, is in the same cultural circumscription.

Finally, to have done with our rich man, seldom does he see even the simple, well-pounded *bifteck* or the *pot-au-feu* itself – the foundation glory of French cooking. Alexandre Dumas the elder wrote in his *Dictionary of Cuisine*: 'French cooking, the first of all cuisines, owes its superiority to the excellence of French bouillon. This excellence derives from a sort of intuition with which I shall not say our cooks but our women of the people are endowed.' This bouillon is one of the two end products of the *pot*. The other is the material that has produced it – beef, carrots, parsnips, white turnips, leeks, celery, onions, cloves, garlic, and cracked marrowbones, and, for the dress version, fowl. Served *in* some of the bouillon, this constitutes the dish known as *pot-au-feu*. Dumas is against poultry 'unless it is old', but advises that 'an old pigeon, a partridge, or a rabbit roasted in advance, a crow in November or December' works wonders. He postulates 'seven hours of sustained simmering', with constant attention to the 'scum' that forms on the surface and to the water level. ('Think twice before adding water, though if your meat actually rises above the level of the bouillon it is necessary to add boiling water to cover it.') This supervision demands the full-time presence of the cook in the kitchen throughout the day, and the maintenance of the temperature calls for a considerable outlay in fuel. It is one reason that the *pot-au-feu* has declined as a chief element of the working-class diet in France. Women go out to work, and gas costs too much. For a genuinely good *pot-au-feu*, Dumas says, one should take a fresh piece of beef – 'a twelve-to-fifteen-pound rump' – and simmer it seven hours in the bouillon of the beef that you simmered seven hours the day before. He does not say what good housekeepers did with the first piece of beef – perhaps cut it into sandwiches for the children's lunch. He regrets that even when he wrote, in 1869, excessive haste was beginning to mar cookery; the demanding ritual of the *pot* itself had been abandoned. This was 'a receptacle that never left the fire, day or night,' Dumas writes. 'A chicken was put into it as a chicken was withdrawn, a piece of beef as a piece was taken out, and a glass of water whenever a cup of broth was removed. Every kind of meat that cooked in this bouillon gained, rather than lost, in flavor.' *Pot-au-feu* is so hard to find in chic restaurants nowadays that every Saturday evening there is a mass pilgrimage from the fashionable quarters to Chez Benoit, near the Châtelet – a small but not cheap restaurant that serves it once a week. I have never found a crow in Benoit's *pot*, but all the rest is good.

A drastically poor man, naturally, has even less chance than a drastically rich one to educate himself gastronomically. For him eating becomes merely a matter of subsistence; he can exercise no choice. The chief attraction of the cheapest student restaurants in my time was advertised on their largest placards: '*Pain à Discrétion*' ('All the Bread You Want'). They did not graduate discriminating eaters. During that invaluable year, I met a keen observer who gave me a tip: 'If you run across a restaurant where you often see priests eating with priests, or sporting girls with sporting girls, you may be confident that it is good. Those are two classes of people who like to eat well and get their money's worth. If you see a priest eating with a layman, though, don't be too sure about the money's worth. The fellow *en civil* may be a rich parishioner, and the good Father won't worry about the price. And if the girl is with a man, you can't count on anything. It may be her kept man, in which case she won't care what she spends on him, or the man who is keeping her, in which case she won't care what he spends on her.'

1959

The Modest Threshold

. . . As I had anticipated, when my family arrived in Paris they did indeed consult me about the scene of our first dinner together. So Maillabuau's it was. When we arrived before the somber, almost lugubrious front, my mother wanted to turn back. It looked like a store front, except for a bit of scrim behind the plate glass, through which the light from within filtered with éclat.

'Are you sure this is the right place?' she asked.

'It's one of the best restaurants in the world,' I said, as if I ate there every day.

My father was already captivated. 'Don't give you a lot of hoopla and ooh-la-la,' he said, with approval. 'I'll bet there are no Americans here.'

We crossed the modest threshold. The interior was only half a jump from sordid, and there were perhaps fifteen tables. Old Maillabuau, rubicund and seedy, approached us, and I could sense that my mother was about to object to any table he proposed; she wanted some place like Fouquet's (not in the *Guide du Gourmand*). But between her and Maillabuau I interposed a barrage of French that neither she nor my sister could possibly penetrate, though each chirped a few tentative notes. 'I have brought my family here because I have been informed it is the most illustrious house of Paris,' I told him, and, throwing in a colloquialism I had learned in Rennes, a city a hundred years behind the times, I added, 'We desire to knock the bell.'

On hearing me, old Maillabuau, who may have thought for a moment that we were there by mistake and were about to order waffles, flashed a smile of avaricious relief. Father, meanwhile, regarding the convives of both sexes seated at the tables, was already convinced. The men, for the most part, showed tremendous *devantures*, which they balanced on their knees with difficulty as they ate, their wattles waving bravely with each bite. The women were shaped like demijohns and decanters, and they drank wine from glasses that must have reminded Father happily of beer schooners on the Bowery in 1890. 'I don't see a single American,' he said. He was a patriotic man at home, but he was convinced that in Paris the presence of Americans was a sign of a bunco joint.

'Monsieur my father is the richest man in Baltimore,' I told Maillabuau, by way of encouragement. Father had nothing to do with Baltimore, but I figured that if I said New York, Maillabuau might not believe me. Maillabuau beamed and Father beamed back. His enthusiasms were rare but sudden, and this man – without suavity, without a tuxedo, who spoke no English, and whose customers were so patently overfed – appeared to him an honest merchant. Maillabuau showed us to a table; the cloth was diaphanous from wear except in the spots where it had been darned.

A split-second *refroidissement* occurred when I asked for the *carte du jour*.

'There is none,' Maillabuau said. 'You will eat what I tell you. Tonight, I propose a soup, trout *grenobloise*, and *poulet* Henri IV – simple but exquisite. The classic *cuisine française* – nothing complicated but all of the best.'

When I translated this to Father he was in complete agreement. 'Plain food,' he said. 'No *schmier*.' I think that at bottom he agreed that the customer is sure to be wrong if left to his own devices. How often had the wives of personal friends come to him for a fur coat at the wholesale price, and declined his advice of an Alaskan seal – something that would last them for twenty years – in favor of some faddish fur that would show wear in six!

The simplicity of the menu disappointed me; I asked Maillabuau about the *pintadou*, fat and anointed with fragrance. 'Tomorrow,' he said, posing it as a condition that we eat his selection first. Mother's upper lip quivered, for she was *très gourmande* of cream sauces, but she had no valid argument against the great man's proposal, since one of the purposes of her annual trips to Europe was to lose weight at a spa. On the subject of wines, M. Maillabuau and I agreed better: the best in the cellar would do – a Montrachet to begin with, a Chambertin with the fowl.

It was indeed the best soup – a simple *garbure* of vegetables – imaginable, the best trout possible, and the best boiled fowl of which one could conceive. The simple line of the meal brought out the glories of the wine, and the wine brought out the grandeur in my father's soul. Presented with one of the most stupendous checks in history, he paid with gratitude, and said that he was going to take at least one meal a day *chez* Maillabuau during the rest of his stay. The dessert, served as a concession to my sister, was an *omelette au kirsch*, and Maillabuau stood us treat to the *marc*, like embalmed gold. Or at least he said he did; since only the total appeared on the check, we had to take his word for it. The *omelette au kirsch* was the sole dessert he ever permitted to be served, he said. He was against sweets on principle, since they were 'not French', but the *omelette* was light and healthy. It contained about two dozen eggs.

The next day we had the *pintadou*, the day after that a *pièce de bœuf du Charolais* so remarkable that I never eat a steak without thinking how far short it falls. And never were the checks less than 'staggering', and never did my father complain. Those meals constituted a high spot in my gastronomic life, but before long my mother and sister mutinied. They wanted a restaurant where they could see some dresses and eat *meringues glacées* and *homard au porto*.

So in 1939, on my first evening in wartime Paris, I went straight from the Louvois to the Rue Sainte-Anne. The Restaurant Maillabuau had vanished. I did not remember the street number, so I walked the whole length of the Rue Sainte-Anne twice to make sure. But there was no Maillabuau; the horses at Longchamp had eaten him.

1959

WAVERLEY ROOT

Piedmont and the Valle d'Aosta

... To speak of Piedmontese cooking is misleading; the gastronomic and political frontiers do not coincide. There are two main cuisines in Piedmont. One is the cooking of certain of the larger cities and of the lower altitudes – say the areas east of Cuneo but not including it, and south of Turin, which does include the capital. Foreigners are likely to think of this as typical of Piedmont, for it is found in the most traveled parts of the country; but it embodies a minimum of local inspiration. It leans heavily on the cooking of Lombardy and more lightly on that of France, whose example is admired and emulated in Piedmont. The cooking of Turin is the most affected of all by these outside influences (Turin has been called 'the most Italian city of France'), which is why you will find more interesting and more characteristic Piedmontese cooking in Cuneo, Asti and Alba than in the capital.

North of Turin, as you get deep into the mountains, you meet a different cuisine, which is really native. It depends on food resources peculiar to the region (white truffles) or concoctions born of the local genius and found nowhere else (*bagna calda*); and when there are echoes of dishes from across the border, they are not so much borrowings as sharings with adjacent areas whose similar geography has produced similar culinary results (*fonduta*). Given that geography, this indigenous Piedmontese cuisine is, of course, mountain cooking – solid food to provide fuel for men who work hard at energy-burning altitudes and for much of the year have to combat cold – hence, roasts and boiled meat, lively seasoning, a goodly amount of garlic, the filling rib-sticking polenta, and a yearning for sweets, since sugar is a quick energy provider; it is no accident that Piedmont is famous for its confectionery. The nature of Piedmontese mountain dishes has also been shaped by what might be called a mechanical accident – it took form at a period when in the mountain areas few persons had ovens. They were dependent first of all on the frying pan and after that on the kettle (for boiling meat or making thick warming soups).

Piedmontese mountain food is heavy but Piedmontese are not heavy eaters. They are preserved from gluttony because they are of sober northern stock, relatively reserved, lacking the exuberance of more southerly peoples, and not given to excess. Their cooking is not sophisticated; it is tasty and (this is the key word) healthy.

The most exclusive food product of Piedmont is the white truffle, whose highly local character is indicated by its name, *trifola d'Alba*, for the region around Alba, especially south of it, is the home ground of the white truffle. It is a rarity, found, so far as I know, nowhere else in Europe, though there are some white truffles in Morocco.

In most truffle-growing areas, the tuber is associated especially with oaks, but the Piedmont white truffle is versatile, growing not only around oaks, but also within the root systems of willows, hazels, poplars, and some other trees. They are less versatile in the matter of altitude, appearing only between 1,300 and 1,950 feet. Some black truffles are found in Piedmont too, but the white ones are more highly prized because they have a stronger flavor. To taste them fresh, at their best, you need to visit Piedmont between November and February. In France, the favorite discoverer and rooter-up of truffles is the hog, but Piedmont prefers dogs – dogs with a college education, for there is a 'university' to train truffle hounds at Rodi. Often truffle hunting is done at night; their odor is stronger then, making it easier to detect a fungus which may be as deep as a foot underground. Some human truffle hunters seem to be able to sniff out truffles unaided, but dogs are better at it.

The white truffles of Piedmont go into many of the region's dishes, including what is perhaps its best known speciality, *fonduta*. This is an Alpine melted cheese dish, found also in the French and Swiss Alps. Piedmont is good cheese country. Roccaverano and Murazzano make a sharp but creamy goat cheese called *robiola*. *Paglierino* is made from cow's milk. The Gressoney valley (in the Valle d'Aosta), which makes the best butter in Piedmont, also produces *tome*, a heavy cheese with a reddish hue, of which the natives say, 'It has three virtues: it sates hunger, quenches thirst, and cleans the teeth.'

None of these goes into *fonduta*. For this Piedmont uses *fontina*, which comes from the Valle d'Aosta, taking its name from Mount Fontin, at Quart. It is a cheese of respectable age. As long ago as 1477 Pantaleone di Confienza wrote in his *Summa lacticinorum*: '*Vallis Augusta casei boni sunt*' ('in the Valle d'Aosta the cheeses are good'). The rich fatty orange *fontina*, which comes in great cartwheels, is made with infinite pains, but the finishing touch comes from a process with which human skill has little to do – its aging in well-aired stone buildings nearly 10,000 feet up.

If *fonduta* is related to the French and Swiss *fondues*, it nevertheless has highly individual characteristics. The melted cheese which is the base for all three is mixed in *fonduta* with butter, milk and beaten egg yolks, none of which appear in the French and Swiss dishes, and is sprinkled liberally with white pepper. Swiss *fondue* uses white wine and kirsch; French practice on alcoholic additions varies; but *fonduta* uses none at all. Finally, *fonduta* is crowned with a layer of white truffles sliced paper-thin, a touch which neither France nor Switzerland can match. Both in France and Switzerland, the bowl of *fondue* is usually placed bubbling over a heater in the middle of the table; the diners spear cubes of bread on their forks, plunge them in the common pot and twirl the bread around to coat it with the melted cheese, and then pop the result into their mouths, repeating the process ad infinitum. In Piedmont the *fonduta*, which has the consistency of a thick cream, is served in individual plates, like soup, or may be poured over slabs of polenta.

Uniquely Piedmontese is *bagna calda* (*bagna caôda* in dialect), which means 'hot bath'. I have never encountered it anywhere else in Italy. Perhaps you have to be born in Piedmont to be able to make it successfully; a Milanese cook told me he had tried to produce it, but always wound up with a slimy thin unappetizing liquid. Yet it seems simple enough. You heat olive oil and butter, about a quarter more butter than oil by weight, together with a generous amount of chopped garlic, in a saucepan, without browning the garlic. When they are well combined, the saucepan is taken off the fire and finely chopped anchovy is stirred into it, along with a bit of salt. The last step is to add thinly sliced white truffles. It is usually placed on the table in little individual bowls over heaters, to keep it hot, particularly important since the vegetables which are dipped in it before being conveyed to the mouth are cold and raw. In Piedmont, the favorite vegetable for *bagna calda* is that local specialty, the cardoon, or edible thistle, but if cardoons are not at hand, you make do with whatever is available – celery, fennel, bits of red or yellow peppers, cauliflower, coarsely chopped cabbage, artichokes, or strips of carrot, singly or in combination.

There is one Piedmontese specialty which you surely know, though perhaps not where it came from – what most people call 'Italian breadsticks'. Italian, yes, since Turin is in Italy, but actually breadsticks (or *batonnets*, as Napoleon, who was fond of them, called them) are purely Turinese even if, like Milan's *panettone*, they have since gotten around. On their home ground these long narrow fingers of a wheat bread that is all crust are called *grissini* and are held to be the most digestible form of bread. Their usual function is to be munched with something else, but if you can lay your hands on a can or jar of white truffles, you can convert them into tasty hors d'oeuvres with the greatest of ease. Mince a truffle fine, crush it in a mortar with a tablespoon of butter, cream a little more butter separately and then mix the crushed truffle with it, with a pinch of salt. Spread this over two-thirds of the length of the breadstick, leaving the other third bare for a handle, and wrap a strip of prosciutto around the truffled spread. This goes nicely with cocktails, but it is perhaps safer served on a plate with other hors d'oeuvres, unless your guests are careful people. The spread acts like paste to hold the ham in place, but there is always danger that it will unwind itself when manipulated by a standing eater whose other hand is occupied by a glass.

One dish that some persons whose geography is good put down as Piedmontese because of its name, though first produced on the soil of Piedmont, was made by a French cook who was only passing through, and does not belong to the Piedmontese school of cooking; for that matter it belongs to no other, including the French, unless you want to create a school of dishes which make do with anything you can find at a moment of near famine. This is chicken Marengo, which has given birth also to veal Marengo. Having defeated the Austrians on June 14, 1800 at Marengo by a miracle of improvisation, Napoleon pursued them with such vigor that he left the commissary, but not his cook, Dunand, far behind. Dunand was desperate. Napoleon as was his habit had not eaten before the battle, to keep his mind clear, and was certain to be famished; and when he called for a meal he demanded immediate service (and bolted it down in a few minutes when he got it). Foragers were sent out and turned up only meager booty – a scrawny chicken, four tomatoes, three eggs, a few crayfish, a little garlic – and a frying pan, for Dunand was also without his cooking utensils. They had been unable to find butter, but had managed some olive oil. The cook cut up the chicken with a sabre and fried it in oil, crushed garlic, and water made more palatable with a little cognac filched from Napoleon's own canteen, together with some emergency-ration bread supplied by one of the soldiers, with the eggs, fried in the same liquid, on the side, and the crayfish, also fried, on top. A measure of Dunand's desperation was the unholy combination of chicken and crayfish; he must really have felt that all the food he had been able to scrape together was none too much. Napoleon found the dish excellent and ordered that it be served him after every battle. On the next occasion Dunand tried to improve the dish by substituting white wine for the water, adding mushrooms, and leaving out the crayfish. Napoleon noted the disappearance, and demanded that they be restored to the dish – not for gastronomic reasons, however. Chicken with crayfish was associated in his mind with victory and he was superstitious. 'You left out the crayfish,' he told Dunand angrily. 'You'll bring me bad luck.' Most French cooks today leave out the crayfish, but in Piedmont, where restaurants responsive to French influence put it on their menus for historical reasons, they respect the tradition by including crayfish. Sometimes they add what Dunand's foragers might have found in this area, but didn't – truffles. Chicken Marengo today is chicken cut into pieces, browned in oil, and then cooked (slowly, not as Dunand did it) with peeled tomatoes, crushed garlic, parsley, white wine and cognac, seasoned with crushed pepper, and served with fried eggs on the side (with or without crayfish, also on the side) and sometimes croutons, doubling for Dunand's army bread.

Although Piedmont produces more rice than Lombardy does, rice has not driven pasta off the menu in Turin as it has in Milan – and this despite the quality of Piedmont rice, already so famous in 1787 that it was there that Thomas Jefferson smuggled some out of the country. This was an illegal act. Piedmont was producing the best rice in Italy, possibly the best rice in the world, and it intended to keep its monopoly. Jefferson got hold of two bags of rice, however, and thus brought the first Piedmontese rice to America.

Though Piedmont has not gone in so exclusively for rice dishes as Lombardy, it nevertheless has a number of local rice dishes. *Riso alla piemontese* proclaims its nationality by including Piedmont's most ubiquitous ingredient, the white truffle, here chopped and combined with a meat sauce, which is poured over the rice; the same sauce also converts *tagliatelle* into a Piedmont dish. *Riso e ceci* is the sort of country fare consistent with the mountaineer tradition, rice and chick peas, seasoned with tomato sauce and hotly spiced. Vercelli has a specialty of risotto with quail. What is called rice and milk soup is not really soup, for the rice is boiled in milk until all of it has been absorbed, when it is served with grated cheese.

The favorite pasta of Piedmont is *agnolotti*, an egg-pasta ring-shaped dough envelope, cooked in boiling water, whose stuffing seems to vary with each cook. The item which appears most consistently in the filling is chopped meat; second is nutmeg; third is spinach; but of three recipes of *agnolotti alla piemontese* which I consulted the first omitted the nutmeg, the second the spinach, and the third the chopped meat. For one which combines all three, try chopped chicken (or veal), chopped prosciutto, chopped purée of spinach, white wine, a little flour, and nutmeg. At the last *Quindicina Gastronomica Piemontese*, the Piedmont gastronomic festival which occurs only every fifteen years, an *agnolotti alla piemontese* had stuffing of minced veal, minced ham, onion, egg, grated cheese, nutmeg – and a minute quantity of finely ground walnut shells! *Tagliatelle* is served not only as noted above but also in a number of other local fashions, for instance cooked in chicken consommé and served with chicken livers. Lasagne becomes so specialized that there is not only a recipe for the lasagne of the town of Cuneo, but even for St Joseph's Day in Cuneo; it is something of a letdown to discover that *lasagne di San Giuseppe alla cunese* is no more exotic than the familiar oven-baked sheet pasta with a combination of chopped meat sauce and béchamel, with grated cheese and butter on top to provide a crust. Piedmont makes gnocchi with potatoes and also with *fontina* cheese, for which semolina flour gnocchi are first cooked in spiced milk to which the cheese is added, and then dipped in beaten eggs, breaded and fried. Much polenta is eaten, especially in the form of *polenta grassa*, a mountain dish of alternate layers of peppered polenta and *fontina* cheese baked in the oven until well browned on top.

1971

Liguria

. . . Of the many specifically Ligurian or Genoese dishes, two stand out particularly for precisely opposite reasons – *pesto*, because it is so sharply localized, unfindable elsewhere; ravioli, because it has spread around the world, and is eaten everywhere by persons who have no idea that it originated in Genoa – or more exactly, on board Genoese ships.

The statement that *pesto* is not found outside of Liguria requires one qualification. On the French Riviera, adjoining Liguria, there is a local variant of *pesto* called *pistou*. It marks the former presence of the Genoese in this area. *Pistou* is much milder than *pesto*. The Genoese sailors, who found in its basil and garlic the green freshness and the earthy pungency they craved after their long odysseys, wanted those qualities in strong, even exaggerated, form. The *pesto* of Genoa is sharp and challenging. When the cookbook of Luigi Carnacini was translated into French, the recipe he had given for *pesto* in the Italian version was toned down because it was 'too aggressive' for the French. It is not always aggressive, even in Liguria. The *pesto* I ate in Genoa's excellent La Santa restaurant seemed to me unaccustomedly mild, and I asked the chef why. He told me he did not use the traditional recipe of Genoa, but that of Nervi, smoother because it adds cream. This is a good example of the localism of Italian food; Nervi is just seven miles south of Genoa, yet it manages to escape the culinary magnetism of the capital and have ideas of its own. Almost every Ligurian town of any importance has developed its own variant of *pesto*.

What is *pesto*? You will often find the name alone on a bill of fare along with the soups; and if you order it, soup is what you will get – usually a thick minestrone. But *pesto*, properly speaking, is not the soup, but the sauce which is added to it at the last moment. The same sauce is also often applied to pasta, in which case the favorite vehicle for it is *trenette*, the local variety of ribbon pasta. After that, *pesto* appears oftenest on gnocchi, of which the two favorite varieties in Liguria are *gnocchi alla genovese*, made with potatoes, and *gnocchi verdi*, made with spinach.

The soul of *pesto* is basil, and the patience and care characteristic of Genoese cooking appear from the very start of *pesto* making in the meticulous preparation of the basil. It is first deprived of its stems and central veins; only the deveined leaves go into the mortar in which it will be ground. *Pesto* makers are adamant on this point: no one can chop the ingredients fine enough; they must be ground, and, it is specified, in a marble mortar (with a pestle 'of good wood', one recipe adds, but does not insist on any specific sort of wood). You begin by crushing the basil leaves carefully with coarse kitchen salt and a clove of garlic. The tender green color of this mixture is your guide for the rest of the process. It should be maintained as the other ingredients are added; if it weakens, put in more basil. Next you add equal parts of young Sardinian pecorino cheese and old Parmesan (if you want a stronger taste, increase the proportion of the sharp Sardinian cheese; if you want it milder, decrease it). As you grind this with the rest, add olive oil (preferably Ligurian) drop by drop, until you have achieved the desired density (you may want it thicker for soup than for pasta). The last ingredient is pine nuts (some persons use walnuts instead), which must also be crushed so thoroughly that they become an indistinguishable part of the whole pungent creamy mass.

When *pesto* goes into minestrone, it must not be cooked with it. This would destroy the fresh sharpness of the sauce. Every recipe I have ever seen says that it should be added at the very end of the cooking, and stirred into the soup – the stirring is indispensable, one of them adds, to prevent the *pesto* from sticking to the bottom of the pan. This contradicts my own experience, which is that I have always been served *pesto* in soup floating raft-like on the surface, like sour cream on borscht or *rouille* on *soupe aux poissons*. Perhaps I was supposed to stir it in myself, but I didn't.

The minestrone with *pesto* which I sampled at La Santa contained peas, potatoes, a little onion, olive oil, garlic, and a few herbs, rather a restrained selection for Genoa. Usually minestrone in Liguria is much richer. One recipe I have, in a Ligurian cookbook, describes *minestrone alla genovese* as containing not only all the ingredients mentioned above, but also squash, cabbage, zucchini, fava beans, red beans, string beans, a ripe peeled pitted tomato, diced eggplant and celery. It also offers a choice of several varieties of pasta to add to the soup, just to make sure it is thick enough – vermicelli, *maccheroncini rigati*, *ditalini* or *penne*, but recommends *tagliatelle*, a rather filling variety.

As for ravioli, its Genoese origin seems confirmed both by the story of its invention and its name. Until the beginning of the nineteenth century, this form of pasta was called *rabiole*, which is a Genoese dialect word meaning things of little value – rubbish, say, or, in the kitchen, leftovers. On shipboard, at least in the days of sail, making use of leftovers was important; if they were thrown away, a ship-might risk running out of food if the voyage were unexpectedly prolonged. The story is that on Genoese ships anything left over at one meal was chopped up together, whatever it might be, stuffed into envelopes of pasta, and served at the following meal. The contents of shipboard ravioli could not have been very exciting; but Genoese ravioli today are often highly elaborate. To begin with, the pasta envelope is made with the finest wheat flour and with eggs. The stuffing called for by my Ligurian cookbook to produce *ravioli alla genovese* is lean veal, heifer's udder, calves' brains, sweetbreads, egg, bread crumbs, grated Parmesan cheese, cropped chard, borage, and nutmeg. This formula can of course be varied, but apparently not very much without losing the right to the name of *genovese*. Another version replaces the veal, including the udders, by chicken and sausage meat or ham, but maintains all the other ingredients. Whatever goes into the ravioli, it is eaten in Liguria either in soup (*pasta in brodo*), or as *pasta asciutta* with a variety of sauces or accompaniments – meat or tomato sauces, mushroom sauce, with truffles, or simply with butter and grated cheese.

Ravioli is an exception in the Ligurian list of dishes, one of the rare travelers. Most Genoese dishes do not turn up elsewhere in Italy. Ligurian cooking is perhaps more distinct from northern Italian cooking in general than that of any other single region of the North, to such an extent that even Italian 'international' restaurants which offer a hodgepodge of regional dishes from other parts of the country generally let Ligurian dishes strictly alone.

1971

M. F. K. FISHER

Young Hunger

It is very hard for people who have passed the age of, say, fifty to remember with any charity the hunger of their own puberty and adolescence when they are dealing with the young human animals who may be frolicking about them. Too often I have seen good people helpless with exasperation and real anger upon finding in the morning that cupboards and iceboxes have been stripped of their supplies by two or three youths – or even *one* – who apparently could have eaten four times their planned share at the dinner table the night before.

Such avidity is revolting, once past. But I can recall its intensity still; I am not yet too far from it to understand its ferocious demands when I see a fifteen-year-old boy wince and whiten at the prospect of waiting politely a few more hours for food, when his guts are howling for meat-bread-candy-fruit-cheese-milkmilkmilk – ANYTHING IN THE WORLD TO EAT.

I can still remember my almost insane desperation when I was about eighteen and was staying overnight with my comparatively aged godparents. I had come home alone from France in a bad continuous storm and was literally concave with solitude and hunger. The one night on the train seemed even rougher than those on board ship, and by the time I reached my god-parents' home I was almost lightheaded.

I got there just in time for lunch. It is clear as ice in my mind: a little cup of very weak chicken broth, one salted cracker, one-half piece of thinly sliced toast, and then, ah then, a whole waffle, crisp and brown and with a piece of beautiful butter melting in its middle – which the maid deftly cut into four sections! One section she put on my godmother's plate. The next *two*, after a nod of approval from her mistress, she put on mine. My godfather ate the fourth.

There was a tiny pot of honey, and I dutifully put a dab of it on my piggish portion, and we all nibbled away and drank one cup apiece of tea with lemon. Both my godparents left part of their waffles.

It was simply that they were old and sedentary and quite out of the habit of eating amply with younger people: a good thing for them, but pure hell for me. I did not have the sense to explain to them how starved I was – which I would not hesitate to do now. Instead I prowled around my bedroom while the house slumbered through its afternoon siesta, wondering if I dared sneak to the strange kitchen for something, anything, to eat, and knowing I would rather die than meet the silent, stern maid or my nice, gentle little hostess.

Later we walked slowly down to the village, and I was thinking sensuously of double malted ice-cream sodas at the corner drugstore, but there was no possibility of such heaven. When we got back to the quiet house, the maid brought my godfather a tall glass of exquisitely rich milk, with a handful of dried fruit on the saucer under it, because he had been ill; but as we sat and watched him unwillingly down it, his wife said softly that it was such a short time until dinner that she was sure I did not want to spoil my appetite, and I agreed with her because I was young and shy.

When I dressed, I noticed that the front of my pelvic basin jutted out like two bricks under my skirt: I looked like a scarecrow.

Dinner was very long, but all I can remember is that it had, as *pièce de résistance*, half of the tiny chicken previously boiled for broth at luncheon, which my godmother carved carefully so that we should each have a bit of the breast and I, as guest, should have the leg, after a snippet had been sliced from it for her husband, who liked dark meat too.

There were hot biscuits, yes, the smallest I have ever seen, two apiece under a napkin on a silver dish. Because of them we had no dessert: it would be too rich, my godmother said.

We drank little cups of decaffeinized coffee on the screened porch in the hot Midwestern night, and when I went up to my room I saw that the maid had left a large glass of rich malted milk beside my poor godfather's bed.

My train would leave before five in the morning, and I slept little and unhappily, dreaming of the breakfast I would order on it. Of course when I finally saw it all before me, twinkling on the Pullman silver dishes, I could eat very little, from too much hunger and a sense of outrage.

I felt that my hosts had been indescribably rude to me, and selfish and conceited and stupid. Now I know that they were none of these things. They had simply forgotten about any but their own dwindling and cautious needs for nourishment. They had forgotten about being hungry, being young, being . . .

In an essay by Max Beerbohm about hosts and guests, the tyrants and the tyrannized, there is a story of what happened to him once when he was a schoolboy and someone sent him a hamper that held, not the usual collection of marmalade, sardines, and potted tongue, but twelve whole sausage-rolls.

'Of sausage-rolls I was particularly fond,' he says. He could have dominated all his friends with them, of course, but 'I carried the box up to my cubicle, and, having eaten two of the sausage-rolls, said nothing that day about the other ten, nor anything about them when, three days later, I had eaten them all – all, up there, alone.'

What strange secret memories such a tale evokes! Is there a grown-up person anywhere who cannot remember some such shameful, almost insane act of greediness of his childhood? In recollection his scalp will prickle, and his palms will sweat, at the thought of the murderous risk he may have run from his outraged companions.

When I was about sixteen, and in boarding-school, we were allowed one bar of chocolate a day, which we were supposed to eat sometime between the sale of them at the little school bookstore at four-thirty and the seven o'clock dinner gong. I felt an almost unbearable hunger for them – not for one, but for three or four or five at a time, so that I should have *enough*, for once, in my yawning stomach.

I hid my own purchases for several days, no mean trick in a school where every drawer and cupboard was inspected, openly and snoopingly too, at least twice a week. I cannot remember now how I managed it, with such lack of privacy and my own almost insurmountable hunger every afternoon, but by Saturday I had probably ten chocolate bars – my own and a few I had bribed my friends who were trying to lose weight to buy for me.

I did not sign up for any of the usual weekend debauchery such as a walk to the village drugstore for a well-chaperoned double butterscotch and pecan sundae. Instead I lay languidly on my bed, trying to look as if I had a headache and pretending to read a very fancy book called, I think, *Martin Pippin in the Apple Orchard*, until the halls quieted.

Then I arranged all my own and my roommate's pillows in a voluptuous pile, placed so that I could see whether a silent housemotherly foot stood outside the swaying monk's-cloth curtain that served as a door (to cut down our libid-inous chitchat, the school board believed), and I put my hoard of Hersheys discreetly under a fold of the bedspread.

I unwrapped their rich brown covers and their tinfoil as silently as any prisoner chipping his way through a granite wall, and lay there breaking off the rather warm, rubbery, delicious pieces and feeling them melt down my gullet, and reading the lush symbolism of the book; and all the time I was hot and almost panting with the fear that people would suddenly walk in and see me there. And the strange thing is that nothing would have happened if they had!

It is true that I had more than my allotted share of candy, but that was not a crime. And my friends, full of their Saturday delights, would not have wanted ordinary chocolate. And anyway I had much more than I could eat, and was basically what Beerbohm calls, somewhat scornfully, 'a host' and not 'a guest': I loved to entertain people and dominate them with my generosity.

Then why was I breathless and nervous all during that solitary and not particularly enjoyable orgy? I suppose there is a Freudian explanation for it, or
some other kind. Certainly the experience does not make me sound very attractive to myself. Even the certainty of being in good company is no real solace.

1946

I Was Really Very Hungry

I

Once I met a young servant in northern Burgundy who was almost frighten-
ingly fanatical about food, like a medieval woman possessed by a devil. Her
obsession engulfed even my appreciation of the dishes she served, until I grew
uncomfortable.

It was the off season at the old mill which a Parisian chef had bought and
turned into one of France's most famous restaurants, and my mad waitress was
the only servant. In spite of that she was neatly uniformed, and showed no
surprise at my unannounced arrival and my hot dusty walking clothes.

She smiled discreetly at me, said, 'Oh, but certainly!' when I asked if I could
lunch there, and led me without more words to a dark bedroom bulging with
First Empire furniture, and a new white bathroom.

When I went into the dining room it was empty of humans – a cheerful ugly
room still showing traces of the petit bourgeois parlor it had been. There were
aspidistras on the mantel; several small white tables were laid with those imitation 'peasant-ware' plates that one sees in Paris china stores, and very good
crystal glasses; a cat folded under some ferns by the window ledge hardly
looked at me; and the air was softly hurried with the sound of high waters from
the stream outside.

I waited for the maid to come back. I knew I should eat well and slowly,
and suddenly the idea of dry sherry, unknown in all the village bistros of the
last few days, stung my throat smoothly. I tried not to think of it; it would
be impossible to realize. Dubonnet would do. But not as well. I longed for
sherry.

The little maid came into the silent room. I looked at her stocky young body, and her butter-colored hair, and noticed her odd pale voluptuous mouth before I said, 'Mademoiselle, I shall drink an apéritif. Have you by any chance –'

'Let me suggest,' she interrupted firmly, 'our special dry sherry. It is chosen in Spain for Monsieur Paul.'

And before I could agree she was gone, discreet and smooth.

She's a funny one, I thought, and waited in a pleasant warm tiredness for the wine.

It was good. I smiled approval at her, and she lowered her eyes, and then looked searchingly at me again. I realized suddenly that in this land of trained nonchalant waiters I was to be served by a small waitress who took her duties seriously. I felt much amused, and matched her solemn searching gaze.

'Today, Madame, you may eat shoulder of lamb in the English style, with baked potatoes, green beans, and a sweet.'

My heart sank. I felt dismal, and hot and weary, and still grateful for the sherry.

But she was almost grinning at me, her lips curved triumphantly, and her eyes less palely blue.

'Oh, in *that* case,' she remarked as if I had spoken, 'in *that* case a trout, of course – a *truite au bleu* as only Monsieur Paul can prepare it!'

She glanced hurriedly at my face, and hastened on. 'With the trout, one or two young potatoes – oh, very delicately boiled,' she added before I could protest, 'very light.'

I felt better. I agreed. 'Perhaps a leaf or two of salad after the fish,' I suggested. She almost snapped at me. 'Of course, of course! And naturally our hors d'œuvres to commence.' She started away.

'No!' I called, feeling that I must assert myself now or be forever lost. 'No!'

She turned back, and spoke to me very gently. 'But Madame has never tasted our hors d'œuvres. I am sure that Madame will be pleased. They are our specialty, made by Monsieur Paul himself. I am sure,' and she looked reproachfully at me, her mouth tender and sad, 'I am sure that Madame would be very much pleased.'

I smiled weakly at her, and she left. A little cloud of hurt gentleness seemed to hang in the air where she had last stood.

I comforted myself with the sherry, feeling increasing irritation with my own feeble self. Hell! I loathed hors d'œuvres! I conjured disgusting visions of square glass plates of oily fish, of soggy vegetables glued together with cheap mayonnaise, of rank radishes and tasteless butter. No, Monsieur Paul or not, sad young pale-faced waitress or not, I hated hors d'œuvres.

I glanced victoriously across the room at the cat, whose eyes seemed closed.

I I

Several minutes passed. I was really very hungry.

The door banged open, and my girl came in again, less discreet this time. She hurried toward me.

'Madame, the wine! Before Monsieur Paul can go on –' Her eyes watched my face, which I perversely kept rather glum.

'I think,' I said ponderously, daring her to interrupt me, 'I think that today, since I am in Burgundy and about to eat a trout,' and here I hoped she noticed that I did not mention hors d'œuvres, 'I think I shall drink a bottle of Chablis 1929.'

For a second her whole face blazed with joy, and then subsided into a trained mask. I knew that I had chosen well, had somehow satisfied her in a secret and incomprehensible way. She nodded politely and scuttled off, only for another second glancing impatiently at me as I called after her, 'Well cooled, please, but not iced.'

I'm a fool, I thought, to order a whole bottle. I'm a fool, here all alone and with more miles to walk before I reach Avallon and my fresh clothes and a bed. Then I smiled at myself and leaned back in my solid wide-seated chair, looking obliquely at the prints of Gibson girls, English tavern scenes, and hideous countrysides that hung on the papered walls. The room was warm; I could hear my companion cat purring under the ferns.

The girl rushed in, with flat baking dishes piled up her arms like the plates of a Japanese juggler. She slid them off neatly in two rows onto the table, where they lay steaming up at me, darkly and infinitely appetizing.

'*Mon Dieu!* All for me?' I peered at her. She nodded, her discretion quite gone now and a look of ecstatic worry on her pale face and eyes and lips.

There were at least eight dishes. I felt almost embarrassed, and sat for a minute looking weakly at the fork and spoon in my hand.

'Perhaps Madame would care to start with the pickled herring? It is not like any other. Monsieur Paul prepares it himself, in his own vinegar and wines. It is very good.'

I dug out two or three brown filets from the dish, and tasted. They were truly unlike any others, truly the best I had ever eaten, mild, pungent, meaty as fresh nuts.

I realized the maid had stopped breathing, and looked up at her. She was watching me, or rather a gastronomic X-ray of the herring inside me, with a hypnotized glaze in her eyes.

'Madame is pleased?' she whispered softly.

I said I was. She sighed, and pushed a sizzling plate of broiled endive toward me, and disappeared.

I had put a few dull green lentils on my plate, lentils scattered with minced fresh herbs and probably marinated in tarragon vinegar and walnut oil, when she came into the dining room again with the bottle of Chablis in a wine basket.

'Madame should be eating the little baked onions while they are hot,' she remarked over her shoulder as she held the bottle in a napkin and uncorked it. I obeyed meekly, and while I watched her I ate several more than I had meant to. They were delicious, simmered first in strong meat broth, I think, and then drained and broiled with olive oil and new-ground pepper.

I was fascinated by her method of uncorking a vintage wine. Instead of the Burgundian procedure of infinite and often exaggerated precautions against touching or tipping or jarring the bottle, she handled it quite nonchalantly, and seemed to be careful only to keep her hands from the cool bottle itself, holding it sometimes by the basket and sometimes in a napkin. The cork was very tight, and I thought for a minute that she would break it. So did she: her face grew tight, and did not loosen until she had slowly worked out the cork and wiped the lip. Then she poured an inch of wine in a glass, turned her back to me like a priest taking Communion, and drank it down. Finally some was poured for me, and she stood with the bottle in her hand and her full lips drooping until I nodded a satisfied yes. Then she pushed another of the plates toward me, and almost rushed from the room.

I ate slowly, knowing that I should not be as hungry as I ought to be for the trout, but knowing too that I had never tasted such delicate savory morsels. Some were hot, some cold. The wine was light and cool. The room, warm and agreeably empty under the rushing sound of the stream, became smaller as I grew used to it.

My girl hurried in again, with another row of plates up one arm, and a large bucket dragging at the other. She slid the plates deftly onto the table, and drew a deep breath as she let the bucket down against the table leg.

'Your trout, Madame,' she said excitedly. I looked down at the gleam of the fish curving through its limited water. 'But first a good slice of Monsieur Paul's *pâté*. Oh yes, oh yes, you will be very sorry if you miss this. It is rich, but appetizing, and not at all too heavy. Just this one morsel!'

And willy-nilly I accepted the large gouge she dug from a terrine. I prayed for ten normal appetites and thought with amused nostalgia of my usual lunch of cold milk and fruit as I broke off a crust of bread and patted it smooth with the paste. Then I forgot everything but the exciting faint decadent flavor in my mouth.

I beamed up at the girl. She nodded, but from habit asked if I was satisfied.

I beamed again, and asked, simply to please her, 'Is there not a faint hint of *marc*, or perhaps cognac?'

'*Marc*, Madame!' And she awarded me the proud look of a teacher whose pupil has showed unexpected intelligence. 'Monsieur Paul, after he has taken equal parts of goose breast and the finest pork, and broken a certain number of egg yolks into them, and ground them *very*, very fine, cooks all with seasoning for some three hours. *But*,' she pushed her face nearer, and looked with ferocious gloating at the *pâté* inside me, her eyes like X-rays, 'he never stops stirring it! Figure to yourself the work of it – stir, stir, never stopping!

'Then he grinds in a suspicion of nutmeg, and then adds, very thoroughly, a glass of *marc* for each hundred grams of *pâté*. And is Madame not pleased?'

Again I agreed, rather timidly, that Madame was much pleased, that Madame had never, indeed, tasted such an unctuous and exciting *pâté*. The girl wet her lips delicately, and then started as if she had been pin-stuck.

'But the trout! My God, the trout!' She grabbed the bucket, and her voice grew higher and more rushed.

'Here is the trout, Madame. You are to eat it *au bleu*, and you should never do so if you had not seen it alive. For if the trout were dead when it was plunged into the *court bouillon* it would not turn blue. So, naturally, it must be living.'

I knew all this, more or less, but I was fascinated by her absorption in the momentary problem. I felt quite ignorant, and asked her with sincerity, 'What about the trout? Do you take out its guts before or after?'

'Oh, the trout!' She sounded scornful. 'Any trout is glad, truly glad, to be prepared by Monsieur Paul. His little gills are pinched, with one flash of the knife he is empty, and then he curls in agony in the *bouillon* and all is over. And it is the curl you must judge, Madame. A false *truite au bleu* cannot curl.'

She panted triumph at me, and hurried out with the bucket.

III

She *is* a funny one, I thought, and for not more than two or three minutes I drank wine and mused over her. Then she darted in, with the trout correctly blue and agonizingly curled on a platter, and on her crooked arm a plate of tiny boiled potatoes and a bowl.

When I had been served and had cut off her anxious breathings with an assurance that the fish was the best I had ever tasted, she peered again at me and at the sauce in the bowl. I obediently put some of it on the potatoes: no fool I, to ruin *truite au bleu* with a hot concoction! There was more silence.

'Ah!' she sighed at last. 'I knew Madame would feel thus! Is it not the most beautiful sauce in the world with the flesh of a trout?'

I nodded incredulous agreement.

'Would you like to know how it is done?'

I remembered all the legends of chefs who guarded favorite recipes with their very lives, and murmured yes.

She wore the exalted look of a believer describing a miracle at Lourdes as she told me, in a rush, how Monsieur Paul threw chopped chives into hot sweet butter and then poured the butter off, how he added another nut of butter and a tablespoonful of thick cream for each person, stirred the mixture for a few minutes over a slow fire, and then rushed it to the table.

'So simple?' I asked softly, watching her lighted eyes and the tender lustful lines of her strange mouth.

'So simple, Madame! But,' she shrugged, 'you know, with a master –'

I was relieved to see her go: such avid interest in my eating wore on me. I felt released when the door closed behind her, free for a minute or so from her victimization. What would she have done, I wondered, if I had been ignorant or unconscious of any fine flavors?

She was right, though, about Monsieur Paul. Only a master could live in this isolated mill and preserve his gastronomic dignity through loneliness and the sure financial loss of unused butter and addled eggs. Of course there was the stream for his fish, and I knew his *pâtés* would grow even more edible with age; but how could he manage to have a thing like roasted lamb ready for any chance patron? Was the consuming interest of his one maid enough fuel for his flame?

I tasted the last sweet nugget of trout, the one nearest the blued tail, and poked somnolently at the minute white billiard balls that had been eyes. Fate could not harm me, I remembered winily, for I had indeed dined today, and dined well. Now for a leaf of crisp salad, and I'd be on my way.

The girl slid into the room. She asked me again, in a respectful but gossipy manner, how I had liked this and that and the other things, and then talked on as she mixed dressing for the endive.

'And now,' she announced, after I had eaten one green sprig and dutifully pronounced it excellent, 'now Madame is going to taste Monsieur Paul's special terrine, one that is not even on the summer menu, when a hundred covers are laid here daily and we have a headwaiter and a wine waiter, and cabinet ministers telegraph for tables! Madame will be pleased.'

And heedless of my low moans of the walk still before me, of my appreciation and my unhappily human and limited capacity, she cut a thick heady slice from the terrine of meat and stood over me while I ate it, telling me with almost hysterical pleasure of the wild ducks, the spices, the wines that went into it. Even surfeit could not make me deny that it was a rare dish. I ate it all, knowing my luck, and wishing only that I had red wine to drink with it.

I was beginning, though, to feel almost frightened, realizing myself an accidental victim of these stranded gourmets, Monsieur Paul and his hand-maiden. I began to feel that they were using me for a safety valve, much as a thwarted woman relieves herself with tantrums or a fit of weeping. I was serving a purpose, and perhaps a noble one, but I resented it in a way approaching panic.

I protested only to myself when one of Monsieur Paul's special cheeses was cut for me, and ate it doggedly, like a slave. When the girl said that Monsieur Paul himself was preparing a special filter of coffee for me, I smiled servile acceptance: wine and the weight of food and my own character could not force me to argue with maniacs. When, before the coffee came, Monsieur Paul presented me, through his idolater, with the most beautiful apple tart I had ever seen, I allowed it to be cut and served to me. Not a wince or a murmur showed the waitress my distressed fearfulness. With a stuffed careful smile on my face, and a clear nightmare in my head of trussed wanderers prepared for his altar by this hermit-priest of gastronomy, I listened to the girl's passionate plea for fresh pastry dough.

'You cannot, you *can*not, Madame, serve old pastry!' She seemed ready to beat her breast as she leaned across the table. 'Look at that delicate crust! You may feel that you have eaten too much.' (I nodded idiotic agreement.) 'But this pastry is like feathers – it is like snow. It is in fact good for you, a digestive! And why?' She glared sternly at me. 'Because Monsieur Paul did not even open the flour bin until he saw you coming! He could not, he *could* not have baked you one of his special apple tarts with old dough!'

She laughed, tossing back her head and curling her mouth voluptuously.

I V

Somehow I managed to refuse a second slice, but I trembled under her surmise that I was ready for my special filter.

The wine and its fortitude had fled me, and I drank the hot coffee as a suffering man gulps ether, deeply and gratefully.

I remember, then, chatting with surprising glibness, and sending to Monsieur Paul flowery compliments, all of them sincere and well won, and I remember feeling only amusement when a vast glass of *marc* appeared before me and then gradually disappeared, like the light in the warm room full of water-sounds. I felt surprised to be alive still, and suddenly very grateful to the wild-lipped waitress, as if her presence had sustained me through duress. We discussed food and wine. I wondered bemusedly why I had been frightened.

The *marc* was gone. I went into the crowded bedroom for my jacket. She met me in the darkening hall when I came out, and I paid my bill, a large one. I started to thank her, but she took my hand, drew me into the dining room, and without words poured more spirits into my glass. I drank to Monsieur Paul while she watched me intently, her pale eyes bulging in the dimness and her lips pressed inward as if she too tasted the hot, aged *marc*.

The cat rose from his ferny bed, and walked contemptuously out of the room.

Suddenly the girl began to laugh, in a soft shy breathless way, and came close to me.

'Permit me!' she said, and I thought she was going to kiss me. But instead she pinned a tiny bunch of snowdrops and dark bruised cyclamens against my stiff jacket, very quickly and deftly, and then ran from the room with her head down.

I waited for a minute. No sounds came from anywhere in the old mill, but the endless rushing of the full stream seemed to strengthen, like the timid blare of an orchestra under a falling curtain.

She's a *funny* one, I thought. I touched the cool blossoms on my coat and went out, like a ghost from ruins, across the courtyard toward the dim road to Avallon.

1937

Dutch Freighter
MS *Diemerdyk*

People who travel on freighters may do so accidentally for the first time, as I did in 1932 from Marseille to Los Angeles on the *Feltre*, later bombed and sunk. Thereafter they do it deliberately, or never again.

They either loathe it and know that they cannot stand it again, or they return like opium smokers to the pipe, never halfheartedly, and almost always with a deliberate plan, a kind of rhythmic pattern, for the long, slow, sleepy voyage.

Either they must have plenty of time and no other pressing use for it than to spend some of it in a little ship, or they must have almost no time at all and an imperative hunger to spend it in this chosen way, moving to the tides' movings and the stars'.

Freighter travel is never forgotten. I was greatly reassured to prove this, lately, when I rode some five weeks on two oceans, two seas, a canal, a couple of bays, and a river, after having been land-bound for more than a decade.

It is true that I pampered myself somewhat, suspecting that my old skill might be too rusty for comfortable practice. I took a clean, efficient little ship toward Europe instead of a grubby if more romantic one headed for the South Pacific, and I chose the easy month of August instead of the obviously more exciting season of an equinox. I was cautious, and slid out under the Golden Gate Bridge in a mood that was definitely timorous.

The minute I *knew*, though, that it would be days and weeks before I touched land again; that I was there on that little Dutch freighter for good or bad or even hell-and-high-water; that if I died on it I would still be a long time from the dust I should return to; that if I lived decently on it the Captain would like me and that if I lived indecently on it he would not; but that in any and all such cases it was basically my own choice – the minute I knew all this again, I was at home.

I slipped unprotestingly into the first trance-like sleepiness which always engulfs me when I put to sea, and which tapers off almost imperceptibly until I land again. It is true that I walk and even talk at the proper times, but inwardly there is little difference between having eyes shut or eyes open; and my first encounters with passengers and officers and general shipside protocol are even less real than my endless untroubled dreams.

Dutch crewmen seem unusually understanding of such mildly neurasthenic procedures, perhaps because they are said to be sons of a phlegmatic nation, and there is no better place to try one's first steps again, one's first deep breaths, than on the scrubbed decks and in the hospitable neat air of a little steamer named anything ending with *-dyk* or *-dam*. From the Captain, coldly and implacably invisible when duty called and very jolly indeed when it did not, to the most impish deckhand or oiler, the men seemed to accept my private reasons for my public behavior just as philosophically as they did the other passengers', and made us all feel, very comfortably, that we were really not much more bother than the tons of canned fruits and precision tools that weighted down the holds and held us to such an even as well as profitable keel. My own actions were steadily somnambulistic, but they caused no more astonishment than if I had stood on my head before every meal, just outside the dining-saloon door, as did a gym teacher from British Columbia, or had dropped my monocle into my full soup plate every night, as did a permanently and politely dead-drunk lecturer from Amsterdam.

Of course, there are always a few mavericks, who get on in a daze and will get off in a state of frustrated ennui. Most of them will never, as God is their witness, let themselves get roped into another tedious crawl over any ocean on this world.

For instance, there was on our little freighter – as there always is – a passenger who either could not or would not accept the fact that for several weeks it would be impossible for him to read the morning and afternoon papers for exactly forty minutes after breakfast and twenty minutes before dinner. He would stand fuming and scowling, plainly miserable, before the two typed sheets of radio news Sparks pinned up each noon on the bulletin board. One was in Dutch, of course, and one in very British American, and the passenger was sure that there were several vitally important bits of news in the Netherlands report which were being deliberately withheld from him as a one-language Yankee. He would waylay a steward or a Dutch passenger and stand suspiciously comparing what he could read with what was being translated.

I felt genuinely pained for him, partly for his present misery and partly because he would never achieve real supercargodom. He had come aboard knowing, but never actually accepting, such irrevocabilities as that the Spokane dailies cannot be delivered, limp from their presses, a thousand miles northeast of Cuba. He would go ashore convinced that it could have been managed somehow.

In the same way there was, this time and always, the passenger who fought a gallant fight for the last twenty-five days of the thirty-three-day voyage to have fresh eggs for breakfast. She was well-read enough to know that very few modern ships travel with chickens aboard, as in the days of Drake and Magellan. But every morning she hoped anew, and assured her table steward that she must have *fresh* eggs, and almost every morning after the first week at sea she sent back what she had ordered with the unbelieving statement that it was *not* fresh at *all*.

Gently, the head steward, a very clever man indeed and one of infinite experience, ordered little omelets and unnamed scrambles for her instead of the undisguisable softboiled eggs she struggled for, until by the time we were heading for the North Sea she was eating highly seasoned dishes that would have seemed impossibly exotic to her in San Diego or Vancouver. The last morning, though, when we all ate an early breakfast and wore our hats and clutched our new passport holders and watched the docks of Antwerp slide by the portholes, I heard her say with a note of dauntless disbelief, 'I *do* insist on having my eggs fresh-fresh-*fresh*.' And she was right: she did insist.

Another common phenomenon of supercargodom, something which even

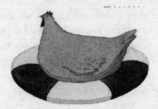

ten years of land exile had not changed for me, was that I soon sniffed out, through the fog of my private snooze, the familiar hunger for new words. It is something shared by all real travelers and can give as much pleasure to a twelve-days-and-all-expenses adventurer as to a raddled old countess who has spent nine-tenths of her life on A Deck, from Hong Kong to Montevideo with stop-offs at will in Plymouth, Skagerrak, Vladivostok.

It takes only a couple of days in Honolulu to enable a Stateside housewife to spend the next ten years rattling off directions to her decorators about *lanais* and *hookalumais* – which she learned in what she knowingly refers to in four, not three, syllables, carefully accented, as Hah-*vah*-ee-ee. In the same enjoyable way, a few days in Paris, especially if helped along by a French Line crossing, can bring out almost voluptuous garglings and rollings of good flat Illinois *r*'s, so that saying '*Trente-trois rue de Rivoli*' to a taxi driver can sound much like the after-treatment of a tonsillectomy.

Even more so, four or five weeks on a Dutch freighter can do fine things to this linguistic *amour-propre* we all wear hidden somewhere until the magic new phonetics brings it to light, and I felt reassured to discover that it was as true in 1954 as it had been decades before, on the *Feltre*, and the *Santa Cerrita* and the *Maréchal Duffroy*, and . . . and . . . and . . .

Very shortly after I went aboard, I learned that, in good Dutch, the barman is called the Buffetchef, pronounced *Puff*ishay (naturally), and that the chief steward, always an equally good man to know, is called the Hof-Meister (*Huff*-Maystuh). Shuttling from one to the other with no pain, it was inestimably satisfying to be able to murmur to the first in supercargo Dutch – which sounds even Dutcher after the second or third small glass of Genever gin – '*Ein Bols*' (Ayn Buhlsh, of course), and then to request knowingly from the second a large bowl of Hodgepodge for lunch.

Hodgepodge is perhaps peculiar to ships out of Rotterdam. Certainly I have never seen it in the same form on land, in Holland or even in France, where it might possibly be called Hochepot. It is a thick, greenish-grey, lumpy, delicious stew of vegetables and bits of unidentifiable meat and sometimes slices of sausage, to be served in soup plates and eaten with large spoons and, if possible, pieces of fresh brown bread for pushing and sopping. Needless to say, it is pronounced, by any old-timer – which means any passenger who has been more than forty-eight hours aboard – Uhdgee-*Puhd*gee. There is something very satisfying about rolling out this word when it has been preceded by a wise modicum of Genever and a few twinkles from the poker-faced, warm-eyed Puffishay.

Cakes (Keks), which apparently are as necessary to the end of a Dutch sea meal as Bols is to the beginning, are based on a batter which is yellow, spongily heavy when baked, and increasingly nutmeggish as the voyage progresses and the fresh *fresh* eggs grow less so. Keks can be anywhere from half an inch to three inches thick, sliced in fingers or rounds, cut in squares, diced or crumbled when stale, and quite possibly used as ballast in a nautical emergency, and they are interesting chiefly as an indication of how the baker feels.

For instance, before our baker's last land-whirl in Cristobal and the long haul toward Antwerp, we were titillated at dinner by his version of a dainty slab named Gâteau d'Amour. The next night, and the only time he let us down in some five weeks, we had to be content with tinned fruit cup and vanilla wafers, but twenty-four hours later he had pulled himself together enough to produce his basic batter again, stripped of the love-cakes' whipped-cream doodads, starkly burned on the starboard side, and entitled Celebration Crumbcake.

And of course the Esperanto of pastry cooks, easy enough to decipher after one or two sorties as supercargo, makes it completely unsurprising to find a cherry on top of anything called Jubilee, or tooth-shattering morsels of nut brittle scattered here and there with the menu cue Noisette, on any ship from a transatlantic liner to a freighter. This lingo is international to the point of banality, and cannot possibly give quite the semantic thrill to a traveler as the ability to recognize, as well as mouth, the word Goudasprits.

Ah, those lovely, dry, flat, whirly Goudapritses, our baker's one deviation from his occasionally faltering but always narrow path of Kek-Kek-Kek!

They meant, on his emotional chart, a period of high-barometer insouciance, with low humidity so that they would stay moderately crisp and unflabby, and a subtropical zing to the air. On the days he served them, the bread too seemed more delicious, and passengers who ordered American Utt-Keks for breakfast reported them to be comparatively airy, which is to say that they were not more than three-quarters of an inch thick, each weighing somewhat less than a pound per Kek. Goudapritses meant, in other words, a general lightness aboard, even in their pronunciation, which according to the Captain was impossible for anyone not born in Holland. (We compromised to our own satisfaction, if not his, by gurgling as genteelly as possible when we said 'Whgh*ooooo*-da-shpritsh,' but there lurked always in our linguistic consciences his firm comment that we simply did not have enough *juice* to speak good Dutch.)

Something that happens at least once on every respectable freighter out of Rotterdam or into it is a Nassi Goreng for luncheon.

Britishers aboard feel about it much as they do about anything even vaguely curried, which a Nassi Goreng is not, and they bandy reminiscences larded with *pukka* and *boy*. Reticent withered Dutch ladies, relics of traders in Surabaya in the old days, grow almost gay again and chat of Rijsttafels, which a Nassi Goreng is not quite. And everybody eats too much and sleeps all afternoon, for the feast is not only tantalizing to several of the senses, but it must be floated down on a heady flood of beer.

A Nassi Goreng is served in an almost hysterical way by every available hand on board, including a few ordinarily invisible oilers squeezed into leftover white jackets. This may be one reason why it is definitely a ceremony performed only when the sea is flat and empty and the ship is on its automatic compass or whatever it is that takes over when the bridge can be left to its own devices.

The Hof-Meister, somewhat glassy-eyed from the general emotional temperature and several amicable Genevers, stands straighter than usual at the pantry door, focusing behind his thick lenses on every one of the loaded platters that whip past him. The stewards, generally a relaxed and merry squad, are frowning, with beaded lips and unaccustomed clattering and crashing. The tables look overcrowded with tall bottles of mango chutney and short bottles of red and black sambal, and soup plates at each place, and the largest size of dinner plates beside the forks, and big stemmed glasses, and the clear green of the Heineken beer bottles.

There seems to be no set pattern for serving, once the rice is there to act as a kind of foundation in the soup plates. The rice is always browned with minced onion, steamed, and then baked slowly, so that it is a little crisp. And then over and around it, and piled on the dinner plate too, is what really amounts to a gastronomical mishmash of grilled and roasted and fried fishes and meats, in chunks and slices and on skewers: chicken, lamb, kidneys, herring, this-and-that. There are even very flabby fried eggs. And on top of all these things, and around them and alongside, go the more or less familiar 'condiments' like chopped roasted peanuts and shaved coconut, steamed raisins, pickled fish, shaved spiced cucumbers, little hot peppers, one or more kinds of chutney of course, grated raw onion . . . on and on. And then, to pull things into focus and to bring real happiness to the world-wanderers who want to go home laden with nonchalant little anecdotes in any language at all besides their own, there is the final fillip, about as subtle as a flash fire in a munitions dump, of sambal.

Sambal, once tasted or even sniffed, can never be compared with Tabasco, or Louisiana hot-sauce, or the *salsa picante* of Mexico, or even the watery, oily, treacherous *sauce forte* splashed cautiously over an Algerian couscous, for it is so much more so that it makes them seem like sweet lemonade or milk.

It is black or it is red, and connoisseurs choose one or the other and shake it with knowing discretion here and there over the general confusion on their plates, at a Nassi Goreng, and then wait happily to fall by accident upon one drop of it, when tears will brim their eyes and they can reach blindly for the beer.

Sambal is, I think I can say without being contradicted, the most thoroughly and incredibly hot flavor in the world. How and why it can somehow, over and above the enjoyable torture it causes, make the basically unattractive clutter of a Nassi Goreng even more entertaining and appetizing than it manages by contradiction to be, I do not try to explain. All I can say is that it is pronounced, surprisingly enough, almost as it is spelled, that it can be found wherever a few old Java hands are gathered together, and that it can add inestimably to the culinary reputation as well as the vocabulary of anyone who has ever added to either, generally, by a trip on a little or big Dutch ship.

So can a Nassi Goreng, of course, even without the red and black sambals!

After five weeks spent contemplating the horizon, the navel, and the Dutch face, things taste better, and memories are good, not sour: the night the Puffishay cried a little because at Panama City he had learned that three weeks earlier his wife in Hille Doornkamp near The Hague had felt a cold coming on; the afternoon a glittering flying fish landed by the engine-room door and Cor of the crew dipped on it like a bird and threw it back into the blue water before it could even open its beak-bill mouth; the morning the Canadian judge came on deck without his orthopedic boot and played a game of deck quoits which everybody pretended not to watch too anxiously, nor cheer with tears too plainly sounding.

There is a kind of sharpening of what wits are left us, on a little ship's slow slide over many waters; and although it demands a certain amount of bravado to attain supercargodom, once done and admitted it is done forever, and like me you can go aboard in San Francisco or Baltimore or Corpus Christi any time at all in your life and get off a few weeks later anywhere at all, and find yourself wide awake again, and stronger and fresher if you want to be, and with a richer, indeed broader, tongue.

SAMUEL CHAMBERLAIN

Clémentine in the Kitchen

... We'll never forget when Clémentine came to us, out of the blue, as the result of a stray telephone number that Mrs Beck had picked up at a Paris dinner party. She had just discharged the fifth cook in eight weeks and was scouting forlornly for a sixth. Clémentine sounded so good over the telephone that my desperate wife at once sent her fifty francs for transportation to our little town north of Paris. One look at the smiling, pink-cheeked Clémentine and we knew that she would be a godsend after the succession of indifferent cooks who had presided in our venerable cuisine. Old Amélie had been too cranky. Noëlie could prepare some toothsome specialties (her *cassoulet* still haunts us), but she was fantastically sloppy. Jeanne had made frequent and abnormal inroads into my wine cellar. But the fair, black-eyed Clémentine seemed to possess all virtues and no faults. She arrived on the five-o'clock local, a demure and smiling little person, and was busy preparing dinner within an hour. The Bęcks heard snatches of song coming from the kitchen and then sniffed the heavenly mélange of shallots, butter, and herbs browning in Clémentine's casserole. Our day of good fortune seemed to be at hand. And when we learned that our rosy discovery was a genuine *Cordon Bleu* and a resident of Beaune, the gastronomic heart of Burgundy, our joy knew no bounds.

The Becks had been in Beaune only a few weeks before and had reveled in the luxurious cuisine of that epicurean stronghold. Would our newly found treasure be able to duplicate the memorable Sunday dinner in Beaune, which we had enjoyed with the Bellon family, *par exemple*? We wondered. If she could, our reputation as Lucullan hosts was everlastingly made. Papa Bellon had spread himself on that memorable Sunday, and the enraptured Becks remembered every detail of the feast. A bourgeois dinner in Burgundy lacks finesse, perhaps, but it is glorious in earthy fundamentals. The menu of Papa Bellon's dinner was simply worded, but it made a more lasting impression upon us than many an ornamental menu of *la grande cuisine française* that we had sampled. *Le voici*:

Escargots de Bourgogne
Truite de la Rivière Nageante dans le Beurre
Coq au Chambertin
Petits Pois à la Française
Pâté en Croûte
Salade de Laitue
Fromage
Tarte aux Mirabelles
Café

Papa Bellon had ordered the dinner two days ahead of time at the leading restaurant in Beaune. From his confident air the Becks knew that auspicious things were in the offing. Besides the plump Monsieur *et* Madame Bellon there were with us two buxom daughters, a solemn son-in-law, and a strapping son of twelve. We sat down for the obligatory apéritif on the terrace while our host went inside to talk to the chef.

A clink of glasses, a few appraising glances at the townspeople walking home from church, and we were ready to go into the restaurant, where our table, decked with red-and-white checkered cloth, shimmering with glassware, and heaped high with crusty bread, had been set for ten guests. The prodigal plenty of that dinner saddens us now, when we think of the daily fare of the Nazi-held Burgundians. At each place were a dozen beautiful *escargots de Bourgogne* in their light ochre shells, very hot and very fragrant, exuding a heavenly aroma of garlic, parsley, and fresh butter. This rare comestible calls for specially designed platters, holders, and forks, but how well worth their acquisition! With the snails we sipped a full-blooded Nuits-Saint-Georges. Some people have the idea that snails, because they live in a shell, are closely related to seafood and therefore must be accompanied by a white wine. *Escargots de Bourgogne* are land snails exclusively, growing fat on the leaves of the grape vines. They never get even close to the sea, and Burgundians prefer them with red wine.

The ancient waiter shifted plates and appeared with a massive oval, copper casserole containing ten handsome trout, deep in a prodigal bath of melted butter. *Nageante dans le beurre* was indeed the expression to use. The wine was a lighter gold than the butter, a clean, tempting Meursault Charmes of 1926. *Coq au Chambertin*, the *pièce de résistance*, could not have been more typical of Burgundy. It is doubtful if any Chambertin went into that delectable dish, which usually is content to be called *coq au vin*, but the sauce wasn't made from just any bottle of red wine, either. Then came a rich and fragrant *pâté en croûte*. Ham, veal, sausage meat, strips of fat, spices, pistachio nuts, and a symphony of herbs had been mixed and encased in a golden crust. This was served hot with a salad of plain green lettuce. We watched the headwaiter with fascination as he mixed the dressing on a flat plate – five parts of olive oil to one of strong wine vinegar, salt, ground pepper, and a generous daub of Dijon mustard. The wine was a lusty Pommard Rugiens 1926, which held over handsomely for the cheese platter, an impressive plank of Camembert, Brie, Roquefort, and Port-du-Salut.

Individual *tartes aux mirabelles* after this, accompanied by a rich Château Chalon poured from its distinctive bottle, then some very black coffee and a trio of liqueurs: Vieux Marc for those who could take it (*papa* and son-in-law), Armagnac for me, and rich purple Cassis for the ladies.

Well, it was quite a Sunday dinner. Do you wonder that we were enthused about the splendors of gastronomy in Beaune?

Would Clémentine, the native Burgundian, give us splurges such as this? Could our figures and my pocketbook take it? The answer, we soon found out, was magnificently in the affirmative. Clémentine was a *Cordon Bleu* in the best tradition. My son Phinney and I began to dream of fabulous banquets, and I began to recall uneasily that one gets gout in Burgundy. Luckily there were two deterrents to shield us from mad, headlong *gourmandise* – Clémentine's mastery of simple dishes, and Mrs Beck's insistence upon a sane and healthy fare. Regardless of our curiosity about exotic dishes and our desire to sample all of Clémentine's sauces, our daily menu contained the same well-balanced fare that prevailed in countless conventional French homes. We had no huge dinners à la Papa Bellon. My unruffled wife saw to that. Our daily living was based, I suppose, upon no more than twenty-five classic French dishes, all of which Clémentine handled with the sure hand of a master. They are elemental dishes throughout France, as fundamental as bread, cheese, and wine. They vary, of course, from one family to the next. But the following list, taken from the most thumb-worn pages in Clémentine's notebook is typical, and eloquent, of the way a civilized French family lives.

EGGS	LAMB
Omelette aux Fines Herbes	Gigot d'Agneau
Soufflé au Fromage	Côtelettes de Mouton

FISH	BEEF
Merlans Frits	Pot-au-Feu
Coquilles Saint-Jacques	Boeuf à la Mode
Turbot au Vin Blanc	Boeuf Bourguignon
Moules Marinière	Faux-Filet Rôti
Truite Meunière	Entrecôte Béarnaise

POULTRY
Poulet Rôti
Coq au Vin
Poule au Riz
Poulet Sauté
Poulet Cocotte
Canard aux Navets

VEAL
Blanquette de Veau
Sauté de Veau
Rôti de Veau
Paupiettes de Veau
Foie de Veau Meunière

PORK AND HAM
Rôti de Porc en Casserole
Jambon, Sauce Madère
Saucissons aux Pommes Purées

Any one of these dishes serves as the *pièce de résistance* in numberless French meals. At lunch time such a *plat* would be preceded by an hors-d'œuvre and followed by the classic *légumes, salade, fromage, et fruits*. The menu varied little at the evening meal, except that it was briefer and began with a hot soup. It was accompanied, of course, by plenty of good crusty bread and an honest, substantial *vin ordinaire*. In view of the present plight of France, the use of the past tense is advisable and eloquent.

Clémentine in the kitchen! The bright-eyed little cook brought new significance to that part of the house, which had waited so long for a presiding genius. It was a neat and ample kitchen. Its red tile floor was worn down in spots but always beautifully waxed. Above the stove was our pride and joy, a shimmering *batterie de cuisine*, fourteen heavy copper pans, polished and tin lined, hanging against the wall in mathematical progression. They ranged from a huge fellow big enough to roast a duck to the tiny vessel just about right for poaching an egg. There was an efficient stove, a commodious and rather ancient soapstone sink, a shelf for a library of cookbooks, from *Tante Marie* to *Ali-Bab*, a massive oak chopping board, and some well-balanced scales with a squad of neat little metric weights. A white marble-topped table stood in the middle of the kitchen, its drawer crammed with sauce whisks, wooden spoons, and a murderous collection of sharp steel knives. In a low cupboard was a mighty assemblage of seasoned earthen casseroles, some with handles, some with covers that could be hermetically sealed. On top of the cupboard was a husky stone mortar with a dark wooden pestle. Hanging near the door were the two invariable adjuncts of a French kitchen – a salad basket and a birdcage.

Here the cheerful Clémentine reigned, not as a despot (like a few French cooks we had known), but as a genial collaborator who, if coddled by the right amount of flattery, appreciated our insatiable interest and didn't mind our incessant intrusions into her domain. Her Burgundian good nature had to stand for a lot. Each of the Becks had a specialty. Diane interested herself (far too much) in the desserts. The young man of the house was absorbed in his vegetable garden and the possibilities for pecuniary profit that it held. The cheese, wine, and cookbook departments were indisputably mine. But there is no question, of course, as to who really holds the reins in a French household. It is *madame la patronne*, and our house was no exception. Once the authority and prestige of Mrs Beck stood unquestioned, this family of incorrigible epicures went at a gallop, but in safe hands, down the road to gastronomic adventure.

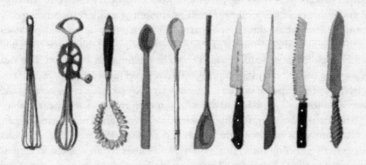

The marketplace in many French towns is a rather dreary affair, usually an open-air edifice of ornamental iron, covered with a tin roof and resounding with the hoarse shouts of local vegetable barons. Numberless early-morning sightseers have been attracted to Les Halles in Paris, of course, but they were looking for atmosphere and onion soup rather than architectural splendor. Even the sad events of 1940 do not dim the memory that most French markets are unlovely. But one notable exception to the rule is the market in our little town of Senlis in the Oise. Located in the disaffected medieval church of St Pierre, this market is an absolute pageant of the picturesque. In its cool, white-washed nave the symphony of color caused by the vegetable and fruit stands and by the brilliantly costumed African Spahi orderlies, buying provisions for their officers, was something to delight the eye of an artist. Rare was the summer day, in fact, when an easel was not set up in some corner of the side aisles, with a painter working feverishly behind it.

The rich Gothic façade of St Pierre looked down upon a small cobblestone square that, on market days, became packed with the umbrellas and stands of ambulatory dry goods merchants. Here sturdy peasant women from neighboring farms would buy strong black cloth with the proceeds of the sale of their *haricots verts*. And here would be stationed the inevitable unshaven accordion player, squeezing out silly, tinkling tunes while his wife tried hard to sell sheet music to a gaping circle of children and rustics from the outlying villages. And here also was our particular joy, the suspender salesman who had the marvelous technique of snapping a pair of suspenders into the air, using the principle of the slingshot, so that they hung on the lamppost, invariably bringing a laugh from the crowd – and, more often than not, a sale.

Market day came twice a week in Senlis, and twice a week the Beck family plunged into this animated picture with joy and abandon. We came laden with market baskets and expanding *filets*, those wonderful nets, gathered together by a handle, that can carry an almost limitless amount of produce, depending only upon the strength of the shopper's arms. Our technique was to buy potatoes first (these filled the bottom of the net), then green vegetables, then fruit, and finally a few heads of lettuce, which could be crammed in at the top. The idea of a paper bag for each vegetable would have been utterly inconceivable. You simply piled your purchases into a given space, keeping the eggs, berries, and cheese on top, and sorted them out when you returned to your kitchen table.

Because of the weight-lifting problem, vegetable and fruit buying usually became my province, with the manly aid of little Phinney. The shrewder business of selecting meat, fish, poultry, and butter fell to *madame*, in earnest consultation with Clémentine. The venerable French custom of maneuvering for special privilege applies equally to the acquisition of a château, a seat in the Chamber of Deputies, or a mere cauliflower. I found a favorite vegetable woman and stuck to her, with the result that she would reserve her choicest produce under the table for the Beck family (and an appreciable *pourboire*). She was a memorable person with a fine moustache, a flashing smile, and more than ordinary displacement. In fact she bulged conspicuously over the chair that she always brought to market. '*Elle a de quoi s'asseoir*,' as I heard an interested observer remark.

Endive, leeks, artichokes, *cèpes* and other mushrooms were cheap and plentiful. So was every sort of fresh herb. Parsnips, lima beans, corn on the cob, and sweet potatoes did not exist. Aside from these differences, the Senlis vegetable market ran very much the way it does in a small American town: potatoes, onions, peas, carrots, string beans, cabbage, tomatoes, cucumbers, eggplant, turnips, broccoli – with the fine distinction that all the French vegetables had been picked when they were young, tender, and not fully grown. Why did those vegetables taste so good on your last trip to France? That is the answer, combined with the fact that they were probably cooked in prodigal quantities of pure butter.

As for fruit, the neat mounds of apples, pears, peaches, apricots, and oranges in the side aisle of this ancient market certainly couldn't compare in size or pulchritude with the pyramids of gorgeousness we now see daily in Mr Fred Popopulous's corner fruit exchange. But when it comes to *flavor*, the Beck family unanimously bestows its palm of excellence upon the small, unbeautiful fruit of France. I hope we don't sound disloyal. But too often the beauty of American 'store' fruit is skin deep. Beneath its superbly tinted cheek frequently lies a wan and listless taste, a hollow texture. Under the peasant roughness of Normandy fruit lurks a Latin ardor, blended with a patrician subtlety offlavor, that our buxom Anglo-Saxon specimens often seem to lack.

The town butchers moved into the apse of St Pierre on market day, lending one more note of color, this time predominantly crimson, to the cool stone vaults. The owner of the *boucherie chevaline* was there (color note: a deep maroon), smiling under a golden horse's head and underselling all his competitors pound for pound. So was the genial *charcutier*, whose ham pies and aromatic *saucissons de Lyon* were the joy of the town. So was the innocent-faced Madame Goujon, all too ready to club one of her pink-eyed rabbits over the head with a wooden stick and then skin it for you. So was the sheepish Monsieur Tarreaux, *marchand de volailles*, the only merchant for whom the peaceful Clémentine regularly reserved a black scowl. It all dated back to the day he sold us a fat, hefty, and expensive duck. Proudly Clémentine brought it back from market, only to find upon closer inspection that it had been stuffed with a roll of wet, heavy newspapers. Monsieur Tarreaux will not soon forget the avalanche of vituperation that descended upon him the next market day.

Steeled by a few such experiences, Madame Beck and Clémentine approached the business of buying meat with great seriousness and knew the cuts of beef, veal, lamb, and pork by heart. This knowledge does them little good now, for the American way of parceling a side of meat is totally different. They also knew how to *marchander*, and this psychological knack of driving a good bargain is far from useless in our new home. The thing we miss most in America is young veal – really young, tender veal with hardly a blush of pink to it, such as sad Monsieur Lesage (the butcher whose wife ran away with the *garçon de café*) used to cut into paper-thin *escalopes* or magnificently thick *côtelettes*. But there are two sides to the picture. No economical French housewife in Senlis ever dreamed of possessing the whole sugar-cured ham that is a happy commonplace in an American home.

One transept of the sixteenth-century building was given over to tables piled high with sweet biscuits, macaroons, and *pain d'épices*. The other transept held the two rival butter-and-cheese magnates of the town: the oily Monsieur Dupuit, whom we distrusted, along with some of his butter, and the plump Madame Veuve Legendre, whom we adored. The perfect *commerçant* will always be personified in my mind by this neat and energetic little woman, surrounded by vast mounds of butter, baskets of fresh eggs, and a glittering terrace of cheese. She made absolutely no compromise with quality. Her prices were invariably fair. When she dexterously scooped off butter with a wire cutter she gave full measure, but no more. The independent Senlis housewives would wait in line for her, but for nobody else – and she could keep four of them in conversation while waiting on a fifth. Madame Legendre had beautiful cheese. Fine, creamy, light-colored Roquefort was her specialty. Often she produced that rarity (even in France), a perfect Camembert or Brie. And her choice of other types, Pont-l'Evêque, Livarot, Coulommiers, Port-du-Salut, and Petit-suisse, was impeccable. We cherish the picture of Madame Legendre, her pouter-pigeon figure silhouetted against a cartwheel of Gruyère, although Wisconsin is helping us to forget.

The cool, sheltered cloisters of the one-time church provided a sequestered courtyard for the fish market, a noticeable convenience in the hot summer months. Here came iced crates of fish – English sole from Boulogne-sur-Mer, *merlans*, turbot, and tuna fish from Douarnenez. For the modest purse there were flat, ugly skates, which French ingenuity has made palatable in the form of *raie au beurre noir*. For the opulent there were fat *langoustes*, crustacean treasures well able to hold their own with Maine's choicest lobsters. In the right season great mounds of rosy shrimp, straight from Brittany, would be piled up on the marble-topped table nearest the exit. This was the final temptation for the Beck family, now heavily laden, and a kilo of *crevettes* would be stuffed into the *filet* before we emerged into the street.

Then came the incomparable moment to watch Gaspard. There are ingenious salesmen in this world, and there are great exponents of low comedy. We believe that Gaspard is a sublime combination of both. Gaspard sold corsets and cheap lingerie in the tiny paved court next to the dry goods store. His voice was hoarse, his manner compelling. With vast earnestness and eloquent gestures he would entreat the housewives to inspect peach-colored slips and pale-lavender rayon panties, bordered with shoddy écru lace. Finally he would assemble a capacity crowd, and then would come the exquisite event for which we had waited. With Chaplinesque subtlety, Gaspard's every gesture suddenly became feminine. He preened; he assumed a languid hauteur. Then, with magnificent mimicry, he snapped on a corset over his street clothes. With delicate poise he stepped into the panties and then slid the gaudy slip over his head. He turned around slowly, so that the farmers' wives could admire, and then, observing an elaborate decorum, he removed slip, panties, and corset, one by one. Then only did he resort to the telling gesture that broke the tension and sent the housewives into roars of hilarity. He scratched himself vigorously in the midriff. And the well-merited sales scramble was on . . .

The Beck family loves to go marketing in America, too. We think it is a *lot* of fun to push a two-decker baby carriage through an old theatre revamped as a serve-yourself grocery store. But without Gaspard, market day is never going to be quite the same.

Though Clémentine was the acknowledged mainspring of our gastronomic life, the town of Senlis generously provided other epicurean touches. One was the neighborhood grocer. Another was the vegetable garden. And most memorable of all was our ancient wine cellar.

Our grocer was a particular delight. Clémentine recognized that perishables had to be bought in the marketplace, but she had her own peasant ideas about staple groceries. She had a deep distrust of the gaudy chain stores, which had sprung up in the twenties, and even the long-established houses of Félix Potin and Julien Damoy could not dispel this suspicion from her thrifty mind. When the Beck larder needed sugar or salt, flour or rice, coffee or tea, Clémentine was convinced that there was only one sensible way of obtaining them – by trotting around the corner to the nearest independent *épicerie*. And thus the colorful Monsieur Aristide Roux and his even more picturesque shop came into our lives. On a timbered side street in our *quartier*, Aristide, a little gnome of a man with a black skullcap, kept a shop whose varied stock satisfied the immediate wants of a hundred or more neighboring families. Few Yankee general stores can boast of greater variety than Aristide stored in his ancient house. The faded sign over his shop window proclaimed that his was a grocery store, a dry goods emporium, a tobacco shop, and a café, all in one.

Finding farm life too strenuous, Aristide had come to town at the turn of the century. His love of the farm had come with him, however, and made itself felt in his merchandise. You could always find a good choice of seed and grain in a far corner of Aristide's store. Dusty saddles hung on the dark brown walls. In the back room was an aromatic assortment of used and new harnesses. Aristide had a particular specialty – secondhand horse collars – which added immensely to the atmosphere of his shop.

Of course, it's fun to buy dried peas and lentils and beans encased in cellophane, as we now do in our New England town. It's a great convenience to order by telephone – sometimes. It's nice to have a date on your coffee, a slogan stamped on your oranges, a chance to add twenty-five words or less to your soap wrapper and thus win a fortune. But we miss Aristide a lot, even though he growled a bit and wrapped everything in old newspapers.

Our vegetable garden was the particular domain of little Phinney, whose eagerness to exploit it for profit augurs well for his economic future. With a zeal patently lacking in his schoolwork, the youngster would begin to spade with the first early blush of spring. By May he was selling us the first fruits of his agricultural efforts, and by September his accrued profits amounted to almost enough to buy that coveted bicycle. Of course we all knew that the real mainstay of the vegetable garden was the genial and faintly simple old Monsieur Beaubernard, who spent three mornings a week there supplementing Phinney's efforts.

Our stone house was situated on the edge of the town, looking out upon open fields and a calm country road. Half a mile away, we could see a sprawling farmhouse framed in trees. Along the edge of this road was Phinney's plot of fertile loam, planted mostly in carrots, peas, string beans, and tomatoes. The outside of our high stone wall formed another boundary, and the two extremities of the plot were barricaded by a double row of assertive cabbages. Phinney's ambition led him to attempt eggplant, sweet peppers, and Brussels sprouts with fair success. He even started to grow corn, but being a sensitive child, gave it up when he overheard a very cruel remark which I quoted from *Le Rire*: '*Le maïs, c'est pour les cochons et les Américains.*' An ample space was given over to lettuce, chicory, and escarole, to the delight of the snails. Cucumber vines wove their way through the tomato plants. Against the inside of the garden wall, espaliered pear trees formed geometric patterns, troubled now and then by an enterprising pumpkin. Close to the wall, where they could get the maximum of reflected heat and sun, were the herbs – chervil, parsley, thyme, sweet marjoram, basil, and especially tarragon. Ah, those prodigal shoots of tarragon. How I wish we could make them grow that way in our new home! The soul of a *sauce béarnaise*, the aromatic secret of a fine vinegar, the fairest flower in many a *bouquet garni*, tarragon is a true aristocrat among herbs. We have never tasted anything better than the tender young chickens Clémentine used to prepare for us, stuffing them generously with branches of fresh tarragon and basting them incessantly until they were roasted a perfect crisp brown. The herbs were removed before serving, when their haunting fragrance had permeated the bird, with sublime results.

Secure inside the garden wall were our chicken yard and rabbit hutch, both enclosed in a cage-like contraption resembling an aviary. Here some tender broilers passed their childhood, in company with a squad of ducks and a few seasoned veterans that had become permanent friends of the family. There was Alfred, the plump pet duck, who was skinny and forlorn when I first won him at the carnival, and Gringoire the goose, who resolutely refused to get fatty degeneration of the liver and thus always escaped the Christmas axe. Clémentine finished the careers of many of our ducks by the rather startling method of driving a pair of scissors through the tops of their heads, and then prying the scissors open. But Alfred and Gringoire always remained serene and unmolested. We also grew sentimental over Marius and Olive, the white rabbits, who finally became enormous, as did the cost of their upkeep. We found a home for all four of them when we left for America, but we worry about them now and then, the food situation being what it is just now in France.

1943

British Bouquet

In these adventurous days when the sky is by no means the limit, travelers set off on all sorts of improbable expeditions. Nobody encounters raised eyebrows if he undertakes a safari into Africa or climbs glaciers in Alaska. It has been our recent experience, however, that the mention of *one* type of pilgrimage meets with a variety of emotions, from scorn and incredulity to raucous hilarity. Just announce that you are contemplating a gastronomic tour of the British Isles and you will see what we mean!

A few years ago, when we sought out some of our friends in England and told them of our projected travels, the reaction was all but unanimous: 'Listen, old boy, you're *not* going to attempt a Bouquet of Britain!' or 'You'll never sell warm beer to the Americans!' A look of consternation, pity, amusement, or pained solicitude passed over their faces, depending upon how each regarded the institution of British cooking. Here and there were glimmerings of hope. After all, they admitted, one dines extremely well in London – in a select group of restaurants. Dover sole, Angus beef, and Stilton cheese are things of un-rivaled splendor. There is nothing quite so good as steak-and-kidney pie when prepared by an English master. And the British are discriminating wine drinkers. But all this did not justify a series of epicurean tours promising the traveler a tempting dinner every night, as similar jaunts in France and Italy had done.

As a consequence, we founded our travels on a different theme – the charm of the British countryside. Now, after rolling through Britain for four leisurely summers and covering uncounted thousands of miles, we are convinced of two things: first, that we have never traveled in a more beautiful country, and second, that life is not so bleak for the gastronome after all. In fact, he frequently fares very well indeed . . .

There is no better way to break up the day on the road than by that noble institution, the roadside picnic. The English shops provide the staples for superlative outdoor feasts. Their Yorkshire ham, cold roast beef, veal, ham and pork pies, smoked tongue and sausage are excellent, and their cheeses are tasty and filling. There is nothing better than the British crackers and cheese biscuits that are exported throughout the world and which make a perfect accompaniment. Small, ripe English tomatoes are delicious, and fruit from the Vale of Evesham – plums, pears, peaches, and apricots – is rich in taste and sweetness. The more fastidious picnicker will find cooked Dublin Bay prawns and rosy boiled shrimps, not to mention cold boiled lobster, at any good fish store. Finally, a bottle of good claret, Burgundy, or Hock is available at the wine shop, where stout, ale, and beer are also for sale. And don't forget a bottle of Sherry for your apéritif! Clearly enough, a small picnic hamper is the motorist's staunch friend in Britain!

In America we are accustomed to a definite pattern of modern accommodations – motels on the outskirts of centers of population, small hotels in the town squares, and multiple-storied hostelries in the cities. A private bath adjoins each room as a matter of course. The hotels are invariably heated, often uncomfortably so. A television set has usually been installed in every bedroom, in addition to the telephone, the radio, the Gideon Bible, the corkscrew on the wall, and the pincushion adorned with buttons, needles, and thread.

The hotels of Britain are far more diverse, more individual, and, usually, older. Some are venerable posting inns that are relics of stagecoach days. Others are converted castles, country estates, or even monasteries. Many vine-grown Tudor buildings or rambling brick relics from Victorian times serve as hotels, and there are half-timbered pubs and thatched village inns scattered over much of the countryside. Modern hotels there are too, especially in the coastal resorts.

Today's transatlantic traveler will find a certain adventure in British hotels, and far greater variety. Private bathrooms, it is true, are not always available, but each bedroom has hot and cold running water. In most hotels the public baths are spotless, and usually the American fetish for a private bath adjusts to the situation. Television there is, but in a special, darkened lounge. Each British hotel that we recommend has one or more hospitable bars, and you really don't need a corkscrew on the wall. The Bible, of course, comes in handy.

The day begins auspiciously in a British hotel. First of all, you have only to indicate your desires upon retiring, and you will be awakened, not by the jangle of the telephone, but by that staunch British institution, early morning tea. Without ceremony, someone (usually a brisk, middle-aged maid) bursts into the bedroom with a passkey and plumps a tray of hot tea, sugar, and milk on the night table. It is uncompromising, perhaps, but it wakes you up, and whets your appetite for the more substantial breakfast that follows. The morning paper from London is under your door if you have requested it, and your shoes are there in the hall, neatly polished, an old European custom.

Breakfast is the most cheerful meal in a British hotel, and many consider it the best. None of that restrained 'Continental breakfast' of a *croissant*, jam, and coffee here! This is a real Anglo-Saxon breakfast, beginning with a fruit or a substantial porridge. A choice of good things follows. One standard dish is Wiltshire or Danish bacon with fresh country eggs, usually fried or scrambled. Another favored combination is spiced sausage with bacon, grilled tomatoes, and mushrooms. Horrifying to the visiting French, but satisfying to solid British citizens, are finnan haddie or kippers, served with boiled potatoes, or grilled kidneys on toast. Following this is the invariably cool but crisp toast in a metal rack, with marmalade and tea or coffee. Substantial is indeed the word for a British breakfast . . .

If the average rural hotel is a friendly and convivial place, it is due largely to its bars, which are gathering places for townspeople and neighboring gentry as well as the hotel guests. The Public Bar is usually the domain of the local citizens. It is their informal club, and the hotel guest may feel like something of an intruder. The Private Bar and the Saloon Bar, with broad comfortable easy chairs and low tables, tend to be more exclusive. In a genuinely old inn, the bar is usually a fascinating place, its ceiling supported by smoke-stained oak beams. Its ancient furniture is highly polished, its walls are bedecked with old prints and polished horse brasses, while a wood fire burns gently in the fireplace. Ladies are always welcome, and the atmosphere is invariably respectable. The barmaid behind the counter is sometimes pert and pretty, but she often resembles a staid, straitlaced schoolteacher. Sensible self-service prevails here. You obtain the drinks for your party at the bar, pay for them at once, and bring them back to your table. It is expeditious, and it couldn't be simpler. The most popular drink is beer, drawn cool from the keg, or ale or stout, both waiting in bottles behind the bar. They are served at room temperature, a fact that disturbs many overseas visitors, who expect their beer to be iced. There is one way out of this dilemma – order iced lager. The barman does consent to ice the fine lager beers that come from Denmark, Germany, and Holland. Time proves the British right about their warm beer, however. After a while it comes to taste quite natural, and delicious.

Sherry is a popular favorite in Britain, where the finest ones, ranging from the old, tawny, and sweet to the highly polished and extremely dry are available. Sherry is usually served in a tall, wasp-waisted glass that doesn't hold very much. This is one way of keeping the price reasonable, but you will be happier with a double Sherry, we think.

There are many gin combinations, of course, and plenty of people order fruit juices or soft drinks. Nothing is better than good Scotch whisky as a key to conviviality, and it is usually served rather frugally in a small glass with water. It seems inadequate, especially since it is only 70-proof Scotch compared to the 86-proof we are used to. But this is another way of cutting down the price – and the consumption. The British barman is notoriously parsimonious with his ice, and it is doubtful if anything can ever be done about it. But he does have an ice bucket with small cubes in it, and if you want some for your Scotch, ask for it in a firm and compelling voice. French brandy is always at hand, but American bourbon is a rarity. Pubs and bars must observe strict closing hours, but they are always open before and after mealtimes.

Statistics of the French wine industry reveal that Great Britain is by far its best foreign customer. Not only for still table wine, but for Champagne, Cognac, Sherry, Port, and Madeira the British are generous importers and conscientious consumers. This is indeed good news for the visiting oenophile, who discovers that even the remote provincial hotels in Britain will produce a respectable wine list. In London, of course, the choice of good wines is extraordinary. A top West End restaurant will display a selection of fine wines from Burgundy, Bordeaux, Alsace, Champagne, and the Rhine that surpasses that of the *caves* of most Paris restaurants. There is often a choice of old years going back to the 1880s in some venerable shrines, although the 1950s now dominate the lists.

A group of hotels such as the Trust House chain buys wine in France in quantity, assuring a most respectable bottle at a reasonable stipend. Time and again we have chosen a Trust House, secure in the knowledge that we would find a reliable bottle of Château Gruaud-Larose for less than a pound.

After this enumeration of the virtues of British hotels and restaurants, we must call attention to a few drawbacks. First of all, although a good French wine seems assured, having it properly chilled is something else again. The red wines offer little complication, but the problem of having a white wine served at the right temperature is a thorny one in most country hotels. Either the ice is in short supply, or the ice bucket is lacking in many rural inns, and the best the flustered waiter can do is to place your bottle in the 'fridge' for an insufficient chilling. The docile British diner usually accepts the situation and allows the waiter to bring an unchilled bottle of Sauternes to the table, where it sits in tepid solitude. We have seen unchilled bottles of Champagne uncorked at the table with a shower of bubbles that doused the guests and completely surprised the waiter. The best way out of the situation is to decide well ahead of time whether you are ordering fish or meat, and in the case of the former insist upon a wine bucket or a speedy transfer to the ice box. Some restaurants keep their white wines under permanent refrigeration, and that isn't good either . . .

The institution of British cooking has long been lampooned by the British themselves. It is the butt of constant sarcasm, and uproariously funny things have been written about it, particularly by P. Morton Shand, whose essay on English boiled cabbage is a classic of all time. The dry, overcooked roast, the tasteless vegetables swimming in water, the tepid brown soup, and the synthetic custards are with us still, beyond a doubt. However, we really don't feel entitled to say much about the defects of the British cuisine, coming from a country,

as we do, where steaks are cooked in a few seconds under infrared rays, where the steam table is the restaurateur's faithful ally, and where TV dinners, hot dogs, hamburgers, dill pickles, soft drinks, and peanut butter sandwiches are among the essentials of life. At least the British don't bake marshmallows on top of sweet potatoes, or roast ham with pineapple.

Britain has come through its long day of austerity with flying colors and trim waistlines. Today the larder is full, and an upsurge of good cooking is under way. To appreciate the plenitude of good things now available, we urge all epicurean travelers in London to pay a visit to two extraordinary food shops. One is the famous Fortnum and Mason store on Piccadilly, where a dashing young man in a morning coat and striped trousers will sell you anything from a gorgeous crock of *pâté de foie gras* to a tin of sardines. The other is the unforgettable Victorian temple of gastronomy at Harrods, in Knightsbridge, surely the most beautiful food shop in the world. These will give an idea of the richness and variety of products available to the public today.

In the realm of seafood, for example, Harrods' marble counters are generously arrayed with the incomparable Dover sole, aristocrat of all restaurant fish, the delectable turbot, the loyal Scottish salmon, and many lesser fry. For breakfast there is smoked haddock which becomes finnan haddie or Arbroath smokie, or smoked herring which becomes either a kipper or a bloater. In season there are some of the world's finest oysters from Colchester or Whitstable. Here are spiny lobsters from the Orkney Islands, rosy shrimps from Cornwall, and tempting Dublin Bay prawns that are gradually acquiring the Italian name of *scampi*.

Nearby are handsome sides of British beef from Aberdeen Angus herds, or perhaps from Hereford or Galloway, and spring lamb from Wales. Ham and bacon from Yorkshire and Wiltshire compete with savory imports from Canada and Denmark. There is veal too, the best being the pale, milk-fed article from Holland. Plump country chickens, geese, turkeys, and Aylesbury ducks await the housewife, who also finds pheasant, quail, and that rare luxury, grouse, in season. The greengrocers' realm is heaped high with the cabbage, sprouts, peas, asparagus, and potatoes that can be so disconcerting when drowned in water, and so good when properly cooked. Nothing is better than the small ripe English tomato, and what can rival their juicy strawberries, cherries, red and black currants, rhubarb, and gooseberries?

The cheese counter is international, of course, but some of the best cheeses are British. The famous Stilton is probably the prima donna of the lot, but Cheddar, Cheshire, Wensleydale, and Double Gloucester can hold their own against the best foreign competition.

Confronted with this panorama of plenty, this choice of fundamentals, one is inclined to wonder about the dismal reputation of British cooking. Is it really possible to ruin such choice materials? The answer cannot be an unqualified yes – some products defy the most indifferent cook. But there are rural hotel kitchens in Britain that can make a shambles out of almost all these delectable things. They can extract the flavor from fish, dry up a good roast, broil a steak to the consistency of shoe leather, and bring a bird to the table roasted to rags.

The questing gourmet traveling in Britain will be surprised to find so few regional specialties available in country hotels. True, there are Cornish pasties and Devonshire cream with strawberries awaiting in the Western counties, but the gourmet will usually search in vain for such specialties as Lancashire hotpot, steak-and-kidney pie, or cock-a-leekie soup. In its stead he encounters a routine menu that soon becomes wearisome. Before long he has it memorized. As hors-d'œuvre: potted shrimps, *pâté maison*, chilled fruit juices. For fish: fried filet of plaice (an absolute fixture), trout *meunière*, cold salmon with mayonnaise. As an entrée: ox tongue and spinach, grilled pork chop, roast lamb, spring chicken, Aylesbury duckling, or grilled steak with the inevitable 'two veg' – potatoes and garden peas or sprouts. For dessert: peach Melba, trifle, ice cream, or cheese and biscuits. There is certainly nothing wrong with this honest choice of viands, but the constant repetition dulls its appeal.

1963

WANDA L. FROLOV

Katish, Our Russian Cook

My Aunt Martha was a woman of firm character and an itching sense of responsibility. Though she was Father's younger sister, she had always felt competent to advise him in matters financial, marital, or moral. Father was used to her and he would nod gravely at her over his pipe and go on with his thoughts, hardly hearing a word she said. But when Father died, Mother was left pretty much at Aunt Martha's mercy, for Mother had always been sorry for this well-intentioned sister-in-law who had never had a husband or children of her own on whom to exercise her passion for management.

Fortunately, a good part of Aunt Martha's improving energies found an outlet in organized charities. Mother felt vastly relieved when she began to take an interest in the Russian émigrés who were arriving on the Pacific Coast in the early twenties. They were some of the refugees from the Russian revolution who had poured into China and Japan and had been among the lucky few to obtain visas for America. But even these charitable interests had a way of backfiring on Mother.

I had just come in from school one afternoon when I saw my aunt's high, old-fashioned electric coupé pull up at our door. She felt that an electric was the only really lady-like mode of transportation still available; she would have preferred a carriage and pair if she could have afforded the outlay and upkeep. Though Aunt Martha must have been hardly forty in 1924, in spirit she belonged to an earlier generation. Her clothes, too, were of another period, for at a time when fashions denied the existence of feminine bosoms and merely hinted at a waistline surprisingly located where it must be sat upon, she presented a well-corseted hourglass figure.

Whenever she visited our white clapboard house in West Los Angeles, her walk up the garden path provided two fine topics for advice. First, there was the extravagantly large garden which Mother insisted upon keeping up, when in the growing city it could have been sold as a building lot; and second, there was the frankly old-fashioned aspect of the house. Aunt Martha insisted that Mother should follow the prevailing mode for putting a plaster false-front on old houses and dubbing them Spanish Colonial. Not to do so was to allow the value of the property to go down. Los Angeles was indulging in an orgy of pale pink, dull orange, and even lavender stucco bungalows that looked more edible than livable. But today, it was easy to see that our relative had more pressing matters to discuss. She nipped up the garden path without so much as a disapproving glance at the bright flower beds.

'I've found just the girl for you, Mary!' she announced breathlessly to Mother the minute she entered the living room.

'Girl? What are you talking about, Martha?'

'Why, a girl to cook for you, and to help with the housework, of course. You know we were discussing the Swedish girl I found last week and you thought she wouldn't be suitable. Now Katish is different – she was made for you.'

Katish, Aunt Martha explained, talking very fast so that Mother couldn't interpose any objections, was Ekaterina Pavlovna Belaev; she was a young Russian woman, of good but simple family, widowed in the war. After the revolution, she had made her way with admirable courage and resourcefulness through Russian Turkestan and the wilder outer regions of China to Harbin and then to America. She knew little English, though she had studied diligently during the months that she had waited in Harbin for her American visa. She had not been trained to earn a living, but she was an excellent cook, and naturally as neat and clean as a new pin. She didn't expect a large salary, but she was in urgent need of a good home, and how could Mother, who claimed to be a Christian, turn her away?

Mother looked uncomfortable. I thought she was weakening. Bub, my fourteen-year-old brother, who had come in by this time, took up the cudgels in defense of the family. 'Aw, Mother, we don't want any old foreign cook,' he protested. 'I like your cooking. Why don't you get this woman a job with some of your rich friends, Aunt Martha?'

Aunt Martha hedged. It was evident that her wealthier friends had been tried and found not wanting an untrained servant. 'Well, Mary,' Aunt Martha said, nettled into imprudence, 'I don't see what you can do but take this poor girl for a time, because I've already promised her that you would.'

At this barefaced statement Mother rallied and said quite firmly that she not only did not need a cook; she wasn't going to have one, and her sister-in-law could get out of the matter in the best way she could.

Bub and I rejoiced in Mother's victory. Aunt Martha's protégés were apt to be peculiar – occasionally they were alarming. The last time Mother had succumbed to her appeal to the Christian spirit, we had found ourselves with a cook who took no pains to disguise her triumphant certainty that the whole family was headed for perdition. This worried us for a week, until we found out that the poor woman was a member of one of those queer religious sects which flourished under the warm Southern California sun. She believed that bodily comfort was a sin and she announced her intention of sleeping on a pallet on her bedroom floor. This was all right with Mother, but it was something of a shock to learn that she had gone so far as to sell the bed which Mother had provided – bedstead, springs, and mattress – and contribute the proceeds to her church. Mother discovered this strange evidence of religious zeal on the same day that the cook discovered that we occasionally used liquor in cooking. The cook departed forthwith, adding the vociferous threat of jail for our liquorous iniquities to her previous threats of damnation. The experience had not left us in a receptive mood toward Aunt Martha's suggestions.

Our redoubtable relative seemed to accept Mother's refusal this time. For a week she was sweet and agreeable and appeared to have forgotten all about the needy Russians. But one afternoon Bub and I came in from school to find Katish established in our kitchen!

Mother hurried us upstairs to explain and admonish us to civilized behavior. Aunt Martha, it seemed, had brought Katish to see her that morning. They had eleven o'clock coffee in the garden and as they chatted pleasantly it had gradually become clear to Mother that Katish still thought that Mother had sent for her and that her belongings were out in front in the electric automobile! Aunt Martha blandly avoided Mother's eye while these amazing facts were sinking in; she knew that Mother, after breaking bread with Katish and hearing the Russian woman's delight in her beloved rose garden, could never deal her the hurt of sending her away.

Katish's English, though odd, had been sufficient to convey her gratitude in being offered this pleasant place to live and work. 'Ai, is nice! I like!'

Mother was stymied and she knew it.

We had to admit that Katish did look jolly. She was a little one side or the other of thirty. Her short, sturdy figure, wide mouth, and snub nose in a round face gave her a look of cheerful reliability. But it was her dancing black eyes that fascinated us. They were large and perfectly round, and resembled the luscious black cherries that the grocer has polished to put in the very front of the window. You couldn't resist them.

And that Katish definitely could cook was immediately apparent.

'Gosh! I'll bet Aunt Martha didn't know that Katish was such a *good* cook!' Bub speculated unkindly as he bit into a piece of creamy cheese cake. 'She probably thought she'd feed us on raw carrots and such junk.' Bub's resentment had been considerably softened by Mother's announcement that he wouldn't have to go to dancing school any longer. Even Katish's small salary would make some adjustments necessary.

The cheese cake that Bub munched so contentedly was the first we had ever tasted that did not have the regrettable texture of peanut butter. That cake was later to win Katish a proposal of marriage, much to Aunt Martha's chagrin. Here is the recipe; I have never found one to compare with it.

KATISH'S CHEESE CAKE. *Cover the bottom of a spring form mold with 18 pieces of finely crushed zwieback mixed with 1½ tablespoons each of butter and sugar. Then cream 1 cup plus 2 tablespoons of sugar with 4 packages of Philadelphia cream cheese. Add 2 level tablespoons of flour, a pinch of salt, a 1-inch length of vanilla bean finely cut, and the beaten yolks of 4 eggs. Mix well and add 1 cup of sour cream. Fold in 4 stiffly beaten egg whites and pour into the crumb-lined pan. Bake in a moderate oven (350°) for about one hour. The crumb crust will be thin and crisp and the cake very light and creamy.*

Katish was tremendously interested in everything she saw about her in this strange country and Bub and I were flattered when she came to us for explanations. On the first Saturday after she was installed in our kitchen I was delegated to take her into the city to shop for some equipment that our late departed cook had allowed to scorch beyond repair during moments of what must have been deep religious abstraction. Katish thoroughly enjoyed our ride in the streetcar. She surprised the harassed conductor by pausing to wish him a pleasant good-morning, and it seemed only natural for me to relinquish to her my usual seat next the window, for she found all the sights of the busy street enchanting. But as the car approached the intersections with its bell clanging a raucous warning she would shut her eyes tightly. '*Boshe moi!* Is miracle we are alive!' she would exclaim with dramatic relief when we had passed safely through the skeins of interlocking traffic.

I took her to the housewares department of a large store and seeing her delight in the gleaming aluminum and gay pottery, I'm afraid I encouraged her to charge more than the minimum necessities to Mother's account. When we left the store, Katish turned and stood looking back into its busy aisles.

'There are thousands of people in the store at any hour of the day,' I told her, seeking to impress. 'Hundreds of clerks alone.'

'So I am thinking,' Katish answered anxiously. 'But I am thinking, what happen if all people decide to go out at the same time?'

I had to admit that I didn't know. It might be pretty disastrous – something like a theatre fire. For a moment the idea was alarming. 'But they never do,' I reassured Katish and myself. 'They just never want to. Let's go have a soda.'

So we went into an Owl Drug Store and had chocolate sodas. Katish was fascinated. She had eaten frozen mousses in Russia and real ice cream in China, but she had never experienced the delight of a soda. At first she wasn't sure that it was proper for a grown-up person to suck up the liquid part through a straw. It seemed a childish thing to do. But the ticklish soda got up her nose and the lump of ice cream rose alarmingly to the top of the glass when she tilted it. She picked up the straws and followed my example, and a smile of pure bliss overspread her friendly face. Sucking happily, she nodded her approval at me over the glass and her conversion to the ice cream soda was complete. She decided that the American drug store was a really wonderful institution when she found that she could buy there an article of kitchen equipment that the housewares department hadn't been able to supply.

When we reached home I went into the kitchen with Katish to see what we were going to have for dinner. Since we children were at home for a hot lunch on Saturdays, Mother had established the custom of a light supper in the evening. 'What are we having, Katish?' I inquired with interest, since an ice cream soda is merely an appetizer to a thirteen-year-old.

'We have mushrooms and ham and the fine salad.' Katish brought out a big basket of mushrooms looking like so many miniature umbrellas fashioned of creamy, delicate silk.

'No dessert!' I yelped in greedy protest, forgetting to express my appreciation of the mushrooms.

'Well, maybe kissel, if no bread and jam now.' Katish shook an admonitory finger. It hadn't taken her long to learn that Bub and I could do with a snack at any hour. But we were pleased that she never said anything foolish about spoiling our appetites for dinner. We had the fine, ferocious appetites of healthy adolescents, and spoiling them was next to impossible.

Her delectable hot sandwiches of mushrooms in sour cream over thin slices of ham were superb, if temporary, appeasement.

MUSHROOMS IN SOUR CREAM. *Wash 1 pound of mushrooms quickly. Never, never let mushrooms stand in water. Cut off the stems just where they cease to be woody; but do not peel. Slice each cap from the top down through the stalk. Heat 3 tablespoons of butter in a heavy pan. When pan and butter are hot, but not burning, put in a layer of the mushrooms. Don't overcrowd the pan and don't bruise the mushrooms with rough stirring; if you do these things the juice will run out and boil away. When the first lot of mushrooms is delicately browned, remove them from the pan, heat a little more fat if necessary, and brown another layer. When all the slices are nicely browned, stir 2 tablespoons of flour into the fat remaining in the pan. Add 1½ cups of milk and stir to form a smooth sauce. Return all the mushrooms to the pan, stir in ½ cup of sour cream, salt and pepper to taste, and add 3 or 4 drops of Maggi Seasoning. Cook over low heat for five or six minutes. Used sparingly, Maggi Seasoning points up the flavor of mushrooms, but too much of it will give a flavor of dried mushrooms.*

MUSHROOM AND HAM SANDWICHES. *Prepare a thin slice of buttered toast for each serving. Over the toast place a thin slice of delicately flavored baked or boiled ham which has been quickly sautéed in a little butter or ham fat. Then pour over each serving a generous amount of bubbling hot mushrooms in sour cream.*

Katish had prepared a large basket of the mushrooms and not all of them would be needed for that night's supper. We were to learn that a generous jar of these mushrooms in sour cream in the icebox was a stand-by of Katish's cuisine. Like most Russians, Katish felt that hospitality was a spontaneous thing. She would have been greatly wounded if ever Mother had been forced to say, 'I do wish we could have urged the Smiths to stay to dinner, but I just don't know what we could have given them.' Katish always had something on hand for unexpected guests and she accomplished it without extravagance or waste.

The mushrooms in sour cream would keep for days and their subtly delicious flavor enhanced and extended a number of dishes to elegance and abundance. If the larder was really low Katish might hard-boil an egg for each person. Then she would open up a can of shrimp or lobster or boned chicken. She would split the eggs in half lengthwise and arrange them in a shallow casserole with the seafood or chicken, then pour the mushrooms over and heat in a moderate oven. With a big salad, this made a meal. Or she might give us the mushrooms hot and savory on tiny circles of toast as a starting course for a light meal. This is one of the best ways to use them. They are worthy of a place by themselves and a receptive palate.

The kissel that Katish promised me is a very common Russian dessert, served alike to children and sophisticates. It is made of fruit juice thickened with potato starch. Some types of juice benefit for adult tastes by the addition of a little good brandy or port. With a few cans of fruit juice in the pantry it can be made up in five minutes' time.

KISSEL. *Apricot, apple, loganberry, and raspberry juice all make excellent kissel. For each cup of juice, use about 2 teaspoons of potato starch. Moisten the starch with a little of the juice and put the remaining juice into a saucepan over a low fire. Stir in enough sugar to sweeten, but take care not to overdo it. When the fruit juice and sugar mixture comes to a boil, stir in the moistened potato starch. Stir briskly for a minute or two and take from the fire. Chill thoroughly before serving.*

A spoonful of brandy stirred into apricot juice after it has been taken from the fire is delicious. Or you may use the brandy to flavor whipped cream to be served with the dessert.

Bottled apple juice makes a wonderful kissel when it is combined with an equal quantity of port and a teaspoon of finely grated lemon peel.

Katish took particular delight in preparing the big wooden bowls of green salad that we had almost every night. Never in her life had she seen such gorgeous displays of fruits and vegetables as those of the California markets.

Oranges, great globes of purest gold, were banked in a lavish splendor that was breathtaking to one who had been accustomed to regard them as a special Christmas treat. Jade-green cabbages and royal-purple eggplants vied in beauty with more exotic vegetables such as delicate avocados, artichokes like great close-hearted emerald flowers, and, in early summer, fat tender spears of asparagus.

A smile of wonder came over Katish's piquant features as she viewed this abundance. 'Ai, Paradise has been given to the Americantzi,' she breathed.

But Katish refused to be dazzled when it came to making her purchases. The market men soon learned that only the freshest and best of their beautiful wares could get into Katish's basket. Mother had suggested that Katish telephone for supplies, but that proved to be more involved than Mother had counted on. Katish's English often needed the aid of her expressive hands and eyes to be comprehensible, for at first she could not remember the American names of all the fruits and vegetables. And besides, she didn't want to be cheated of that delightful daily excursion. It was some distance from our house to the shopping center, and the only car in the family at that time was a deplorable, cut-down affair known as The Menace, and belonging to Bub. This unreliable chariot was not always available.

Katish took the difficulty in stride. '*Nitchevo*. It is nothing. I go on my foot.' And so she did.

She displayed a mind of her own when it came to selecting foods and planning menus. Mother solved the problem of a suitable budget by giving her a certain sum of money at the beginning of each week and letting her spend it as she thought best. It wasn't a large sum, but hardly a month was to pass without Katish's appearing with a present that she had bought for Mother with the money she had saved. It never seemed to occur to either of them that she might have returned the money instead. Katish loved giving presents and Mother loved getting them, so that was that.

A thing we'd better get straight right away, if we're going to understand each other and Katish, is just what is the sour cream she used in preparing so many of her fine dishes. Katish's horror knew no bounds when she ordered it days ahead of time from our grocer and then found that the well-meaning but benighted soul had simply put aside a bottle of fresh cream to sour for her! Sour cream is especially prepared and packaged at the dairy. When properly fresh, it has a very delicate sour taste, and none of the unpleasant odor of stale cream. It is thick, almost as thick as whipped cream, and much more delicious. One very good use for the uncooked sour cream (*smetana* is the Russian word for it) that we learned from Katish is as a condiment for snappy radishes. You dip the radish in sour cream and then in salt, and it is really very good.

Americans look surprised when Russians put butter on their radishes; but it's all right, they only do this when sour cream isn't offered!

Among Americans it is usually safer to refer to sour cream by some euphemism. Katish simply called it Russian cream after one or two disappointing encounters with timid souls.

1947

BARBARA KAFKA

Tempest in a Samovar

My father loved storms, water pounding into already muddy earth, the rich scent of the wet ground carrying a hint of mold, god-bearing cracks of light-ning and body-shaking thumps of thunder. He would sit on an awninged terrace to be spectator, possessed and possessor of nature's big effect. Frightened, I would join him, trying to live up to his exhilaration. I loved my father, was an acolyte trying to share his vision and not be afraid of his storms. I have never been ill on a boat; he boasted of his years on ocean liners when only he and the captain arrived for dinner. In the wind's shout, I heard his voice and tensed against alarm.

This is how I learned about food, amid the alarms of the dinner table, his pleasure surrounded by the family fights. The food sheltered me; I grew round as I built a wall against their anger, which sought to shred me between the talons of competing ambitions, assign me roles and set goals that if achieved could only displease one while satisfying the other. The food covertly put me on my father's side. He took the steak bone from the platter and gnawed it, smearing his mouth with fat and flecks of charred bone, his teeth grating into the hard surface, his tongue seeking out bits of marrow and shreds of sweet flesh, to my mother's flesh-fearing disgust. I learned that the sweetest meat lies near the bone.

He drank and his many brothers drank. Together they drank, challenging each other with their ice-cold native vodka. The clear liquid was a booby trap, hot with long-soaked small red peppers, but clear as rainwater. Who would gag, who would reel? When he drank with them, the bitter arguments, the arm wrestling were softened by love and shared memories. They listened to news from the Russian front and ate herring in cream with sliced onions, smoked salmon, sturgeon, and a fish they called *kipchunkie* (which I later learned to call sable) and, finally, smoked black cod. There were bagels too hard for me to bite, black Russian pumpernickel, and what they called cornbread, a throwback to Europe where wheat was 'corn'. The bread was dense and heavy and has dis-appeared. No one will any longer make the dough, too thick for machines. He ate the heel, the crumb of bread was for the effete, along with white meat of chicken and desserts.

He taught me to eat pickles from the barrel, the juice running down my arm, and took me to restaurants when I was mother-abandoned. She was out of town, often in Washington, doing important work – beyond objection – for the government during the great war. His was the ultimate revenge and seduction. We had lunch at Lüchow's. His office was nearby, and he was proud of his charge card: number 1. We ate herring in dill mustard sauce and puffy, plate-sized apple pancakes, boiled beef with lots of horseradish, and I sipped his beer.

At Chambord, we sat outdoors on a spring night, beyond the copper-pot view of the kitchen, a kitchen where they would prepare, if you would wait, any dish from the classic French repertoire, and my father ordered – the whole restaurant stopped to stare – a nineteen-dollar bottle of wine in 1945 when I was twelve. I remember the bottle shape, a Bordeaux, the year a '29; but the name is clogged in memory. I fell in love with the idea of France, the country vital to my father's business but whose language remained arcane to him. Later, that was my victory, my French.

My mother did not, does not cook. Like learning to type, it was something for servants. She scrambled to success with education as grappling tool and was moving always upward, bringing sometimes a memory of a tasted recipe for Rachel, a recipe reflecting the ever-increasing image of the better life, first, *moules marinière*, then fillet of sole *bonne femme*. She liked chocolate ice cream and tried French with a clumsy accent. I learned that food was part of travel and distant places.

Rachel was not a nice person, and why should she be, a black woman living in a tiny room – a maid's room – in the Fifth Avenue apartment without a view of self-proclaimed liberals? But she was a superb natural cook and always there from the time I was four until the apartment with the view could be bought and she didn't fit. My mother fought her leaving. My father was remorseless and Rachel went to work in his factory. I didn't miss her. By then I was leaving as well, glad to escape the escalating sound of fighting, the several glasses of Scotch too many, and the disappointment of a woman whom the end of Depression and war left without a clear cause.

I didn't spend time in the kitchen with Rachel. I lived in Barsetshire, Jane Austen's Hampshire, Joyce's Dublin, Swann's attar-of-roses Paris, and Stendhal's provinces. I swallowed the sentimental sour of Edna St Vincent Millay and Dorothy Parker. I gobbled Yeats, Eliot, and Mallarmé and wandered lonely through picture galleries learning the strange green faces of gold-framed madonnas, the melodrama of red in El Greco, the tear-provoking response of

Cézanne's solid geometry, and the liquid geometry of Dali. I danced, and a savage in music, I could hear only the insistent beat of ballets, the enticements of my father's gypsy records, and the voice-carried sweetness of opera. And what I wrote I hid.

But Rachel did teach me that cooking was an improvisation and a response. My mother's hints of dishes produced, from Rachel's pots, wonderful flavors, and, for the few people Rachel liked, there were mysteriously good chocolate cakes to eat late at night with whole bottles of milk.

Refuge in the mind-world of college brought no relief. I courted favor, writing other people's papers, better than my own. To produce was too frightening, a challenge to my father's fragilely male repudiation of my mother's achievement, a challenge to my mother's expansive competition, her flight through six degrees. It was to risk annihilation, and I graduated with a cum, summa generals, and a summa thesis written late at night in the last hurried hours before the deadline in the less frightening, public space of my dorm's living room.

I worked, I married, and I fled again from my parents' house as I tried to learn, awkwardly, what a home might be, a place that was not perpetually neat and ready to be viewed, one filled with the smell of onions and garlic and welcoming to hoped-for friends. I learned to cook. It was not frightening. It was all there in my friends the books, often wrapped in the festivity of French. I spread six or seven on the floor and learned of food as I had learned to learn. Comparing recipes, I tried to see through them to the times when they were written, the personalities of the cooks, and to an ultimate version of whatever dish I would serve, a try at loving, too late at night. I was still not able to judge the time and space of recipes, had not yet learned to listen to the changing sound of bubbles in the pot, the varying smells from the oven.

I had found the way to invert and supersede my father's intrusive pleasures, avoid my mother, and reject their worlds. I worked with my hands. I was a cook. I learned a new language, recipes.

In this new language I found work. I had wanted to write great poetry, but my fears of competing in my parents' worlds crippled my ambition. As if by happenstance, but surely by the intuition of others, I found that people would pay me to write about food, about what I had traveled and tasted, what my hyperacuity – honed in staying short of danger in those nightly dinner-table battles – made me taste and replicate and feel. In that work, everything I knew and the ways I had learned to see was of use. If we look, food has the structure of linguistics and religion. It is sociology and economics, politics and cultural definition; it is history, memory, and passion interwoven with style as clearly as painting, literature, dance, music, and architecture. Yet it is without the risks of high art.

Food is about loving and giving and performance and applause. It is poly-morphous, combining what had been the professional work of men with what had been the largely invisible, perhaps because ubiquitous, labors of women. It is essential and sensuous. I found a home where my father's storm could be tamed to the bubbles and steam of my grandmother's samovar.

1992

ROBERT FARRAR CAPON

Water in Excelsis

. . . Consider first the teetotalers. They began, no doubt, by observing that some men use wine to excess – to the point at which, though the wine remains true to itself, the drinker does not. That much, I give them: Drunks are a nuisance. But they went too far. Only the ungrateful or the purblind can fail to see that sugar in the grape and yeast on the skins is a divine idea, not a human one. Man's part in the process consists of honest and prudent management of the work that God has begun. Something underhanded has to be done to grape juice to keep it from running its appointed course.

Witness the teetotaling communion service. Most Protestants, I suppose, imagine that it is part of the true Reformed religion. But have they considered that, for nineteen centuries after the institution of the Eucharist, wine was the only element available for the sacrament? Do they seriously envision St Paul or Calvin or Luther opening bottles of Welch's Grape Juice in the sacristy before the service? Luther, at least, would turn over in his grave. The WCTU version of the Lord's Supper is a bare 100 years old. Grape juice was not commercially viable until the discovery of pasteurization; and, unless I am mistaken, it was Mr Welch himself (an ardent total abstainer) who persuaded American Protestantism to abandon what the Lord obviously thought rather kindly of.

That much damage done, however, the itch for consistency took over with a vengeance. Even the Lord's own delight was explained away. One of the most fanciful pieces of exegesis I ever read began by maintaining that the Greek word for wine, as used in the Gospels, meant many other things than wine. The commentator cited, as I recall, *grape juice* for one meaning, and *raisin paste* for another. He inclined, ultimately, toward the latter.

I suppose such people are blessed with reverent minds which prevent them from drawing irreverent conclusions. I myself, however, could never resist the temptation to read raisin paste for wine in the story of the Miracle of Cana. 'When the ruler of the feast had tasted the water that was made raisin paste . . . he said unto the bridegroom, "Every man at the beginning doth set forth good raisin paste, and when men have well drunk [*eaten*? – the text is no doubt corrupt], then that which is worse: but thou hast kept the good raisin paste until now."' Does it not whet your appetite for the critical *opera omnia* of such an author, where he will freely have at the length and breadth of Scripture? Can you not see his promised land flowing with peanut butter and jelly; his apocalypse, in which the great whore Babylon is given the cup of the ginger ale of the fierceness of the wrath of God?

The secularists, on the other hand, are no better. They classify wine as an alcoholic beverage, which makes about as much sense as classifying cheese as a salted food. Alcohol occurs all over the place; bread has its share, rotten apples do very well by it, hard cider is amply provided with it, and distilled spirits are full of it. How foolish, therefore, to encourage people to think of alcoholic content as the principal identifying note of wine. The general classification, of course, is legitimate enough as far as it goes. But it is hardly more than slightly relevant. Apart from an intellectual fascination, I have no *consuming* interest in alcohol; nor, I think, does any sane man. It is tasteless, odorless, indigestible, and, in sufficient doses, blinding. Far from being the only, or even the most notable, ingredient in wine, it is simply one member of a vast committee – and not the most responsible member at that.

Nothing appalls me more than to hear people refer to the drinking of wine as if it were a forbidden and fascinating way of sneaking alcohol into one's system. My flesh creeps when I hear the legitimate love of the fruit of the vine treated as if it were a longer-winded way of doing what the world does with grain neutral spirits and cheap vermouth. With wine at hand, the good man concerns himself, not with getting drunk, but with *drinking in* all the natural delectabilities of wine: taste, color, bouquet; its manifold graces; the way it complements food and enhances conversation; and its sovereign power to turn evenings into occasions, to lift eating beyond nourishment to conviviality, and to bring the race, for a few hours at least, to that happy state where men are wise and women beautiful, and even one's children begin to look promising. If someone wants the bare effects of alcohol in his bloodstream, let him drink the nasty stuff neat, or have a physician inject it. But do not let him soil my delight with his torpedo-juice mentality.

Wine is not – let me repeat – in order to anything but itself. To consider it otherwise is to turn it into an idol, a tin god to be conjured with. Moreover, it is to miss its point completely. We were made in the image of God. We were created to delight, as He does, in the resident goodness of creation. We were not made to sit around mumbling incantations and watching our insides to see what creation will do for us. Wine does indeed have subjective effects, but they are to be received gratefully and lightly. They are not solemnly important psychological adjustments, but graces, super-added gifts. It was St Thomas, again, who gave the most reasonable and relaxed of all the definitions of temperance. Wine, he said, could lawfully be drunk *usque ad hilaritatem*, to the point of cheerfulness. It is a happy example of the connection between sanctity and sanity.

Once wine is defined as an alcoholic beverage, however, sanity is hard to come by. As a nation, we drink the way we exercise: too little and too hard. Our typical gala dinner party is a disaster: three or four rounds of martinis followed by a dinner with two tiny glasses of middling Burgundy. The food is wolfed without discernment, the wine is ignored, and the convivialities come on so early that no one is up to the profundities when they arrive.

How much better if we would forget, at least in our dinnering, the alcoholic idiocy – if we would provide our guests with long evenings of nothing but sound wine, good food, and fit company. Try it sometime. Sherry or Cinzano or Dubonnet – or, best of all, a good rainwater Madeira before dinner. No gin, no whiskey – and, in the name of all that's holy, no vodka. More important still, no dips, no crackers, no de-appetizers at all. Only a mercifully brief apéritif, followed by a long and leisurely meal, with one wine or many, but with whatever wine there is dispensed with a lavish wrist: a minimum of half a bottle per person, if you are dealing with novices, or a whole bottle if you have real guests on your hands. Your party will reach an *O Altitudo*, an *Ecce, quam bonum!*, to which wine is the only road. Hard liquor is for strong souls after great dinners; it is the grape that brings ordinary mortals *usque ad hilaritatem*.

And ordinariness is the right note on which to sum up the case for wine. It is precisely the foolishness of classifying wine as an alcoholic beverage that keeps so many of us from taking it with our lunches, suppers – and even breakfasts, if you like. Whiskey, gin, and rum are sometime things. A man who takes them too often courts disaster. But wine is simply water that has matured according to nature's will. It is the ordinary accompaniment of a grown man's food. How sad, then, that the secular conscience sweeps Sherry into the same category as vodka and looks on Zinfandel as liquor. God gave us wine to make us gracious and keep us sane. The light apéritif *en famille*, and the half-bottle or bottle split between husband and wife over cold meat loaf and brawling children, are not solemn alcoholic dosages. They are cheerful minor lubrications of the frequently sandy gears of life. Properly underrated – that is, taken for what they are, and not as great problem-solving idols – they are on the side of the angels; they can hardly be overrated at all. *À ta Santé!*

To say much more, however – to provide you with a detailed directory of wines and their uses – is too large a task for any book that does not give itself entirely to the subject. I commend you the standard works. If you want the full treatment, start with the *Britannica*, and read your way in. Here you will have to be content, or discontent, with personal observations and prejudices.

My own tastes would, I suppose, have to be described as classic or ortho-dox. I have long since stopped apologizing for them. From time to time, well-intentioned authors write articles which urge novices of wine to ignore everybody's advice and drink what they like. To be sure, there is a substantial grain of truth in that. No man ever knows just how good the best is until he is familiar enough with the mediocre to appreciate the greatness of the achieve-ment. One must drink a lot of wine before one is an expert.

Unfortunately, however, the articles lead some people to think that exper-tise is simply a matter of letting untutored personal preference have its head. I have little patience, of course, with wine snobs who look down their noses at anything but Romanée-Conti, Montrachet, and the four great Clarets. But I have even less patience with the man who implies that a middle-priced California red is really just as good as Château Latour. It is as if he were to tell me that the strings of the local high school orchestra are in the same league with those of the New York Philharmonic. (No gentleman should ever utter it, of course, but the proper rejoinder to such a man is the remark of the guide to the lady who said she didn't think much of the paintings in the Louvre: 'The paintings are not on trial, Madame; you are.')

Accordingly, a balance must be struck. Exercise your own taste; trust it, even when it is less than perfect. Like conscience, it is the only personal guide you have. There is a point in every art beyond which no one can go without at least a modest supply of pretensions. Don't be ashamed, therefore, to be a *pretender* to the kingdom of wine. You cannot come into your own unless you do. On the other hand, however, be sure that your taste, like your conscience, has ample opportunity for instruction. Better men than you or me have drunk wine before us. No one needs instruction more than the man who thinks he needs none.

With that in mind, go to it. Remember, for example, that the wines of France and Germany do not enjoy unearned reputations. If all you know is Chilean Riesling, don't close your mind to the great Rheingaus and Moselles. Or, if your drinking experience is limited to Chianti (however good), don't speak too quickly against Rhônes, Burgundies, and Clarets. Every man will have his lawful preferences, of course, but in great wines, preference is a question of Stern or Heifetz – a matter of informed taste judging between goods, not a choice between good and bad.

Remember, too, that while the great European wines are unquestionably in a class by themselves, American wines can be very good indeed, and many of them, especially the California varietals, get better every year. One important note, however. American wines fall into two categories: California and Eastern. The California growers make their wines chiefly from European grape varieties – that is, from species of *Vitis vinifera*, the classic wine grape – the grape which, from the Bible to the present, has made the world's heart glad. The best California wines, accordingly, are named after the grape varieties themselves. If you want the best, you will buy, not a Burgundy, but a Pinot Noir; not a Claret, but a Cabernet Sauvignon; not a Rhine wine, but a Riesling.

Eastern wine growers, however, do not normally plant European varieties at all. Instead, they make their wines from domesticated strains of the native American grape, *Vitis labrusca* – the so-called fox grape, or slip-skin grape. That is the reason why New York State wines, for example, taste so very different from California or European ones – why they taste, to Americans, more 'grapey' than the classic types. We have not been raised on peanut butter and Concord grape jelly for nothing: Quite naturally, the preferences of a large part of the nation lean to the 'foxy' taste of wines made from Concord, Delaware, or Niagara grapes.

To me, however, such wines present a problem. For drinking neat, they are passable enough; but for use with food, they lack the graces and subtleties of the classic types. That applies especially to cooking: Concord-flavored sweetbreads are a mistake; a 'foxy' fillet of sole is simply tragic. I would almost be willing to make a firm rule that, of domestic wines, only the California ones should ever be allowed to see the inside of a pot. As an Easterner, I wish I could say something kinder; but there it is. I shall never be governor of New York.

As long as I am putting my reputation on the block, let me close by declaring myself on one of the most controversial matters in the world of wine: corkscrews. If you have never considered the subject carefully, you no doubt think that a corkscrew is just a corkscrew, and that one will do as well, or as badly, as another. The truth is, however, that there are more tin-fiddle manufacturers in the corkscrew business than anywhere else. So much so, that you could live a whole lifetime and never come across a good one – unless, of course, you learned what to look for. Herewith, therefore, a short course on how to find a real corkscrew in a world of fakes.

The principal tool you will need to enable you to discern between the useful and the useless in the corkscrew department is an ordinary ⅛-inch-wide paper match. If you can insert such a match lengthwise up through the middle of the screw, or worm, it has passed the first test. Such a screw will grip the cork over the widest possible area. Above all, unlike a screw with a solid shaft running up the middle, it will not act as a drill, tearing holes both in the cork and in your patience.

Next, be sure that the worm passes these other tests: It should be made of wire, not flat metal (which simply cuts what it should be lifting); the wire should be just about ³/₃₂ of an inch in diameter, making the whole worm a shy ³/₈ of an inch across; the helix formed by the wire should make at least six complete turns along the length of the worm; its working length should be between 2¼ and 2½ inches; and finally, the point of the worm should be sharp, smooth, and *not centered* – it should simply lie in the regular path of the rest of the helix.

If you are a stout fellow, and if this paragon among worms has a good handle attached to it, your shopping is over. All you need to do is insert the screw into the cork, place the bottle firmly on the floor between your feet, put your back into it, and pull. If, however, you were looking for something your wife or child might use, you had better continue your search until you find just as good a worm attached to a screw or lever mechanism which will make the work go easier.

Perhaps the best and most available of these is the (usually) French model which looks (roughly) like a toilet paper tube with two handles set crosswise at one end, and with a worm protruding from the other. The upper handle drives the worm into the cork, and the lower one (via a left-handed thread) lifts upper handle, worm, and cork out of the bottle and into the barrel of the device. It is commonly made of wood, but elegant ones in bone are available. I recommend it because it is one of the few corkscrews which combines useful mechanical advantage with a (normally) good worm. If you want something more stylish, go ahead and look. I wish you luck. The world is full of utterly intriguing corkscrews – most of them just as utterly hopeless.

Just to prove, however, that I am not one of the finest minds of the sixteenth century, I shall also recommend to you the most modern corkscrew of all, the carbon dioxide cork extractor. As you might expect, this one has no worm, but rather a long, hollow needle set at the end of a handle containing a CO_2 cartridge. The needle is simply pushed all the way through the cork, the handle is activated, and the pressure of the gas forces the cork out, Champagne-bottle style. The CO_2 does nothing to the wine, but there is hardly a cork anywhere which it will not unseat. The gadget is particularly useful in the cases of young wives, old corks, or both.

One sad note, however. Once a cork has made up its mind to go *into* the bottle, no corkscrew on earth can persuade it to do otherwise. If you can't lick 'em, join 'em: Push the cork all the way in with a pickle fork, hold it back while you pour the wine into a pitcher, and then glare at the empty bottle in triumph. A good cook must never lose the upper hand.

RICHARD OLNEY

Wine in Cooking

I do not want to suggest that cooking with wine is a special kind of cooking in a world apart – it is not (any more so than cooking with onions, cooking with herbs, cooking with carrots, eggs, or bread). It is as natural and as logical a moistening agent in viticultural country as is milk in dairy country or water the world round. And yet, be it the responsibility of innocence, cynicism, or a super, but questionable refinement, the concept seems sometimes hopelessly clouded.

In innocence, many believe that a product designated as 'cooking wine' has a place in the kitchen (nor are foreigners the only sinners – many a Frenchman is convinced that if a recipe calls for 'very good wine', it means a cheap wine that titles 12 or 13 per cent alcohol rather than a meagre 10 or 11 per cent). To taste a dish in which a dishonest wine has been used is conclusive, but that should not be necessary; it is only too reasonable to assume that a wine not good to drink can bring no positive quality to a cooked preparation. There should be no question of using a wine in the kitchen that one does not consider good enough to serve at one's table (which is not to say that wine should not be kept in the kitchen for cooking purposes – ends of bottles should certainly be kept, wines of a colour poured together and corked in bottles or half-bottles, protecting them as nearly as possible from contact with the air).

The cynic – he whose chicken boiled up in *gros-rouge* is labelled *coq-au-Chambertin* – may really believe that it makes little or no difference, finding it more practical to pay lip service to a 'noble' tradition that he privately believes to be a lot of pretentious hocus-pocus, but, more often, his own palate is not that naïve; he is convinced that the client (alas, he often wears chef's clothing) cannot tell the difference. In any case, if a restaurant menu lists *coq-au-Beaujolais* (or *coq-au-vin de Chinon, de Nuits*, etc.), it is a near certainty that it will be prepared with a wine superior to the one used in the *coq-au-Chambertin*, for no restaurant owner is crazy enough to pour a ruby fortune over an old cock.

Super refinement, whose seat is more often cerebral than 'palatal', is peopled by a number of precepts, some of which are valuable and many of which are deceptively plausible: Good wines are rightly used in cooking, but great wines are often recommended, and repeated insistence is placed on the importance of serving the same wine at table that has been used in the confection of a dish, an eminently artistic conceit, mainly unrelated to the palate, although it is often possible to respect the form without inconvenience. Few, however, are those who would complain if their lobster, poached in a Pouilly-Fumé, were accompanied by a Montrachet; few, on the other hand, would willingly drink a white wine with a pheasant *salmis* or with beef braised in white wine.

One may respectfully find a place in the kitchen for a great wine only if heat never comes into contact with it, the wine's unique personality defining a dish – sparking its general character with a personal note in much the same way that a slight detail in a sketch may rescue it from impersonal abstraction (meat jellies, fresh fruits macerated in wine, and dessert jellies are cases in point, and it is to avoid the blunting effect of heat that the chosen wine should never be added to a jelly until it is nearly cold but before the jell stage).

Heat cannot efface the offensive qualities of a bad wine and it can, indeed, put to good use those of a robust and honest wine with a frank fruit, a solid structure, and a firm, uncomplicated bouquet, but, depending on the length or the intensity of the cooking process, it nonetheless alters or completely transforms the wine's original nature.

If one refuses to judge a wine's greatness by the dent it makes in one's purse, it is not easy to find a satisfactory yardstick: What precisely differentiates a perfect bourgeois growth in Pauillac from its seignorial neighbour – or a Vosne-Romanée from La Tache? It is the same thing that separates de Hooch from Vermeer. It can only be sensed, but one knows that between the two is an abyss; the one is terrestrial, the other divine. And the mystery remains intact.

The mystery has it, also, that a good wine, loyal and solid, will remain exactly that in our memories whereas a great wine will continue to evolve, barely perceived nuances and, if it is a very old wine, distant associations taking fuller form, unveiling fragile complexities – and that without bringing the slightest deception to a subsequent tasting.

Relegated to the kitchen, all wine becomes earthbound; the mystery is erased. If a great wine is thus sacrificed, we have destroyed a marvellous thing.

The eye often betrays the palate and preconceived ideas confuse it. A system of rules has been more or less consciously elaborated concerning the roles of red wine and white wine in the kitchen that is more closely allied to a cerebro-visual aesthetic than to a sapid reality.

Classical recipes for fish cooked in red wine (one of the most celebrated being *sole au Chambertin* – the words' consonance must surely be the main factor in its choice) are well known but usually considered as curiosities (the uses of white wine in the preparation of meats – red and game – are far more common but less known, simply because the eye fails to detect the presence).

Among the whites and the reds alike, each, after all, runs the gamut from light-bodied, fruity, and refreshing to muscular, chewy, powerful, and richly bouqueted. Yet, in a general way, and above all when we think of wines for cooking, the first run of adjectives means 'white wine' and the second 'red wine' and the laws are smugly laid down: Fish and white meats should be treated with white wine, red meats and game with red.

But, as a matter of fact, any dish traditionally prepared with white wine can as well be prepared with red and conversely; depending on the qualities of the chosen wine (assuming them to be positive) the result will be different but good. The only real reason – and it is valid – to insist absolutely on a white wine, for instance, in a creamed sauce bound by egg yolks is to avoid the dull and shadowy, violet-brown cast lent by the red wine; nor, even with the blood, will one ever have a richly velvet, nearly black civet with white wine.

1974

KEITH BOTSFORD

Something So Deliciously Corrupt About Them

Joseph Conrad's characters (I have been rereading him lately) do not seem to eat. Too busy with typhoons, laying down bombs or being Garibaldi in unspecified parts of Central America, think I. But in fact the explanation is far simpler and lies in the fact that many of them live out their complicated lives where there is no cheese, as for instance the South China Sea and the Straits of Malacca.

There is something gastronomically missing in a cheeseless society. The idea that you might be sitting by a mountain lake in south-central Mexico, eating excellent grilled huachinango and not have something to chase away one taste and finish the wine with is somehow dispiriting. There are parts of the tropical river system of Venezuela and northern Brazil where you will be fortunate to find anything to eat at all, but when hunger sets in, that sort of intermediate hunger which is not gung-ho for a real meal but can use some dampening down, I have a genuine nostalgia for cheese.

Nor are the triste tropics the only places where this want is felt. Poland has a lot of pigs; pigs don't get milked (piglets get the entire supply); so Poles don't have cheese. Certainly one of the reasons I hated my gastronomic trip to China two years ago is that except in the remoter regions of the north and east, cheese is not part of their culture.

Then there are those countries – say Spain and Portugal and Greece – that have a cheese or two but don't really have cheeses; and others (Scandinavia and the Netherlands come to mind) that eat cheese in quantity, but produce cheeses they have done their best to ensure taste of nothing at all.

I speak here as something of a renegade for, in common with my whole family, I am – apart from butter and cheese – a strictly non-dairy man. I have had a lifelong fear of developing an ulcer from being forced to drink milk. I like ice cream little; I will not touch yoghurts; I tolerate cream only with fruit. I can think of not one of my children who has not spurned breakfast cereals because of the milk required to make them soggy. Yet we have always loved cheese. Why?

I cannot say that cheese played an important part in my early diet, apart from parmesan on pasta or in risottos and minestra. Yet from very early I can remember at least three striking cheese flavours. First the little silverfoil-wrapped, round Bel Paese cheeses that were universal before the war, filling, creamy and delicious; then that weird and wonderful, all-but-vanished hard, Swiss, mountain-herb green cheese called sapsago, whose principal flavour comes from melilot, a sweet form of clover; and finally real, deep-golden gruyère of which, my mother assures me, I would insist on eating only the parts around the holes.

What did these cheeses have in common? I think in childhood they provided a contrast to the rest of my diet, a salt, chalky, savoury contrast, and they were vaguely exotic. I never saw the parmesan that was added to our Italian dishes, but these three cheeses were visible and tangible.

It was not until I grew up that I began to appreciate cheese as the embodiment of a superior corruption: that is, as something that mysteriously grew better as it aged and ripened. This must be a reflection of my tendency to like food on the borderline of perishability. I am known for not stopping short even when the gorgonzola is about to walk across the table. I like my meat well hung, my game high, my cheeses ripe. In short, whatever is just short of disintegration.

Thus it comes about that I have much less feeling for those stable cheeses, from cheddar to gouda, that seldom really ripen. Camembert and brie and reblochon and roquefort will all convert themselves into runny extremes, and it is then that they show themselves most fully individual. For though all cheeses start with milk (cow, ewe or goat) some of them stay in their original, bland state; others have corruption in them from the start, whether natural or induced by additives that bring about the ripening.

The fact that eating cheese does wonders for the digestion and goes wonderfully with the last few glasses left in the bottle may have something to do with it; but ultimately I suspect ripeness is indeed all, and that in the same way I like my bananas near-soft and certainly darkening, I have a natural affinity for the decaying part of our lives, for autumn, the rot of vegetation, the conversion of life into death.

1995

JEFFREY STEINGARTEN

Primal Bread

> Wherefore do ye spend money for that which is not bread? . . . Eat that
> which is good, and let your soul delight itself in fatness.
>
> Isaiah 55:2.

The world is divided into two camps: those who can live happily on bread alone
and those who also need vegetables, meat, and dairy products. Isaiah and I fall
into the first category. Bread is the only food I know that satisfies completely,
all by itself. It comforts the body, charms the senses, gratifies the soul, and
excites the mind. A little butter also helps.

Isaiah was a first-class prophet but untrained as a dietitian. A good loaf of
bread will not delight your soul in fatness. It contains almost no fats or sugars
– mainly proteins and complex carbohydrates – because it is made from three
elemental ingredients: flour, water, and salt. If you wonder why I left out the
yeast, you have discovered the point of my story.

Every year I have an intense bout of baking, but these episodes now seem
just a prelude, a beating around the bush, a period of training and practice for
this year's assault on the summit: *le pain au levain naturel*, naturally leavened
bread. I have slipped into a foreign language here because this is a bread most
commonly associated with the Paris baker Lionel Poilâne and his ancient
wood-fired oven at 8 rue du Cherche-Midi, the most famous bakery in the
world. When the baking is going well, Poilâne's bread defines the good loaf: a
thick, crackling crust; a chewy, moist interior; the ancient, earthy flavors of
toasted wheat and tangy fermentation; and a range of more elusive tastes –
roasted nuts, butterscotch, dried pears, grassy fields – that emanate from
neither flour, water, nor salt, but from some more mysterious source. This is
the true bread of the countryside, Poilâne writes, the eternal bread. This is the
bread I can eat forever, and often do.

Pain au levain was the first leavened bread, probably discovered in Egypt six
thousand years ago. Professor Raymond Calvel, in his definitive *La boulangerie
moderne*, places this breakthrough '*chez les Hébreux au temps de Moïse*', which is when

les Hébreux were enslaved by *les Egyptiens*. I would love to believe this account but find it improbable. My own *pain au levain* adventure began much more recently.

Saturday, October 7, 1989 I amass thirty recipes for creating a starter, or as the French call it, *le chef*. This is a piece of dough in which wild yeast and lactic acid bacteria live happily in symbiosis, generating the gases, alcohols, and acids that give this bread its complex taste and chewy texture. Commercial yeast is bred to produce clouds of carbon dioxide for a speedy rise, at the expense of other aromatic compounds. But your first loaf of *pain au levain* can take six days to make from start to finish.

Then each new batch of bread is leavened with a piece of risen dough saved from the previous baking. Compared with using commercial yeast, *pain au levain* is unpredictable, slow, and prey to variations in weather, flour, temperature, and the seasons. 'Playing with wild yeast is like playing with dynamite,' I was warned by the technical manager of a giant US milling company.

Chez Panisse Cooking has a lucid and detailed recipe contributed by Steve Sullivan, owner of the Acme Bread Company in Berkeley and a stupendous baker; he uses organic wine grapes to activate the starter. I am in luck: the New York State grape harvest is under way. I order a variety of excellent flours from Giusto's Specialty Foods in San Francisco, which supplies flour to Acme, and when they arrive I walk around the corner to the Union Square Greenmarket, buy several bunches of unsprayed Concord grapes, tie them in cheesecloth, lower the cheesecloth into a batter of flour and water, squeeze the grapes to break their skins, put the bowl near a pilot light on the stove, and go away for the weekend.

Two days later What a mess! My mixture of flour and grapes has overflowed, sizzling and seething over the stove and running into those little holes in the gas burners from which the flames are supposed to emerge. I start again. There is something terrifying about the violent life hiding in an innocent-looking bowl of flour and grapes, and I lie awake at night wondering where it comes from.

My computer has collected 236 scientific abstracts on naturally leavened bread, but none has a definitive answer – as many as 59 distinct species of wild yeast and 238 strains of bacteria have been spotted in sourdough cultures. The truth is vital to me. Wild yeast living on the wheat berry would make Montana-Idaho country bread, because that's where Al Giusto says his wheat is grown. If they live on the grapes, it would be upstate New York country bread. But my goal is to bake *Manhattan* country bread with a colony of wild bacteria and yeast that can grow and flourish only here. I apply to *Vogue* for the funds to run DNA traces and gas chromatographs on all my breads and starters. I have received no reply as of the present writing. Maybe tomorrow.

Saturday, October 14 I have made a few loaves of bread with my grape starter – the early ones were pale purple – but must abandon the project in a few days when I leave New York to eat in Paris for three weeks. Besides, I am extremely suspicious of yeast that live on grapes. They are too fond of wine rather than wheat. I am looking for yeast that love bread as much as I do.

Monday, April 2, 1990 In the August 1989 issue of his indispensable newsletter, *Simple Cooking,* John Thorne gives instructions for *pain au levain* based on the methods that Poilâne himself employs. But I will wait until I can get hold of Poilâne's paperback handbook, *Faire son pain.* My friend Miriam promises to find one for me in Paris.

Meanwhile, I turn to *The Laurel's Kitchen Bread Book* . . . and its recipe for *desem* (the Flemish word for *levain*), which is fastidiously designed to develop the yeast that live on stoneground whole-wheat. Everything must be kept below 60 degrees until the final rise to discourage the growth of acid-generating bacteria that thrive at higher temperatures, and everything must be sealed to avoid colonization by airborne yeast.

I telephone Giusto's and ask them to send me a sack of whole-wheat flour by overnight mail the moment it is milled. Then I walk around the house testing the temperature. Bread writers who live in the country typically tell you that the perfect place for this rising or that is on the creaky wooden stairs going down to your root cellar. Don't they know that most people live in apartments? At last I create a zone of 55 degrees by piling a twenty-four-quart stockpot on a cardboard box at the edge of my desk with the air conditioner set to turbofreeze.

Late April It is a balmy spring, but I am wearing a winter coat at my desk so that *Laurel's Kitchen desem* will feel comfortable. My wife has the sniffles.

Early May Both of us have come down with serious colds, complete with fever. The *desem* starter smells terrific, a fresh fruity scent unlike anything I've made before, and the bread is rough and wheaty, full of complex aromas. But like all whole-grain breads, the strong taste of unrefined flour obscures the more delicate flavors I am after. Long ago I concluded that the only bread worth its name is made with good white flour; small amounts of barley, whole-wheat, or rye can be added for their flavor and color. John Thorne calls whole-grain bread 'a kind of aerated gruel'. If Isaiah were alive today, I'm sure he would agree.

Friday, June 1, late morning Miriam and *Faire son pain* have arrived from Paris. Step One: create a bowlful of life. Poilâne's instructions have you make a small piece of dough with one-ninth of the total flour and water and leave it covered for two to three days while the wild yeast and bacteria awaken and multiply to form an active culture.

Bakers weigh everything because flour can be packed densely or lightly in a measuring cup and doughs can be tight or aerated; it is their weight that matters. I dust off my electronic kitchen scale and set it to grams. Poilâne says that all ingredients at all stages should be between 22 and 24 degrees centigrade, which equals 72 to 75 degrees on Dr Fahrenheit's thermometer – a nice, moderate room temperature. Now I can turn off the air conditioner.

I weigh 42 grams of water and 67 grams of unbleached white flour, about a half cup, put them in a large bowl, and squish them together with the fingers of my right hand until the dough comes together into a rough ball.

I knead the *chef* with extra flour on my wooden counter for two minutes, put it into a rustic brown ceramic bowl, cover the bowl with a wet kitchen towel, secure the towel with a rubber band, and go about my business. This nonchalance lasts for five minutes, and then I am back in the kitchen, peeking under the towel to see if anything is happening. Twenty peeks and several broken rubber bands later, I scrape the *chef* into a clear glass bowl. It looks less like something from a French farmhouse but does facilitate obsessive observation.

I wash my rustic bowl in hot water and learn a lasting lesson: utensils coated with flour or dough are easily washed in *cold* water; hot water makes the starch and gluten stick to everything, including itself. If the dough has hardened, *soak* the utensils in cold water. If you leave them long enough, your wife may get disgusted and clean them up herself. Do it too often and there will be a price to pay.

For the rest of the day, at three-minute intervals, I search for the appearance of tiny bubbles against the glass.

Saturday, June 2, immediately after waking In just twenty-four hours, the kitchen towel has grown dry and stiff, the dough has darkened and crusted over, and two spots of pale blue mold have appeared on it. This is not the life-form I had in mind.

I make the morning coffee and start all over. This time I use bottled spring water. New York City tap water is rated among the most delicious in the nation, but chlorinated water of any kind can inhibit the growth of yeast. And weeks later, when I grow attuned to small differences in the taste of my breads I find that you can recognize things like chlorine in the crust, where flavors are concentrated.

Instead of white flour I weigh out some organic whole-wheat flour: organic because pesticides and fungicides deal death to microbes, and whole-wheat because if yeast do actually live on the wheat berry, it is on the outer bran layer that they will, I figure, be found. Instead of a colorful, charming kitchen towel, I use plastic wrap this time. It may prevent a friendly airborne microbe or two from settling on the *chef*, but it keeps the dough from crusting over.

Sunday, June 3 Is that a bubble in the *chef* or a flaw in the glass of the bowl? The *chef* still smells like wet whole-wheat flour, nothing more.

Monday, June 4 The *chef* has swelled and smells tangy, somewhere between beer and yogurt.

Tuesday, June 5 No further change. Maybe I have failed. Maybe my *chef* is dead. But it is time for Poilâne's Step Two, doubling the earlier quantities and building the *chef* into what Poilâne calls the *levain*, which you leave from twenty-four to forty-eight hours to ferment.

Wednesday, June 6, bright and early The thing is alive! I think it is trying to talk to me. In only twenty-four hours the *levain* has risen to the top of the bowl and is pressing up against the plastic wrap. Large bubbles proudly show themselves through the glass. There can be no doubt about it: I have created life in a bowl in my kitchen!

In Step Three you build the *levain* into two pounds of bread dough, tripling its weight by dissolving it in 252 grams of water and working in 400 grams of flour and 15 grams of salt. Now that a happy fermentation has begun, I shift to Giusto's white organic unbleached bread flour. The kneading begins, twenty long minutes of it, stretching the dough away from my body with the heel of my hand, folding it back toward me, giving the dough a quarter turn, and doing it again and again. Besides aerating the dough, this motion unkinks the protein molecules and lines them up next to each other, where they link into a network of gluten. The dough becomes satiny and elastic so that as the yeast produces more carbon dioxide it can stretch and expand around bubbles of gas.

I find twenty minutes of kneading unendurable. Mine is not the attitude of a true artisan. Hand kneading puts the baker in touch with his living dough, you read, endows him with responsibility for his bread. Soon I will switch to my KitchenAid K5A heavy-duty home mixer equipped with a dough hook. It pummels and whirls instead of kneading, but it does produce acceptable results, especially when I take over for a few minutes at the end.

Seven o'clock that evening Poilâne is fuzzy on forming a round loaf, so I follow the standard procedure – flattening the dough with the smooth domed surface facedown and rolling and stretching it into a tight spherical package. I have bought a *banneton*, a professional linen-lined rising basket, from French Baking Machines to replace my makeshift two-quart bowl lined with a kitchen towel. I flour it heavily and lower the loaf into it, smooth side down. Then, to create a moist, draftless environment, I inflate a large Baggie around the whole thing and tie it tightly. My loaf will rise until midnight.

I spend part of the evening in a state of wonder. The first miracle is that a handful of wheat flour contains everything needed to create the most satisfying and fundamental of all foods. Then I marvel a while about yeast. Why does the yeast that feeds on wheat produce a harmless leavening gas and appealing flavors rather than poisons? And why does wild yeast seem to do best at room temperature? Yeasts were created long before rooms were. Is this a coincidence or part of Somebody's master plan? Last, I wonder at the role of salt. Nearly all recipes call for about 1 percent salt by weight – much more and you kill the yeast and bacteria, much less and the yeast grow without restraint and exhaust themselves too soon. Is it mere chance that the chemically ideal level of salt is precisely the amount that makes bread taste best?

Midnight The loaf has barely budged and I am getting worried. Better give it another two hours. My wife has already gone to bed. She sees this as a dangerous precedent. But several weeks will pass before my compulsive baking threatens to destroy the marriage.

2 a.m. Through the inflated Baggie I can see that the loaf has swelled by half. I have preheated the oven to 500 degrees with a thick 16-inch terra cotta tile on the oven shelf and a Superstone backing cloche on top of it. This device, manufactured by Sassafras Enterprises, is an unglazed ceramic dish with a domed cover that creates something like the even, penetrating, steamy heat of a brick oven. The tile underneath increases the stored heat in the oven and protects the bottom of the bread from burning. Elizabeth David's *English Bread and Yeast Cookery* has a photograph of a nearly identical baking cloche from 500 B.C., excavated from the Agora in Athens.

I invert the *banneton* on the fiery base of the cloche, slash the top of the loaf in a checkerboard pattern with a razor blade to encourage a good rise in the oven, pour a quarter-cup of warm water over the loaf to create extra steam (a frightening but successful gesture I learned from *The Laurel's Kitchen Bread Book*), sprinkle flour over the top for decoration, and cover with the preheated dome.

2:30 a.m. I lower the heat to 400 an uncover the bread to let it brown. It has not risen as much as I would have liked and my slashes have become deep valleys.

3:00 a.m. My first *pain au levain* is done! When I tap the bottom of the loaf with my forefinger, it sounds hollow, a sign that the starch has absorbed all the excess water, turning from hard crystals into a soft gel.

As I know unequivocally from both book learning and experience, bread is not at its best straight from the oven. Complex flavors develop as it cools, and if you love your bread warm, you should reheat or toast it later.

3:05 a.m. Just this once, I cut a slice of hot bread. The crust is crisp and tender, the aroma and taste are complex and nutty if a little bland. But it is overly sour and its crumb is dense and gray. Yet I am not disappointed. Butter improves matters, as it does everything in life but one's health, and I know that the flavor will improve by the morning. Which it does.

3:20 a.m. I am falling toward slumber when my heart starts racing and a wave of dread washes over me. I forgot to hold back part of the dough as the *chef* for my next loaf!

3:21 a.m. I can't fall asleep. I drag myself into the kitchen and whip up a new *chef*. This time it takes two minutes, and I am confident it will work perfectly. I eat another piece of bread and sleep contentedly. In the morning, my wife objects to crumbs on the pillow.

Thursday, June 21 I am baking as fast as I can, six generations so far with my new *chef*. With each baking the *chef* grows more vigorous and its flavor more assertive but a bit less acidic.

My wife feels that my baking schedule has prevented us from going away on sunny summer weekends. She says it is like having a newborn puppy without the puppy. She has always wanted a puppy. And she is unhappy that every surface in the apartment has a delicate dusting of Giusto's bread flour. But it is only when I nearly turn down tickets to the Madonna concert for fear that Madonna will interfere with my first rising that she puts her foot down. I refrigerate the dough overnight, as I've done with other breads, and find that the final flavor has, if anything, improved. But my bread is still too dense, and I do not know what to do about it.

Tuesday, July 31 I throw myself upon the mercy of experts. Noel Comess left the post of chef de cuisine at the Quilted Giraffe four years ago, at the age of twenty-eight, to start the Tom Cat Bakery in an abandoned ice cream factory in Queens, and his sourdough *boule* is the best in the city. He agrees to let me snoop around one evening. His room temperature is 85 degrees, much warmer than Poilâne's, and the proportion of old risen dough to new at each stage is less than I have learned to use. I watch him form several loaves and realize that beating down the dough is the last thing that naturally leavened bread needs. We pore over his books. Noel loves baking bread and the continuous, self-renewing process of *pain au levain*.

Back at home I round my loaves more gently and find that they bake higher and with a more varied texture. But they still look like my bread, not like Noel's. A warmer rising temperature sometimes helps and sometimes doesn't. And my *chef* is simply not active enough to use the proportions that Noel does.

I turn to Michael London. From 1977 to 1986 Michael and his wife, Wendy, ran a patisserie in Saratoga Springs, New York, called Mrs London's Bake Shop – Craig Claiborne once compared their creations favorably to Wittamer's in Brussels and Peltier's in Paris – and now from the makeshift kitchen of their Federal-period brick farmhouse in nearby Greenwich they run the Rock Hill

Bakehouse, where they bake three times a week. I cannot count the mornings I have rushed down to Balducci's or over to the Greenmarket to buy a giant loaf of Michael's Farm Bread before they disappear.

An unstable and sweltering little plane carries me to upstate New York. I am bearing a Baggie filled with 4 ounces of *chef* and my latest loaf of bread. Michael and Wendy critique the loaf I have brought, and then we eat it with butter from their cow. Their percipient and blonde seven-year-old daughter, Sophie, loves my bread. I watch Michael make his *levain*, and he shows me how to invigorate my starter. As you build the dough from one stage to the next, the *chef*, the *levain*, and the dough should always be used just at the peak of their activity. We sleep for a few hours, wake at one in the morning, make a ton of dough, sleep until five, when his four helpers arrive, and begin shaping loaves for the final bake.

Michael builds my 4 ounces of strengthened starter into *levain* and then into 20 pounds of dough. He bakes several loaves with it, and they look just like Michael's other breads, not like mine at all. The secrets, it seems, lie in the baker's art and intuition, not just in the bacterial composition of the air, the flour, or the grapes. A professional French hearth oven does not hurt either.

Thursday, September 6 My baking schedule is less frenzied, twice a week now, and my wife eagerly awaits the finished product. My *chef* is happy and strong and aromatic, the man from UPS has got used to lugging up a 50-pound bag from Giusto's every week or two, and I have vacuumed most of the organic bread flour out of my word processor. Most days the bread is more than good enough to eat, and some days it is so good that we eat nothing else.

1990

EDWARD BEHR

The Goodness of Salt

It's sad that the unclouded enjoyment of salt is a thing of the past. Salt is win-some when a few grains of it are tasted in a tiny pinch, although that hardly begins to address the health campaign against this nutrient. Salt does raise blood pressure in the seventh or tenth of the population whose blood pressure is salt-sensitive. However, there is no evidence that people with normal blood pressure who avoid salt are reducing the chance of a future problem. The whole truth about salt is only beginning to be widely understood. Bureaucrats who issue alarmist guidelines see not individuals but an ill-informed mass of least common denominators, to be treated all alike. Ironically, until recently salt has been a metaphor for value, preservation, and permanence. Only during the last decade did partial new knowledge turn the old symbol on its head. Now hardly anyone praises salt.

No passion like that for chocolate or champagne has ever declared itself for salt. Yet salt's potency in heightening the taste of food is unmatched and has been honored since ancient times. One of its simplest and most satisfying uses is to fix the beautiful green color of vegetables in an open pot of boiling water. It also conveniently lowers the freezing point of water in the salt and ice mix of old-fashioned ice cream freezers – an application that has been exploited with increasing sophistication since the early vogue of fruit ices in the time of Catherine de Médicis. Salt enhances nearly every food, but its culinary signific-ance is seen most clearly when it seasons breads, potatoes, and grains. They taste flat and almost metallic without it.

Without salt there would be none of the delicious foods it preserves: ham, sausage, bacon, corned beef, smoked salmon, salt cod, anchovies, pickles, sauerkraut, cheeses, olives. Salting is often combined with two other funda-mental means of preservation, drying and smoking, as in meats and fish. Some salt-cured foods are soaked for a day to rid them of enough salt to bring them back into the range of palatability, but the salt pungency of prosciutto that would be alarming in quantity sharpens the appetite in a small serving of thin slices over ripe melon or figs.

Nineteenth-century Americans ate more salt pork than they did fresh meat. The salty palate that resulted may explain the peculiar saltiness of American baked goods. The current generation of cookbooks has reduced the salt but until recently our pie pastry, Toll House cookies, sticky buns, banana bread, and other sweets have contained four times or more salt than their European equivalents. And the salt in our recipes is usually intensified by the alkali taste of baking soda or powder and by the salt in salted butter. In the Old World, eggs and yeast are preferred leavenings to powders, and salted butter for baking is all but unheard of on the Continent. Even in England, unsalted butter was always used for the finest baking. The salty taste of our traditional baked goods is not so much good or bad as it is characteristic.

Salt has minor but worthy variety in type and flavor. Gray salt is the un-refined sea or bay salt, sometimes found in health-food and fancy-food shops, that looks dirty and has the stimulating flavor of the ocean. This salt has all the mingled salts of the sea and correspondingly less plain sodium chloride than refined salt. The French prefer a small sacrifice in flavor on behalf of delicate style: gray salt in the kitchen, white salt at the table, with occasional exceptions such as gray salt served with pot-au-feu.

Of the half-dozen kinds of salt currently on my shelf, gray Armorican salt made near the mouth of the Loire is the most interesting. Close behind are two kinds of coarse white crystals from Mediterranean France, as well as Maldon sea salt from Essex, England (from the Maldon Crystal Salt Company, the only remaining maker of sea salt in England). The usual refined white sea salt sold by health-food stores is more reasonably priced but has about half the desirable sea taste of the other four. A box of flaked kosher salt sat unused until it hardened and I threw it out; it was undistinguished and contained additives: contrary to the common impression, most brands of kosher salt do. Morton's plain salt for pick-ling (not iodized because iodine turns pickles black) also lacks interest, like its table salt. Once I had some Hawaiian salt, and it was the most boring of all. Good gray salt is two dollars or more a pound, too expensive for most uses; I use the health-food store's refined sea salt for bread and most everyday seasoning, although one imported salt or another is used at my table. It is a shame that for curing, where the kind of salt matters most, the cost of good gray salt is prohibitive.

Early in this century, when more scattered saltworks still survived, there was more variety to salt. The suffix *-wich* in an English place name – Norwich, Middlewich, Droitwich, Greenwich – means the site of a saltworks or brine spring. A native of the Kanawha River valley in West Virginia once wrote a book in which he lamented the passing of the Kanawha red salt that was no longer boiled from the brine springs in the town of Malden. It was colored by iron oxide and its strong taste was prized for curing meat.

Salt deepens flavors and to an extent unites them, and it balances acidity and sweetness, helping to restore equilibrium when they are in excess. Salt plays against not just these basic tastes but against aromatic flavors, and it cuts the oily taste of fat. A vinaigrette for salad is a careful balance between oil and vinegar – a balance that turns on salt. It is famously difficult to achieve, easier with a prodigal use of oil, and the amount of salt is as often awry as that of the two liquids.

It is confusing that a set volume of salt weighs more or less depending on the variety. Coarse flaked salt weighs about half as much as a spoonful of granulated white salt, gray salt about two-thirds as much. Most recipes calculate for the granulated white, and any adjustments are up to the cook. A few otherwise knowledgeable cooks have the notion that sea salt is saltier than regular salt and that less is needed. To my palate, that just isn't so.

A salt grinder is sometimes used to grind coarse crystals 'fresh' at the table, but I don't believe this freshness has any value. Rather, the appeal of grinding comes from the immediate lively effect of the fine salt particles and powder when they hit the tongue (the fineness depends on the grinder). Unfortunately, gray salt clumps with humidity and works poorly in either a grinder or shaker; it must be pinched.

Although the liking for salt is universal, each of us has a taste for a certain amount of it, based on what we are used to. And we often like more than we think we do. We clearly enjoy a good deal more than we need. For the cook, the correct amount of salt is no more than an average of individual tastes. Some professional cooks fail to recognize their immoderate preferences and so don't reduce their salting to the average. Home cooks tend to underestimate the average, and they are often inconsistent. Or, in the face of the campaign against salt, they don't salt at all. They may not realize that part of the pleasure they take in a meal at a good restaurant comes from well salted – skillfully salted – food.

A salt grinder, shaker, or dish should always be on the table so that individuals can season food to taste, especially such foods as roasts, which don't come fully salted from the kitchen. I respect and sympathize with those who have to restrict their use of salt, but some zealous puritans would like everyone to cut down on salt because a small percentage would benefit from abstinence. These fearful proselytizers have no spirit, no *joie de vivre*. Does the sensual, the aesthetic, have no value in life? To those with high blood pressure it may be an injustice on the part of Fate, but it is impossible to enjoy food fully without salt. Salt is part of the structure of taste. Its use isn't a weakness, but an intelligent application of the senses.

CHARLES PERRY

Medieval Near Eastern Rotted Condiments

Kamakh, *murri* and *bunn* were highly praised by medieval Arab poets, but their very description makes us marvel and shiver with horror simultaneously. They were emphatically decayed substances, most of them made from *budhaj*, which was thoroughly rotted barley dough.

BUDHAJ

This, like its variant, *fudhaj*, is an Arabized form of the Persian word *pudeh*, 'rotten'. We have recipes in both the tenth-century *Kitab al-Tabikh* and the thirteenth-century *Kitab Wasf* which concur that it was made from barley flour, optionally mixed with wheaten flour, kneaded without leaven or salt. Raw loaves of this dough, optionally wrapped in fig leaves, were rotted in closed containers for forty days and then dried, optionally being baked as well, and ground for use as flour.

These are the only explicit recipes, but the murri recipe appended to *A Baghdad Cookery Book* (thirteenth century) ends with some sentences which make no sense in context but sound like garbled instructions for budhaj: 'Take pennyroyal [*sc.* budhaj] and wheaten or barley flour, make into a dry dough with hot water, using no leaven or salt, and bake into a loaf with a hole in the middle. Wrap in fig leaves, stuff into a preserving jar, and leave in the shade until fetid. Then remove, and dry.'

It should be noted that Professor Arberry's translation is based on a manuscript that spelled budhaj as budhanj, which is also a variant spelling of the word for 'pennyroyal'. It should be clear that budhaj must have been meant; the 'n' is intrusive, as it is in the recipes in *Kitab Wasf* where budhaj is spelled fudhanj.

Kitab al-Tabikh also gives instructions for making rotted bread that closely parallel those for the rotting of barley dough. It uses this flour of rotted bread in condiments where later books use plain flour.

MURRI

The Arab lexicographers suspected this word of being foreign and reported that the common people pronounced it with a single 'r': *al-muri*. This encourages us to derive the word from the Greek *halmyris*: a salty thing.

Whether an actual Greek sauce or technique is the origin of murri is extremely problematic, however. Conceivably murri represents the Greek idea of a salty liquid seasoning as interpreted in the basically Persianized – and fish-poor – Near Eastern environment. The picture is clouded by the fact that *Kitab Wasf* describes a 'Byzantine murri' made *without* rotted bread, based on toasted bread and caramelized honey. Apparently the same unrotted 'murri' was also known among the Christians of Spain, because the *Manuscrito Anónimo* notes its use disapprovingly.

Two basic recipes for rotted murri are known to us, one Iraqi and the other North African. 'Murri of the Iraqis' given in *Kitab Wasf* is virtually identical to the recipe appended to *A Baghdad Cookery Book*: Flour ground from (apparently unrotted) unleavened bread is added to equal amounts budhaj flour and salt, moistened and stored in a vessel in the summer sun for forty days. When it is black, more water is added and it is allowed to ferment for two weeks 'until it bubbles and settles'. The liquid is strained off and flavored with cinnamon, saffron and herbs or more spices. A second or even third infusion can be made from the lees.

The other version, the 'infused murri of the North Africans' which *Anónimo* invidiously compared to non-rotted murri, is exhaustively described in *Kitab Wasf*. This recipe uses no wheat flour, only budhaj and a smaller, though not stated, proportion of salt. It is flavoured with a number of spices, along with broken carob, fennel stems, citron leaves, pith of bitter orange wood and pine nuts, wetted to the consistency of treacle and stored in the sun. After forty days the mixture is strained, fresh bread is added and this new mixture is left in the sun ten days and then strained. A second, third and even fourth infusion from the lees may also be made in the same way.

BUNN

The only recipe for this relatively rare condiment is the one given in *Kitab al-Tabikh*. One part budhaj flour and nine parts flour of rotted bread are mixed together and put in a vessel with water to cover. Nigella and fennel are thrown in. The next day salt, no more than one-tenth the total amount, is added. It is eaten after a week.

A rather similar product in *Kitab Wasf* called *barhuma* of murri, made with fresh rather than rotted flour and salt to the proportion of one third, is stored for forty days. In other words, it is a murri recipe used to produce a table condiment like bunn rather than a liquid seasoning.

KAMAKH

This is the obsolete Persian word *kaameh*. There were several kinds. Not all were made with rotted grain, but the most important was red kamakh. One part budhaj to four or five parts fresh bread were mixed with milk and ripened in the sun, with more milk being added daily until it turned red.

From this foundation were made a variety of kamakhs: clove, cinnamon, caraway, rose petal, anise, *nanakhwa* (probably nigella), or condiments flavoured with any of a variety of herbs such as basil or thyme.

AN EXPERIMENT IN ROTTING

[*Note*: It is strongly advised not to eat any of these preparations. They are highly carcinogenic.]

On February 28, 1987, I began rotting barley and bread with the aim of making bunn. I used raw loaves, each about a quarter of a cup, of barley dough and barley-wheat dough for the budhaj, and also rotted and preservative-free whole-wheat flatbread from a health-food store. In the absence of fig leaves, I used bottled grape leaves, soaked to leach out the benzoate of soda. I also rolled some loaves in bran and wrapped others in plastic film as an experiment. All were stored in plastic containers.

There are always mysteries in old cookbooks, because even the most un-poetical depend on the existence of a living tradition for the cook to know when the result is correct. With a totally unfamiliar process such as this, we are on very uncertain ground. How should the result look and feel and smell? How much is dependent on Near Eastern microbes? How much on microbes that might conceivably be extinct? I found that balls of dough of different degrees of moistness rotted differently, as did those wrapped in grape leaves versus those merely rolled in bran. Some did not develop external signs of rot, but only turned a reddish tan. At the end of forty days, each batch seemed to have rotted – and come to smell – differently.

I decided that the most likely candidate was the barley dough wrapped in leaves in a loosely lidded container. These loaves were surprisingly white throughout most of their volume, and smelled faintly but not unpleasantly of rot. The bread had rotted vigorously and in the end looked like a furry black kitten with pink patches. I ground and sifted both budhaj and rotted bread, mixed them and made bunn.

I tasted all three products, in very gingerly fashion (see the warning at the head of this section). The rotted barley had a faint barley flavour. The rotted bread had a slight saltiness but was neutral in taste. Surprisingly, though, it had an extremely plush feel in the mouth, I supposed because the gluten had been consumed. The bunn, which at first smelled strongly of the spices, developed a curious richness of aroma, like that of a ripe salami, after a week. It had a loathsome appearance, but was agreeable to taste, if not a delicacy by my standards.

The bunn also developed some sourness, and I concluded that the 'sharpness' mentioned in *Manuscrito Anónimo* and the pungency described by poets must have been a combination of the spice flavors and the acetic fermentation that bunn and murri undergo, being moist enough for the vinegar bacteria to flourish – to say nothing of the concentrated lactic acid of the long-aged yogurt of red kamakh (which must have smelled like high cheese as well) – rather than a flavor due to the original rotted bread or dough.

I had also made bunn with some of the reddish-tan loaves rolled in bran; this batch quickly produced a foul-smelling layer of mold and scum not mentioned in the bunn recipe. From this I concluded that the barley dough had rotted incompletely and that the rotting of budhaj was probably a process intended to reduce the nutritive contents of the barley so that the fermentation of products made from budhaj would be slower and more controlled.

Still, it will not do to say that the flavour of, say, murri, was essentially sour. *Kitab Wasf* remarks, after the recipe for 'Byzantine murri', 'Our only aim was the amusing sorts of food found in books, like omelet made without eggs and milk without milk'. In other words, this recipe was felt to mimic the flavor of genuine murri to some degree; yet it contained nothing that could make it sour. It would take considerably more experimentation, and the courage to taste these strange and definitely unhealthful substances, to get a clearer idea what the medieval condiments were like.

WHY DID THESE CONDIMENTS DISAPPEAR?

The rotted preparations enjoyed varying popularity. About 30 per cent of the recipes in the *Manuscrito Anónimo* call for murri, but less than 7 per cent in those of *A Baghdad Cookery Book*. At various periods the elegant disdained them for their dark and unpleasant colors. They are completely extinct now, and there is no certain evidence of them after the fourteenth century.

All these products, being based on rotted grain, are rich in the compounds called aflatoxins which are considered among the most virulent carcinogens known. It is highly unlikely that these condiments fell out of favor because it was discovered that they were unhealthful – medieval life expectancy was so short that the carcinogenic effects would in most cases never have been noticed.

The influence of the new Ottoman cuisine emanating from Istanbul from the fifteenth century on is not enough to explain their disappearance either. As has been mentioned, they are already missing in the pre-Ottoman fifteenth-century book *Kitab al-Tibakhah*, and they have died out even in formerly murri-loving areas like Morocco, which was never under Ottoman control.

My guess is that it was a combination of factors: the depression that settled over most of the Arab world after the fifteenth century and helped to erode various aristocratic traditions, the example of the new Ottoman cuisine that disdained the use of spices, and perhaps the influence of the new ingredients from the New World, which perhaps went ill with the old condiments.

At any rate, one thing is sure: of all medieval foods, these are the least likely to experience a revival.

1987

SIDNEY MINTZ

Sweetness and Power

... Most people in the Caribbean region, descendants of the aboriginal Amerind population and of settlers who came from Europe, Africa, and Asia, have been rural and agricultural. Working among them usually means working in the countryside; getting interested in them means getting interested in what they produce by their labor. Because I worked among these people – learning what they were like, what their lives were made into by the conditions they lived under – I inevitably wanted to know more about sugar and rum and coffee and chocolate. Caribbean people have always been entangled with a wider world, for the region has, since 1492, been caught up in skeins of imperial control, spun in Amsterdam, London, Paris, Madrid, and other European and North American centers of world power. Someone working inside the rural sectors of those little island societies would inevitably be inclined, I think, to view such networks of control and dependence from the Caribbean vantage point: to look up and out from local life, so to speak, rather than down and into it. But this insider's view has some of the same disadvantages as the firmly European perspective of an earlier generation of observers for whom the greater part of the dependent, outer, non-European world was in most ways a remote, poorly known, and imperfect extension of Europe itself. A view that excludes the linkage between metropolis and colony by choosing one perspective and ignoring the other is necessarily incomplete.

Working in Caribbean societies at the ground level, one is led to ask in just what ways beyond the obvious ones the outer world and the European world became interconnected, interlocked even; what forces beyond the nakedly military and economic ones maintained this intimate interdependence; and how benefits flowed, relative to the ways power was exercised. Asking such questions takes on a specific meaning when one also wants to know in particular about the histories of the products that colonies supply to metropolises. In the Caribbean case, such products have long been, and largely still are, tropical foods: spices (such as ginger, allspice, nutmeg, and mace); beverage bases (coffee and chocolate); and, above all, sugar and rum. At one time, dyes (such as indigo and annatto and fustic) were important; various starches, starch foods, and bases (such as cassava, from which tapioca is made, arrowroot, sago, and various species of *Zamia*) have also figured in the export trade; and a few industrial staples (like sisal) and essential oils (like vetiver) have mattered; bauxite, asphalt, and oil still do. Even some fruits, such as bananas, pineapples, and coconuts, have counted in the world market from time to time.

But for the Caribbean region as a whole, the steady demand overall and for most epochs has been for sugar, and even if it is now threatened by yet other sweeteners, it seems likely to continue to hold its own. Though the story of European sugar consumption has not been tied solely to the Caribbean, and consumption has risen steadily worldwide, without regard to where the sugar comes from, the Caribbean has figured importantly in the picture for centuries.

Once one begins to wonder where the tropical products go, who uses them, for what, and how much they are prepared to pay for them – what they will forgo, and at what price, in order to have them – one is asking questions about the market. But then one is also asking questions about the metropolitan homeland, the center of power, not about the dependent colony, the object and target of power. And once one attempts to put consumption together with production, to fit colony to metropolis, there is a tendency for one or the other – the 'hub' or the 'outer rim' – to slip out of focus. As one looks at Europe the better to understand the colonies as producers and Europe as consumer, or vice versa, the other side of the relationship seems less clear. While the relationships between colonies and metropolis are in the most immediate sense entirely obvious, in another sense they are mystifying.

My own field experiences, I believe, influenced my perceptions of the center-periphery relationship. In January 1948, when I went to Puerto Rico to start my anthropological fieldwork, I chose a south-coast municipality given over almost entirely to the cultivation of sugar cane for the manufacture of sugar for the North American market. Most of the land in that municipality was owned or leased by a single North American corporation and its landholding affiliate. After a stay in the town, I moved to a rural district (*barrio*); there, for slightly more than a year, I lived in a small shack with a young cane worker.

Surely one of the most remarkable things about Barrio Jauca – and, indeed, about the entire municipality of Santa Isabel at the time – was its dedication to sugar cane. In Barrio Jauca, one stands on a vast alluvial plain, created by the scouring action of once-great rivers – a fertile, fanlike surface extending from the hills down to the Caribbean beaches that form Puerto Rico's south coast. Northward, away from the sea and toward the mountains, the land rises in low foothills, but the coastal land is quite flat. A superhighway from northeast to southwest now passes nearby, but in 1948 there was only a single tarred road, running due east-west along the coast, linking the roadside villages and the towns – Arroyo, Guayama, Salinas, Santa Isabel – of what was then an immense, much-developed sugar-cane-producing region, a place where, I learned, North Americans had penetrated most deeply into the vitals of pre-1898 Puerto Rican life. The houses outside the town were mostly shacks built on the shoulders of roads – sometimes clustered together in little villages with a tiny store or two, a bar, and not much else. Occasionally, an unarable field could be found, its saline soil inhibiting cultivation, on which a few woebegone goats might graze. But the road, the villages stretched along it, and such occasional barren fields were the only interruptions to the eye between mountains and sea; all else was sugar cane. It grew to the very edge of the road and right up to the stoops of the houses. When fully grown, it can tower fifteen feet above the ground. At its mature glory, it turned the plain into a special kind of hot, impenetrable jungle, broken only by special pathways (*callejones*) and irrigation ditches (*zanjas de riego*).

All the time I was in Barrio Jauca, I felt as if we were on an island, floating in a sea of cane. My work there took me into the fields regularly, especially but not only during the harvest (*zafra*). At that time most of the work was still done by human effort alone, without machines; cutting 'seed', seeding, planting, cultivating, spreading fertilizer, ditching, irrigating, cutting, and loading cane – it had to be loaded and unloaded twice before being ground – were all manual tasks. I would sometimes stand by the line of cutters, who were working in intense heat and under great pressure, while the foreman stood (and the *mayordomo* rode) at their backs. If one had read about the history of Puerto Rico and of sugar, then the lowing of animals, the shouts of the *mayordomo*, the grunting of the men as they swung their machetes, the sweat and dust and din easily conjured up an earlier island era. Only the sound of the whip was missing.

Of course, the sugar was not being produced for the Puerto Ricans themselves: they consumed only a fraction of the finished product. Puerto Rico had been producing sugar cane (and sugar in some form) for four centuries, always mainly for consumers elsewhere, whether in Seville, in Boston, or in some other place. Had there been no ready consumers for it elsewhere, such huge quantities of land, labor, and capital would never have been funneled into this one curious crop, first domesticated in New Guinea, first processed in India, and first carried to the New World by Columbus.

Yet I also saw sugar being consumed all around me. People chewed the cane, and were experts not only on which varieties were best to chew, but also on how to chew them – not so easy as one might expect. To be chewed properly, cane must be peeled and the pith cut into chewable portions. Out of it oozes a sticky, sweet, slightly grayish liquid. (When ground by machine and in large quantities, this liquid becomes green, because of the innumerable tiny particles of cane in suspension within it.) The company went to what seemed like extreme lengths to keep people from taking and eating sugar cane – there was, after all, so much of it! – but people always managed to lay hands on some and to chew it soon after it was cut, when it is best. This provided almost daily nourishment for the children, for whom snagging a stalk – usually fallen from an oxcart or a truck – was a great treat. Most people also took the granular, refined kind of sugar, either white or brown, in their coffee, the daily beverage of the Puerto Rican people. (Coffee drunk without sugar is called *café puya* – 'ox-goad coffee'.)

Though both the juice of the cane and the granular sugars were sweet, they seemed otherwise quite unrelated. Nothing but sweetness brought together the green-gray cane juice (*guarapo*) sucked from the fibers and the granular sugars of the kitchen, used to sweeten coffee and to make the guava, papaya, and bitter-orange preserves, the sesame and tamarind drinks then to be found in Puerto Rican working-class kitchens. No one thought about how one got from those giant fibrous reeds, flourishing upon thousands of acres, to the delicate, fine, pure white granular food and flavoring we call sugar. It was possible, of course, to see with one's own eye how it was done (or, at least, up to the last and most profitable step, which was the conversion from brown to white, mostly carried out in refineries on the mainland). In any one of the big south-coast mills (*centrales*), Guánica or Cortada or Aguirre or Mercedita, one could observe modern techniques of comminution for freeing sucrose in a liquid medium from the plant fibers, the cleansing and condensation, the heating that produced evaporation and, on cooling, further crystallization, and the centrifugal brown sugar that was then shipped northward for further refining. But I cannot remember ever hearing anyone talk about making sugar, or wonder out loud about who were the consumers of so much sugar. What local people were keenly aware of was the *market* for sugar; though half or more of them were illiterate, they had an understandably lively interest in world sugar prices. Those old enough to remember the famous 1919–20 Dance of the Millions – when the world market price of sugar rose to dizzying heights, then dropped almost to zero, in a classical demonstration of oversupply and speculation within a scarcity-based capitalist world market – were especially aware of the extent to which their fates lay in the hands of powerful, even mysterious, foreign others.

By the time I returned to Puerto Rico a couple of years later, I had read a fair amount of Caribbean history, including the history of plantation crops. I learned that although sugar cane was flanked by other harvests – coffee, cacao (chocolate), indigo, tobacco, and so on – it surpassed them all in importance and outlasted them. Indeed, the world production of sugar has never fallen for more than an occasional decade at a time during five centuries; perhaps the worst drop of all came with the Haitian Revolution of 1791–1803 and the disappearance of the world's biggest colonial producer; and even that sudden and serious imbalance was very soon redressed. But how remote this all seemed from the talk of gold and souls – the more familiar refrains of historians (particularly historians of the Hispanic achievement) recounting the saga of European expansion to the New World! Even the religious education of the enslaved Africans and indentured Europeans who came to the Caribbean with sugar cane and the other plantation crops (a far cry from Christianity and uplift for the Indians, the theme of Spanish imperial policy with which the conventional accounts were then filled) was of no interest to anyone.

I gave no serious thought to why the demand for sugar should have risen so rapidly and so continuously for so many centuries, or even to why sweetness might be a desirable taste. I suppose I thought the answers to such questions were self-evident – who doesn't like sweetness? Now it seems to me that my lack of curiosity was obtuse; I was taking demand for granted. And not just 'demand' in the abstract; world sugar production shows the most remarkable upward production curve of any major food on the world market over the course of several centuries, and it is continuing upward still. Only when I began to learn more Caribbean history and more about particular relationships between planters in the colonies and bankers, entrepreneurs, and different groups of consumers in the metropolises, did I begin to puzzle over what 'demand' really was, to what extent it could be regarded as 'natural', what is meant by words like 'taste' and 'preference' and even 'good'.

Soon after my fieldwork in Puerto Rico, I had a chance for a summer of study in Jamaica, where I lived in a small highland village that, having been established by the Baptist Missionary Society on the eve of emancipation as a home for newly freed church members, was still occupied – almost 125 years later – by the descendants of those freedmen. Though the agriculture in the highlands was mostly carried out on small landholdings and did not consist of plantation crops, we could look down from the lofty village heights on the verdant north coast and the brilliant green checkerboards of the cane plantations there. These, like the plantations on Puerto Rico's south coast, produced great quantities of cane for the eventual manufacture of granulated white sugar; here, too, the final refining was done elsewhere – in the metropolis, and not in the colony.

When I began to observe small-scale retailing in the busy marketplace of a nearby town, however, I saw for the first time a coarse, less refined sugar that harked back to earlier centuries, when haciendas along Puerto Rico's south coast, swallowed up after the invasion by giant North American corporations, had also once produced it. In the Brown's Town Market of St Ann Parish, Jamaica, one or two mule-drawn wagons would arrive each market day carrying loads of hard brown sugar in 'loaves', or 'heads', produced in traditional fashion by sugar makers using ancient grinding and boiling equipment. Such sugar, which contained considerable quantities of molasses (and some impurities), was hardened in ceramic molds or cones from which the more liquid molasses was drained, leaving behind the dark-brown, crystalline loaf. It was consumed solely by poor, mostly rural Jamaicans. It is of course common to find that the poorest people in less developed societies are in many regards the most 'traditional'. A product that the poor eat, both because they are accustomed to it and because they have no choice, will be praised by the rich, who will hardly ever eat it.

I encountered such sugar once more in Haiti, a few years later. Again, it was produced on smallholdings, ground and processed by ancient machinery, and consumed by the poor. In Haiti, where nearly everyone is poor, nearly everyone ate this sort of sugar. The loaves in Haiti were shaped differently: rather like small logs, wrapped in banana leaf, and called in Creole *rapadou* (in Spanish, *raspadura*). Since that time, I have learned that such sugars exist throughout much of the rest of the world, including India, where they were probably first produced, perhaps as much as 2,000 years ago.

There are great differences between families using ancient wooden machinery and iron cauldrons to boil up a quantity of sugar to sell to their neighbors in picturesque loaves, and the massed men and machinery employed in producing thousands of tons of sugar cane (and, eventually, of sugar) on modern plantations for export elsewhere. Such contrasts are an integral feature of Caribbean history. They occur not only between islands or between historical periods, but even within single societies (as in the case of Jamaica or Haiti) at the same time. The production of brown sugar in small quantities, remnant of an earlier technical and social era, though it is of declining economic importance will no doubt continue indefinitely, since it has cultural and sentimental meaning, probably for producers as well as consumers. Caribbean sugar industries have changed with the times, and they represent, in their evolution from antecedent forms, interesting stages in the world history of modern society.

I have explained that my first fieldwork in Puerto Rico was in a village of cane workers. This was nearly my first experience outside the continental United States, and though I had been raised in the country, it was my first lengthy encounter with a community where nearly everyone made a living from the soil. These people were not farmers, for whom the production of agricultural commodities was a business; nor were they peasants, tillers of soil they owned or could treat as their own, as part of a distinctive way of life. They were agricultural laborers who owned neither land nor any productive property, and who had to sell their labor to eat. They were wage earners who lived like factory workers, who worked in factories in the field, and just about everything they needed and used they bought from stores. Nearly all of it came from somewhere else: cloth and clothing, shoes, writing pads, rice, olive oil, building materials, medicine. Almost without exception, what they consumed someone else had produced.

The chemical and mechanical transformations by which substances are bent to human use and become unrecognizable to those who know them in nature have marked our relationship to nature for almost as long as we have been human. Indeed, some would say that it is those very transformations that define our humanity. But the division of labor by which such transformations are realized can impart additional mystery to the technical processes. When the locus of manufacture and that of use are separated in time and space, when the makers and the users are as little known to each other as are the processes of manufacture and use themselves, the mystery will deepen. An anecdote may make the point.

My beloved companion and teacher in the field, the late Charles Rosario, received his preparatory education in the United States. When his fellow students learned that he came from Puerto Rico, they immediately assumed that his father (who was a sociologist at the University of Puerto Rico) was a *hacendado* – that is, a wealthy owner of endless acres of tropical land. They asked Charlie to bring them some distinctive souvenir of plantation life when he returned from the island at the summer's end; what they would relish most, they said, was a machete. Eager to please his new friends, Charlie told me, he examined countless machetes in the island stores. But he was dismayed to discover that they were all manufactured in Connecticut – indeed, at a factory only a few hours' drive from the New England school he and his friends were attending.

As I became more and more interested in the history of the Caribbean region and its products, I began to learn about the plantations that were its most distinctive and characteristic economic form. Such plantations were first created in the New World during the early years of the sixteenth century and were staffed for the most part with enslaved Africans. Much changed, they were still there when I first went to Puerto Rico, thirty years ago; so were the descendants of those slaves and, as I later learned and saw elsewhere, the descendants of Portuguese, Javanese, Chinese, and Indian contract laborers, and many other varieties of human being whose ancestors had been brought to the region to grow, cut, and grind sugar cane.

I began to join this information to my modest knowledge of Europe itself. Why Europe? Because these island plantations had been the invention of Europe, overseas experiments of Europe, many of them successful (as far as the Europeans were concerned); and the history of European societies had in certain ways paralleled that of the plantation. One could look around and see sugar-cane plantations and coffee, cacao, and tobacco haciendas, and so, too, one could imagine those Europeans who had thought it promising to create them, to invest in their creation, and to import vast numbers of people in chains from elsewhere to work them. These last would be, if not slaves, then men who sold their labor because they had nothing else to sell; who would probably produce things of which they were not the principal consumers; who would consume things they had not produced, and in the process earn profit for others elsewhere.

It seemed to me that the mysteriousness that accompanied my seeing, at one and the same time, cane growing in the fields and white sugar in my cup, should also accompany the sight of molten metal or, better, raw iron ore, on the one hand, and a perfectly wrought pair of manacles or leg irons, on the other. The mystery was not simply one of technical transformation, impressive as that is, but also the mystery of people unknown to one another being linked through space and time – and not just by politics and economics, but along a particular chain of connection maintained by their production.

1985

HAROLD McGEE

From Raw to Cooked: The Transformation of Flavor

Why do we like our foods cooked? In the modern world, with its stoves and barbecues, toasters and microwave ovens, that may sound like a peculiar question. But step back for a moment into the natural world, and what seems strange is that the human animal could ever enjoy morsels that have been heated just this side of pure carbon. Cocoa and coffee beans, for example, or the crust on a roast. Very strange! After all, the earth's entire animal population had eaten its foods raw for thousands of millions of years. Then a mere million years ago or so, some early humans began to apply fire to a variety of objects, including plants and animals that their ancestors had eaten raw for aeons. By and large, the new charred version prevailed. And now it's sushi and steak tartare and crisp vegetables that punctuate our meals with occasional novelty.

True, anthropologists have pointed out that cooking serves several very practical purposes: it generally makes foods easier to chew, more digestible, less likely to cause illness, slower to spoil. On these grounds alone it would have caught on as 'adaptive' behavior. In fact, the purely mechanical advantages of cooking have influenced the very shape of the human face: our jaws are smaller and protrude less than the jaws of our ancestors and primate relatives. But humans had never eaten cooked foods before, and cooked flavors are not only stronger but often very different from the raw originals. So why would we have come to enjoy them?

One answer might be that as omnivores, humans are equipped to exploit a wide variety of foods. Perhaps our tastes are flexible enough that we can learn to like anything, provided there's a good reason to learn to like it. Another answer might be Brillat-Savarin's religious formulation: 'The Creator, while forcing man to eat in order to live, tempts him to do so with appetite and then rewards him with pleasure.' Certainly if one hungers for evidence that a benign Intelligence rules the universe, one could do worse than contemplate coffee, chocolate, and the roast.

But such answers don't offer much to chew on. Surely there's more to be said about so important a part of our life! A third approach is to look in some detail at the chemical changes caused by cooking. Perhaps a comparison of raw and cooked flavor molecules can offer a hint as to why cooked foods are so appealing. In fact, it does. The chemistry may at first seem rather esoteric and even hopelessly complicated: around six hundred different flavor compounds have been identified to date in cooked beef, for example. But the exercise is worth it. When we get down to basics, to the lowest common denominators of flavor, some very interesting patterns emerge, and with them an unexpected insight into gastronomical pleasure.

The modern-day chemistry of food flavor dates from around 1912 and the discovery of the browning reaction, also known as the Maillard reaction, which generates much of the characteristic color and aroma of foods cooked over a flame, in the oven, or in oil. It's fitting that a French scientist was at the heart of the matter, though he hadn't actually set out to build on the heritage of Thouvenel and Chaptal, Thenard and Proust, those early chemists who had explored the essence of meat flavor. The flavor of foods was far from the mind of the young doctor Louis-Camille Maillard as he pursued biochemical research at the University of Nancy. Rather, Maillard was interested in how living things string together proteins from their subunits, the amino acids. An eminent German chemist, Emil Fischer, had already succeeded in linking amino acids together in the test tube, but he did so using such unbiological means as pure alcohol, concentrated ammonia, and high temperatures. Maillard tried limiting the materials to common constituents of cells, and had some success when he heated amino acids together with glycerol, which is a part of every fat molecule.

Because glycerol has some features in common with sugars, Maillard repeated his experiment using sugars and amino acids. He observed that when these two materials were heated together, the solution in the test tube slowly turned brown. When he tried to analyze the substance responsible for the color, he found that it wasn't soluble in water, which suggested that its molecules were very large. It also contained some nitrogen, which derived from the amino acids. In this respect, as well as in the lower temperatures required to create it, the colored substance differed from the brown products of caramelized sugar, which contain no nitrogen. In his initial report of 1912, Maillard told the French Academy of Sciences that his discovery had consequences 'not only in human physiology and pathology, but also in plant physiology (cyclic alkaloids, etc.), agronomy (maturation of manures, humus, diverse industries), in geology (combustible minerals, etc.)'.

Maillard's report makes no mention whatever of foods or flavor. One of these oversights is remedied in a second report of the same year, in which Maillard includes the sugar, gingerbread, and beer industries among those that should be interested in the reaction, since they use 'materials of biological origin' and 'are led to bring together sugars and amino acids (or the starches and proteinaceous substances capable of giving birth to them)'. As one of his footnotes makes clear, Maillard was educated on this point by an English expert on brewing beer, one Arthur Robert Ling. In 1908, at a professional meeting at the Criterion Restaurant in Piccadilly, London, Ling had read a paper on malting, the process of germinating barley grain for several days and then kilning it to dry it. Much of a beer's color and flavor are generated when the barley is kilned. The initial germination was thought to involve the barley's 'autodigestion', or breaking down of stored starches and proteins to their fundamental building blocks, which could then be rearranged by the growing seedling. Ling imagined that these building blocks might be responsible for both the color and flavor of malted barley. So he tried the experiment of heating amino acids and sugars together, and noticed the development of a brown color and an aromatic odor.

Ling published his observations in 1908, but he never followed up on them. Maillard did devote some eight years to studying the combination under heat of amino acids and sugars, which is why the reaction was named after him, not Ling. Surprisingly, however, this countryman of Brillat-Savarin and the students of osmazome never made much of the flavorsome aspects of the browning reaction. And when Maillard died suddenly in Paris in 1936, at the age of fifty-eight, his work on browning was little remembered. For the last fifteen years of his life he had served as a professor of biological and medical chemistry at the University of Algiers, largely devoting his career to the analysis of urine and its diagnostic usefulness.

Although Maillard didn't realize how important the browning reaction is to the preparation of foods, he appears to have been quite right about a different connection that puts cooking in an interesting and unlikely perspective. As early as 1912 he pointed out the similarity between the brown compounds he could produce in the test tube and the substances that give rich organic soil its dark color. These soil substances had been studied since around 1800, when they were given the name *humic acids*: *humic* because found in humus, the Latin for 'soil'; and *acid* because they could be dissolved only in alkaline solution. Nowadays, it's thought that humic acids are created by bacteria, fungi, algae, and other soil microbes that decompose the plants' structural materials, cellulose and lignin, into phenolic substances. The phenolic substances are then oxidized by enzymes that have been released into the soil from dead plants and microbes, and bond together in large, colored structures. (The same browning enzymes in plants affect the color of many of our foods.) In addition, the microbial breakdown of proteins and carbohydrates generates large quantities of amino acids and sugars, which then undergo the Maillard reaction at the relatively low temperature of the soil, thanks to the presence of minerals, which may act as catalysts, and frequent changes in moisture and temperature.

To my knowledge, no one has investigated the possible contribution of the Maillard reaction to the characteristic odor of humus, which is generally attributed to a few chemicals secreted by soil bacteria. But it's an intriguing parallel: that the main chemical pathway for producing attractive colors and flavors in our foods is traveled naturally when the earth reclaims its own. Is it possible to detect a hint of fertile soil in the vapors of a roast, or a suggestion of brown-black coffee beans as one turns over the first spadefuls in the spring?

Apart from occasional studies in the brewing and sugar industries, the Maillard reaction received little attention until World War II, when American troops in the Pacific tropics complained that their powdered eggs were turning brown and developing unappetizing flavors. Laboratories assigned to analyze the problem discovered the culprit to be relatively low-temperature browning reactions made possible by the concentration of sugars and amino acids in dehydrated foods. The remedy was to remove the small quantities of glucose present in the eggs before drying them. Once browning had been identified as a cause of deterioration in processed and stored foods, the Maillard reaction became an object of great interest for both commercial and government-sponsored research. Of the many studies published in the late 1940s and the 1950s, most focused on ways to prevent browning.

A few scientists, however, bucked the trend of viewing the Maillard reaction as little more than a nuisance. One of the earliest and most notable dissents was a report issued in 1946 by H. M. Barnes and C. W. Kaufman, two chemists at General Foods Corporation. In order to piece together a basic understanding of browning in foods, they had begun by studying the reactions between individual amino acids and sugars. In doing so, they noticed that 'the flavors and odors developed were apparently characteristic of the particular amino acid being used.' A mixture of serine or threonine and glucose, for example, smelled like maple syrup. Such observations led Barnes and Kaufman to suggest a positive role for browning:

The present authors now believe that, in addition to being responsible for many deteriorative changes that occur in food products, the Maillard reaction may also be the contributing factor in the development of many of our characteristic food flavors. Although no evidence is as yet available, there is reason to suspect that the distinctive flavor differences in breakfast foods, the crust of baked bread, roasted coffee, etc., may be attributed to chemical combinations brought about during the heat treatment operation.

Chocolate, maple syrup, beer, soy sauce, and roasted, broiled, and fried meats also belong on this list. And Barnes and Kaufman ended their report with a prediction that has since been fulfilled in spades: 'Fundamental research on this aspect may provide a means of chemically synthesizing some flavors which will nearly approximate the natural flavors.'

Within a year of this forecast, the first patent for an artificial flavor – maple – had been granted, and others were being vigorously pursued. The quality of meatiness, the erstwhile osmazome, was perhaps the most sought-after flavor of all. Before the importance of the Maillard reaction had sunk in, industrial laboratories had approximated meatiness by means of MSG (monosodium glutamate) and certain nucleotides, or compounds related to the components of DNA and RNA. These created a 'brothy' flavor, and when one added vegetable protein that had been hydrolyzed (broken down into smaller chains of amino acids), a meaty aroma developed. But in 1960 a chemist at Lever Brothers patented a simpler formula based on the Maillard reaction: Heat either cysteine or cystine, two related sulfur-containing amino acids, with furan, a substance derived from sugar, and you get a meaty flavor. The amino acids arginine, glutamic acid, and proline improve the effect. Certain additional sugars produce a specifically beefy flavor. The reaction 'may be carried out by adding the reagents to a food product in which a meatlike flavor is desired, e.g., deflavored codfish hydrolyzate'.

The Lever Brothers' patent created a sensation. According to one reviewer, it precipitated 'a flood of grantings and applications' for similar patents. There were dozens of amino acids, dozens of sugars, and endless ways of combining them, each formula holding the promise of another desirable flavor. With the development in the mid-1960s of instruments that could analyze in great detail the chemical composition of natural aromas, the science of flavor chemistry reached full stride.

Today, any curious cook can explore the virtuosic nature of the Maillard reaction, thanks to those strange modern emporiums known as 'health food' stores. Many of them sell capsules of individual amino acids in powdered form. The idea that they're valuable nutritional supplements is nonsense – anyone who can afford to pay five dollars for thirty half-gram capsules probably already consumes more than enough protein. But the amino acids are fun to play with on the stove. Try tapping some of the powder into a small pan of boiling water. You'll smell a faint whiff of ammonia as the molecule breaks down, and if you use cysteine, which contains sulfur, you'll detect an odor reminiscent of boiled eggs, which is mainly hydrogen sulfide. Now add some of the powder to a pan (ideally nonstick) of gently bubbling corn syrup. Almost instantly the clear liquid will begin to turn a rich brown, and you'll smell some remarkable things. With cysteine, I notice the essence of fried onions – probably more sulfur compounds – as well as ammonia, hydrogen sulfide, and a general 'brothiness'. With lysine the effect is much milder, something like lightly toasted bread. And with phenylalanine, an aroma strangely reminiscent of melting plastic, followed in a minute or so by essence of almonds!

Experiments like these give a vivid sense of the Maillard reaction's vast potential for creating flavor. Heat a single odorless amino acid in water, and you produce a simple aroma; heat together a single amino acid and a mixture of two sugars, the glucose and fructose in corn syrup, and you can rouse an olfactory image of an actual food, like fried onions, maple syrup, or almonds. The image may be one-dimensional rather than *trompe-le-nez*, but it's still recognizable, even uncanny. Now, even the most unadorned of raw foods – a piece of meat, a potato, a green pea, some wheat flour – contains a score of amino acids and a handful of various sugars, as well as other molecules that may contribute in other ways to the aroma. It's evident, then, that cooking must generate very complex mixtures of flavor molecules.

Just how complex the flavors of cooking are has become evident only with the development of highly sensitive analytical instruments in the last two or three decades. As of 1963 some 500 flavor compounds had been laboriously catalogued from a variety of foods. A couple of years later the gas chromatograph, which separates a mixture of volatile compounds into its pure components, was married to the mass spectrometer, which makes it possible to identify a compound even in the tiny amounts typical of food aromas. By 1984 this technology had raised the number of identified flavor compounds to 4,300. The current estimate is that perhaps 10,000 such compounds exist, with the typical cooked food containing between 300 and 800.

Here, perhaps, is our first clue to the great appeal of cooked foods. Their flavors are intricate composites of many individual aromas and are certainly much richer in taste than such uncooked originals as a handful of grain, a tuber, a share of the hunt. (This is also true of such uncooked but fermented foods as wine and cheese.) There is, however, a major exception to this rule. Ripe raw fruits also tend to have very complex flavors. The strawberry has more than 300 component aromas, the raspberry 200 or more. Fruits probably provided our evolutionary ancestors with refreshing sensory interludes in an otherwise bland and dull diet. Perhaps cooking with fire was valued in part because it transformed blandness into fruitlike richness. The English essayist Walter Pater once said that 'All art constantly aspires to the condition of music'; perhaps the appropriate culinary paraphrase is 'All cooked foods aspire to the condition of fruit.'

The subtle complexity of food flavors has thwarted the chemists who have tried to produce convincing synthetic flavors. Vanillin doesn't really taste like vanilla, and imitation maple syrup seems duller than the real thing, precisely because imitations can't provide us with the fullness and depth that character-ize the originals. Where a real food gives us a rich chord of sensations, the imitation product gives us only a few of the more prominent notes.

This complexity also threatens to thwart our understanding of cooked flavors. Given that modern flavor chemists have catalogued some six hundred components of beef aroma, the rest of us may wonder how such a tedious exercise could possibly illuminate the pleasure we take in a bite of roast beef. As it turns out, among all these analyses are some promising clues to the nature of that pleasure. Several important flavor components have turned up in what might otherwise seem quite unrelated biological puzzles. This common currency suggests that the puzzle of culinary pleasure is itself interlocked in a larger pattern, one that offers a new perspective on our fondness for the cooked.

The best way to get to know the flavor compounds produced by cooking is to look at their origins and family resemblances. Let's take a single simple pro-genitor, table sugar, and see what families arise during caramelization. Plain crystalline sucrose has no odor. Heat it to about 320°F (160°C) and it melts; to 335°F (168°C), and it begins to color and develop a rich aroma. At this point, from the initial pure population of sucrose molecules we have generated more than a hundred reaction products – probably several hundred; the cataloguing is still in progress. These products arise when the carbon, hydrogen, and oxygen atoms in sugar molecules interact with each other and with oxygen in the air at high temperatures. The heat causes the atoms in the sugar molecules to move with such force that the bonds holding them together are readily broken. The molecules fragment in a variety of ways, and these fragments then react with each other in a variety of ways: and so on throughout the cooking. The result is sucrose's myriad progeny, the substances that constitute caramelized sugar. (Fats contain the same three elements, and generate many of the same aroma molecules when heated.)

Among the reaction products, many have a low boiling point. Significant numbers of these molecules escape into the air, reach the nose, and contribute to the aroma. The volatile products of caramelization can be divided into two general groups, according to the structure of their molecules: the chains and the rings. Principal among the chain families are simple acids, alcohols, alde-hydes, and esters. These each consist of a row of linked carbon atoms that is decorated with hydrogen atoms and an occasional oxygen or two. We're all familiar with representatives of each family. The acids include acetic acid, which gives vinegar its characteristic aroma. We know the alcohols from vodka, a mixture of ethyl alcohol and water, and whiskey, whose pungency comes from the presence of several longer-chain alcohols. One of the common aldehydes produces the aroma that distinguishes sherry from ordinary white wine. And the flavor of bananas is due largely to several esters.

That's already quite a heady mixture! But caramelized sugar also contains ring compounds, which are closed circles of carbon atoms, sometimes with one carbon replaced by an oxygen, again decorated with hydrogen and the odd oxygen. *Furans*, five-cornered rings that include one oxygen, can have sweet, fruity, nutty, or butterscotch flavor notes. *Pyrones* are six-cornered, with one oxygen in the ring and another attached to the opposite carbon. Maltol, a prominent pyrone, contributes a strong flavor of caramel itself. Then there are six-carbon rings, which include benzene and various derivatives, and are most familiar to us as the solvents in spot removers.

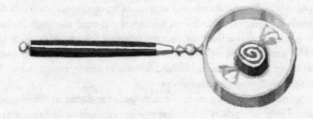

Fruits, nuts, alcohol, sherry, vinegar, spot remover, caramel – the mixture somehow spells caramel. Each of the hundred-plus flavor compounds is produced in a very small but characteristic quantity, and the relative proportions are essential to the overall effect they create. It's the composite impression, the chord, that we register.

It turns out that several of the flavor notes in caramel are contributed by chemical families that are common in nature, particularly in the fruits. Organic acids, alcohols, aldehydes, and esters are ubiquitous in the living world because they are all associated with the universal processes of energy production. The cook generates them by breaking up sugar molecules and scrambling the atoms with heat; fruits generate them during ripening (and microbes – yeasts, molds, and bacteria – during fermentation) by means of enzymes, which accomplish the same kinds of atomic rearrangements at lower temperatures. So at least some of the components of caramel aroma are flavors that would have been familiar to our preculinary ancestors from raw and fermented – that is, partly spoiled – fruits.

So much for browning plain sugar. Of course, nearly all our foods contain both carbohydrates and proteins, so most kitchen browning entails the Maillard reaction between sugars and amino acids. When heated, these chemical ingredients will give rise to the products typical of caramelization (if the temperature is at least 335°F, or 168°C), plus products typical of heated amino acids alone, plus the Maillard products proper. The amino acids bring two new elements into the picture: nitrogen, a constituent of all amino acids, and sulfur, a constituent of two. Heat any amino acid in boiling water and you'll detect the faint smell of ammonia as the nitrogen is torn away; heat a sulfur-containing amino acid like cysteine, and you'll also detect hydrogen sulfide, that eggy note. Both of these simple volatile compounds contribute to the aromas of cooked eggs, meats, and dairy products, all rich in proteins and especially in sulfur-containing amino acids.

The Maillard reaction proper begins when a nitrogen atom on an amino acid attacks one of the carbon atoms on a sugar. A large composite molecule forms, rearranges itself internally, and then breaks up into pieces. Each piece continues to metamorphose until the heating stops or the molecule escapes into the air. The participation of nitrogen seems to be a great encouragement to such metamorphoses, because Maillard browning takes place at much lower temperatures than does caramelization.

The important families of aroma compounds produced in the Maillard reaction are all rings of carbon atoms that may also include one or two nitrogens, sometimes an oxygen, and sometimes a sulfur. Each of these basic ring structures may be surrounded by a variety of other atoms or groups of atoms. Sometimes two or more rings will fuse together into one large molecule. The principal families include several five- and six-membered rings. The five-membered rings are the *pyrroles*, with one nitrogen; the *thiophenes*, with one sulfur; the *thiazoles*, with a nitrogen and a sulfur; and the *oxazoles*, with a nitrogen and an oxygen. The six-cornered rings are the *pyridines*, with one nitrogen, and the *pyrazines*, with two nitrogens. Currently, it's thought that the pyrazines and thiazoles are primarily responsible for the characteristic flavor of browned foods.

These ring compounds add another dimension to the flavors produced in sugar caramelization. Several contribute a nutty note, the sulfur rings a suggestion of browned onion and meatiness, and certain pyrazines and thiazoles a general 'roasted' impression, even hints of chocolate. But there are some surprises. Several oxazoles contribute floral odors. And many pyrazines and thiazoles, the two families that seem to be most essential to the typical browned flavor, together with the pyridines, are reminiscent of green leaves and vegetables. In fact, several of the particular compounds produced by the action of heat on our foods remind us of the flavors that we encounter in plants, and that our ancestors would have encountered long before they had mastered fire.

Let's look at a few examples of characteristic roasting products whose aromas are reminiscent of plants. Two 'green'-smelling pyridines, 3-methylpyridine and 2-ethylpyridine, are found in roast lamb, and 2-ethylpyridine is also found in roast beef.* Also reminiscent of green vegetables is 2-methylthiazole, formed during the cooking of beef, as is 5-ethyl-4-methylthiazole, which has nutty, green, and earthy overtones. A green note is contributed by the 2-propylpyrazine found in roast coffee and peanuts; the green, nutty 2,3-dimethylpyrazine has been noted in roast beef, cocoa, coffee, popcorn, potato chips, and a variety of nuts, as has the earthy, raw-potato aroma of 2,5-dimethylpyrazine.

This mingling of the animal and vegetable, the raw and the cooked, may seem like a remarkable coincidence. It's one thing to find shared features in browned sugar and in fruits, which also contain sugar. But by comparison to those simple acids, esters, and so on, these nitrogen- and sulfur-containing rings, which are known as heterocyclic compounds, are rather exotic. It's harder to see how these structures would have any connection with the world of natural flavors.

In fact, many of these typical 'artificial' flavor molecules have also been found in the raw natural world. They are by no means common, but they're not all that rare either. Information is scattered and preliminary at the moment, but it's also quite intriguing. Furans have been found in pineapples and strawberries, oxazoles in ryegrass and members of the aster family. There's a thiazole in passion fruit and two others in the tamarind, a tropical pod-fruit with a rich flavor reminiscent of prunes. And 2-isobutylthiazole contributes to the flavor of the tomato.

The most extensive and exciting findings have to do with the pyrazines. One regular reviewer of the field has said that 'to date no other class of flavoring compounds has been shown to be as important to our foods.' Members of this chemical family were first recognized in the test tube in the middle of the nineteenth century, and first found in foodstuffs – molasses and then coffee – at the beginning of the twentieth century. Around 1950, a fungus-produced antibiotic, aspergillic acid, proved to be a pyrazine derivative, and in 1962

---

* In these chemical names, the prefix indicates by number the atom of the central ring at which a 'side group' of atoms is attached, and then names the side group.

pyrazines were extracted from fermented soy beans. In the late 1960s and early 1970s, pyrazines were identified in cocoa products, green peas, cooked beef, Gouda and Emmenthal cheeses, tamarind, wine grapes, dried red beans, soil-inhabiting bacteria, and then in a number of raw vegetables, including asparagus, green beans, beets, carrots, lettuce, and potatoes. Perhaps most renowned among flavor chemists is the potent 2-isobutyl-3-methoxypyrazine, which is found in fairly large quantities in bell peppers and is thought to be responsible for the 'vegetative' or 'herbaceous' character of some wines. The 'bell-pepper' pyrazine can be smelled at a concentration in air of one part in a trillion, and is now a favored experimental tool for probing the mysterious means by which our olfactory cells detect aroma molecules.

So the pyrazine family is well known to microbes and plants. These organisms even synthesize some of the same pyrazines that we create when we roast meats, cocoa and coffee beans, and nuts. This is true, for example, of the earthy 2,5-dimethylpyrazine found in dried red beans and tamarind fruit. Tamarin also contains the nutty, roasted 2-methylpyrazine as well as 2,6-dimethylpyrazine, both of which are found in a wide range of browned foods. Cooking with fire may have been a great human innovation, but our ancestors and other animals have been encountering molecules characteristic of the roast for much, much longer, probably for hundreds of millions of years.

And not just in their food plants. It turns out that some animals produce their own heterocyclic aroma molecules. In 1973 a group of entomologists noticed that when ants of several species are disturbed, they secrete a chocolate-smelling substance that induces nearby ants either to retreat or to attack. That is, the substance seems to operate as an alarm pheromone. When the secretion was analyzed, it turned out to consist of several pyrazines, some of which have been found in cocoa products. Another species of ant employs a different pyrazine in its trail pheromone, which helps individual ants follow each other; that pyrazine is found in fried beef, cocoa, coffee, and roasted nuts. It's now thought that the use of pyrazines as chemical signals is widespread among the many thousands of species of ants, and perhaps among other insects as well. Recent studies have detected pyrazines in ladybugs, moths, beetles, and butterflies. Several butterflies, including the monarch, selectively extract and store pyrazines from their food plants and release them, apparently as a defensive gesture or a warning signal, when their bodies are pinched. In another sensory realm, some squids and coelenterates – including certain jellyfish, the sea pen, sea pansy, and sea cactus – incorporate the pyrazine ring in a light-emitting complex that generates visual signals. And a thiazole ring is at the core of the substance luciferin, which is responsible for the glow of the firefly.

A consistent theme emerges among these animal anecdotes: communication. Animals exploit molecules in the pyrazine and thiazole families as signals, just as they've done with alcohols, esters, aldehydes, terpenoid substances, and other volatile molecules. Odor signals are involved in a variety of important activities, from mating and egg laying to feeding, the marking of trails and territories, aggregation, and warnings and defense against predators. In the case of the insect pheromones, the efficiency of the odor-molecule signals has been well established: only small quantities of energy are required to generate them and, because the odors travel freely in the air and can be detected even when very dilute, they can be effective at distances of a few millimeters or a hundred feet.

To date, almost nothing is known about the function of pyrazines and thiazoles in plants, but it's likely to resemble their role in the animal world. These molecules are classified along with thousands of others found in plants as *secondary products*: that is, compounds that don't seem to have a direct role in the primary activities of growth, energy production and storage, and reproduction. It's thought that most of these secondary products have a defensive function. Some clearly do – for example, the poisonous alkaloids and cyanide-producing compounds – and most of the substances that we value as flavorings, the essential oils of the herb and spice plants, repel many insects and other predators. Circumstantial evidence suggests that pyrazines may have a similar function. In both insects and wild plants, the presence of pyrazines is usually associated with a defensive toxin. For example, the monarch butterfly borrows from its food plant, the milkweed, both a bitter poison and a strong-smelling trio of pyrazines. The pyrazines themselves aren't toxic. So it appears that for both plant and butterfly, the poison is the actual weapon used to deter predators, while the pyrazines are a memorable early warning signal. Once a predator has gotten sick on a bite of milkweed or monarch, the mere whiff of pyrazines is probably sufficient to cut short any subsequent attack.

The study of pyrazines in monarch butterflies was led by Miriam Rothschild, an English entomologist who has long been interested in the odorous secretions of insects. She pointed out decades ago that a number of insects emit very similar odors when handled, and many of these odors have turned out to involve pyrazines. In any event, the exploitation by insects of protective plant pyrazines, and the variety of messages carried by the pyrazine secretions of ants, are two indications that these molecules are quite versatile. They may have originated in plants as purely defensive compounds, but as life has evolved, so has their significance. Rothschild has ventured some stimulating thoughts about the versatility of the pyrazine odors:

Certainly their evocative qualities make them ideal ingredients of a generalized warning system, but we may speculate that they probably also act as enhancers or boosters of other 'interesting' signals, perhaps even heightening the attractive elements of various animal and plant secretions. Furthermore all evocative scents of this type – vanilla and chocolate are other examples – possess a certain subtle quality which stirs, if it does not actually sharpen, memory, and possibly also assists or hastens the process of learning.

Rothschild's speculations raise fascinating questions. What does it say about gastronomical pleasure that evocative odors help plants and insects survive, that the aroma of chocolate can be so important in the lives of organisms as different as ants and humans? Can biology make sense of the powerful impression that certain foods make on us?

We don't yet know enough to venture any confident answers. But it's worth noting that in the matter of smell, there's not as much difference between us and some insects as we might think. For example, in a series of remarkable experiments running from the 1920s through the 1960s, Karl von Frisch proved that the olfactory sensitivities of the bee are quite similar to those of humans. Not only do both species detect the same classes of odors, but they detect them at about the same concentrations in the air. The insects, being invertebrates, are by no means our evolutionary predecessors; the last ancestor that humans and ants had in common was nothing much like either. But that very distance indicates how important it has been for all animals to detect a wide variety of aroma molecules, and particularly molecules that are generated by plants and other animals. Maybe we're simply lucky that cooking with fire happens to create aroma molecules very similar, and sometimes identical, to those found in nature. If for some reason it hadn't turned out that way, then roasted cocoa beans might strike us as quite abominable.

Of the evocativeness of aromas, no one has written more eloquently than Marcel Proust in his *In Search of Lost Time*. 'And the orange squeezed into the water seemed to yield to me, as I drank, the secret life of its ripening growth . . . countless mysteries unveiled by the fruit to my sensory perception, but not at all to my intelligence.' Such moments take the narrator 'deep down in that region more intimate than that in which we see and hear, in that region where we experience the quality of smells, almost in the very heart of my inmost self.' It's no doubt a crime of some sort to have Proust consort on the same page with insects! But if there is something to Miriam Rothschild's musings, then our powerful response to odors may in part be a legacy of their prehistoric importance for animals, which have used them to recall and learn from their experiences. Just as an evocative odor dilates our nostrils and deepens our breath as we try to capture it and its significance, so perhaps it dilates our receptiveness and deepens our attentiveness to the circumstances of the moment as it gives that moment an indelible mark. We may come to associate a particular aroma with a particular experience, and a very familiar aroma may impart a fundamental sense of security. But initially, odors are empty of associations, and their significance can change over time. Perhaps the same element of indeterminacy that makes them so versatile also accounts for their penumbra of significant mystery.

Our quest to understand the pleasures of cooked foods has taken us quite some distance from Louis-Camille Maillard and his test tube of sugars and amino acids. But it was the census of the chemical progeny of the browning reaction that expanded our perspective to include ants and fireflies, milkweed and butterflies. These parallels remind us that the detection of useful and dangerous chemicals, the active invention of chemical signals, and their deployment for a variety of purposes have been important elements in the mutual accommodation of plant and animal life on earth. And this biochemical saga has engendered many of the table's pleasures. Spice plants have strong flavors because they are effective deterrents to many plant-eating insects; flowers have pleasant odors because long ago beetles proved to be useful agents of cross-pollination; fruits have pleasant flavors because, somewhat later, small mammals proved to be useful dispersers of seeds. It seems that browned foods taste good partly because they develop a complexity comparable to that of the fruits, and partly because the major families of aroma chemicals created by heat had already been in active use by plants and animals for millions of years.

Perhaps, then, the great triumph of cooking has not been just a matter of its mechanical and hygienic advantages. Heat transforms our foods by enriching their flavors tremendously, and by evoking, at some level, different foods and different times. In a sip of coffee or a piece of crackling there are echoes of flowers and leaves, fruit and earth, a recapitulation of moments from the long dialogue between animals and plants. The simplest morsel offers much to savor.

1990

COLMAN ANDREWS

Chicken à la King and Bidimensional Piranha

'On no account should new terms or names [for dishes] be created.'
L. Saulnier, *Le Répertoire de la Cuisine*

In a Leo Cullum cartoon in *The New Yorker* in 1984, one Eskimo offers another a platter bearing a single, unadorned whole fish. 'It's called fettuccine Alfredo,' the first Eskimo announces.

Well, now, a plate of fish is obviously not fettuccine Alfredo – but then neither is most of what's served under that name in the restaurants of America today. Food nomenclature in this country in general, in fact, has degenerated in recent years into a hash of misnomer, a stew of garbled terminology.

Back in the Dark Ages of American gastronomy, say fifteen or twenty years ago, the food we ate in restaurants may well have been frozen (or canned), over-cooked, and underseasoned. But at least we knew what to call it – or, rather, when we saw what the restaurant called it, we knew more or less what it was going to be. Certain names implied certain ingredients and/or cooking methods, and any reasonably experienced diner knew which names meant what. Chicken à la king, for instance, was always chicken in a cream sauce with pimentos, served on toast or in a puff-pastry shell; veal parmigiana was cloaked in tomato sauce, with gooey cheese melted on top; sole Véronique involved green grapes. The particulars might have varied from one restaurant or chef to another, but standard definitions did exist.

Such definitions were given almost statutory weight by the French, in such books as the *Larousse Gastronomique*, *Le Répertoire de la Cuisine*, and Escoffier's *Le Guide Culinaire*. Culinary nouns, verbs, and adjectives had meanings that could no more be tampered with than weights and measures could be arbitrarily changed. Thus, *hongroise* implied paprika; Parmentier, potatoes; Vichy or Crécy, carrots. Even if he couldn't quote the textbook definitions of several hundred garnishes or sauces, anyone who went out to dinner regularly probably knew, for instance, that a dish described as *provençale* wasn't likely to be made with sour cream and dill.

Practical value aside, old-style food names in general – French and otherwise – are colorful, poetical, evocative. Some dishes are named after professions: *maître d'hôtel* butter, *poulet chasseur*, diplomat pudding; others are named for famous personalities – musicians (tournedos Rossini, steak Sinatra), writers (*poulet* George Sand, the Châteaubriand), statesmen (*jambon* Metternich), and both monarchs and their lady friends (the Napoléon; crêpes Suzette).

English food names, for instance, are often more interesting than the food they describe: angels on horseback (grilled oysters wrapped in bacon on toast), bubble and squeak (reheated mashed potatoes with cabbage or other greens), toad in the hole (sausage baked in pastry), tipsy parson (a relative of trifle).

The Italians like naughty food names. The best known of these is the famous Roman pasta dish, spaghetti *alla putanesca* – 'whore style'. In several parts of Italy, gnocchi, or potato dumplings, are known as *strangolopreti* or *strozzapreti*, meaning 'priest stranglers', the implication being that even holy men consume them gluttonously. Then there are the notorious Sicilian convent pastries dubbed *fedde del cancelliere* (chancellor's buttocks) and *minni di virgini* (virgins' breasts), and the tiny Roman pasta called *cazzetti d'angeli*, which it is possible to translate no more delicately than as 'little angels' penises'.

The Chinese like metaphorical food names – Dragon and Phoenix (made with seafood or reptiles and chicken), Ants Climbing a Tree (minced pork with glass noodles, in which bits of meat are supposed to resemble ants), Lion's Head (pork with curly cabbage – the cabbage thought to resemble a lion's mane). Sometimes, metaphor becomes euphemism: In *Food in History*, Reay Tannahill notes that poor Chinese workers in medieval times ate such things as 'brushwood shrimps' and 'household deer' – grasshoppers and rats, respectively.

Another whole category of food names is intentionally ironical – names that make a joke out of the poverty of their ingredients. The most famous of these is 'Welsh rabbit', made from melted cheese, ale, and mustard, implying that this blend of ordinary ingredients is what the Welsh eat when they haven't been able to shoot or trap any four-footed bunnies. (On the rabbit/rarebit question, I refer the reader to Ambrose Bierce, in *The Devil's Dictionary*: 'RAREBIT, n. A Welsh rabbit, in the speech of the humorless, who point out that it is not a rabbit. To whom it may be solemnly explained that the comestible known as toad-in-a-hole is really not a toad, and that *ris-de-veau à la financière* is not the smile of a calf prepared after the recipe of a she banker.')

There are countless other examples of this genre: Britain's Scotch wood-cock (toast with anchovy paste and scrambled eggs); the Italian *uccelli scappati*, or 'escaped birds', and the Niçois *alouettes sans têtes*, or 'larks without heads', both of which are little bundles of flattened beef or veal rolled around herbs and breadcrumbs; the Sicilian *fegato ai Sette Cannoli*, a dish of sliced yellow squash in a garlicky sweet vinegar sauce, said to be the closest thing to liver *fegato* that the poor Palermo neighbourhood of Sette Cannoli can afford. I wonder, too, if there isn't similar irony implied by the Catalan and Provençal words for omelet – *truita* and *troucho*, respectively – identical to the words in those languages for trout. The fisherman who comes home with an empty creel, that is, might have to settle for eggs for dinner.

About the most imaginative dish names I've seen in recent years are the surrealistic Spanish ones coined by Jimmy Schmidt and Ricardo Jurado-Solares at the original Rattlesnake Club in Denver in the mid-1980s.* These included *calamares atacados por pirañas bidimensionales* (squid attacked by bidimensional piranhas), *aquarium vacio encostalado y frito con lava* (empty aquarium encrusted and fried with lava), and *explosion nuclear en el campo de calabezas* (nuclear explosion in the pumpkin patch). These were, respectively, fried squid with tomatillo sauce, spicy seafood wontons, and chicken and mushroom empanadas with pumpkin–blue cheese sauce. These names might have had no logic to them, and they certainly weren't traditional – but they were sure fun.

In contrast, the typical 'New American' menu today is apt to offer (to pick from several real ones at random) such things as 'lobster with Scotch whisky and white bean ravioli in leaves of green chard', 'chicken salad with baby lettuces, roasted peppers, sun-dried tomatoes, pine nuts and goat cheese', 'braised veal ribs in white wine, roma tomatoes, apricots and fresh herbs, served with great northern white beans', and 'charcoal grilled Szechuan beef, thinly sliced, with hot chili oil and cilantro shallot sauce'. Those aren't dish names, those are recipes – or at least shopping lists.

At least with names like that, though, you know pretty much what you're going to get. Maybe old-style food terminology has lost its appeal simply because it has been so often and egregiously misapplied over the years in America, either through ignorance, laziness, or some misapprehension about the nature of 'creativity' in the kitchen. As many times as you may have eaten 'eggs Benedict,' for instance, I'll wager you that you've never eaten *eggs Benedict*, the real thing, served on Holland rusk with a slice of tongue instead of ham, and garnished with thick slices of black truffle. Tournedos Rossini, beef Wellington, and dishes as simple as the Cobb salad or the *salade niçoise* are similarly misinterpreted as a matter of course.

---

* The Rattlesnake Club in Denver was subsequently renamed Adirondacks, and Schmidt was bought out by his partner, Michael McCarty. At this writing, the restaurant is closed. Schmidt today owns the Rattlesnake Club in Detroit, along with several other restaurants in that city.

And then there's fettuccine Alfredo: Supposedly invented in 1920 in Rome by Alfredo di Lellio at his Alfredo restaurant on the via della Scrofa ('street of the Sow'), and supposedly named in his honor by Mary Pickford and Douglas Fairbanks, Jr, who ate the dish while in Rome on their honeymoon, fettuccine Alfredo has become one of the most popular of all pastas in America. But fettuccine Alfredo isn't what you think it is.

Let's not even mention the peas or mushrooms or prosciutto that often get stirred into something masquerading under Alfredo's name; the fact is that real fettuccine Alfredo contains *no cream*. Here is a contemporary description (from 1931) of the way Alfredo himself used to make the dish, from *Conducted Tour* by Gil Meynier:

When steaming platters of *fettucini* [*sic*] were brought in, Alfredo himself came and stood at the head of the table . . . A spoon in one hand, a fork in the other, he made a few graceful passes over the dishes on which butter, cheese and *fettucini* were waiting to be mixed by the master. The spoon delved into the heap of flat, golden, ribbon-like spaghetti [*sic*] and lifted it toward the caress of the fork which in its rapid movements carried a piece of fast-melting butter. The grated cheese penetrated into the lower layers of the deftly malaxated mass. Alfredo was no longer smiling. A minute longer and it would be ready to serve. An almost imperceptible gesture of the head warned his attentive aide to have the plates ready. One more stroke . . . he dug into the dish and with an upward gesture drew from it a first portion which he piously deposited on the first plate. In three movements he emptied the dish in three miraculously equal shares. And started on the next lot.

There was originally nothing in the dish, in other words, but noodles, cheese, and butter. Of course, the cheese was the finest Parmigiano Reggiano, and the butter was extraordinarily rich. Most accounts of the dish maintain that cream was first added because American butter wasn't rich enough. Nonetheless, what was probably the first recipe ever given for the dish in this country, in restaurateur George Rector's *The Rector Cook Book* (1928), was a pure one, calling for cheese and butter only. (Rector calls the dish simply 'noodles Alfredo', without specifying the kind of pasta to be used, and appends the recipe to something called marinated beef Alfredo.)

As food changes and develops, of course, so do dish names and their interpretations. But I think there have to be some commonly agreed-upon definitions – perhaps not as stringent or all-encompassing as those of Escoffier or Larousse, but at least ballpark meanings. I think we ought to have at least some menu shorthand, colorful or not, and that we ought to agree on what that shorthand stands for. And I think that while chefs certainly have the right to improvise, they don't have a right to call any old thing by a famous name.

It's not just a matter of cream in the fettuccine Alfredo. It's the whole idea of re-establishing some kitchen basics around here. Otherwise the day will soon and surely come when we'll order steak tartare and get beef stroganoff – or order fettuccine Alfredo and get a plate of fish.

1992

MARGARET VISSER

Dinner Is Served

. . . The recent fashion for *nouvelle cuisine* is a social expression of the modern ideal that successful people ought to contrive to be not only very rich but also very thin. Food is not mounted in an extravagant and copious display, to be divided among the guests; modern individualists receive individual plates, each already bearing its exquisite and exotic, though meager, portion. This might consist, for example, of a scattering of colorful shreds of vegetables and flowers. Or there may be three slices of duck breast lying on a sheet of concentrated but unthickened sauce; this sauce may be streaked or dotted with sauce of a different shade, *ton sur ton*. Sauces go under, not over, the food, lending it background and visual enhancement rather than comfortably cloaking it; the sophisticated skimpiness, expensive simplicity, and image-consciousness of *nouvelle cuisine* remind us of the fashionable clothes designed for its consumers. Japanese restraint and refinement of taste are suggested by layout, conscious juxtapositions, and the attention to color, shape, and texture. Restaurants love *nouvelle cuisine* because anyone tempted to pander to an appetite must order several artistic creations in order to make up a meal.

The ancient threefold pattern of the formal European dinner, even the dinner *à la française* – overture, climax, sweet final flourish – provides the structure for much simpler, and more simply filling, family meals: soup, meat and two veg (notice the threefold principle in microcosm for this central course), and dessert. Tea and a biscuit do not constitute a proper meal; nor would a series of sweet dishes, or nothing but greens. Soup is a meal, but only if it is thick enough, and accompanied, say, by bread and cheese. Breakfast often fails to be considered a meal. The French are amazed by the British breakfast because – unlike the 'Continental' repast consisting of coffee and a roll – a traditional British breakfast is a real meal, with cereal and milk or grapefruit in the place of soup or *hors d'œuvres*, then eggs and bacon, and finally toast and jam (for dessert). For many people a meal is not really a meal unless it features something hot. And leaving out meat changes the entire structure of the proceedings. Vegetarian dishes cost less, are shared more easily, and can be cooked more quickly, in spite of the peeling and chopping, than meat. But they generally force us (to whom vegetarianism is not traditional) to use considerable imagination and effort to keep everyone happy, and convinced that they are eating a *meal*.

An airline dinner is a useful device to keep passengers pinned to their places and occupied for an appreciable length of time. People hurtling through the air in a metal tube, both uneasily aware of what could go wrong and stupefied with boredom, are deemed to require solace. Eating is comfort – provided that nothing untoward or unexpected occurs during dinner. In the early days of air travel, until the early thirties, travelers ate at tables set out in the plane, as in a restaurant. There were wine bottles, flowers, cloths on the tables, and male stewards (then called couriers) in white jackets, serving the meals. The shuddering and dipping of the aircraft caused spills, and the noise was so infernal that conversation had often to be carried on by means of written notes – but still things were done 'properly', which is to say as far as possible as they were done on earth.

The first passenger aircraft in service after World War II fitted people into planes as though they were in a bus: airline management had realized that the future lay in cutting corners, increasing the numbers on board, and relying on the prestige of technology to make up for any loss in luxury. The gamble paid off. The new air travelers packed themselves into small spaces with a sense of fun, awe, and excitement. At first, seats were reversible so that passengers could turn them round and sit facing each other for meals; soon even that kind of encouragement to companionship was denied. But a three-course dinner with a hot meat component is still provided for everybody (except those who exempt themselves on health or vegetarian grounds), whether they are ready to eat or not, on the fold-out flap which anchors us to our places while dinner is served.

No effort is spared to impress upon us that we might be cramped and uncomfortable, but we are certainly experiencing a technological miracle. A tray is usually the receptacle for dinner, with pre-molded compartments or fitted containers keeping every course separate. The separateness is spatial, not sequential: an airline meal is one course of a tiny dinner *à la française*. There will be cellophane coverings and plastic lids (we are hygienic, we are safe) and cutlery, pepper, salt, and paper napkin in a neat bundle. Until air travel became entirely banal, people used to save their little plastic knives, their mustard packets, and swizzle-sticks stamped with airplane motifs, as souvenirs; they were familiar objects, but small and sufficiently odd-looking to remind us of those strange meals aloft, and to prove to others that we had been there. The knife, for instance, often has an almost triangular blade: its bizarre shape looks convincingly modern, but it is actually designed so that we can eat with elbows so tightly compressed to our sides that the blade must descend almost vertically upon the meat. Nobody with any sense would eat the *hors d'œuvres* of an airplane meal first. They are almost always cold, and the heated meat and two vegetables will cool off in a matter of minutes. We therefore attack the main course first, then rip open the *hors d'œuvres*, toy with the stiff lettuce (most of us leave this *'entremets'* uneaten), then attempt the block of cake.

For the higher price of their tickets, first-class and 'business' class passengers get better food as well as wider seats. In their anxiety to please their richer customers, and to mark as clearly as possible the difference between them and the mere 'economy' or 'coach' class, airlines spend as much as four times the amount on meals for the well-heeled in their curtained-off enclosure up front as for those in more straitened circumstances behind. In North America food service is becoming an important selling point on aircraft, now that the few airline companies which are left have agreed among themselves to refrain from the turbulence that used to be caused by competitive fare cuts. So more imagination is being tried when compiling menus, china and metal cutlery are increasingly supplied, and meals, especially in the upper class, may even be served in courses (*à la russe*).

The 'companions' close to our sides (we face other people's backs) are likely to be strangers. Meals are provided in strict accustomed sequence: breakfast, lunch, dinner, with 'proper' tea-breaks and drinks, in spite of time changes, and regardless of the fact that eating events may take place with very short periods of sedentary time between them. An airline meal is not large: who would expect a large meal in our cabined and confined state? But it is invariably complete, and as complex as possible. It tries to carry all the connotations of a shared, comforting, 'proper' dinner. It is supposed to supply a nostalgic link with the cultural presuppositions with which flying conflicts, such as warm kitchens, stable conditions, and the products of the earth. Manners, here, impose passivity and constraint; ornamentation is taken care of by the oddity of our being served dinner at all in such circumstances. There is no question of argument, and only very limited choice. Airline passengers are extraordinarily docile and uncomplaining. They give up space and ceremony, believing that this is only fair since they are gaining time and ought to be grateful for safety.

The three-part meal turns up again in another 'food event', the time-saving hamburger. Here we have a meal wherein all references to companionship have been firmly deleted. Circles are symbols of completeness and self-sufficiency. The traditional European plate is round: diners at table are separated from one another, marked off by the cutlery, and expected not to trespass upon others' places. Circular hand-held hamburgers make the most individual and unshared of meals; table, tablecloth, conversation, and cutlery are all unnecessary. Utterly round buns (giant hamburger industries destroy every imperfectly circular bun) enclose disks of ground meat, every one of them exactly alike in weight, consistency, and color. Subordinate to bread and meat, but colorful, glistening, and frilly, are the tomato slices and lettuce leaves. Trimmings may be chopped onions, ketchup, pickles, or mustard; a slice of processed cheese can supply an extra course.

Every burger is as self-contained, as streamlined and as replete as a flying saucer, and just as unmistakably a child of the modern imagination. Yet its substance is no more novel than hot meat and two veg, with sauce, condiments, and bread; and the roundness is not only self-sufficient but also old-fashioned, plump, and comforting. The middle section of the traditional three-course meal is piled up, each part clearly identifiable and contrasted with each, the whole symmetrically bracketed with bread. Our teeth bite down through the lot, as we skilfully hold it all together with fingers which must simultaneously contrive not to get bitten or to let parts slide out from the whole. The formality of hamburgers lies in their relentlessly predictable shape, and in the superimposed and separate layers of food which make sophisticated references to parts of the sequential model for a formal meal. Hamburgers are ready very fast (we do not see, and therefore discount, all the work which this speed and availability presuppose), and they take only a few minutes to eat: informality in this case cuts away time and clearly signals a disinclination to share.

The native Cantonese institution of *sihk puhn* uses informality to achieve something very different. A *sihk puhn* (literally 'eat pot') takes the sequence of nine courses which make up a formal Chinese banquet and collapses them all into one mass of food. (The English word 'mess' originally designated a portion of food or a course; then it came to mean a portion shared among two, three, or four people; then a number of people eating together; and finally – perhaps because of a set of ideas similar to that expressed by *sihk puhn* – it signifies structure destroyed.)

Into a large wooden basin go bits of fatback pork, white turnips, chicken, dried beancurd skin, fish balls, dried pork skin, dried fish, fresh fish, and dried squid. Each ingredient is fried separately in peanut oil, and all are mixed together at the last moment – rather as a hamburger is assembled before the customer's eyes. A sauce is made of chopped green onions, sugar, black peppercorns, dried cassia bark, cloves, fennel, star anise, rice wine, fermented soy beans, fermented beancurd paste, garlic, and water; this is poured over all. *Sihk puhn* is consumed at a great concourse of people, and each bowl is shared among about eight of them. Every person takes a pair of chopsticks and an individual portion of rice. A party might sit at a table or squat on the ground;

the first to come are the first served. People root about in the bowl with their chopsticks for bits of food; they eat at their own pace, and leave whenever they feel like it. There are no hosts for the groups, there are no speeches, very little talking, no toasts, no precedence or places of honour, no dressing up, no head table, no waiters.

The point about a *sihk puhn* is that it is most emphatically not formal; and this expresses the intention of everybody at the feast to practise equality. As a local rice merchant told the anthropologist James Watson, 'It shows that we all trust each other.' Factory workers, bank managers, and farmers sit or squat side by side; the destruction of sequence is symbolic of the (temporary) collapse of distinction among the people present. *Sikh puhn* banquets are used to legitimize social transitions, such as marriages, the birth of male children, the 'coming to personhood' of all babies thirty days after birth, and the adoption of male heirs.

While hamburgers demonstrate an agreement to be separate, *sihk puhn* signifies cohesion and trust. In both cases, equality is expressed not only through informality but also through careful attention to the principle of simultaneity, in one case through the careful stacking of the ingredients, and in the other through the wanton mixing of them. Hierarchy, both in America and in the Canton Delta, is expressed by formality, and therefore informality breaks down rank. And where formality takes time, its relaxation requires speed.

1991

PART TWO

THE OLD WORLD

ALAN DAVIDSON

Funeral Cookbooks

There is a custom which I have met only in Thailand, whereby a person composes a small cookbook before her or his death, so that it can be distributed as a keepsake to the mourners attending the funeral.

The recipes, typically no more than a score, are likely to be those which the deceased especially enjoyed. They need not have been composed or used by the deceased, but often are. Sometimes they incorporate little anecdotes and attributions.

The design of the booklets, and the specifications to the printer, may reflect very careful consideration. I have one with a beautiful white card cover on which appears a luminous red sun. The typography and layout are such that a professional designer had clearly been at work.

I know of only one person, a Thai lady, who made a point of collecting these hard-to-find ephemera. She was murdered by her gardeners in Bangkok and I never learned what happened to the collection. The items are hard to find because they are printed in small editions, just enough for the expected number of mourners; and those who receive them usually keep them.

The idea is attractive. With what better keepsake could one depart from a funeral? What other would equally well keep one's memory green among friends? If one is to issue some sort of posthumous message, avoiding anything egotistical or hortatory, is not a simple message about enjoyable food the best that could be devised? It is true that one could equally well compose a list of 'books I have enjoyed', but that might seem didactic, even patronizing; whereas a little bouquet of recipes arrives on a more relaxed note: 'take them or leave them, it's up to you, I just wanted you to have them.'

So I have thought about this, off and on, for years. If I was in the Thai cultural framework, I would long ago have put together my favourite family recipes and worked out an exquisite design and cover for them. Every two or three years I would be updating it, modifying the design, thinking of even greater refinements, perhaps adding an appendix giving biographical particulars of my forebears whose recipes would be used, maybe even a tiny index; and would there be scope for some drawings, and who should do them?

However, I am not in the Thai culture, and I hesitate to import this item from it, with the attendant risk of causing surprise and perhaps even criticism in the damp and muddy driveway of the crematorium. Although, naturally, hoping that the hypothetical booklet would not be printed until long hence, I am prey to gloomy imaginings about its reception.

'A bit odd, don't you think?'

'Yes, but of course he *was* a bit odd.'

'I think I'll give mine to Oxfam tomorrow.'

'Hmm, wouldn't it be more correct to keep it for a while?'

'Yes, but what for? We're knee-deep in cookbooks already. Still, you may be right. By the way, did you say anything to the family about it?'

'No, I wondered whether to, but I thought not. Between ourselves, I heard that the whole business of getting it printed in three days had been a nightmare for them.'

'Yes, I'm sure it was. It's all rather embarrassing, isn't it?'

Yet sometimes I hear other voices, surprised in a pleasant way, enthusiastic, warm in the autumn sunshine which plays on the group at the crematorium door.

'My dear, I think it was a wonderful idea! And so original! I'm going to treasure my copy . . .

What, then, will happen? Something or nothing? Time will have to tell. But will anyone be listening when time tells? Probably not, save perhaps a lone ethnologist collecting data on the transferral or non-transferral of funeral customs from one culture to another.

1988

GEORGE ORWELL

Below Stairs in a Paris Hotel

. . . Our *cafeterie* was a murky cellar measuring twenty feet by seven by eight high, and so crowded with coffee-urns, breadcutters and the like that one could hardly move without banging against something. It was lighted by one dim electric bulb, and four or five gas-fires that sent out a fierce red breath. There was a thermometer there, and the temperature never fell below 110 degrees Fahrenheit – it neared 130 at some times of the day. At one end were five service lifts, and at the other an ice cupboard where we stored milk and butter. When you went into the ice cupboard you dropped a hundred degrees of temperature at a single step; it used to remind me of the hymn about Greenland's icy mountains and India's coral strand. Two men worked in the *cafeterie* besides Boris and myself. One was Mario, a huge, excitable Italian – he was like a city policeman with operatic gestures – and the other, a hairy, uncouth animal whom we called the Magyar; I think he was a Transylvanian, or something even more remote. Except the Magyar we were all big men, and at the rush hours we collided incessantly.

The work in the *cafeterie* was spasmodic. We were never idle, but the real work only came in bursts of two hours at a time – we called each burst '*un coup de feu*'. The first *coup de feu* came at eight, when the guests upstairs began to wake up and demand breakfast. At eight a sudden banging and yelling would break out all through the basement; bells rang on all sides, blue-aproned men rushed through the passages, our service lifts came down with a simultaneous crash, and the waiters on all five floors began shouting Italian oaths down the shafts. I don't remember all our duties, but they included making tea, coffee and chocolate, fetching meals from the kitchen, wines from the cellar, and fruit and so forth from the dining-room, slicing bread, making toast, rolling pats of butter, measuring jam, opening milk-cans, counting lumps of sugar, boiling eggs, cooking porridge, pounding ice, grinding coffee – all this for from a hundred to two hundred customers. The kitchen was thirty yards away, and the dining-room sixty or seventy yards. Everything we sent up in the service lifts had to be covered by a voucher, and the vouchers had to be carefully filed, and there was trouble if even a lump of sugar was lost. Besides this, we had to supply the staff with bread and coffee, and fetch the meals for the waiters upstairs. All in all, it was a complicated job.

I calculated that one had to walk and run about fifteen miles during the day, and yet the strain of the work was more mental than physical. Nothing could be easier, on the face of it, than this stupid scullion work, but it is astonishingly hard when one is in a hurry. One has to leap to and fro between a multitude of jobs – it is like sorting a pack of cards against the clock. You are, for example, making toast, when bang! down comes a service lift with an order for tea, rolls and three different kinds of jam, and simultaneously bang! down comes another demanding scrambled eggs, coffee and grapefruit; you run to the kitchen for the eggs and to the dining-room for the fruit, going like lightning so as to be back before your toast burns, and having to remember about the tea and coffee, besides half a dozen other orders that are still pending; and at the same time some waiter is following you and making trouble about a lost bottle of soda-water, and you are arguing with him. It needs more brains than one might think. Mario said, no doubt truly, that it took a year to make a reliable *cafetier*.

The time between eight and half-past ten was a sort of delirium. Sometimes we were going as though we had only five minutes to live; sometimes there were sudden lulls when the orders stopped and everything seemed quiet for a moment. Then we swept up the litter from the floor, threw down fresh saw-dust, and swallowed gallipots of wine or coffee or water – anything, so long as it was wet. Very often we used to break off chunks of ice and suck them while we worked. The heat among the gas-fires was nauseating; we swallowed quarts of drink during the day, and after a few hours even our aprons were drenched with sweat. At times we were hopelessly behind with the work, and some of the customers would have gone without their breakfast, but Mario always pulled us through. He had worked fourteen years in the *cafeterie*, and he had the skill that never wastes a second between jobs. The Magyar was very stupid, and I was inexperienced, and Boris was inclined to shirk, partly because of his lame leg, partly because he was ashamed of working in the *cafeterie* after being a waiter; but Mario was wonderful. The way he would stretch his great arms right across the *cafeterie* to fill a coffee-pot with one hand and boil an egg with the other, at the same time watching toast and shouting directions to the Magyar, and between whiles singing snatches from *Rigoletto*, was beyond all praise. The *patron* knew his value, and he was paid a thousand francs a month, instead of five hundred like the rest of us.

The breakfast pandemonium stopped at half-past ten. Then we scrubbed the *cafeterie* tables, swept the floor and polished the brasswork, and, on good mornings went one at a time to the lavatory for a smoke. This was our slack time – only relatively slack, however, for we had only ten minutes for lunch, and we never got through it uninterrupted. The customers' luncheon hour, between twelve and two, was another period of turmoil like the breakfast hour. Most of our work was fetching meals from the kitchen, which meant constant *engueulades* from the cooks. By this time the cooks had sweated in front of their furnaces for four or five hours, and their tempers were all warmed up.

At two we were suddenly free men. We threw off our aprons and put on our coats, hurried out of doors, and, when we had money, dived into the nearest *bistro*. It was strange, coming up into the street from those firelit cellars. The air seemed blindingly clear and cold, like arctic summer; and how sweet the petrol did smell, after the stenches of sweat and food! Sometimes we met some of our cooks and waiters in the *bistros*, and they were friendly and stood us drinks. Indoors we were their slaves, but it is an etiquette in hotel life that between hours everyone is equal, and the *engueulades* do not count.

At a quarter to five we went back to the hotel. Till half-past six there were no orders, and we used this time to polish silver, clean out the coffee-urns, and do other odd jobs. Then the grand turmoil of the day started – the dinner hour. I wish I could be Zola for a little while, just to describe that dinner hour. The essence of the situation was that a hundred or two hundred people were demanding individually different meals of five or six courses, and that fifty or sixty people had to cook and serve them and clean up the mess afterwards; anyone with experience of catering will know what that means. And at this time when the work was doubled, the whole staff were tired out, and a number of them were drunk. I could write pages about the scene without giving a true idea of it. The chargings to and fro in the narrow passages, the collisions, the yells, the struggling with crates and trays and blocks of ice, the heat, the darkness, the furious festering quarrels which there was no time to fight out – they pass description. Anyone coming into the basement for the first time would have thought himself in a den of maniacs. It was only later, when I understood the working of the hotel, that I saw order in all this chaos.

At half-past eight the work stopped very suddenly. We were not free till nine, but we used to throw ourselves full length on the floor, and lie there resting our legs, too lazy even to go to the ice cupboard for a drink. Sometimes the *chef du personnel* would come in with bottles of beer, for the hotel stood us extra beer when we had had a hard day. The food we were given was no more than eatable, but the *patron* was not mean about drink; he allowed us two litres of wine a day each, knowing that if a *plongeur* is not given two litres he will steal three. We had the heeltaps of bottles as well, so that we often drank too much – a good thing, for one seemed to work faster when partially drunk.

Four days of the week passed like this; of the other two working days, one was better and one worse. After a week of this life I felt in need of a holiday. It was Saturday night, so the people in our *bistro* were busy getting drunk, and with a free day ahead of me I was ready to join them. We all went to bed, drunk, at two in the morning, meaning to sleep till noon. At half-past five I was suddenly awakened. A night-watchman, sent from the hotel, was standing at my bedside. He stripped the clothes back and shook me roughly.

'Get up!' he said. '*Tu t'es bien saoulé la gueule, pas vrai*? Well, never mind that, the hotel's a man short. You've got to work today.'

'Why should I work?' I protested. 'This is my day off.'

'Day off, nothing! The work's got to be done. Get up!'

I got up and went out, feeling as though my back were broken and my skull filled with hot cinders. I did not think that I could possibly do a day's work. And yet, after only an hour in the basement, I found that I was perfectly well. It seemed that in the heat of those cellars, as in a Turkish bath, one could sweat out almost any quantity of drink. *Plongeurs* know this, and count on it. The power of swallowing quarts of wine, and then sweating it out before it can do much damage, is one of the compensations of their life.

. . . It was amusing to look round the filthy little scullery and think that only a double door was between us and the dining-room. There sat the customers in all their splendour – spotless table-cloths, bowls of flowers, mirrors and gilt cornices and painted cherubim; and here, just a few feet away, we in our disgusting filth. For it really was disgusting filth. There was no time to sweep the floor till evening, and we slithered about in a compound of soapy water, lettuce-leaves, torn paper and trampled food. A dozen waiters with their coats off, showing their sweaty armpits, sat at the table mixing salads and sticking their thumbs into the cream pots. The room had a dirty mixed smell of food and sweat. Everywhere in the cupboards, behind the piles of crockery, were squalid stores of food that the waiters had stolen. There were only two sinks, and no washing basin, and it was nothing unusual for a waiter to wash his face in the water in which clean crockery was rinsing. But the customers saw nothing of this. There were a coco-nut mat and a mirror outside the dining-room door, and the waiters used to preen themselves up and go in looking the picture of cleanliness.

It is an instructive sight to see a waiter going into a hotel dining-room. As he passes the door a sudden change comes over him. The set of his shoulders alters; all the dirt and hurry and irritation have dropped off in an instant. He glides over the carpet, with a solemn priest-like air. I remember our assistant *maître d'hôtel*, a fiery Italian, pausing at the dining-room door to address an apprentice who had broken a bottle of wine. Shaking his fist above his head he yelled (luckily the door was more or less soundproof):

'*Tu me fais chier.* Do you call yourself a waiter, you young bastard? You a waiter! You're not fit to scrub floors in the brothel your mother came from. *Maquereau!*'

Words failing him, he turned to the door; and as he opened it he farted loudly, a favourite Italian insult.

Then he entered the dining-room and sailed across it dish in hand, graceful as a swan. Ten seconds later he was bowing reverently to a customer. And you could not help thinking, as you saw him bow and smile, with that benign smile of the trained waiter, that the customer was put to shame by having such an aristocrat to serve him.

... Undoubtedly the most workmanlike class, and the least servile, are the cooks. They do not earn quite so much as waiters, but their prestige is higher and their employment steadier. The cook does not look upon himself as a servant, but as a skilled workman; he is generally called '*un ouvrier*', which a waiter never is. He knows his power – knows that he alone makes or mars a restaurant, and that if he is five minutes late everything is out of gear. He despises the whole non-cooking staff, and makes it a point of honour to insult everyone below the head waiter. And he takes a genuine artistic pride in his work, which demands very great skill. It is not the cooking that is so difficult, but the doing everything to time. Between breakfast and luncheon the head cook at the Hôtel X. would receive orders for several hundred dishes, all to be served at different times; he cooked few of them himself, but he gave instructions about all of them and inspected them before they were sent up. His memory was wonderful. The vouchers were pinned on a board, but the head cook seldom looked at them; everything was stored in his mind, and exactly to the minute, as each dish fell due, he would call out, '*Faites marcher une côtelette de veau*' (or whatever it was) unfailingly. He was an insufferable bully, but he was also an artist. It is for their punctuality, and not for any superiority in technique, that men cooks are preferred to women.

The waiter's outlook is quite different. He too is proud in a way of his skill, but his skill is chiefly in being servile. His work gives him the mentality, not of a workman, but of a snob. He lives perpetually in sight of rich people, stands at their tables, listens to their conversation, sucks up to them with smiles and discreet little jokes. He has the pleasure of spending money by proxy. Moreover, there is always the chance that he may become rich himself, for, though most waiters die poor, they have long runs of luck occasionally. At some cafés on the Grand Boulevard there is so much money to be made that the waiters actually pay the *patron* for their employment. The result is that between constantly seeing money, and hoping to get it, the waiter comes to identify himself to some extent with his employers. He will take pains to serve a meal in style, because he feels that he is participating in the meal himself.

I remember Valenti telling me of some banquet at Nice at which he had once served, and of how it cost two hundred thousand francs and was talked of for months afterwards. 'It was splendid, *mon p'tit, mais magnifique!* Jesus Christ! The champagne, the silver, the orchids – I have never seen anything like them, and I have seen some things. Ah, it was glorious!'

'But,' I said, 'you were only there to wait?'

'Oh, of course. But still, it was splendid.'

The moral is, never be sorry for a waiter. Sometimes when you sit in a restaurant, still stuffing yourself half an hour after closing time, you feel that the tired waiter at your side must surely be despising you. But he is not. He is not thinking as he looks at you, 'What an overfed lout'; he is thinking, 'One day, when I have saved enough money, I shall be able to imitate that man.' He is ministering to a kind of pleasure he thoroughly understands and admires. And that is why waiters are seldom Socialists, have no effective trade union, and will work twelve hours a day – they work fifteen hours, seven days a week, in many cafés. They are snobs, and they find the servile nature of their work rather congenial . . .

In the kitchen the dirt was worse. It is not a figure of speech, it is a mere statement of fact to say that a French cook will spit in the soup – that is, if he is not going to drink it himself. He is an artist, but his art is not cleanliness. To a certain extent he is even dirty because he is an artist, for food, to look smart, needs dirty treatment. When a steak, for instance, is brought up for the head cook's inspection, he does not handle it with a fork. He picks it up in his fingers and slaps it down, runs his thumb round the dish and licks it to taste the gravy, runs it round and licks it again, then steps back and contemplates the piece of meat like an artist judging a picture, then presses it lovingly into place with his fat, pink fingers, every one of which he has licked a hundred times that morning. When he is satisfied, he takes a cloth and wipes his fingerprints from the dish, and hands it to the water. And the waiter, of course, dips *his* fingers into the gravy – his nasty, greasy fingers which he is for ever running through his brilliantined hair. Whenever one pays more than, say, ten francs for a dish of meat in Paris, one may be certain that it has been fingered in this manner. In very cheap restaurants it is different; there, the same trouble is not taken over the food, and it is just forked out of the pan and flung onto a plate, without handling. Roughly speaking, the more one pays for food, the more sweat and spittle one is obliged to eat with it.

Dirtiness is inherent in hotels and restaurants, because sound food is sacrificed to punctuality and smartness. The hotel employee is too busy getting food ready to remember that it is meant to be eaten. A meal is simply '*une commande*' to him, just as a man dying of cancer is simply 'a case' to the doctor. A customer orders, for example, a piece of toast. Somebody, pressed with work in a cellar deep underground, has to prepare it. How can he stop and say to himself, 'This toast is to be eaten – I must make it eatable?' All he knows is that it must look right and must be ready in three minutes. Some large drops of sweat fall from his forehead onto the toast. Why should he worry? Presently the toast falls among the filthy sawdust on the floor. Why trouble to make a new piece? It is much quicker to wipe the sawdust off. On the way upstairs the toast falls again, butter side down. Another wipe is all it needs. And so with everything. The only food at the Hôtel X. which was ever prepared cleanly was the staff's, and the *patron*'s. The maxim, repeated by everyone, was: 'Look out for the *patron*, and as for the clients, *s'en fout pas mal!*' Everywhere in the service quarters dirt festered – a secret vein of dirt, running through the great garish hotel like the intestines through a man's body.

Apart from the dirt, the *patron* swindled the customers wholeheartedly. For the most part the materials of the food were very bad, though the cooks knew how to serve it up in style. The meat was at best ordinary, and as to the vegetables, no good housekeeper would have looked at them in the market. The cream, by a standing order, was diluted with milk. The tea and coffee were of inferior sorts, and the jam was synthetic stuff out of vast unlabelled tins. All the cheaper wines, according to Boris, were corked *vin ordinaire*. There was a rule that employees must pay for anything they spoiled, and in consequence damaged things were seldom thrown away. Once the waiter on the third floor dropped a roast chicken down the shaft of our service lift, where it fell into a litter of broken bread, torn paper and so forth at the bottom. We simply wiped it with a cloth and sent it up again. Upstairs there were dirty tales of once-used sheets not being washed, but simply damped, ironed and put back on the beds. The *patron* was as mean to us as to the customers. Throughout that vast hotel there was not, for instance, such a thing as a brush and pan; one had to manage with a broom and a piece of cardboard. And the staff lavatory was worthy of Central Asia, and there was no place to wash one's hands, except the sinks used for washing crockery.

In spite of all this the Hôtel X. was one of the dozen most expensive hotels in Paris, and the customers paid startling prices. The ordinary charge for a night's lodging, not including breakfast, was two hundred francs. All wine and tobacco were sold at exactly double shop prices, though of course the *patron* bought at the wholesale price. If a customer had a title, or was reputed to be a millionaire, all his charges went up automatically. One morning on the fourth floor an American who was on diet wanted only salt and hot water for his breakfast. Valenti was furious. 'Jesus Christ!' he said, 'what about my ten per cent? Ten per cent of salt and water!' And he charged twenty-five francs for the breakfast. The customer paid without a murmur.

According to Boris, the same kind of thing went on in all Paris hotels, or at least in all the big, expensive ones. But I imagine that the customers at the Hôtel X. were especially easy to swindle, for they were mostly Americans, with a sprinkling of English – no French – and seemed to know nothing whatever about good food. They would stuff themselves with disgusting American 'cereals', and eat marmalade at tea, and drink vermouth after dinner, and order a *poulet à le reine* at a hundred francs and then souse it in Worcester sauce. One customer, from Pittsburgh, dined every night in his bedroom on grape-nuts, scrambled eggs and cocoa. Perhaps it hardly matters whether such people are swindled or not.

. . . For, after all, where is the *real* need of big hotels and smart restaurants? They are supposed to provide luxury, but in reality they provide only a cheap, shoddy imitation of it. Nearly everyone hates hotels. Some restaurants are better than others, but it is impossible to get as good a meal in a restaurant as one can get, for the same expense, in a private house. No doubt hotels and restaurants must exist, but there is no need that they should enslave hundreds of people. What makes the work in them is not the essentials; it is the shams that are supposed to represent luxury. Smartness, as it is called, means, in effect, merely that the staff work more and the customers pay more; no one benefits except the proprietor, who will presently buy himself a striped villa at Deauville. Essentially, a 'smart' hotel is a place where a hundred people toil like devils in order that two hundred may pay through the nose for things they do not really want.

1933

DOROTHY HARTLEY

Some English Kitchens

My first kitchen was a stone-floored cottage in the Yorkshire dales. It had a thick rag rug on the hearth and a ceiling rack that held thin brown oatcake. When soft and newly made, the oatcake hung in loops, which later dried out stiff and brittle. The stone slab where it was baked made a little separate hearth at one side of the fireplace. The high mantelpiece had a polished gun over it, and on it two china dogs and brass ornaments. The window, almost blocked by red geraniums in flower-pots, was set deep in the thick stone wall; and most of the light came through an open door that gave onto the moor. Fresh mountain air and the smell of cooking always filled this brightly polished kitchen. I can remember a basin of mutton broth with a long-boned chop in it. A man reached up to lift down a flap of oatcake to crumble into the broth, and I remember the warm, safe feel of the big sheepdog I leant against. I remember, too, being carried high on the farmhand's shoulder, and feeling him drop down and rise up as he picked white mushrooms out of the wet grass. Once a week a wagonette ran to Skipton to take people to market.

My next kitchen was in a convent of French nuns at Skipton. It had a high ceiling and a sense of space and peace. The wooden tables were scoured white as bone, scrubbed along the grain with sharp river sand and whitening. The wide range shone like satin; the steel fender and stands were rubbed bright with emery cloth. In the wintry sunshine brass pans and silver dishcovers glittered on the cream plaster walls. To prevent clogs slipping the flags were lightly sanded, and the hearthstone was white as drifted snow. At one side of the fireplace stood an iron coffee-grinder; at the other sat a black-gowned little Sister, with white coif and blue apron, slicing vegetables, her clogs laid beside her and her white-stockinged feet on the rolled-back hearthrug.

All morning the kitchen was alive with stir and bustle, the clatter of clogs and pails, and the aroma of breakfast coffee. The range fire roared away like an imprisoned dragon behind his long bars, and the meat jack clicked and clicked as steadily as the rosary of the old Reverend Mother who slept away her last days in the warm armchair by the window. From ten o'clock to twelve the jack clicked before the fire, while on top sizzled and bubbled the pans and the big pot. Interesting noises came from scullery and pantry: the clank of the soft-water pump by the sink, the gurgle of the new boiler, the whirr of beating eggs, the clonking thump of the heavy bread pancheons, and the scurried prayers and ejaculated responses with which the kitchen Sisters timed their cooking.

The long afternoon was still. The sunlight shone through the window, the opened range smoked gently, the clock ticked loudly, a cricket chirped. The woollen rug was spread out before the hearth and a yellow cat was asleep in the middle of it with the little 'vegetable Sister' asleep at the side. At five o'clock a bell rang, and the kitchen woke up. The big kettle began to sing, the rhythmical tump-tump of the bread slicer sounded, and a yellow bowl of butter was put to warm on the fender. Sometimes the big fire front was dropped right down, and around it sat the four or five lucky girls who had drawn lottery numbers for that honour. (Others' numbers allocated prayers for the Holy Souls, weeding the grotto, or cleaning the altar candlesticks.) The toasters, armed with long wire forks, handed the brown slices back to the kitchen Sister, who at once ran them through the mangle: it was more economical to crush the crusts than to cut them off, and it allowed the butter to soak in more easily. Then the slices were arranged in a line along the hotplate, held upright between two flannel-covered bricks that looked like book-ends. Afterwards they were buttered and piled on plates on the refectory table. In each urn the tea hung in bags, with an attendant basin behind, into which the bag could be lifted after 'three Hail Marys and grace' had been said, as it was bad to drink tea that 'had stood'. When the first missionaries brought back tea from China they reported it should stand as long as it took to say the Pater Noster slowly. (The jugs of milk were rich with cream and crystallized sugar stood in stemmed glass bowls.) When tea was over the 'charge girls' carried round a bowl of soapy water and a clean tea towel. We turned round to wash our knives and spoons, dried them and replaced them in our silver goblets rolled up in our napkins. In true mediaeval exclusiveness we each kept our own table-ware as the mediaeval people kept their 'Neps'.

Nightfall in the convent kitchen was redolent of broth. The big iron pot with the screwed-on lid (called a digester) which had chuckled unmoved at the back of the stove since dinnertime, was now laid, washed and empty, on a newspaper by the hearth. 'Piggy's dinner' was steaming in a bucket on the dying fire. The little 'vegetable Sister' had gone to chapel. The voice of Thomas the gardener called through the backdoor, 'Will you be wanting anything more tonight, Mother?' before he clumped off home leaving the watchdog under the table for the night . . . The yellow cat and a long-legged child are drinking milk together on the hearthrug.

My largest kitchen, masculine and enterprising, was at a boys' school. Being 'northern' the bread was homemade, rising each week in a huge tub set before the fire. Piles of Yorkshire teacakes came daily from the baker, and a new gas-stove supplemented the oven range. It was here I first realized the specialities of England, for my enterprising mother sent away to her Welsh home for small Welsh mutton, as she thought the large Yorkshire sheep very coarse. We had bilberries from the mountains in leaking purple crates. From the east coast came barrels of herrings and boxes of bloaters, and cream cakes in wooden shelved hampers from 'Buzzards of London'. Apples came from Gloucestershire, and cream, in hygienic containers that weighed a ton, from Devon. From the north came sacks of oatmeal. Oxfordshire sent crates of wonderful fruit, Moorpark apricots, and apricot hams. The beef was local: all the pressed beef and brawn moulds were learned in that kitchen and are genuine Yorkshire recipes from the dale farms. At sheep shearings huge flat baskets of beef sandwiches were carried round, each with a mustard pot tied to the handle. No one eats mutton at a sheep shearing. At cattle fairs there were rounds of beef, snowy under tufts of shaved horseradish, and big tins of Yorkshire pudding, golden crisp, with tortoiseshell markings where dripping had splashed onto them. The Craven Heifer Inn served a massive Yorkshire tea with ham, game pies, apple pies, parkin and cheese, hot teacakes, jam and honey and black treacle, and tea.

But the most wonderful memories of Yorkshire are the old-fashioned Victorian dinner parties. I remember best the desserts, the really beautiful sweet dishes of those parties. Avalanches of snowy cream deluging a sherried mixture of macaroons and candied fruits. Hedgehogs of sponge-cake, spiked with almonds, and swimming in custard yellow with egg yolks. There were junkets, looking virginal in silver; apricot creams moulded like Milan Cathedral; and damson cheese, crimson in a pool of port wine on a gold-washed dish, and apple cheese. There were jellies, trembling in glass, with maidenhair fern; white blancmanges garnished with scarlet geranium; apple pastry, a pleasant mixture of apples, candied peel, raisins, spice and wine, baked in a square crust, iced smooth as marble, and decorated with geometrical designs of red cherries, green angelica, and black Carlsbad plums. There was gingerbread, heraldic with gilding and cloves, and Dublin rock that always vaguely reminded me of John the Baptist. In spring, blue-veined Wensleydale cheese; in winter, Stilton, sedate in a white napkin. There were piled dishes of dessert fruit: plums, grapes, peaches and small oranges set around a spiky pineapple. And once, real strawberries growing in boxes on the table! These sweets and creams have spilled over into this book.

My next kitchen was in a country rectory in the shires between Nottingham and Leicestershire. A rambling Elizabethan house with a garden and orchard,

pigsties and barns; more like a small farm than a rectory. It had an apple loft with slatted shelves, and a meat larder with a pulley to lift a carcase of mutton to the ventilated roof. Strange bleached frogs swam in the underground soft-water tanks; and all the water, which was as hard as iron and corroded the kettles, had to be pumped up. The kitchen, over thirty feet long and twenty feet wide, contained a Queen Anne dresser that had twenty-four brass handles and twelve knobs to polish. There were six steps down to the larder and five up to the scullery; three steps down to the dining-room and two up from the entrance hall. Counting coal-houses and outside pumps and passages you walked about a mile per meal. We had neither gas nor electricity, and during the dark winter months there were seventeen lamps a day to be lit and trimmed, and each night a dozen flat brass candlesticks were cleaned and ranged on the oak chest at the foot of the stairs. A lovely old house with every mediaeval inconvenience. The nearest shop was five miles away, and we had no car. A butcher called once a week, a grocer once a fortnight; and the wine, coal and brewery every six months. With one maid and a weekly washerwoman it was not an easy house to run.

It was here we 'did' our first pig. After the bleak north everything in the Midlands seemed warm and rich and ripe. The mutton was fat, the cakes full of eggs, and in September we made wonderful wines and jams and rich preserves. Most of the fruit and vegetable sections were learnt in this district.

Another kitchen was in a row of semi-detached houses in a small mining town near Wigan. It was barely twelve feet square, and its one window looked on a yard and directly faced an identical window opposite. In one corner a huge built-in cupboard made almost another room: the top part held stores and grocery, the middle part china, and the lower cooking pots and pans. A shallow brown earthenware sink, with a hen-bucket beneath, was fitted in the opposite corner. Over it hung the tin milk can – the milk was delivered from a churn with a brass tap – and a spring balance to weigh the meat and fish, which came to the back door in carts. Between the big cupboard and the sink was a smaller built-in cupboard. Its top served as a general work table; beneath were the shoe and blacklead boxes, the gas meter, the knife board and bath brick, and the cat's kitten basket. The treadle sewing machine was set against the far wall, and overhead was a rack for airing clothes. Being a collier's home, the wash-house was extra large and led directly into the kitchen. The miner used to leave his clogs outside and come in through the wash-house where he would swill down in the tub. His clean shirt was handed out hot from the kitchen rack; then he would come for tea at the table by the fire. Only the women and children used the upstairs bath; though one miner *did* run a slatted board from his hencoop to the bathroom window, and persuaded his favourite drake to use the bath for mating purposes. (A Wigan man can do anything with poultry.)

The cooking in this mining community was good, especially the 'snapins' and the food that will keep hot without spoiling. The Wakes were always celebrated with traditional dishes, and many trotter and shellfish recipes, as well as Lancashire Hotpot and Hindle Wakes, came from this kitchen.

Today I live on the Welsh border where the mutton is good, the beef bad, and the best fruits are the wild ones. Here there are a profusion of small fine damsons, and the blackberries hang like bunches of grapes over the Dee. Welsh cookery is based on the mountain grazing farm, the Hafod; only in the valleys do you get rich food. But now a noisy chemical works has invaded our peaceful valley. Our old big house has been divided and let, and I have lived for twenty years in a workman's cottage, with a gas-stove in one room and a log fire and pot crane in the other, and cooked – as convenient – on each. It's been a happy time, for –

'Better is the life of a poor man in a cottage . . . than delicate fare in another man's house; and better a dry morsel and quietness therewith, than a house full of sacrifices with strife' (Ecclesiasticus).

1954

FAY MASCHLER

Sole Food

Eating is such a gregarious activity that to do it alone seems almost as barmy as talking to yourself. But just as, no doubt, you have caught yourself wandering down the street having a nice little chat or maybe even indulging in a gentle nag at yourself, there will be times when you have to eat alone. There may even be long periods when you have to do so but then it will become a routine and you may, after a while, love it, as indeed talking to yourself can become rewarding when you realize what a lot of sense you make and what very sound views you hold.

What is much more distressing is the sudden or occasional lonesome meal or the prospect of, for example, a fortnight of them. Eating alone is one meal that should never be left to chance. Peering in the fridge and rummaging through cupboards will suggest the odd culinary idea but it will be one all too easy to reject and you will settle for eggs. People on their own eat far too many eggs and we know what effect that has. Eating alone needs planning. By this I don't mean you should spend a long time cooking, getting stuck into things like simmering and braising and marinating, all of which serve to mock your single state. It is too easy to move from Was It Worth It? (the braising) to What Is It All Worth? which is no subject to contemplate as you chew through your solitary *coq au vin*.

What you must do is serve yourself delicious food that takes practically no preparation and is extravagant enough a buy to make you thankful it needn't be shared. Very few people have had too much smoked salmon. It is worth testing yourself to see if you could number among those few. Do not make the mistake, however, of thinking two halves of an avocado are better than one. Believe me, the second half can pall. Also, don't treat yourself to a duck or wild goose or anything that divides neatly into two. Partridges, woodcock or grouse make better lonesome meals and they avoid the lunacy of carving for yourself: 'White meat or dark? A little of both I think.' 'Could you manage a bit more? Yes, just a smidgin.' It's easy to go over the edge and start to use words like smidgin.

Eating alone requires reserves of willpower and behaviour that have previously never been called upon. Your self-respect is at stake. Those colonial johnnies who changed each night for dinner while pushing their way through the Borneo jungle were merely showing you the way to setting the table properly for your quiet meal. You will need a knife, maybe two, a fork, a glass, a linen napkin. You mustn't crouch over the sink stuffing the food into your mouth with your fingers on the grounds that it will save washing up. That must be done thoroughly too. A person on their own can get a lot of satisfaction from a clean kitchen and there is no one to check how often you visit it later in the evening to inspect those surfaces so thoroughly wiped with your J Cloth.

Eating on your own enables you to eat whatever you like and expurgate long remembered slights and grudges. If your ex- or absent partner used to give you the cold shoulder after you'd had a spoonful or two of the aïoli, now is the time to eat it until you are *humming* with garlic. If looks have been sent your way because you like ketchup with filet mignon, now is the time to bang it on. The sense of elation resulting from these defiant acts can take you through an evening. A very good thing to eat alone is nuts that require shelling. You can do it while reading or watching television and every now and then you realize what a pleasure it is not to have to crack them for anybody else. A meal of nuts could start with salami. There will be no one else around who requires the rind to be peeled off for them. It is a time to stray from any diet you have been pretending to follow and secret passions like Sara Lee Frozen Chocolate Cake will stay secret.

Eating alone in restaurants is the worst kind of eating alone but that too can be handled. Waiters are unpleasant to people on their own partly because they know the diner to be at a grave psychological disadvantage but mainly because the bill will not be big. And if the bill is not big, *neither is the tip*. Therefore, if you are eating on your own you should choose the kind of place where the staff are not counting on the tips – for example, family-run Indian restaurants – or you should go somewhere ineffably grand where the bill is sure to be astronomical even for one. If you are caught on your own at any other kind of restaurant chew the food thoughtfully and make little notes on your cheque-book and it will be thought that you are a restaurant critic.

A certain amount of sympathy can be attracted by posing as someone who has been stood up. The drawback to this is that you must wait at least twenty minutes before ordering and keep glancing anxiously at the door. Also the sympathy can all too easily turn to contemptuous understanding of your predicament. Never try to pick up another lone diner in a restaurant. It doesn't go down well. If you find yourself having to use restaurants on your own a good deal, it is worth joining a club where such behaviour is accepted and even admired. I believe some men's clubs have a large table where single eaters can sit together, which is a practice restaurants might like to copy. Women diners on their own can sometimes win out by ordering an expensive bottle of wine but it is a short-lived victory since drinking a whole bottle of good wine on your own can be depressing. Eating alone in restaurants is a no-win situation.

My husband says that when he was single and had to cook for himself he would frequently have a meal of haddock cooked in milk. He added thoughtfully, 'It didn't need to be watched'. I think when you get to that point it is time to look around for some company.

1978

NORMAN DOUGLAS

Venus in the Kitchen

The following recipes were collected not in a hurry, nor with the intention of publishing them. They were collected slowly, one by one, for the private use and benefit of a small group of friends, most of whom, I am sorry to say, are older than they want to be, and all of them anxious – who is not? – to preserve for as long as may be possible the vitality of their youth and middle age.

I began one night twelve years ago after we had enjoyed a succulent dinner with several bottles of old red wine, followed by bitter lamentations on the part of the older members of the party over their declining vigour, in the course of which one of them remarked: 'Something might be done in the way of culinary recipes,' adding that a well-known authority, Liebault, had written upon the rejuvenating effects of certain condiments and certain dishes. I was then and there deputed, or rather implored, to look into the subject and to note down such recipes as might apply to their case. This I did, supplying them with copies.

Twelve years is a long period of time, and no doubt I could have made a larger selection in the interval, but my leisure is not wholly given up to researches of this kind, important as they may be to persons of mature age. I have other 'hobbies', as they are called, such as the collecting of Persian carpets and the writing of a book, begun in 1902, on the varieties of Central Asian melons, which are the finest in the world – whatever certain American friends may say to the contrary (I have been to their country; they have not been to Khiva) . . .

In spite of that artistic encouragement I kept the recipes at the bottom of my trunk, adding a fresh one every now and then and also an occasional freak-dish of an aphrodisiacal nature. There they would have stayed but for a member of that group of friends whom I have mentioned, and who lived at Smyrna before the Turkish occupation and has since died. He tried one or two of them, and was favourably impressed by their subsequent effects. They worked, he said. He begged me to have them printed, and said that in so doing I might confer a benefit on some poor devil. The poor devil, he explained, must be a rich one, else he had better abandon all hope of encountering Venus, and retain that frigidity of temperament for which the economical recipes of ordinary cookery books are responsible. Well, I hope the poor devil, whoever he is, will follow his example and achieve the same happy results.

PILAFF BEY

P.S. – The foregoing pages and all that follows were written not later than 1936.

BROAD BEAN SOUP

Cook the broad beans in salted water with a ham bone. Add a pinch of chopped parsley and a pinch of saffron. When the beans are well cooked, pass through a sieve, leaving some whole ones behind which you will add to the soup later. Put the liquid again on the fire and when boiling add a handful of rice and the few beans left over. When the rice is cooked, serve with grated Parmesan cheese. Highly recommended.

CELERY CREAM

Peel the celery, cut in small pieces, scald it, and drain in a colander.

Now put it in a saucepan over the fire with a piece of butter; sprinkle it with a pinch of flour; moisten it with some good thickened stock; bind it with the yolk of eggs mixed with cream, flavour it with a little nutmeg and serve hot.

CRAYFISH À LA SYBARITE

Fry lightly in butter two onions and three carrots already sliced finely, with chopped parsley and thyme. Throw in the crayfish, which you must have already cut into pieces. Cook the pieces on both sides, then add some spice as: a small pinch of cinnamon, a little grated nutmeg, and a pinch or two of paprika. Add a spoonful of butter, and when this is melted, throw in half a bottle of dry champagne, which must never boil. Cook for half an hour and serve hot.

EELS À LA DEL SBUGO

A big eel is necessary, from which you remove the inside. Wash well and skin, leaving the head attached to the skin. Put the skin in vinegar and water, and leave it there till you have done the next operation.

Boil the flesh of the eel in water together with a slice of lemon, a piece of celery, a small carrot, and a few cloves. When you see that it can be detached from the bone, take it out from the water, let it cool and then bone it, being careful not to break the bone, which you put aside.

Now pulp the flesh in a mortar, together with a few blanched almonds, a spoonful of sultana raisins, a pinch of sugar, one of cinnamon, and some finely chopped aromatic herbs, pepper and salt.

Take the skin out of the infusion, dry it well, and put it first on a board. Make a layer of the pulp inside it, place in the middle the bone and cover it with the rest of the pulp. Roll it up and stitch it, seeing that it gets the same form of the eel as before.

Brush it with olive oil all over, place it on a baking dish, and cook it in a hot oven till the skin is crisp.

Serve hot after having sprinkled with sugar and cinnamon.

SNAILS À LA C.C.C.
N. I

Feed your snails for a fortnight on milk. This is not difficult; you have only to put the snails in an earthen vessel and cover it with a lid. Every morning just pour a glass of milk on the snails.

When the time for cooking them has arrived, put the snails in an infusion composed of water, vinegar, and salt, and leave them there over-night. In the morning wash them well under the tap and then boil them in water.

After this take them out of their shells, dip them in beaten eggs and fry them in olive oil. Before serving flavour them with elaeologarum, which is a sauce much used by the old Romans, and composed of lovage, coriander, rue, oil, and fish-stock.

My friend C.C.C. knows how to make this sauce to perfection.

SNAILS À LA C.C.C.
N. II

Put in a stewpan four ounces of butter for fifty snails, and set it on a good fire; when melted, sprinkle in it a teaspoonful of flour, stirring awhile; then add a teaspoonful of parsley chopped fine, two sprigs of thyme, a bay-leaf, a pint of white wine, and then the snails, which you have previously put back into their shells; cover the whole with warm broth, boil gently till the sauce is reduced and the snails are cooked, and serve them mouth upwards, and filled with the sauce.

SNAILS À LA C.C.C.
N. III

Boil the snails for about twenty minutes in salt water. Then take them out of the shells.

Chop some rosemary, an onion, garlic, and parsley, and put them to fry in olive oil in a saucepan; place the snails in it and season with pepper and salt. After a few minutes add a handful of fresh or dry mushrooms, half a cup of broth, and a little tomato sauce dissolved in water.

Let them boil for about a quarter of an hour and then pour in a glass of strong red wine and let the snails cook.

An old friend ate this dish in Bolgidinga when he was there, and declares that he found himself at least ten years younger!

SNAILS À LA CINQUECENTO

Take thirty snails ready for cooking. Put them in a pot with red wine and water half and half, a glass of vermouth, a little thyme, two bay-leaves, a clove of garlic, some parsley. Season with pepper and salt.

Boil them in the above for about an hour. Then take them out and shell them, cleaning them of the dark part at the bottom.

Now beat an egg with olive oil in a plate, together with a pinch of salt and pepper, and place your snails in it, leaving them there for a few hours. After this take them out and roll them in bread-crumbs.

Take some silver skewers and fix on each of them eight or nine of the snails. Grill them lightly, and finish cooking in a hot oven.

ANDOUILLES

Take some pig's guts. Wash them well, and cut them into pieces about seven inches long. Put them in water with a fourth part of vinegar, some thyme, bay-leaves, a crushed clove of garlic, and keep them there over-night in order to lose the smell of pork.

The next morning take your guts, cut some of them into thin slices; leave the others uncut, in order to fill them in. Cut some fat and some lean meat of pork into thin fillets, mix them together with the sliced guts, add a pinch of salt and pepper, and fill the guts which you have left apart. Be careful to fill them only about a third, otherwise they will burst in cooking. Tie them with string at both ends.

When this is done, put them to boil in an equal mixture of water and milk with a little salt, thyme, bay-leaves and cloves, and also a little fat. Cook them for at least three hours, then let them cool in the liquid in which they have been boiled.

When you want to eat them, take them out and grill them.

This recipe works in the opposite direction, with me.

P.B.

1952

ELIZABETH DAVID

South Wind through the Kitchen

'A venerated Queen of Northern Isles reared to the memory of her loving Consort a monument whereat the nations stand aghast.' Thus Norman Douglas on the Albert Memorial. All Norman's friends must, as did I, have stood aghast when they saw what had been perpetrated on his posthumously published *Venus in the Kitchen*. 'Decorations by Bruce Roberts' announced the title-page. Decorations? Defacements would have been a more accurate description. Had not any director or editor at Messrs Heinemann's ever glanced at so much as a paragraph of even one of the Douglas books before publishing *Venus in the Kitchen*? Did they simply take it on trust from Mr Graham Greene (whose brief, moving and purposeful introduction to the book would, had anyone in the publishing house taken the trouble to study it, have provided all the necessary clues) that Norman Douglas was a rather famous writer and that they would be lucky to get his final work? Did they hand a typescript or a set of galley proofs to their illustrator? Or did they think it sufficient to commission him to provide 'decorations' for what they innocently supposed was a cookery book which would sell on a title and illustrations with an erotic twist? If so, then their intentions were cruelly foiled by Mr Roberts. Anything more anaphrodisiac than his simpering cupids (in bathing trunks), his bows and arrows and hearts, his chefs in Christmas cracker hats, his amorphous fishes and bottles and birds, his waiters in jocular poses, his lifeless, sexless couples seated at tables-for-two, it would be hard to envisage. One would not dwell upon the dismal blunder were it not that these so-called decorations (where was the necessity for decorations?) have given to *Venus in the Kitchen* an image of Valentine-card mawkishness so absurdly alien to the author's intentions that potential buyers of the book (now reissued in an American paper-back with, intact, alas, the English illustrations plus a gigantic scarlet heart on the cover thrown in for good measure) should be warned that the contents of the little book have nothing whatsoever to do with its appearance.

Cupids in the kitchen? Whatever next? The book is no more, and also no less, than an instructive and entertaining little collection of recipes mainly (as was to be expected from an author who had spent some forty years of his life in Italy, who was rather more than familiar with the Greek and Latin classics and had written a treatise dealing with every bird and beast mentioned in the Greek Anthology) of ancient Mediterranean lineage. To those even a little versed in the history and literature of cookery the recipes are unastonishing. In varying versions they are to be found in a number of books in French, Italian, Spanish, Latin, English, Greek. What makes this particular little anthology notable is not the recipes. It is the characteristically irreverent Douglas spirit which imbues them, and the style in which they are presented; a style which gives the impression that they were written not with a pen, but with a diamond-cutter; and then, appended to many of them – and they are the ones to be looked for – the typical deflating comment. There is nothing erotic here, much less anything with the slightest sniff of the sentimental. It is as plain as the nose on your face that at the age of eighty-two or thereabout, Norman Douglas was back at his old game of mocking at superstition and the superstitious. He regarded the whole business of aphrodisiac recipes as comical and bawdy. And to be frank, he did not know, nor pretend to know, very much about the practical aspects of cooking. Many of the recipes were, I believe, collected by Pino Orioli, the bookseller who was Norman's great friend and, at one time, his partner in the Florentine publishing venture which produced some of Norman's own books; and in the postscript to his preface he acknowledges technical assistance received from one of his oldest friends, the late Faith Compton Mackenzie, and from that magical writer, Sybille Bedford. What Norman Douglas did know about, and better than most, was the importance of the relationship between the enjoyment of food and wine and the conduct of love affairs, and for that matter of most other aspects of life.

I was, myself, once inducted onto a panel, somewhat uncertain and disorganized, of ladies and gentlemen thought to be capable of presiding over a kind of gastronomes' brains-trust at a certain English country food festival. Among the more resourceful worthies on the platform upon that memorable occasion was Mr Osbert Lancaster. A member of the audience demanded to be informed whether the panel considered good food to be possessed of aphrodisiac properties. And if so, what food in particular. A tricky question. The panel was silent. From the audience came shouts and derisive taunts. The whole meeting looked like breaking up in pandemonium. With faultless timing Mr Lancaster rose to his feet and boomed, in authoritative tones, that while he did not feel empowered to pronounce upon what food might or might not be prescribed for those in need of an aphrodisiac, he was prepared to commit himself to the point of declaring that if anyone wanted a sure-fire *an*aphrodisiac then it would be badly cooked food presented with a bad grace. An opinion with which Norman Douglas would have concurred.

'Indigestion and love will not be yoked together.' 'No love-joy comes to bodies misfed, nor shall any progress in knowledge come from them.' 'A man's worst enemy is his own empty stomach.' 'Be sober; let the loved one drink.' 'Good intentions – no . . . Gastritis will be the result of good intentions.' 'I have been perusing Seneca's letters. He was a cocoa-drinker, masquerading as an ancient.' 'The longer one lives, the more one realizes that nothing is a dish for every day.' 'The unseemly haste in rising! One might really think the company were ashamed of so natural and jovial a function as that to which a dining-room is consecrated.' 'To be miserly towards your friends is not pretty; to be miserly towards yourself is contemptible.'

The last maxim of Norman's was one he was particularly fond of enlarging upon when it came to a question of whether we could or should afford an extra treat in a restaurant or a more expensive bottle of wine than usual. It was a lesson from which I have derived much benefit. Eating alone in restaurants, as I have often in the pursuit of gastronomic researches been obliged to, I never fail to recall Norman's words (a recollection which has resulted in a surprise for many a haughty maître d'hôtel and patronizing wine waiter, expecting a lone woman to order the cheapest dish and the most humble wine on the list). More important, to treat yourself to what you want, need, or are curious to taste, is the proper, and the only way, to learn to enjoy solitary meals, whether in restaurants or at home.

And let nobody waste his time looking into *Venus in the Kitchen* for advice on love-potions. Not once in the entire book does Norman suggest that he regards the idea of aphrodisiac recipes as anything more than a jovial diversion. A certain artichoke dish is 'appetizing, even if not efficacious'. Salad rocket is 'certainly a stimulant'. A 'timid person is advised to sustain himself' with 'leopard's marrow cooked in goat's milk and abundant white pepper'. Pork chops with fennel seeds (an interesting dish. I know it well. Fennel seeds figure frequently in the country cooking of Tuscany) makes 'a stimulant for sturdy stomachs'. A piece of loin of pork simmered in milk (a method of meat-cooking well known in certain parts of central and northern Italy) is 'a good restorative'. Restoratives, stimulants, sustaining dishes, one notes. Why are they restorative, stimulating, sustaining? Because this is good cooking; interesting, well-seasoned, appetizing, fresh, unmonotonous. Nothing is a dish for every day . . . Certainly not that concoction of the intestines of a sucking pig stuffed with pieces of eel, peppercorns, cloves and plenty of sage (evidently an uncommonly grisly form of chitterling sausage) concerning which Norman is at his most teasing: 'This is an extremely appetizing and stimulating dish. The eel goes very well with pork, because it is among fish what the pig is among quadrupeds.' A simultaneous right and left to certain religious observances and to inherent prejudices with which he had no patience.

'Anchovies have long been famed for their lust-provoking virtues' is the piece of information appended to a recipe for anchovy toast. Ha! This recipe, which sounds a good one, consists of an emulsion of four ounces of butter and the yolks of four eggs plus one tablespoon of anchovy sauce and a seasoning of Nepal pepper. Hardly enough anchovy to provoke a mild thirst, let alone a lust. Anyone who hopes that *Venus in the Kitchen* is going to provide a roll on the dining-room floor would do well to reconsider. And to buy the book for a different kind of fun. For the fun, that is, of reading about the spices and wines and herbs, the fruit and flowers, the snails, the truffles, the birds, animals and parts of animals (the crane, the skink, the testicles of bulls) which went into the cooking pots of ancient Rome and Greece and of Renaissance Europe; for a glimpse, just enough to send us looking for more of the same kind, of the cinnamon and ginger and coriander flavoured game dishes, of the rose- and saffron-spiced sauces and meats, of the pistachio creams, the carnation conserves, the gentian- and honey-flavoured wines, the Easter rice, the Sardinian pie of broad beans, the rolls of beef marbled with hard-boiled eggs and ham, the fennel and the almond soups which have all but vanished from European cooking.

To students of *Venus in the Kitchen* it may come as a disappointment to learn that Norman Douglas did not himself go in for the little extravaganzas he was fond of describing. Authentic food (if you can lay hands on a copy, see the passage in *Alone* describing his search in wartime Italy for genuine *maccheroni*, those *maccheroni* of a lily-like candour made from the correct hard fine white wheat flour), wine properly made, fruit from the trees he knew to have been well tended and grown in the right conditions – such things were his concerns. Gourmets' solemnities and sippings were not for him.

His tastes in food, in his last years, had become more than a trifle idiosyncratic. His explosive denunciations concerning the fish of the Mediterranean waters were familiar to all his friends (and to readers of *Siren Land*). 'Mussels? Of course, if you *want* to be poisoned, my dear. You know what happened to the consul in Naples, don't you? *Palombo?* No fear. But have it your way, my dear, have it your way. If you *care* to eat shark . . .' Then there was that business of the saffron. 'Liz, now take another glass of wine, and go into the kitchen; just see that Antonio puts enough saffron into that risotto. A man who is stingy with the saffron is capable of seducing his own grandmother.' From his pocket would come a brilliant yellow handkerchief. 'When the rice is that colour, there's enough saffron.' Enough! I should say so. For me the taste of saffron was overpowering long before the requisite colour had been attained. Just another of Norman's kinks, like his mania for hard-boiled eggs, of which he ate only the whites. How many discarded hard-boiled egg yolks did I consume in those weeks spent with him on Capri during the last summer of his life?

'For Liz. Farewell to Capri,' Norman wrote in the copy of *Late Harvest* which he gave me when I said goodbye to him on 25 August 1951. For me it was not farewell to Capri. It was farewell to Norman. On a dark drizzling London day in February 1952 news came from Capri of Norman's death. When, in the summer of that year, I spent six weeks on the island all I could do for Norman was to take a pot of the basil which was his favourite herb to his grave in the cemetery on the hill-road leading down to the port. I went there only once. I had never shared Norman's rather melancholy taste for visiting churchyards. A more fitting place to remember him was in the lemon grove to be reached only by descending some three hundred steps from the Piazza. It was so thick, that lemon grove, that it concealed from all but those who knew their Capri well the old Archbishops' palace in which was housed yet another of those private taverns which appeared to materialize for Norman alone. There, at a table outside the half-ruined house, a branch of piercingly aromatic lemons hanging within arm's reach, a piece of bread and a bottle of the proprietor's olive oil in front of me, a glass of wine in my hand, Norman was speaking.

'I wish you would listen when I tell you that if you fill my glass before it's empty I shan't know how much I've drunk.'

To this day I cannot bring myself to refill somebody else's glass until it is empty. A sensible rule, on the whole, even if it does mean that sometimes a guest is obliged to sit for a moment or two with an empty glass, uncertain whether to ask for more wine or to wait until it is offered.

In the shade of the lemon grove I break off a hunch of bread, sprinkle it with the delicious fruity olive oil, empty my glass of sour white Capri wine; and remember that Norman Douglas once wrote that whoever has helped us to a larger understanding is entitled to our gratitude for all time. Remember too that other saying of his, the one upon which all his life he acted, the one which does much to account for the uncommonly large number of men and women of all ages, classes and nationalities who took Norman Douglas to their hearts and will hold him there so long as they live. 'I like to taste my friends, not eat them.' From his friends Norman expected the same respect for his privacy as he had for theirs, the same rejection of idle questioning, meddling gossip and rattling chatter. From most of them he knew how to get it. The few who failed him in this regard did not for long remain his friends. Habitually tolerant and generous with his time, especially to the youthful and inexperienced, he had his own methods of ridding himself of those who bored him. I once witnessed a memorable demonstration of his technique in this matter.

In the summer of 1951 there was much talk on Capri, and elsewhere in Italy, of a great fancy-dress ball to be given in a Venetian palace by a South American millionaire. The entertainment was to be on a scale and of a splendour unheard of since the great days of the Serene Republic. One evening Norman, a group of young men and I myself were sitting late at Georgio's café in the Piazza. Criticism of the Palazzo Labia ball and the squandered thousands was being freely expressed. Norman was bored. He appeared to be asleep. At a pause in the chatter he opened his eyes. 'Don't you agree, Mr Douglas?' asked one of the eager young men. 'All that money.' He floundered on. 'I mean, so many more important things to spend it on . . .'

'Oh, I don't know.' Norman sounded far away. Then, gently: 'I like to see things done in style.'

And he stomped off. Evaporated, as he used to put it. The reproof had been as annihilating as any I ever heard administered.

In Graham Greene's words 'so without warning Douglas operates and the victim has no time to realize in what purgatorio of lopped limbs he is about to awaken, among the miserly, the bogus, the boring, and the ungenerous'.

It was when Norman Douglas was in his very early fifties that, one night after a convivial dinner, he 'was deputed or rather implored' by those of his companions who had been bemoaning their lost vigour, 'to look into the subject of aphrodisiac recipes and the rejuvenating effects of certain condiments and certain dishes'.

Some twelve years later Norman put his collection of recipes together in book form and wrote a preface signed 'Pilaff Bey'. (On the spine of the present American edition 'Bey' appears as the author's name. A circumstance which may lead to some confusion among booksellers and their customers.) As a frontispiece for the book Norman still had in his possession a drawing done some years previously by D. H. Lawrence. The spasmodic friendship, doomed, one would suppose, from the first, between these two men of almost ludicrously opposed temperaments, had ended in the pillorying in print of each by the other. The illustration Lawrence had done for the aphrodisiac book was so perversely hideous, so awful an example of Lawrence's gifts as an artist that Norman thought it a good joke. He decided to use it. When, eighteen years later, the book at last was published Messrs Heinemann did at least respect their lately dead author's wishes in the matter. In juxtaposition to the febrile drawings commissioned by the publishers the frontispiece looked startling enough. For those who had eyes to see it indicated also something of the tone of the book and of the intentions of the author. The preface, left as it was written 'not later than 1936' told them the rest. The book had originated as an exposition of the absurdities, the lengths 'to which humanity will go in its search for the lost vigour of youth'. In spirit it was a send-up, a spoof. As such Norman intended it to remain. He was reckoning, for once in his life, without his publishers. He was reckoning, perhaps, without Death. With the present American publishers he could hardly be expected to have reckoned. In what spirit of prudery one can only guess, these worthies have relegated the Lawrence frontispiece (there would appear to be matter in it to interest the Warden of All Souls and other students of Lawrence-Mellors-Lady Chatterley mythology) to the last page of the book, facing the index. That, at least, Norman would have found a capital joke.

1964

Have It Your Way

'Always do as you please, and send everybody to Hell, and take the consequences. Damned good rule of Life. N.' I think we must both have been more than a little tipsy the evening Norman wrote those words on the back page of my copy of *Old Calabria*. They are in a pencilled untidy scrawl that is very different from the neat pen-and-ink inscription, dated 21 May 1940, on the flyleaf of the book, and from the methodical list of 'misprints etc.' written on the title page when he gave me the book. 'Old-fashioned stuff, my dear. Heavy going. I don't know whether you'll be able to get through it.'

I have forgotten the occasion that gave rise to Norman's ferociously worded advice, although I fancy the message was written after a dinner during which he had tried to jolt me out of an entanglement which, as he could see without being told, had already become a burden to me. And the gentleman concerned was not very much to his liking.

'You are leaving with him because you think it is your duty. Duty? Ha! Stay here with me. Let him make do without you.'

'I can't, Norman. I have to go.'

'Have it your way, my dear, have it your way.'

Had I listened to Norman's advice I should have been saved a deal of trouble. Also, I should not, perhaps, have seen Greece and the islands, not spent the war years working in Alexandria and Cairo, not have married and gone to India, not have returned to England, not become involved in the painful business of learning to write about food and cookery. And I should not now be writing this long-overdue tribute to Norman Douglas. Was he right? Was he wrong? Does it matter? I did what I pleased at the time. I took the consequences. That is all that Norman would have wanted to know.

When I met him first, Norman Douglas was seventy-two. I was twenty-four. It was that period in Norman's life when, exiled from his home in Florence and from his possessions, he was living in far-from-prosperous circumstances in a room in the place Macé in Antibes.

Quite often we met for drinks or a meal together in one or another of the cafés or restaurants of the old lower town, a rather seedy place in those days. There was little evidence of that bacchanal existence that legend attributes to all Riviera resorts.

The establishment Norman chose when he fancied a pasta meal was in a narrow street near the old port. 'We'll meet at George's and have a drink. Then we'll go and tell them we're coming for lunch. No sense in letting them know sooner. If we do, they'll boil the macaroni in advance. Then all we shall get is heated-up muck. Worthless, my dear. We'll give them just twenty minutes. Mind you meet me on the dot.'

At the restaurant he would produce from his pocket a hunk of Parmesan cheese. 'Ask Pascal to be so good as to grate this at our table. Poor stuff, my dear, that Gruyère they give you in France. Useless for macaroni.' And a bunch of fresh basil for the sauce. 'Tear the leaves, mind. Don't chop them. Spoils the flavour.'

Now and again Norman would waylay me as I was buying provisions in the market. 'Let's get out of this hole. Leave that basket at George's. We'll take the bus up toward Vence and go for a little stroll.'

The prospect of a day in Norman's company was exhilarating; that little stroll rather less so. A feeble and unwilling walker, then as now, I found it arduous work trying to keep up with Norman. The way he went stumping up and down those steep and stony paths, myself shambling behind, reversed our ages. And well he knew it.

'Had enough?'

'Nearly.'

'Can you tackle another half kilometre?'

'Why can't we stop here?'

'*Pazienza.* You'll see.'

'I hope so.'

At that time I had not yet come to understand that in every step Norman took there was a perfectly sound purpose, and so was innocently impressed when at the end of that half kilometre, out in the scrub, at the back of beyond, there was a café. One of those two-chair, one-table, one-woman-and-a-dog establishments. Blessed scruffy café. Blessed crumbling crone and mangy dog.

'Can we deal with a litre?'

'Yes, and I'm hungry too.'

'Ha! You won't get much out of *her*. Nothing but bread and that beastly ham. Miserable insipid stuff.' From out of his pocket came a hunk of salami and a clasp knife.

'Do you always carry your own provisions in your pocket?'

'Ha! I should say so. I should advise you to adopt the same rule. Otherwise you may have to put up with what you get. No telling what it may be, nowadays.'

Certain famous passages in Norman Douglas's work, among them Count Caloveglia's dissertation in *South Wind* on the qualities necessary to a good cook, in *Siren Land* the explosive denunciation of Neapolitan fish soup, in *Alone* the passage in which he describes the authentic pre-1914 macaroni, 'those macaroni of a lily-like candour' (enviable phrase – who else could have written it?), have led many people to believe that Norman Douglas was a great epicure in matters gastronomical, and so he was – in an uncommon way; in a way few mortals can ever hope to become. His way was most certainly not the way of the solemn wine sipper or of the grave debater of recipes. Connoisseurship of this particular kind he left to others. He himself preferred the study of the original sources of his food and wine. Authenticity in these matters was of the first importance to him. (Of this, plenty of evidence can be found by those who care to look into *Old Calabria, Together, Siren Land, Alone*, and *Late Harvest*.) Cause and effect were eminently his concerns, and in their application he taught me some unforgettable lessons.

Once during that last summer of his life, on Capri (he was then eighty-three), I took him a basket of figs from the market in the Piazza. He asked me from which stall I had bought them. 'That one down nearest to the steps.'

'Not bad, my dear, not bad. Next time, you could try Graziella. I fancy you'll find her figs are sweeter; just wait a few days, if you can.'

He knew, who better, from which garden those figs came; he was familiar with the history of the trees, he knew their age and in what type of soil they grew; he knew by which tempests, blights, invasions, and plagues that particular property had or had not been affected during the past three hundred years; how many times it had changed hands, in what lawsuits the owners had been involved; that the son now grown up was a man less grasping than his neighbours and was consequently in less of a hurry to pick and sell his fruit before it ripened . . . I may add that it was not Norman's way to give lectures. These pieces of information emerged gradually, in the course of walks, sessions at the tavern, apropos a chance remark. It was up to you to put two and two together if you were sufficiently interested.

Knowing, as he made it his business wherever he lived and travelled to know, every innkeeper and restaurant owner on the island (including, naturally, Miss Gracie Fields; these two remarkable human beings were much to each other's taste) and all their families and their staff as well, still Norman would rarely go to eat in any establishment without first, in the morning, having looked in; or if he felt too poorly in those latter days, sent a message. What was to be had that day? What fish had come in? Was the mozzarella cheese dripping, positively dripping fresh? Otherwise we should have to have it fried. 'Giovanni's wine will slip down all right, my dear. At least he doesn't pick his grapes green.' When things did not go according to plan – and on Capri this could happen even to Norman Douglas – he wasted no time in recriminations. 'Come on. Nothing to be gained by staying here. Can you deal with a little glass up at the Cercola? Off we go then.'

Well-meaning people nowadays are always telling us to complain when we get a bad meal, to send back a dish if it is not as it should be. I remember, one bleak February day in 1962, reading that a British Cabinet Minister had told the hotel-keepers and caterers assembled at Olympia for the opening of their bi-annual exhibition of icing-sugar buses and models of Windsor Forest in chocolate-work, 'If the food you have in a restaurant is lousy, condemn it . . .'

At the time Norman Douglas was much in my mind, for it was round about the tenth anniversary of his death. How would he have reacted to this piece of advice? The inelegance of the phrase would not have been to his taste, of that much one can be certain. And from the Shades I think I hear a snort, that snort he gave when he caught you out in a piece of woolly thinking. 'Condemn it? Ha! That won't get you far. Better see you don't have cause for complaint, I'd say. No sense in growling when it's too late.'

1969

An Omelette and a Glass of Wine

Once upon a time there was a celebrated restaurant called the Hôtel de la Tête d'Or on the Mont-St-Michel just off the coast of Normandy. The reputation of this house was built upon one single menu which was served day in day out for year after year. It consisted of an omelette, ham, a fried sole, *pré-salé* lamb cutlets with potatoes, a roast chicken and salad, and a dessert. Cider and butter were put upon the table and were thrown in with the price of the meal, which was two francs fifty in pre-1914 currency.

But it wasn't so much what now appears to us as the almost absurd lavishness of the menu which made Madame Poulard, proprietress of the hotel, celebrated throughout France. It was the exquisite lightness and beauty of the omelettes, cooked by the proprietress herself, which brought tourists flocking to the mère Poulard's table.

Quite a few of these customers subsequently attempted to explain the particular magic which Madame Poulard exercised over her eggs and her frying pan in terms of those culinary secrets which are so dear to the hearts of all who believe that cookery consists of a series of conjuring tricks. She mixed water with the eggs, one writer would say, she added cream asserted another, she had a specially made pan said a third, she reared a breed of hens unknown to the rest of France claimed a fourth. Before long, recipes for the *omelete de la mère Poulard* began to appear in magazines and cookery books. Some of these recipes were very much on the fanciful side. One I have seen even goes so far as to suggest she put *foie gras* into the omelette. Each writer in turn implied that to him or her alone had Madame Poulard confided the secret of her omelettes.

At last, one fine day, a Frenchman called M. Robert Viel, interested in fact rather than surmise, wrote to Madame Poulard, by this time long retired from her arduous labours, and asked her once and for all to clear up the matter. Her reply, published in 1932 in a magazine called *La Table*, ran as follows:

6 June 1932

Monsieur Viel,
    Here is the recipe for the omelette: I break some good eggs in a bowl, I beat them well, I put a good piece of butter in the pan, I throw the eggs into it, and I shake it constantly. I am happy, monsieur, if this recipe pleases you.

Annette Poulard

So much for secrets.

But, you will say, everyone knows that the success of omelette making starts with the pan and not with the genius of the cook. And a heavy pan with a perfectly flat base *is*, of course, a necessity. And if you are one of those who feel that some special virtue attaches to a venerable black iron pan unwashed for twenty years, then you are probably right to cling to it.

Cookery does, after all, contain an element of the ritualistic and however clearly one may understand that the reason for not washing and scouring omelette pans is the risk of thereby causing rust spots and scratches which would spoil the surface of the pan and cause the eggs to stick, one may still have a superstitious feeling that some magic spell will be broken if water is allowed to approach the precious pan. Soap and water, come not near, come not near our omelette pan . . . (Personally, I keep my old iron omelette pan, the surface protected by a film of oil, for pancakes, and use an aluminium one for omelettes and wash it up like any other utensil. This is not perversity, but simply the ritual which happens to suit me and my omelettes.)

As to the omelette itself, it seems to me to be a confection which demands the most straightforward approach. What one wants is the taste of the fresh eggs and the fresh butter and, visually, a soft bright golden roll plump and spilling out a little at the edges. It should not be a busy, important urban dish but something gentle and pastoral, with the clean scent of the dairy, the kitchen garden, the basket of early morning mushrooms or the sharp tang of freshly picked herbs, sorrel, chives, tarragon. And although there are those who maintain that wine and egg dishes don't go together I must say I do regard a glass or two of wine as not, obviously, essential but at least as an enormous enhancement of the enjoyment of a well-cooked omelette. In any case if it were true that wine and eggs are bad partners, then a good many dishes, and in particular, such sauces as mayonnaise, Hollandaise and Béarnaise would have to be banished from meals designed round a good bottle, and that would surely be absurd. But we are not in any case considering the great occasion menu but the almost primitive and elemental meal evoked by the words: 'Let's just have an omelette and a glass of wine.'

Perhaps first a slice of home-made pâté and a few olives, afterwards a fresh salad and a piece of ripe creamy cheese or some fresh figs or strawberries . . . How many times have I ordered and enjoyed just such a meal in French country hotels and inns in preference to the set menu of *truite meunière, entrecôte, pommes paille* and *crème caramel* which is the French equivalent of the English roast and two veg. and apple tart and no less dull when you have experienced it two or three times.

There was, no doubt there still is, a small restaurant in Avignon where I used to eat about twice a week, on market days, when I was living in a rickety old house in a crumbling Provençal hill-top village about twenty miles from the city of the Popes. Physically and emotionally worn to tatters by the pandemonium and splendour of the Avignon market, tottering under the weight of the provisions we had bought and agonized at the thought of all the glorious things which we hadn't or couldn't, we would make at last for the restaurant Molière to be rested and restored.

It was a totally unpretentious little place and the proprietors had always been angelically kind, welcoming and generous. They purveyed some particularly delicious *marc de Champagne* and were always treating us to a glass or two after lunch so that by the time we piled into the bus which was to take us home we were more than well prepared to face once more the rigours of our mistral-torn village. But even more powerful a draw than the *marc* was the delicious cheese omelette which was the Molière's best speciality. The recipe was given to me by the proprietress whose name I have most ungratefully forgotten, but whose omelette, were there any justice in the world, would be as celebrated as that of Madame Poulard. Here it is.

OMELETTE MOLIÈRE

Beat *one* tablespoon of finely grated Parmesan with three eggs and a little pepper.

Warm the pan a minute over the fire. Put in half an oz. of butter. Turn up the flame. When the butter bubbles and is about to change colour, pour in the eggs.

Add *one* tablespoon of very fresh Gruyère cut into little dice, and *one* tablespoon of thick fresh cream. Tip the pan towards you, easing some of the mixture from the far edge into the middle. Then tip the pan away from you again, filling the empty space with some of the still liquid eggs. By the time you have done this twice, the Gruyère will have started to melt and your omelette is ready. Fold it over in three with a fork or palette knife, and slide it on to the warmed omelette dish. Serve it instantly.

With our meals in Avignon we generally drank local wine, pink or red, which was nothing much to write home about (the wine of our own village *was* notable though: the worst I have ever consistently had to drink) but what I would choose nowadays if I had the chance would be a deliciously scented Alsatian Traminer or a white burgundy such as the lovely Meursault –

Genevrières of 1955, or a Loire wine, perhaps Sancerre or a Pouilly-Fumé – anyway, you see what I mean. I like white wines with all cheese dishes, and especially when the cheese in question is Gruyère. No doubt this is only a passing phase, because as a wine drinker but not a wine expert one's tastes are constantly changing. But one of the main points about the enjoyment of food and wine seems to me to lie in having what you want *when* you want it and in the particular combination you fancy.

1959

Chez Barattero

From 1956 to 1961 I contributed a monthly cookery article to London Vogue. *In those days cookery writers were very minor fry. Expenses were perks paid to photographers, fashion editors and other such exalted personages. Foreign currency allowances were severely restricted, so cookery contributors didn't come in for subsidized jaunts to Paris or marathons round three-star eating cathedrals. They were supposed to supply their articles out of some inexhaustible well of knowledge and their ingredients out of their own funds. At a monthly fee of £20 an article (increased at some stage, I think, to £25) it was quite a struggle to keep up the flow of properly tested recipes, backed up with informative background material, local colour and general chatter. So it was with gratitude that one year I accepted an offer from my editor, the original and enlightened Audrey Withers, to go on the occasional trip to France, provided with £100 from Condé Nast to help cover restaurant meals, hotels, petrol and so on. To be sure, £100 wasn't exactly princely even in those days, but it was double the ordinary currency allowance, and even though those trips were very much France on a shoestring, the knowledge I derived from them was valuable. In French provincial restaurants at that time local and regional dishes weren't always double-priced on a 'menu touristique'. Some, incredible as it now seems, would be listed as a matter of course on the everyday menus of quite ordinary restaurants. Asked nicely, a* patron *might come up with a speciality based, say, on some local farmhouse pork product, or on a cheese peculiar to the immediate district, perhaps an omelette of the chef's own devising, or a simple fish dish with an uncommon sauce. It was for ideas and stimulus that I was looking, not restaurant set pieces.*

On one trip, however, I came to make the acquaintance of Madame Barattero and her Hôtel du Midi at Lamastre in the Ardèche. Now, a hotel with a Michelin two-star restaurant attached might not seem exactly the appropriate choice for people on a restricted budget. As things turned out, that particular two-star restaurant-hotel proved, in the long run, very much cheaper, infinitely better value, and far more rewarding than most of the technically cheap places we'd found. Staying at Lamastre on half-pension terms was restful and comfortable. Every day we drove out to the countryside, usually taking a picnic, or lunching at a small town or village restaurant. In the evening we were provided by Madame Barattero with a delicious dinner made up of quite simple dishes geared to the price charged to pension-naires. *Prime ingredients and skilled cooking were, however, very much included in our* en pension *terms. That lesson was a valuable one, and seemed well worth passing on to my readers.*

My account of the Hôtel du Midi was published in Vogue *in September 1958. I should add that while much of the material published in* Vogue *as a result of my trips to France in the fifties was incorporated in* French Provincial Cooking, *this was one of several articles which got away. There did not seem to be a place for it in the book, and in fact it was, in its day, unique for a* Vogue *food article in that it included no recipes. It was, again, Audrey Withers who took the decision to publish an article quite unorthodox by the rules prevailing at the time. I appreciated her imaginative gesture. With Madame Barattero I remained on friendly terms for many years, receiving a moving welcome every time I visited her hotel. Two years ago, after a brief retirement, Madame Barattero died. Her declining years had been clouded by increasing deafness, by the withdrawal of one of her Michelin stars, and I believe other untoward happenings. The restaurant of the Hôtel du Midi is now in the hands of the same chef who was in charge of the kitchens all those years ago, and who had long since become a partner in the business. I have not visited Lamastre for several years now, so cannot express any opinion on the cooking. I am glad though to be able to republish my article, as a tribute to Madame Barattero's memory.*

Rose Barattero is the euphonious name of the proprietress of the Hôtel du Midi at Lamastre in the Ardèche. Slim, elegant, her pretty grey hair in tight curls all over her head, the minuscule red ribbon of the Legion of Honour on her grey dress, Madame Barattero is an impressive little figure as she stands on the terrace of her hotel welcoming her guests as they drive into the main square of the small provincial town whose name she has made famous throughout France.

Here, in this town, in the modest hotel which stands back to back with her own, she was born. Her parents were hotel-keepers, her brother inherited, and still runs, the old Hôtel de la Poste. Her sister has a hotel at St-Vallier down on the Rhône. Her husband, a *niçois*, and a relation of the Escoffier family, started his career as an apprentice at the Carlton in London, and was already making a name for himself as a promising chef when she married him and they set up on their own at the Hôtel du Midi.

When M. Barattero died in 1941 the hotel was already celebrated for its cooking. His young widow took over the running of the hotel and the restaurant, putting the kitchen in the charge of a hard-working and modest chef who had started as Barattero's apprentice. His wife looks after the accounts and the reception work. During the past fifteen years or so the fame of Barattero's at Lamastre has spread throughout France; Madame Barattero's name is among the most respected in the entire French restaurant industry.

In the fiercely competitive world of the French catering business this is no ordinary achievement. Lamastre is a town of little over three thousand inhabitants. It is not on a main road; the country round about, although magnificent and infinitely varied, is not known to tourists in the way in which, let us say, Provence or the château country of the Loire are known, for there is not very much left in the way of architectural or historical interest for the ordinary sightseer. In other words, a place like Barattero's must rely, not on the local population and the passing tourist, but upon those customers who make the journey to Lamastre expressly for the cooking.

Michelin awards Madame Barattero two stars. Now, although Michelin one-star restaurants are very much on the chancy side, both as regards quality and price, and such of their three-star establishments (there are only eleven in the whole of France) into which I have penetrated, either a little too rarefied in atmosphere for my taste – or, as Raymond Mortimer observed recently of a famous Paris house, the food is too rich and so are the customers – it is rare to find the two-star places at fault. As far as the provinces are concerned these two-star establishments (there are fifty-nine of them in the whole country, about twenty of which are in Paris) offer very remarkable value. I do not mean to suggest that they are places for the impecunious, but rather that while the cooking which they have to offer is unique, the charges compare more than favourably with those prevailing in hundreds of other French establishments where the surroundings vary between the grandiose and the squalid and where the cooking, while probably sound enough, is uneven or without distinction.

I have often heard the criticism that these modest establishments of two-star quality, offering, as most of them do, no more than half a dozen specialities at most, are places whose resources are exhausted after a couple of meals, or alternatively that the accommodation which they have to offer is not up to the standard of the cooking. So tourists make their pilgrimage to eat a meal at a place like the Midi at Lamastre, the Chapon Fin at Thoissey, or the Armes de France at Ammerschwihr and move on without knowing that they could have stayed for several days, not only in comfort and quiet and enjoying a variety of beautifully cooked dishes, but quite often at considerably reduced prices for pension or half-pension terms.

Early last summer we drove from Lyon down the western bank of the Rhône towards St-Péray, and there turned off up the steep and beautiful road which leads to Lamastre and St-Agrève. We had been warned that the forty-odd kilometres from St-Péray to Lamastre would take us twice as long as we expected because of the sinuous road, so we had allowed plenty of time, and arrived in front of the Hôtel du Midi while the afternoon sun was still shining over the little *place*. Our welcome from Madame Barattero was so warm and the rooms we were shown so airy, light and sympathetically furnished, the bathroom so immense and shining, the little garden below our terrace so pretty and orderly, that we decided there and then to stay several days. We discussed half-pension terms with Madame and then made ourselves scarce until dinner time.

Now it must be explained that chez Barattero there are five special dishes for which the house is renowned. They are *galantine de caneton*, a *pain d'écrevisses sauce cardinal*, a *poularde en vessie*, a *saucisse en feuilletage* and a dish of artichoke hearts with a creamy sauce which they call *artichauts Escoffier*. If you were really trying you could, I suppose, taste them all at one meal (indeed four of them figure on the 1,800 franc menu, the most expensive one, the others being 1,600 and 1,200) but we could take our time and enjoy them gradually. We left the choice of our menus to Madame. Indeed, there was little alternative but to do so. For although she does not herself do the cooking Madame has been studying her guests and composing menus for them for thirty-four years and she neither likes being contradicted nor is capable of making a mistake in this respect. She knew without being told that we didn't want to overload ourselves with food, however delicious; with an unerring touch she provided us night after night with menus which I think it is worth describing if only to demonstrate one or two important points about French restaurant cooking. First, how varied the food can be even in a place where the advertised specialities are very limited; secondly, how well worth while it is eating even the simplest of the routine dishes of French cookery produced in an absolutely first-class manner. ('One does not come here to eat something as ordinary as *œufs en gelée*,' the archbishop-like head waiter in a famous Paris restaurant once said to me. He was wrong. Such simple things are the test of a really good establishment.) And thirdly, how very much a good dish gains by being served quite on its own, without fussy garnish or heaps of vegetables to overfill you and to get in the way of your sauce, to distract from the main flavours of the chicken or the fish and to sicken you of the sight of food long before the end of the meal.

We could have started every meal with soup had we so wished, but in fact we did so only once or twice because they were so good that we should have eaten too much. And the last part of the meal always consisted of a fine platter of cheeses and either strawberries, cherries or an ice, so I will leave those items out of the following account of our menus.

The wines we drank were mostly recent Rhône vintages, the current wines of the house, for many of which, especially the red Hermitages, the Cornas and the Côte Rôtie, I have a particular affection. Among the whites we tried were St-Péray, Chapoutier's Chante Alouette, Jaboulet's La Chapelle Hermitage 1950; for those who prefer, and can afford, old burgundies and bordeaux there is a well-stocked cellar of fine vintages.

TUESDAY

Galantine de caneton: The name is misleading to English ears. It is a whole boned duck, its flesh mixed with finely minced pork, truffles, brandy and *foie gras*, sewn up in the skin of the duck and cooked in the oven; the result resembles a long fat sausage with the feet of the duck protruding at one end. This pâté has a flavour of very great delicacy, and is served sliced and quite unadorned. The lettuce leaves and the little heap of potato salad which, I have an uneasy feeling, would be the inevitable garnish provided by an English restaurateur, is simply unthinkable here.

Sole meunière: Perfectly cooked whole sole with quantities of hissing and foaming butter. Again, no garnish of any kind, and none needed.

Blettes à la crème au gratin: Blettes, or chard, that spinach-like vegetable with fleshy white stalks is, to me, only tolerable when cooked by a master hand, but as the Barattero chef has that hand, and makes a particularly excellent cream sauce, all was well.

WEDNESDAY

After an exhausting day's driving in bad weather, and a good and not expensive lunch at the Cygne (but unsettling contemporary decor in an old hotel) in the rather depressing town of Le Puy, we returned to dinner at Lamastre.

Potage de légumes: The routine vegetable soup of the day, but the mixture of carrots, potatoes and other vegetables was so delicate, so buttery, so full of flavour, that this alone would serve to make the reputation of a lesser restaurant. Note: although so full of flavour this soup was quite thin. I think we make our vegetable soups too thick in this country.

Ris de veau à la crème: I have eaten too many ambitiously conceived but ill-executed dishes of sweetbreads ever again to order them of my own accord, so I was grateful to Madame Barattero for showing me how good they can be when properly done. There were mushrooms in the sauce. Perfect.

Petit pois à la française: A big bowl of very small fresh peas (even in good restaurants it is rare nowadays not to get *petit pois de conserve*) cooked with little shreds of lettuce but without the little onions usually associated with the *à la française* manner of cooking them. The result was very creamy and good. I doubt if I shall ever again put onions with my peas.

THURSDAY

Pain d'écrevisses sauce cardinal: A very remarkable dish. A variety of *quenelle*, but unlike the pasty *quenelles* one eats elsewhere, even in the much cracked-up Lyon restaurants; as light as a puff of air, with the subtle and inimitable flavour of river crayfish permeating both *quenelle* and the rich cream sauce. The garnish of the dish consisted of a few whole scarlet crayfish and crescents of puff pastry.

Poularde en vessie: A three-pound Bresse chicken, stuffed with its own liver, a little *foie gras* and slices of truffle, is tied up inside a pig's bladder and cooked extremely gently in a marmite of barely simmering water for one and a half hours. As Madame Barattero said, a chicken poached in the ordinary way, however carefully, cannot help but be '*un peu délavé*', a trifle washed out. By this system, which is an ancient one, the chicken, untouched by the cooking liquid, emerges with all its juices and flavours intact. When it is cold, as it was served to us, these juices formed inside the bladder have solidified to a small amount of clear and delicately flavoured jelly. Madame asserted that nothing was easier to cook than this dish – 'What do you mean, why can you not get a pig's bladder in England? You have pigs, do you not?' – and upheld her point by adding that the chef's eight-year-old son already knows how to prepare the *poulardes en vessie.* A green salad with cream in the dressing was the only accompaniment to the chicken.

FRIDAY AND SATURDAY

The most important part of Friday's meal was a sad disappointment. It was a dish of tiny grilled lamb cutlets, obviously beautiful meat, but much too undercooked for our taste.

On Saturday evening, when *épaule d'agneau* was announced, I explained the trouble. The little shoulder appeared cooked to what was, for us, perfection. A beautiful golden brown on the outside and just faintly pink in the middle. It had been preceded by a delicious *omelette aux champignons* and was accompanied by a *gratin* of courgettes and tomatoes, just slightly flavoured with garlic and cooked in butter instead of olive oil as it would have been in Provence. It went admirably with the lamb, and this was a good example of a very nice dinner of quite ordinary French dishes without any particular regional flavour or speciality of the house.

SUNDAY

Next day was Whitsunday and we stayed in to lunch as well as to dinner, for, as the weekend drew near, we had been observing with fascinated interest the preparations afoot for the large number of customers expected for the *fêtes*. The chef had prepared fifteen of his boned and stuffed ducks and by lunchtime on Sunday dozens of *poulardes* tied up in pig's bladders and scores of *pain d'écrevisses* were ready, all gently murmuring in their respective copper marmites.

Until now the service at meal times had been performed entirely by Marthe and Marie, the two pretty, expertly trained young girls in black frocks and starched white aprons who also brought our breakfasts and looked after our rooms. Now two waiters and Madame's sister from St-Vallier appeared upon the scene. There was no bustle and no panic or noise. Everything went like clockwork. And this I think partly explains what must seem a mystery to many visitors: how these unassuming places, in which the hotel part of the business is only incidental, can manage to maintain, day after day, cooking of a quality which simply could not be found in England and which is rare even in France. The answer is that they are organized and run in a way which a Guards sergeant-major would envy, and are as well equipped to deal with a banquet for three hundred people or a steady stream of holiday visitors as they are to provide comfort and an intimate atmosphere for a handful of regular guests out of season.

From a peaceful Sunday morning gossip in the charming blue and turquoise and cream tiled *charcuterie* run by M. and Madame Montagne (where there is a good restaurant in a French town or village you may be sure that a good *charcuterie* is not far away), I returned to Barattero's for the promised Sunday feast. Customers were arriving from Valence, from Marseille, from Lyon. A huge shining silver-grey Rolls-Bentley was parked in the square (it was the first English car we had seen). A party of young people flung themselves off their Lambrettas and clattered round a large table. They evidently took the cooking and its reputation for granted, for they hadn't dressed up or put on Sunday voices as we would have here for such an occasion. It was enjoyable to watch them, and all the other customers who were there simply because they were going to enjoy the food, for there was none of that holy hush which to some of us makes the grander eating places such a sore trial.

This was our luncheon menu:

Saucisse en feuilletage: This might be called the apotheosis of the sausage roll. A fresh, pure pork sausage (from the Montagne establishment, as I had already learned), coarsely cut and weighing about ¾ lb, is poached and then encased in flaky pastry, baked, and served hot, cut in slices. Both sausage and pastry were first class. A delicious hors-d'œuvre.

Pain d'écrevisses sauce cardinal: This seemed even better, if possible, than the first time we had eaten it, and this is quite a test, for one is inclined to be more critical when tasting a famous dish for the second time. The chef at Barattero's has been cooking the *pain d'écrevisses*, and the other specialities of the house, almost every day for some thirty years, but even so I suppose it is possible that they might vary.

Artichauts Escoffier: I am always in two minds about dishes of this kind. The cream sauce with mushrooms was very light and did not overwhelm the artichoke hearts, but all the same I wonder if they are not better quite plain; at La Mère Brazier's in Lyon we had had a salad of whole artichoke hearts and lettuce dressed simply with a little oil and lemon, which, in its extreme simplicity, was quite delicious and the best artichoke dish I have ever eaten.

Poulet rôti: A *poulet de grain* (the equivalent of a spring chicken) for two people, perfectly roasted in butter, already carved but reconstituted into its original shape, served on a long platter with a nest of miniature *pommes rissolées* beside it. No other garnish.

For dinner that evening we tasted again the wonderful duck pâté, to be followed by a little roast *gigot* and another dish of those tender little *petits pois*. When we told the waiter how much we had enjoyed the lamb, he replied yes, certainly, it must be a treat to us after the mutton boiled with mint of English cookery. Some very quaint notions of English food are current in France.

The last customers were only just leaving as we ourselves said goodby to Madame Barattero after dinner, for we were leaving early next morning. The place had seemed full to us, but it was the time of the Algerian crisis, and had it not been for *les événements*, Madame said, there would have been twice as many people. Customers would have come even from Paris. In her long, arduous and successful career as restaurateur and hotel-keeper she has learned that you can never be quite sure what to expect, and even with her tremendous experience it is impossible to know how many people to cater for. As she says: 'Thirty-four years in the hotel business, what a stint, hein?'

Since writing my introductory note to the above I have received reassuring news of the food at the Hôtel du Midi. In June 1983 a reader who had stayed at Lamastre as a result of reading about Madame Barattero in French Provincial Cooking *wrote me a charming letter telling me that the dinner had been 'most delicious'. The first course had been a* salade tiède – 'ce que nous avons ici de la nouvelle cuisine', *she was told – but as you would expect subtle and different, followed by the celebrated* pain d'écrevisses *(the crayfish now come from Hungary)), then there were cheeses, and a* chariot de desserts, *stylish, original* 'd'un goût très raffiné'. 'Tout est léger ici' *said the maître d'hôtel. There was an iced* soufflé aux marrons, *a pistachio sorbet, oranges in grenadine,* tuile tulips *filled with a cream of strawberries served with a* coulis. *Bernard, son of maître Perrier, the chef who became Madame Barattero's partner, and inherited from her the restaurant and hotel, of which he is now in charge, has succeeded his father as chef. It was Bernard, I learned, who had added the delicious desserts. The maître d'hôtel had said that they were the only missing elements in the range of dishes in the old days, and they are Bernard's contribution. I remember Bernard Perrier as a small boy, and I remember also how Madame Barattero predicted that in time he would follow in his father's footsteps. It was good to hear that the young man is fulfilling Madame's prophecy and that the Hôtel du Midi continues to flourish.*

1984

QUENTIN CREWE

Eels

The village of Passay, not far from Nantes, has a deserted and faintly sinister air about it. Whether this is due to the fact that so many of its inhabitants have moved away in search of employment, or to the enduring effects of an ancient curse, is not easy to determine.

Whatever the case, in a narrow back street of this wan village lives a delightful old couple, almost the last of a traditional group of fisherfolk, Monsieur and Madame Baudray. He is a red-faced man with grey hair and bright eyes tinged with green, and she is an equally lively person of a most hospitable nature.

Passay sits at the edge of the Lac de Grand-Lieu, the largest lake in France, although it varies in size from 6,300 hectares in the winter to 2,600 in the summer (from 15,750 to 6,500 acres) and is nowhere much more than 1.5 m (5 ft) in depth. It has a pleasantly inviolate feeling about it, the lonely stretch of water surrounded by virgin groves of trees. Nothing disturbs the peace, except for the cries of the water birds and the occasional splash of a fish jumping for a fly.

The lake used to belong to Monsieur Guerlain, the head of the family famous as the makers of the best scent in France. A few years ago, the old gentleman, who is now 87, gave the lake to the nation. It was decided to keep it as a nature sanctuary. No tourism is allowed – no water sports, no shooting, no fishing.

M. Guerlain made two conditions when he gave the lake. First, that he should be allowed to come to shoot the duck, which he does nearly every Saturday during the season; secondly, that the fishermen of the village, whose livelihood depended on the lake, should be allowed to continue to fish as they had always done. There were, not very long ago, 120 fishermen, but now there are only ten, of whom André Baudray is one. Soon there will be none, for the right to fish is not heritable and the few remaining who are entitled to the privilege are not young.

There are many kinds of fish in the lake, but the principal catch is eels. These curious, primeval-seeming creatures, that appear to be the victims of some evolutionary hiccough with their fatiguing life-cycle, are by no means like other fish. There is much dispute and, even today, a fair measure of mystery about this life-cycle. I felt confident that anything M. Baudray told me about eels was bound to be right since he had spent his whole life watching them and earning his living from them, but experts contradict many of the things he believes.

As every schoolboy knows, European freshwater eels spawn in the Sargasso Sea in the Atlantic (to the south-west of Bermuda) and it is there that the young hatch. M. Baudray assured me that it was only the impregnated female that had to make the long journey out to the Sargasso, which struck me as the ultimate in animal male chauvinism, but apparently he is quite mistaken on this point. Both males and females cross the ocean, the males going when they have been in Europe for about six to nine years. The females go from one to three years later when they may be as much as 60 cm (24 in).

The eels, which are sluggish when in fresh water, become active swimmers when in the sea, covering as much as 40–50 km (25–31 miles) a day and reach their breeding ground in three to four months. The precise area is between latitudes 22 and 30 degrees north, centred on 26 degrees north and 56 degrees west. There, at a depth of 100–300 m (330–990 ft), where the water is at a constant 20°C, a colossal nuptial feast takes place.

The young that result (*leptocephali*) are leaf-shaped and transparent. They develop very slowly, taking three years to grow to a length of 7–9 cm (2¾–3¼ in). During that time, both as eggs and as *leptocephali*, they are borne by the Gulf Stream across the Atlantic towards Europe. The crossing is slow, taking about three years. During it, the creatures lose their transparency and become smaller, measuring only 6 cm (2¼ in). They arrive in the first three months of the year, transformed now into elvers. It is a fascinating sight to watch them, in so close a single file that they look like an endless black thread, making their way up a river, hugging the bank for safety. At some point they scatter, the males peeling off earlier than the females. Some make their way overland for considerable distances, until they reach a suitable lake or pond in which to live. Eels can survive out of water for several hours but, as they are vulnerable to predators, they prefer to travel on wet moonless nights.

The eel-fishing season lasts only from March to November, because eels hibernate – at least, M. Baudray says they hibernate, while some experts say they do not, though they do burrow down into the mud to escape cold weather, which seems to me much the same thing. While they are carnivorous and voracious eaters, they can go without food for long periods.

For the first two months of the season, M. Baudray catches his eels with a rod and line. After that the water becomes too warm and so, for reasons that were not clear to me, but partly due to the fact that the area of the lake navigable by boat is reduced to a seventh of what it is in winter, the eels no longer take the bait. Instead, M. Baudray uses nets, which he keeps at a small cabin in the woods by an inlet where his boat is moored. The nets are odd-looking, something like a triple hourglass, with three compartments. In the lake, across a current, he has constructed a 50 m (55 yd) dam that encourages the eels to swim into the nets.

Baudray's boat is a flat-bottomed craft, not unlike a punt, except that on board he has a small *'vivier'* or tank in which to put his catch, which must be kept alive as eels turn very quickly when dead. Back at his cabin, he transfers them to a larger tank, where they stay until it is time to sell them.

He expects his annual catch to be about 30 tons, which is a lot of eels when you realize that a kilo consists of something between nine and thirteen of the wriggling creatures, which means a minimum of 270,000 eels. I thought these figures preposterous until I discovered that each female produces 1.3 to 1.5 million eggs.

Several mysteries remain about eels. The European eel is a widespread species, with no sub-species. They are found in plenty in Italy, Greece and Turkey. If these eastern eels have to go to the Sargasso Sea to breed, they must pass through the Straits of Gibraltar but, according to the Italian expert Paola Manfredi, no one has ever caught an eel in the Straits. She may have been being too emphatic in saying 'never', but certainly it is virtually unheard of for any-one to see an eel there. But then, there is no record of anyone's seeing an eel on its outward journey in the Atlantic. No one knows either what becomes of the parent eels after breeding. Do they live on at a great depth, or do they die? As their entire guts regress just before migration to allow space for the rapidly maturing gonads, ovaries and testes, it is unlikely that they survive for long.

Baudray used to deliver his eels all over France, but now the demand has dropped, and he and his wife are inclined to do rather less than they used to. They do, however, go on adventurous holidays, having an unexpected admiration for Britain and in particular Scotland, though not for British food.

Madame Baudray is an enthusiastic cook with a liking for the old traditional ways of cooking eels – in a *matelote*, with Malaga grapes, Agen prunes and red wine, stewing them for up to two hours. Baby eels she cooks *à la Provençale* with lots of oil and garlic. Otherwise she grills them with *gros sel* 'as always at the Grand-Lieu'.

It is Madame Baudray who likes to half-believe in the story of the curse, while her husband looks benignly sceptical. 'There was once a village here, called Herbauges, and St Martin came to visit it. He was badly received. It was a bit like the story of Sodom and Gomorrah.' At this point Madame Baudray looked a little shy and asked if I knew that story, but she went on. 'So St Martin cursed the village and it was submerged beneath the lake with its church and all its houses. And at midnight on Christmas Eve, one can hear the bells of the church ringing out from below the water.'

There are not many first-class restaurants that serve eels now. The one supreme exception is Charles Barrier in Tours, in many ways the most distinguished chef in France. He is now 75 and has run his eponymous restaurant for nearly 50 years, gaining three Michelin stars for many of them. The restaurant has been reduced a little in size and M. Barrier now spends fewer hours in the kitchen, but he watches carefully over everything. He is still inventive, but amusingly trenchant in his criticism of anything gimmicky.

He says that not long ago he asked the editors of the *Guide Michelin* whether he should go on producing old-fashioned dishes like stuffed pig's trotters and his glorious *matelote d'anguilles*, for which he gave us the recipe. The response was: 'Please, M. Barrier, never stop because, if you do not do these things, surely, nobody else will.'

There is a sad comparison to be made between these two charming and elderly gentlemen. They are the last of their kind. M. Baudray is one of the last fishermen on the Lac de Grand-Lieu. And Charles Barrier, who was a chef of distinction long before Paul Bocuse and his *bande* were ever heard of, represents an age and a style that he has kept alive for so long and that will disappear completely when he finally retires. We will miss them.

1993

JANE GRIGSON

Marcel Proust (1871–1922)

I have always maintained a reserve towards the famous mixture of lime tea and madeleine. Proust, after all, did not claim much for it as food. It acted as a trigger precisely because he had forgotten it. As an adult he did not bother with tea, so that when he came in cold and depressed one day, and his mother offered him tea and a madeleine, he at first refused, then took it, and without thinking raised a spoonful of madeleine crumbs soaked in tea to his lips. As he tasted it, as it 'touched my palate . . . a shudder ran through my whole body, and I stopped, intent upon the extraordinary changes that were taking place. An exquisite pleasure had invaded my senses, but individual, detached, with no suggestion of its origin . . . I put down my cup and examine my own mind . . . What an abyss of uncertainty whenever the mind feels that some part of it has strayed beyond its own borders.' So he bullied his memory, tried a few more spoonfuls of madeleine and tea without success, fought a natural laziness to step back from the abyss and leave undisturbed 'the vast structure of recollection'.

'And suddenly the memory returns. The taste was that of the little crumb of madeleine which on Sunday mornings at Combray . . . my aunt Léonie used to give me, dipping it first in her own cup of real or of lime-flower tea.' The slow search, the painful search for time past had begun.*

Reserve seemed the proper attitude for a respectful reader. But one winter the dried flowers from our lime tree in France smelled more fragrant than usual (we sit under the tree every day in summer, looking down from the cliff to the Loir below, which is also Proust's Loir running through his family's town of Illiers, that became Combray). They tempted me to make madeleines to have with lime tea in the evening. Hoping for nothing, sceptical even, we were surprised by the gentle delicacy they made together.

We talked of a visit many years ago to the house at Illiers. It had been got up as a shrine, smelling of new paint, a shell of vacancy and loss. 'In the empty

* Most quotations in this chapter come from *À la recherche du temps perdu.*

kitchen a terrine in the shape of a rabbit might have held the meats potted by Françoise. The emptiness upstairs might have been the theatre and have known the drama of the child's going to bed; the door knob in one room or another might have taken around its slope the coloured Merovingian images from the child's magic lantern.' It might, but it was no longer the real thing. Not even the tinkle of the garden bell announcing Swann's arrival was real. In the church that smelt of rose-scented peonies – we were too late for hawthorn flowers – we felt closer to Proust.

Closer still, for a few moments, when we visited friends recently at midday, on the other side of the Loir. As we drank coffee in the *salon*, the meal over, our host said, 'Did you know that Proust sometimes sat here in this room? He came over from Courtanvaux with Robert de Montesquiou' – the chief model for Charlus – 'and wrote to my great-grandmother on mauve paper in gold ink.'

I reflect that there was nothing mauve and gold about Proust's enjoyment of food, even if in later life he savoured it only in memory. He loved the good, simple dishes that characterize the Loir valley, where the favourite summer entertainment is a meal under the trees. The holidays of May and June at Illiers-Combray were ruled by Aunt Léonie from her bed upstairs, and by her energetic deputy Françoise whose particular kingdom was the kitchen and dining-room. In her white starched bonnet, she was an awesome rather than a lovable figure, and valued for her unforgettable meals of pure and seasonal quality.

That part of France is not especially famous for its food, any more than it is for its landscape. It takes time, and – or so I like to think – a discernment that comes only from experience, to perceive the unsensational harmony of both. Everyone visits Chartres. They rush in, then away, as if the cathedral lay in a desert. Few understand that the windows keep the memory of brilliant corn weeds now banished from the plain of the Beauce by fertilizers – cornflower blue, poppy red, corn marigold, corn cockle purple. Or that the two spires are the summation of the Beauce, of its rich flatness broken elsewhere by smaller spires, a flatness that suddenly drops into small delightful valleys, before it suddenly and finally tips over into the wider valley of the Loir. Here unvisited small towns, as Illiers once was, present opportunities for fine eating in their markets, cooked-pork shops, cake shops and bakeries.

From this unflashy ground, Proust was well able to appreciate the *nouvelle cuisine* of his day; if one can give a date for such changes in cookery, which in truth are made gradually, I suppose it would have to be 1883 when Auguste Escoffier and César Ritz started their partnership at Monaco at the Grand Hotel. They worked to combine luxury, simplicity and elegance of food and setting. For the first time, dining out became possible for women of the upper classes and bourgeoisie, dining out in public that is. Dishes, especially sweet ones, were named after them by Escoffier, so that his *Art Culinaire* index reads like a register of the Belle Époque. Ritz saw to it that lighting, a civilized sense of ease and shine in the decor and service, flattered their appearance.

Concentration on quality rather than quantity was an inevitable result of the new service *à la russe*, that became the norm with Urbain Dubois and Escoffier. When course succeeded course, with only a choice between two dishes at each one, any lack in the basic ingredients or the skill of the chefs was far more noticeable than it had been under the old buffet style of service.

After the success of the Savoy and Carlton Hotel restaurants in London, Escoffier and Ritz turned towards Paris. In 1896, in good time for the great exhibition planned for 1900, the Ritz Hotel opened in the Place Vendôme. Proust was at the opening gala dinner. He had written little but, since his meeting with Robert de Montesquiou three years earlier, he had become more and more part of that Parisian society of intellect, wealth and aristocracy which he had despaired of encountering when he had first glimpsed it as a child at Illiers.

At his own dinner parties, he adopted the delightful habit of moving round the table with each course, to make sure none of his guests should feel neglected by the host. Towards the end of his life, during the last eight years when he became almost a voluntary prisoner in his cork-lined room, his last housekeeper, Céleste Albaret, has recorded how carefully he chose the wines for the single guest he occasionally invited to dinner. By that time, he was living on little more than a litre of milk a day, flavoured with coffee. Céleste knew he had been a great gourmet from his precise tastes, and from the way he talked about the food of his childhood, but by then he could only enjoy it in his memory, '*gourmand de ses souvenirs*'.

ASPARAGUS

As summer came along at Combray, shelled peas would be ranged in platoons of different sizes by the little kitchen maid, for exact cooking so that the largest should be as tender as the tiny ones. The next job for 'poor Giotto's Charity', as Swann had named her, was the asparagus which lay beside her in a basket. She sat with a mournful air, as though all the sorrows of the world were heaped upon her; and the light crowns of azure which capped the asparagus shoots above their pink jackets would be finely and separately outlined, star by star, as in Giotto's fresco are the flowers banded about the brows, or patterning the basket of his Virtue at Padua.'

No wonder she looked so wretched. She had an allergy to asparagus, and Françoise was making her clean it every day, and putting asparagus into every dish she could think of, hoping to get rid of her. In this she succeeded, though not until after the girl had had her baby.

All this Proust discovered later. At the time he only saw their rainbow-loveliness 'tinged with ultra-marine and rosy pink which ran from their heads, finely stippled in mauve and azure, through a series of imperceptible changes to their white feet, still stained a little by the soil of their garden-bed'.

Although asparagus in France is different from ours, both are cooked and served in the same way, with melted butter or a hollandaise or mousseline sauce. Or cold with vinaigrette.

If you are concerned to stretch a small quantity, combine them with another of Proust's favourite things, scrambled eggs. And remember Escoffier's tip – when you beat the eggs, spear a clove of garlic on the end of your knife or fork – it gives them a most delicately appetizing flavour.

SOLE MEUNIÈRE AUX POIREAUX
Sole Fried in Butter with Leeks

Sole is everyone's favourite fish – or so you will conclude from this book – and the *meunière* method is one of the best ways of cooking it. This is what Proust liked. Indeed fried sole was the only dish ever finished, during the last years of his life.

Proust: My dear Céleste, I think I could manage a fried sole. How quickly do you think I could have one, if it's not too much trouble?
Céleste: Straightaway, Monsieur.
Proust: How kind you are, Céleste.

And good, kind, patient Céleste would rush out to a fishmonger's nearby in the place Saint-Augustin, run back with the sole, cook it and present it to Proust on a clean, doubled napkin – to soak up any fat that might remain – with four lemon halves, one at each napkin corner.

Had Proust been alive today, and a young man, he would I think have appreciated a new French version of *sole meunière*, a version with lightly cooked, shredded leeks, not too many, just enough to make the fish even more appetizing than usual. The two secrets are clarified butter and finely cut leek. Other fish can be substituted, obviously other flatfish, from turbot down to plaice, or small filleted whiting.

> *1 packet butter*
> *1¹/₂ kilos (3 lb) skinned sole, preferably two large ones, or 2 kilos (4 lb) other fish*
> *seasoned flour*
> *Cayenne pepper*
> *4 medium leeks, trimmed to their white stalks*
> *salt*
> *lemon quarters (optional)*

Cut up the butter into a small pan. Bring it slowly to the boil, stirring as it melts. When it has separated into golden oil and white crust, strain it through damp muslin into two fish pans, large enough to accommodate one sole each, with room to spare.

Turn the fish in seasoned flour, to which you have added Cayenne according to taste: I added enough just to make the flour slightly pink. Heat the pans, shake any surplus flour from the fish, and put in to cook – not too fast. After 3–4 minutes, according to the thickness of the fish, see if it is nicely browned underneath. Turn it over, if so, otherwise leave a little longer.

As it cooks, slice the leeks thinly so that they tumble into green and white shreds.

Add the leeks to the turned fish, and stir them about carefully so that they cook lightly in the butter. They should not entirely lose their crispness, neither should they brown – a few patches of light gold are all right, but no more. Salt the leeks, and leave them in the pan for a minute as you remove the sole to its warmed serving dish. Remove the leeks with a slotted spoon and put them round the sole in little piles or in a circle. Arrange the lemon quarters at intervals among the leeks. Serve immediately with bread, and a dry white wine.

Note Unfortunately the new French cookery depends for its light effect on brief cooking and prompt service. Easy to manage if you have help in the kitchen that you can trust, or if you always eat in the kitchen and do not mind leaving the table to cook between courses. If your problem is the lack of a second fish pan, remember that the sole will survive waiting around better than the leek shreds. Brown the sole in turn, using half the butter, over a slightly higher heat (golden-brown, not black-brown), and put them on their dish in the oven set at mark 2, 150°C (300°F) to complete their cooking while you cook the leeks in their juices, refreshed with the remaining butter.

If something is served before the sole, this really must be done between courses.

BARBUE RADZIWILL

Brill Radziwill

'Upon the permanent foundation of eggs, cutlets, potatoes, preserves, biscuits . . . Françoise would add as the labour of fields and orchards, the harvest of the tides, the luck of the markets, the kindness of neighbours, and her own genius might provide' – a turkey perhaps, or brill 'because the fishwoman had guaranteed its freshness'. Here is a good recipe for brill from a book published in Paris when Proust was fourteen: it can be adapted to other flatfish, chicken halibut or chicken turbot, Dover, or Torbay sole.

I do not know which Radziwill was honoured in this way (there were a lot of them, scattered across Europe). Perhaps it was Prince Constantin, who owned the château at Ermenonville with its famous eighteenth-century garden, where Rousseau was buried on an island in the lake. Much of the Prince de Guermantes was drawn from him. Léon, his son, the contemporary and friend of Proust, and one of the originals for Saint-Loup, would have been too young. So would his distant cousin, Michel, who married Proust's childhood love, Marie de Bernadaky from whom so much of Gilberte was taken.

2 kilos (4 lb) brill, trimmed
100 g (3½ oz) butter
1 heaped tablespoon finely chopped onion
bouquet garni, *salt, pepper*
300 ml (½ pt) béchamel sauce
2–3 tablespoons grated Parmesan
1 heaped tablespoon breadcrumbs

Cut down the centre of the dark-skinned side of the fish, and cut the fillets away from the bone to make a pocket. Push in a quarter of the butter. Scatter a flameproof dish with the onion, *bouquet* and seasoning. Place brill on top, cut side down. Spread a third of the remaining butter over the top. Pour a tumbler of water round the sides. Either put into the oven, mark 4–5, 180–190°C (350–375°F), until cooked, or cover and simmer on top of the stove. Transfer the cooked fish to a warm plate.

Reduce the cooking juices to a small amount of concentrated flavour, stir in the béchamel, then flavour to taste with 1–2 tablespoons of Parmesan, tasting as you go. Off the heat, whisk in the rest of the butter, and strain the sauce over the fish. Mix the last of the cheese with the crumbs, scatter on top of the fish and brown lightly under the grill.

ROAST CHICKEN

One morning Proust – or rather the Narrator as a child – took his usual pleasant way to the kitchen to see how lunch was coming along, and had a painful surprise. Françoise was on her own – the poor little maid, Giotto's Charity, was recovering upstairs from having a baby – and was trying to kill a chicken without much success. '"Filthy creature! Filthy creature!" she screamed with rage. It made the saintly kindness and unction of our servant rather less prominent than it would do next day at dinner when it made its appearance in a skin gold-embroidered like a chasuble, and its precious juice was poured out drop by drop as from a pyx . . . I crept out of the kitchen and upstairs, trembling all over; I could have prayed, then, for the instant dismissal of Françoise. But who would have baked me such hot rolls, boiled me such fragrant coffee, and even – roasted me such chickens?' Well, yes.

Those chickens were undoubtedly fattened on maize, as they still are in those parts. It gives them an excellent flavour and a golden tinge. Françoise roasted them on a spit, which some people will be able to do, but one can manage a lot with our farm chickens even without a spit, to make them almost as succulent as hers.

Using a sharp knife, carefully raise the skin from the neck end of the chicken, and wriggle your fingers into the gap until the skin is free of the breast and the top of the legs. Mash about a third of a packet of butter with salt and pepper; add a shallot or tablespoon of onion and a large clove of garlic, chopped together to a pulp. Using a broad knife or your fingers, spread this butter between the skin and meat of the chicken.

Make a stuffing, by mixing the following together:

60 g (2 oz) dry white crumbs
2 tablespoons chopped parsley
pinch oregano, salt, pepper
grated rind of half a lemon
1 tablespoon lemon juice
60 g (2 oz) melted butter
1 egg

Place the stuffed bird on a roasting rack in a pan and cook at mark 5, 190°C (375°F) for 15–20 minutes per half-kilo or pound, plus 20 minutes. No need to baste, or turn the chicken about. Should the breast become brown too quickly, protect it with a butter paper.

Remove surplus fat from the pan juices, and boil them up with giblet stock and a glass of wine. Aim at a small quantity of concentrated juice. The French do not have our passion for jugs of gravy.

Vegetables

A couple might accompany the chicken – or the roast mutton and any other large pieces of meat. Cooked chicory, or spinach, and always mashed potato (though sometimes to make an exciting change, Tante Léonie would order boiled potatoes with béchamel sauce). Proust loved chips, though rather as a snack, and when he was hardly eating anything – towards the end of his life – would occasionally ask his housekeeper, Céleste, to make some for him. Like everything else, they had to be exactly to his taste, though in fact they could not compete with the way such dishes had tasted in the past. If he asked for something he remembered enjoying, he might take a couple of spoonfuls – that was all.

One vegetable of Françoise's kitchen that is no longer familiar to us is the cardoon, cardoon served with beef marrow sauce. If you grow such things, here is the recipe for the sauce, which can also be served with boiled celery or chicory:

100 g (3–4 oz) beef marrow
2 tablespoons butter
1 heaped tablespoon flour
4 tablespoons meat jelly, glaze or juice from roast meat
about ½ litre (¾ pt) beef, or other appropriate stock
lemon juice, salt, pepper, parsley

Slice and poach the marrow for about 10 minutes in a very little water (or boil the bones, upright, as usual, and extract marrow when cooked). Make a sauce with the butter, flour, meat jelly etc., and stock. Boil down to a good consistency. Add lemon and seasonings, then the marrow to reheat, and finally the parsley. Pour over the cooked cardoon stalks.

BOEUF À LA MODE

À l'ombre de jeunes filles en fleur, the second part of Proust's novel, starts in comic irony, with dinner given by the parents to the old but still powerful ambassador, the Marquis de Norpois. The routine diplomatic charm is misunderstood, too much is hoped for – by the father anxious about his clever child's future, by the schoolboy son who longs for nothing but an invitation to Gilberte's house (and who understands to his amazement the emptiness of Monsieur de Norpois's mind). Social comedy against an excellent meal of *boeuf à la mode*, baked York ham, truffle and pineapple salad – the mother has counted greatly upon the salad, but the guest made no comment – and Nesselrode pudding.

Françoise, in Paris now since Aunt Léonie's death, had been for two days in an 'effervescence of creation'. In honour of the distinguished visitor, she had herself gone to Les Halles 'to procure the best cuts of rumpsteak, shin of beef, calves'-feet, as Michelangelo passed eight months in the mountains of Carrara choosing the most perfect blocks of marble for the monument of Julius II'. Monsieur de Norpois was delighted with the cold beef spiced with carrots, which had 'made its appearance couched by the Michelangelo of our kitchen upon enormous crystals of jelly, like transparent blocks of quartz'. Though perhaps there was a hint that it was not quite the thing, when he added that he would like to have seen how the family Vatel would have tackled *boeuf Stroganoff*.

My own favourite piece of beef for *boeuf à la mode* is not easy to get outside Scotland, and I have to order it by special-delivery post, then store it in the freezer: Charles MacSween & Son, 130 Bruntsfield Place, Edinburgh, supply it – plus superb Aberdeen Angus beef of all kinds, fruity and mealy puddings, haggises and so on. This special cut is the long lean muscle from the inside of the blade bone, known by many names, principally as the shoulder fillet, but also as the salmon cut or fish tail. I first saw it in our butcher's shop in France, and cannot understand why English butchers do not provide it. Pared of external fat, it is a beautiful looking piece of meat, which tastes especially good and carves beautifully. Alternatives are rump and silverside.

Another point to bear in mind is the weight of the meat. If you intend to serve the beef cold, then you will find that a piece weighing about 1¼–1½ kilos (2½–3 lb) trimmed weight, will do for 6–8 people depending on the rest of the meal. If you intend to eat the beef hot, you would be wise to buy from 2–3 kilos (4–6 lb), and then make the beef mould from the leftovers. The cooking time will not be much increased, as the piece of beef will be longer rather than thicker and it is thickness that decides the matter. If you possess a slow electric casserole cooker, it will produce a tender piece of beef, and you will have no worries about it cooking too fast.

piece shoulder fillet, rump or silverside
250 g (8 oz) piece pork back fat, chilled
bouquet garni
2 chopped onions
1 chopped celery stalk
3 crushed cloves garlic
4 tablespoons olive oil
white wine
2 pig's trotters or one calf's foot
kilo (2 lb) carrots
½ kilo (1 lb) sliced onions
beef stock, barely salted
250 g (8 oz) shin beef (see *recipe*)
2 egg whites (see *recipe*)

First lard the beef. Cut long strips of pork fat, push a lardoire with a u-shaped groove through the length of the piece, push a strip of fat into the groove and pull the lardoire back so that the fat is introduced into the meat. Repeat regularly. Not only will this help the tenderness, it also gives each slice an attractive appearance. I find that the small larding needles sold by kitchen shops are no good for a big piece of meat: they should only be used for poultry and small pieces of game and meat. Tie up the beef, if necessary.

Put it into a close-fitting bowl, with the *bouquet*, chopped onions and celery, garlic, oil and enough wine to cover. Put a piece of foil over the top and leave for a few hours to marinate, or in the refrigerator overnight.

Next cut the pork skin into squares about 3 cm (generous inch). Put them into a pan with the trotters or calf's foot, add enough cold water to cover and bring to the boil. Leave for 2 minutes, then drain and rinse under the cold tap.

Dice half the carrots. Put them into the base of a flame-proof casserole that is barely larger than the beef and trotters. Add the onions. Cover and put into a really hot oven, mark 7–8, 220–230°C (425–450°F) for half an hour; remove the lid and give them another 5 minutes. This 'pinches' the vegetables, making them slightly brown, and for a braised dish it works better than browning the vegetables in fat.

Remove the casserole and lower the oven temperature to mark 2, 160°C (300°F). Strain the marinade – remove the meat first – on to the carrots and onion, and scrape about with a wooden spoon to dislodge the brown bits. Place the beef, pork skin and trotters or foot into the pot. Add enough beef stock barely to cover. On top of the stove bring the whole thing to boiling point, put on the lid and transfer to the oven for about 3 hours – test with a skewer or small larding needle. Towards the end of cooking time, simmer the remaining carrots, neatly sliced, in a little extra beef stock. If you intend to serve the beef hot, you can also glaze a few onions and turnips to go with the carrots.

To serve hot: remove the beef to a dish, cut away the string, and keep it warm. Cut the meat neatly from the trotters or foot, and put with the pork skin, the freshly cooked carrots etc., around the meat. Strain the cooking liquor into a wide shallow pan. Degrease it, and boil steadily for 20–30 minutes. Remove scum and skin as they rise, until the sauce is reduced to a clear, syrupy glaze. Slice some of the meat, pour over the glaze and serve.

To serve cold: leave the beef to cool down in the pot for 3 hours. Take a little of the liquor, put it into the refrigerator and see how well it sets. If the jelly is weak, reduce the stock. If it is strong, you can proceed straightaway to clarifying it with shin of beef (not essential, but desirable to add flavour and colour) and egg whites.

Strain the liquor through a damp double muslin into a pan, and whisk in the 2 egg whites and the minced shin of beef. Continue whisking as the pan comes slowly to the boil. Boil for 10–15 minutes, until the white of egg and beef form a thick, unpleasantly grey layer with a spongy look. The scummy look comes from the impurities in the stock, which below this layer will be crystal clear. Pour it out gently through another clean piece of double muslin.

Put a thin layer of this clarified stock into the bowl or terrine in which you intend to mould the beef. Leave it to set in the refrigerator. When it is firm, arrange some of the separately cooked carrot slices on top. Gently pour a little stock round the slices, and transfer again to the fridge until the pieces are set in place. Cut away the string from the meat and put it into the bowl or basin on top of the carrots (keep the pork skin and pork trotter meat for a separate meal, heating them through and serving them with a sauce tartare . . .).

Arrange the rest of the sliced carrots round it and pour in the rest of the stock. Return to the refrigerator and leave to set firm – until next day if possible.

Turn out and serve with a salad. Or else follow Françoise's style, and separate the meat from the jelly when you turn the whole thing out: chop the jelly and carrots into large cubes and surround the beef with them. This is easier for carving, and easier for larger pieces of meat altogether.

Note The instructions above are based on Richard Olney's recipe for *boeuf à la mode*, in the Time-Life book *Beef and Veal*, in the Good Cook series. There are many versions, as you would expect for so classic a dish, but I find his the best.

RIZ À L IMPÉRATRICE

As a child, Proust was already a lover of the theatre, 'a Platonic lover, of necessity, since my parents had not yet allowed me to enter one'. When they were living in a street near the Madeleine, he would study the playbills stuck on to the nearest Moriss column, imagining fantastic performances. At last his parents told him to choose between two plays. 'I had shewn myself such vivid, such compelling pictures of, on the one hand, a play of dazzling arrogance, and on the other a gentle, velvety play, that I was as little capable of deciding which play I should prefer to see as if, at the dinner-table, they had obliged me to choose between rice *à l'impératrice* and the famous cream of chocolate.' Anyone who feels an aversion to rice puddings, may be encouraged to try this one and think again.

> *125 g (4 oz) long grain rice*
> *600 ml (1 pt) milk*
> *half a vanilla pod*
> *4 egg yolks*
> *125 g (4 oz) sugar*
> *2 heaped teaspoons gelatine*
> *300 ml (½ pt) double cream*

Boil the rice in water for 3 minutes, then drain and rinse it under the cold tap. Return to the pan with half the milk, cover and simmer until very tender. Bring rest of the milk to the boil with the vanilla pod, then whisk into the yolks and the sugar. Pour back into the pan and stir over a lowish heat until the custard thickens (use a double boiler if you are not accustomed to making egg custards). Melt the gelatine in 2 tablespoons of hot water and add to the hot custard. Strain into a bowl, and add the cooked rice which will have absorbed all the milk. Cool. Whip cream and fold in. Turn into a lightly oiled mould. Chill, and serve with soft fruit or stewed pears that have been lightly poached in syrup.

CRÈME AU CHOCOLAT
Chocolate Cream

When the main part of the meal was over, Françoise would bring in 'a work composed expressly for ourselves, but dedicated more particularly to my father, who had a fondness for such things, a cream of chocolate, inspired in the mind, created by the hand of Françoise'. It was as 'light and fleeting as an "occasional piece" of music, into which she had poured the whole of her talent. Anyone who refused to partake of it, saying: "No, thank you, I have finished; I am not hungry" would at once have been lowered to the level of the Philistines . . . To have left even the tiniest morsel in the dish would have shewn as much discourtesy as to rise and leave a concert hall while the piece" was still being played, and under the composer's very eyes.'

The recipe that Françoise invented is lost for ever, but here is a light version of the favourite *mousse au chocolat*, by Édouard de Pomiane, who visited friends in that part of the world, or a little further to the west (and was often grateful for what it could still provide in the shortage of the last war).

180 g (6 oz) plain chocolate, bitter for preference
6 egg yolks
6 teaspoons sugar
125 ml (4 fl oz) double cream
6 egg whites

Break up the chocolate or grate coarsely into a pudding basin. Add 3 tablespoons water. Set over a pan of simmering water, and stir until the mixture is smooth and melted and fairly hot (though nowhere near boiling – if you overheat chocolate, it turns to mud). Remove the basin from the pan, and rapidly beat in the egg yolks and the sugar. Whisk the cream until thick, and stir it quickly into the cooled chocolate. Finally whisk the egg whites until stiff and fold them in with a metal spoon last of all. These last two operations should be done delicately, so that the cream will be as airy and light as possible. Divide between one large shallow dish, or eight glasses. Chill until set. Serve with plain or almond biscuits.

CREAM CHEESE WITH STRAWBERRIES

At Combray, the hawthorn. '"Just look at this pink one; isn't it pretty?" And it was indeed a hawthorn, but one whose flowers were pink, and lovelier even than the white . . . it was attired even more richly than the rest, for the flowers which clung to its branches, one above another, so thickly as to leave no part of the tree undecorated, like the tassels wreathed about the crook of a rococo shepherdess were every one of them "in colour" and consequently of a superior quality, by the aesthetic standards of Combray, to the "plain", if one was to judge by the scale of prices at the "stores" in the Square, or at Camus's, where the most expensive biscuits were those whose sugar was pink. And for my own part I set a higher value on cream cheese when it was pink, when I had been allowed to tinge it with crushed strawberries. And these flowers had chosen precisely the colour of some edible and delicious thing . . .'

Even in that celebrated paean to the hawthorn – the flower of love from the porcelain shepherdesses of Chelsea or Meissen to Gilberte framed in an arch of pink hawthorn, imagining that unknown world of her existence which Proust thought never to penetrate – food has its place. I cannot think of a passage in our literature, English literature, where such a comparison is made. And so perfectly, so naturally. But then, he had Ronsard before him, another poet of the Loir, comparing the pale skin of his love's neck and breast to the cream cheese that they had brought to the meadows on its rush mat for their picnic.

And the best, richest cheese, especially the goat cheese after the kids have been born, comes in spring, at hawthorn time when you may see the pink here and there in an otherwise creamy fall of flowers.

Proust had a passion for it, to the extent that his father warned him against eating too much, when he was grown up and not too healthy.

To get the cheese right, as close as can be to the dish that appears on every table in the Loir valley, you should buy an imported *fromage frais* or quark from Germany. English brands of curd and cream cheese are too much dried, the wrong texture. To half a kilo of this (1 lb) – assuming a family party – add a small fresh goat's cheese if possible; such things are easier to find now at a health-food shop than they were even a year ago.

Whisk 150 ml (5 fl oz) of double cream with 3 heaped tablespoons of caster or icing sugar. Fold into the cheese mixture, and add more sugar to taste. Icing sugar dissolves in more easily than caster sugar or granulated.

If you want to make the whole thing lighter, and bulkier, whisk 1 or 2 egg whites until stiff, and fold in last of all. Turn into a large and beautiful bowl.

Serve with strawberries and sugar. Later in the year with raspberries, peaches and so on. In winter it can be eaten with home-made apricot or strawberry jam, the kind with big pieces of fruit in it.

There is always a biscuit of some kind to go with the cream cheese and fruit.

Tuiles amandes, or tiny biscuits from the *pâtissier*, or sponge fingers of a kind superior to the normal brand of boudoir biscuits on sale, with their over-rigid shape, are the most popular.

PITHIVIERS ALMOND CAKE

The other great dessert of the region is the famous almond cake from Pithiviers. Sometimes cream cheese is served with it, and well they go together. Years ago I bought one in Illiers, and a long loaf of bread shaped like an ear of corn in the *épi* style; and I have since wondered whether it was from these shops that Françoise had ordered her almond cake, or 'a fancy loaf, because it was our turn to "offer" the holy bread'. If you take a swing round from Chartres towards the east, rather than south-west to Illiers-Combray, you will find Pithiviers on the map. Its cake is unchanged after nearly two centuries at least. The town smells of honey on the Chartres side, from the factory where they make *pain d'épice*. In the centre, shops and restaurants try to rival Chartres, the capital of the great corn plain of the Beauce, with lark pâtés and pies. So expensive has a Pithiviers become, that we see it less frequently in the small Loir towns than we did when we first went to live there. Nowadays I make it at home in England. We eat it more often in Wiltshire than we can afford to do in the Loir valley.

½ kilo total weight (1 lb) puff pastry
beaten egg to glaze
icing sugar

FILLING
125 g (4 oz) ground almonds
125 g (4 oz) caster sugar
60 g (2 oz) melted butter
2 large egg yolks
2 generous tablespoons double cream
2–3 tablespoons rum or brandy (or malt whisky)

Roll out half the pastry, and cut a circle about 25 cm (10 inches) in diameter. Place it on a moistened baking sheet. Brush a 2½-cm (1-inch) rim with beaten egg.

Mix the filling ingredients in the order given, to make a thick but not completely stiff paste. Put it on the pastry. Spread it almost to the rim. Roll out the other half of the pastry to a slightly larger circle, and place it on top, lining up the two edges and pressing gently but firmly all round the rim (the extra size of the top circle will be taken up by the mound of filling). Make a small central hole, knock up the edge so that it looks like the edge of a book with its leaves, and brush over with beaten egg. Leave 5 minutes.

Using a knife, nick the edge twelve times at regular intervals. It is easier to judge if you make the first two nicks opposite each other, then give the sheet a half turn, and make two more nicks, so that the whole thing is quartered; the other eight nicks can be judged perfectly after that. With your thumbs press in and upwards to form a petal effect at every nick, Tudor-rose style. Score light inner scallops with the point of a knife, being careful not to go right through the pastry. Then score curving lines from the central hole to the scallops to make a swirling design.

Bake for 15 minutes at mark 8, 230°C (450°F). Check to see how the pastry is colouring, and leave the temperature as it is unless the brown is already pronounced, for a further 15 minutes. Or else lower the temperature to mark 6, 200°C (400°F).

Remove the Pithiviers, raise the heat again to mark 8 if necessary. Spread out some newspaper on the table, put the baking sheet on top and dredge the cake with icing sugar. Try not to make a very thick layer, and confine it to the cake if you can (easier said than done). Return it to the oven for the sugar to melt to a rich brown shiny glaze. Open the door frequently to see how it is going. If there are runnels of white where you scored the pastry, it does not matter, as long as the main effect is dark and glassy and rich. Serve warm.

The cake can be made in advance and reheated.

POIRES BOURDALOUE

A classic dish of fine flavour and straightforward ingredients. It can look unimpressive, but to eat, it is a delight. Céleste Albaret would sometimes bring in a *poire Bourdaloue* from a restaurant nearby, hoping Proust would try to eat this favourite dish of his early days. But no, he would take a couple of spoonfuls and that was that.

Why Bourdaloue? I do not know. Bourdaloue was one of the greatest of seventeenth-century preachers, but he went on for so long that the ladies of the court became uncomfortable before he had finished. Prudently they equipped themselves, or so it is said, with flowery pots of a waisted, pear- or kidney-shaped design, that could be discreetly used. These pots became known as Bourdaloues (Madame de Sévigné had an especially pretty one; it's on show at her much loved home, Les Rochers, in Brittany).

This brings us no nearer the answer, unfortunately. Let us return to the ingredients – the choice of macaroons needs care, as often these days bought ones consist of ground rice or something of the kind and almond essence: the best solution is those tiny macaroons imported from France, under the BN label. They are in any case a useful store-cupboard item. For six to eight people, you will need:

6–8 fine ripe dessert pears
lemon juice
375 g (12 oz) sugar
vanilla pod
sweet shortcrust flan case, 22–25 cm (9–10 inches), baked blind
375 ml (12 fl oz) milk
75 g (2½ oz) caster sugar
1 large egg
3 large egg yolks
50 g (scant 2 oz) flour
2 heaped tablespoons macaroon crumbs
60 g (2 oz) lightly salted or unsalted butter

Peel, core and halve the pears, and rub them over with lemon juice to prevent discolouration and enhance their flavour. Stir the sugar into 600 ml (1 pt) water, and when it has dissolved, allow it to boil, then simmer for 4 minutes with the vanilla pod. Slip in the pear halves, and simmer until they are tender. Remove, drain and keep warm in the oven, set at mark 2, 150°C (300°F); at the same time put in the pastry case to heat through.

Make a frangipan cream. Extract the vanilla pod from the pear syrup and bring it to the boil slowly with the milk. Strain on to the caster sugar, egg, yolks and flour that have been well beaten together. Whisk as you do this, to avoid lumps. Tip back into the pan, and stir over a moderate heat for the custard to thicken. It should boil very gently indeed, but only for a minute or two (the flour prevents the eggs curdling disastrously; should the mixture look slightly lumpy, blend it in the liquidizer and it will smooth out). Keep stirring. Remove from the heat and add half the macaroon crumbs and just over half the butter. Put a layer into the pastry case, arrange the pears on top, and cover with the remaining frangipan.

Scatter the last of the macaroon crumbs over the top, and sprinkle with the last of the butter which you have melted. Place under a hot grill to glaze and brown slightly. Serve at once with whipped cream.

Variations

(1) Cook the pears and frangipan in advance, as well as the pastry. Assemble just before the meal, leave in the low oven to reheat and glaze at the last minute.

(2) Omit the pastry case, and prepare the dish in an attractive but grill-proof shallow pot.

(3) To make a more elaborate looking dish, for a larger number of people, increase the number of pears appropriately and arrange them, when cooked, on a rather thicker bed of frangipan cream; omit the top layer of cream and the glaze, but decorate by brushing the pears over with the much reduced syrup they were cooked in, and distributing angelica leaves, lightly toasted split almonds and a few glacé cherries in between them.

NESSELRODE PUDDING

An iced pudding flavoured with chestnuts and dried fruit was invented by Monsieur Mony, chef for many years to the Russian diplomat, Count Nesselrode, in Paris. He passed the recipe on to Jules Gouffé who published it in his *Livre de Cuisine* of 1867. Glacé fruit and peel were a further embellishment to the Nesselrode by the time Proust was old enough to notice such things.

1 tablespoon sugar
60 g (2 oz) mixed currants and raisins
60 g (2 oz) mixed glacé fruits, angelica, candied orange peel
Maraschino liqueur (or Madeira, Marsala etc.)
300 ml (10 fl oz) single cream
vanilla pod
4 large egg yolks
125 g (4 oz) sweetened chestnut purée, or unsweetened with vanilla sugar to taste
300 ml (10 fl oz) double cream
marrons glacés and whipped cream (optional; see recipe)

Bring the sugar to the boil with 3 tablespoons of hot water and simmer the dried fruit in this syrup for a minute. Remove from the heat and leave to cool. Put in a basin with the chopped glacé fruits etc., and add enough Maraschino to cover. Leave several hours or overnight.

Bring single cream to the boil slowly with the vanilla pod, and pour on to the beaten egg yolks, whisking. Return to the pan and cook slowly, without allowing the custard to boil, until it thickens. Cool slightly, then strain on to the fruits, and add the chestnut purée (it will mix more easily if the custard is still tepid). Whip the double cream, fold into the chestnut mixture, and freeze in the usual way at the lowest possible temperature.

Turn out and decorate with the marrons glacés and whipped cream, if you like: Monsieur Mony served a cream and egg custard, chilled and flavoured with Maraschino, but the habit of serving a custard sauce with ices is not popular any more.

Note Rhapsodizing about ice-cream in *La Prisonnière*, Albertine mentions chocolate and lemon ices, also raspberry, vanilla and strawberry.

MADELEINES AND LIME TEA

Madeleines, said to have first been made in Lorraine at Commercy, are plump little cakes that look 'as though they had been moulded in the fluted scallop of a pilgrim's shell'. Special tins are needed, which not only shape the base of the cakes in the characteristic way, but cause the mixture to rise into a central dome. If you use ordinary bun tins, madeleines will look as gently curved as any other small plain cake. It also follows that you can bake a variety of mixtures in the tin and achieve the same effect: I sometimes feel that the many brands of madeleines on sale in France in plastic bags – some of quite good quality – have been made from an easier pound-cake mixture (4 oz each of butter, sugar, self-raising flour, eggs – i.e. 2 eggs). Indeed, if you flavour this with orange-flower water, you can get a good result, although the following is closer to the real thing:

> *scant 100 g (3 oz) butter*
> *125 g (4 oz) caster sugar*
> *3 large eggs*
> *120 g (scant 4 oz) self-raising flour*
> *1 tablespoon orange-flower water (or milk)*

Cream butter, add sugar, and cream again. Beat in eggs one at a time, alternating with the flour. Stir in the orange-flower water. Fill buttered and floured tins to their rim, then bake until golden brown at mark 7, 220°C (425°F). About 10–15 minutes.

Lime tea is made from dried lime blossoms. Every year people pick the flowers on a warm day at the height of their scent, and spread them out on

newspapers in a dry place until they are brittle. Store in plastic bags if you are confident that all the moisture is gone, or in brown paper bags; close them well. When you want to make the *tisane*, or lime tea, remove enough dried flowers to fill a large stoneware jug; don't ram them in, just put in enough to fill the jug lightly. Pour on boiling water almost to the top, and leave to infuse for about 5 minutes. Strain this *tisane* into a warmed jug, and serve with madeleines. A soothing end to a Proustian evening, or a pleasant tea in winter time. Health-food shops and delicatessens often sell packages of lime tea from France. They will be labelled *tisane*, with *tilleul* underneath, meaning lime, as opposed, say, to mint or vervain.

1979

ÉDOUARD DE POMIANE

Cooking with Pomiane

THE DUTIES OF A HOST

It is much easier to accept an invitation to dinner than to receive guests at your own table.

To accept an invitation to dinner may or may not be pleasant but, in any case, it is only a question of passing pleasantly, or unpleasantly, an hour or two.

On the other hand, to invite relations, friends or business contacts to a meal is a most complicated business. You must, according to Brillat-Savarin's formula, be responsible for their entire happiness whilst they are under your roof.

But the guest's happiness is a matter of infinite complexity. It depends on the host himself, on his humour, his health, his business interests, his pastimes, the character of his wife, his education, his appetite, his attitude towards his neighbour at table, his artistic sense, his inclination to mischief, his good nature, and so on and so forth.

So it is really not worth worrying too much, or the problem of inviting guests to dinner would become insoluble.

First of all, there are three kinds of guests: 1. Those one is fond of. 2. Those with whom one is obliged to mix. 3. Those whom one detests.

For these three very different occasions one would prepare, respectively, an excellent dinner, a banal meal, or nothing at all, since in the latter case one would buy something ready cooked.

To prepare a dinner for a friend is to put into the cooking pot all one's affection and good will, all one's gaiety and zest, so that after three hours' cooking a waft of happiness escapes from beneath the lid.

A dinner prepared for a business contact is meant to impress him and to 'pay back' hospitality. Horrible expression!

For my part, I have never 'paid back' a dinner. The people who invite me are richer than I am. They would find my table too modest, and they don't come, because they are not invited.

Those whom I do invite like my savoury casserole and *they* don't pay *me* back because they prefer to return and enjoy it another time.

To make a dinner for people one can't bear is to try and keep up with the Joneses, as you say in English. Whatever you do, you are bound to be criticized, so it is better to buy ready-cooked food and let the supplier be criticized instead.

Having established these facts, let us begin.

For a successful dinner there should never be more than eight at table. One should prepare *only one good dish*. This should be preceded and followed by some little thing, then cheese and a sweet course if you are in France or pudding and cheese if you are in England. Finally dessert, good coffee, and a glass of cognac or natural spirits.

For the dinner to be really good the host must feel a glow of inward joy during the whole of the week which precedes it. He must await with impatience the day of the party. He must ask himself every day what he can do to improve it, even if it is only a question of a simple *pot-au-feu*.

Whatever such a host offers to his guests, I am sure that it will be good, because he will have enjoyed the anticipation of it for a week beforehand and he will feel this same joy for a week afterwards in his pleasure at having charmed his guests.

The dinner which you are obliged to give is almost always banal, but one should take trouble with it all the same, for perhaps amongst the guests there is someone who is worth while and perhaps the host will find in him a future friend.

In spite of this, however, such a dinner is never outstanding because one can never really please people whom one doesn't know.

The menu should be varied and the dishes neither insipid nor too highly spiced; neither too colourful, too classic nor too exotic. The guests must be able to talk about them as one talks about the latest film for which one has to book seats weeks in advance.

Poor host. I really pity you!

And now for the third category, the 'smart' dinner. I can assure you that on such a day my telephone works overtime. My wife is still in bed. She rages at the telephone exchange who have cut her off between ordering Lobster Thermidor and Chicken Demidoff. 'Engaged again. Just my luck. I shall never have time to arrange this wretched dinner . . .'

And yet, in the evening, when the guests arrive, the hostess will say to them smiling, 'How nice of you to come! Let me have your coat, darling . . .'

THE DUTIES OF A GUEST

In my youth I always said, and later on I repeated, that one should never refuse an invitation to lunch or dinner, for one never knows what one may have to eat the next day.

This being established, I, like all the believers in this maxim, have very frequently found myself at other people's tables.

As soon as one is seated at table between fellow guests, one is torn by conflicting feelings – a desire to enjoy the meal to the full whilst respecting the claims of good manners, and a reluctance to ruin one's digestion.

My considerable experience authorizes me to offer a little advice to young *gastronomes*, on the way in which they should conduct themselves at table.

First of all, don't expect too much. In this way you will not be disappointed at the end of the meal – a thing which is very harmful to the digestion. The day before the party, assess your host at his true value. Calculate, and I am afraid this is a little cynical, just what you are likely to get.

If your host cooks himself, if he is a *cordon bleu* . . . see that your preceding meal is a very light one, or skip it altogether.

On the other hand, if you have accepted, from a sense of duty, the invitation of a culinary ignoramus, have a drink before you leave home and a small snack. In this way you will arrive suitably fortified and you will avoid the pangs of hunger, so delightful before a good dish but so dangerous a prelude to a doubtful dinner.

Don't make a bloomer on arrival. If the house is luxurious, let your coat fall carelessly into the hands of a waiting servant, pull off your gloves and make your *entrée*.

If the household is a modest one your hostess will greet you in the hall, which is much more cosy. In this case, have the courage to air your opinions and if a delicious smell of roast meat is seeping under the kitchen door, dilate your nostrils, sniff it appreciatively and express your delight to your hostess. This behaviour, and you know this as well as I do, would be very much out of place if the occasion were more formal because then it would be very bad form to talk about food at all, and especially about what you could smell in the hall.

Now you sit down to table. What do you do with your table napkin? I always slip the corner between my neck and my collar. It is a matter of taste, but a matter on which no one agrees with me. Personally, I feel that the moment one tucks in one's napkin is one of the joys of the meal . . . Now one waits.

One waits for the soup . . . or one doesn't wait, if it is already in one's soup plate. In this case, it will be cold – and detestable.

If the soup is piping hot and fragrant, compliment your hostess, but don't ask for more. You would overload your stomach. Hold back for what is to follow. As to what follows, you may or may not like it. You must know how to restrain yourself and accept things gracefully.

Whoever may be your neighbour at table, remember that you came for the purpose of eating. Keep your attention fixed on this weighty occupation, but, at the same time, take care. Very often the day after such a dinner is spoilt by a bad night. So watch how you go at table.

Above all, drink very little. For a *gourmet* wine is not a drink but a condiment, provided that your host has chosen it correctly.

And what about conversation? The art is not to neglect either of your neighbours. And this is not easy. Generally, one talks to them in turn, but as soon as the less agreeable of the two begins to talk to her other neighbour, one leaves her to him and becomes unilateral.

First of all, talk about what is on your plates. The subject is there under your nose and will suggest all sorts of reminiscences and anecdotes. According to the temperament of your neighbour you will steer the conversation in one direction or another – but beware of the fumes of the wine. They are very dangerous . . .

A WORD OR TWO ABOUT THE MENU

During the past fifty years there has been a trend towards simplicity in all the arts and the art of cooking is no exception. For years doctors have been of the opinion that over-indulgence was the cause of many ailments and now the price of food has obliged all but the rich to cut down their meals to a more modest level. It is no longer possible for an ordinary family to offer their friends the lavish dinners of years ago. The educated public is far more sensitive than before, and recognizes as art the inventive spirit which finds new and interesting ways of presenting various materials.

The young housewife is now as proud of the dish which she has produced as of the embroidery she may have designed or the sweater she has knitted. This dish which she has created must be appreciated by her guests, so she tries to provide a suitable background for it. She must not distract attention by numerous dishes each better than the last. The chosen dish must not, of course, constitute the whole meal. It must be framed by something very light and simple, carefully chosen as a foil to the principal course, which is the highlight of the meal.

It is not easy to choose this main dish. It must please each of the guests.

Have they all the same tastes? The hostess must know this. In this matter of choosing the dish she must call into play all her perspicacity and her instincts as a psychologist.

She must know how to blend her guests and group them according to common characteristics which so often lead to similar tastes in food. Having first done this, she must make her choice. The dish can be, according to the circumstances, rustic and copious or subtle and exquisite.

Don't be afraid of departing from the classic menu. If your guests love fish and sunshine, prepare a *bouillabaisse* which need not be followed by any meat dish. Your guests will not complain, and they will take away with them an unforgettable memory of your party.

Don't blush to offer a *cassoulet*. Have the courage to serve the most homely dish provided it is perfect of its kind.

It is usual to begin lunch with *hors d'œuvres* and dinner with soup. Stick to these customs provided you don't overdo the *hors d'œuvres* as they do in restaurants. Such an excess of rich salads and sausage and so on requires the accompaniment of quantities of bread and makes the beginning of the meal too heavy.

As for soup, portions are getting smaller and smaller. Serve a good *consommé* which is always welcome and, according to the physiologists, stimulates the digestive juices.

These preliminaries to the meal can be followed at lunchtime, if you wish, by a dish of scrambled eggs, and by a little boiled fish in the evening. Don't tax your ingenuity over these dishes. The simpler and more natural they are, the better.

Concentrate all your efforts on the main dish and let it be abundant. Your guests will enjoy a second helping since you will have used all your art in its preparation.

Follow this with a few leaves of salad and, in the order in which you prefer them, cheese and your sweet dish. Remember that men, in general, are greedier than women, and will enjoy a pudding. To be strictly fair, the women may have been out to tea and eaten all sorts of cakes and would really be quite happy with some fruit . . .

Serve with the meal your usual wine supplemented by a bottle of something special to accompany the main dish which you will have illuminated, *Madame*, with your own special grace and your charming smile.

CULINARY TRADITIONS

What would our lives be like without tradition? What terrible fatigue would overwhelm humanity if it only had to concern itself with the future? Tradition represents a momentary pause in the course of toil – repose and the backward glance towards the past – the comparison of today with yesterday. Tradition is the memory of happy moments which have vanished, and their ephemeral return to life.

Without tradition the past would be dead. Tradition brings back to life those whom we have loved, those to whom we owe the present and, by consequence, the future.

What, after all, is a museum? It is just an exhibition of monuments of the past. In every age civilized men collected mementoes of the past so that living and future generations could draw from them inspiration founded on a solid basis.

Daily life is a struggle. Tradition is peace of mind. And that is why we continually create new traditions by instinct if not through feeling.

All artistic manifestations are somehow based on tradition. Tradition perpetuates the moralistic religions. Tradition elevates everything it touches. Tradition even directs the art of eating. Each country has its own culinary traditions, even if they only consist in the arrangement of meals. An English breakfast is quite different from the French morning *café au lait*. Why? By tradition. One might say that the difference is due to climate. But no, since the traditional Englishman, even when he is living in Bangkok or Bahrein, sticks doggedly to his eggs and bacon, toast, and so on.

It is tradition which makes us eat pancakes on Shrove Tuesday. It was tradition which, for centuries, obliged Russians of all levels of society to exchange hard-boiled eggs at Easter saying as they did so '*Khristós Voskrése*' – Christ is Risen.

Sometimes culinary traditions are dictated and transmitted by religions. Sometimes, older even than our present religions, they are relics of paganism. The *Galette des Rois* is a relic of the Roman Saturnalia and there are many other survivals of pagan traditions.

The various religions laid down gastronomic restrictions and obligations the origins of some of which we shall never know. In some cases certain animals or forms of vegetable life were held to be sacred and it was naturally forbidden to eat them.

In other cases the prohibition of certain foods, perhaps on special days, were based on rules of hygiene dictated by the great moral legislators who were the founders of the religions.

What does it matter? It is a fact that in France even the most lukewarm Christians go without meat on certain days of the year, and especially on Good Friday. On Good Friday even unbelievers eat *morue*, and during Holy Week formidable quantities of this excellent dried and salted cod are consumed.

Is this culinary tradition based upon hygiene? Certainly, since it is a very good thing to go without meat from time to time. This is both a prevention and a cure for arterio-sclerosis, high blood pressure and other pathological states aggravated by over-eating. The Jews and the Mahommedans are forbidden to eat pork. This is a wise prohibition in countries where trichinosis and other maladies transmitted from pigs to humans are prevalent.

Let us respect these traditions, therefore, both because they represent religious obligations and because they are customs whose benefits have been demonstrated by their survival through the centuries.

By following traditions we commemorate those who have transmitted them. We bring back to life those who are no longer with us and we perform a good deed, since the Dead are not altogether dead as long as there are those amongst the living who evoke their memory.

THE PSYCHO-PHYSIOLOGY OF GOURMANDISE

If gluttony is a deadly sin, a certain healthy greed or a love of good food which we in France call *gourmandise* is a most important instinct since it prompts us to choose food which we enjoy.

Certainly, this choice could be considered to satisfy desires which are quite unrelated to the needs of the body. This, however, is not the opinion of the physiologists who have studied, in the case of animals, the relation between the psyche and the digestion.

The experiments of Pavloff are quite convincing on this point. The celebrated Russian physiologist operated on dogs to create an opening from the stomach to the exterior. When the dogs were completely restored, and after months during which they had lived and eaten like other dogs, it was possible to collect the secretions from their stomachs and study them at will, both as regards quantity and quality.

These secretions consist of gastric juices. Now it is well known that the gastric juices contain both hydrochloric acid and pepsin, that is to say the substances necessary for the digestion of meat and anything containing albumen.

If there is a scarcity of gastric juice in the stomach, digestion will be poor. This is easy to understand.

Furthermore, the gastric juices secreted by the stomach flow into the intestines. When they come into contact with the mucous lining of the intestine they provoke the formation of a substance called secretine. This is absorbed by the intestine, passes into the blood and stimulates the liver and the pancreas. Bile, reaching the intestine from the liver, emulsifies the fats. The pancreatic juices digest albumen, starch and fat, that is to say all foodstuffs.

Thus the digestion of a meal is governed by the quantity of gastric juice produced in the stomach.

Now let us return to Pavloff's dog. Let us watch it and observe its preferences for different kinds of food. This dog, ignorant of the list of deadly sins, is frankly greedy. He loves meat soup and doesn't try to hide it. When he sees it he quivers with excitement and his delight is perfectly evident as he hurls himself on the bowl and devours his meal.

The next day, try showing him a bowl of boiled rice or simply some starch paste. Our poor dog, unless he is starving, will simply sniff it and leave it severely alone.

This dog has definite preferences. He is greedy for meat and a total abstentionist as regards boiled rice.

How does his stomach react to these very different meals?

At the sight of the meat the gastric juices flow freely into his stomach. Faced with the boiled rice, his stomach does not react at all, or at the most yields a few drops of gastric juice.

Thus just the sight of a good meal is enough to prepare one's organism for digestion. A bad meal, once taken, will be poorly digested.

In this experiment the greed of our dog paid off. Another dog might, perhaps, have preferred a meal without meat. But why does one dog prefer meat, and another prefer bread? Because, for the sake of his organism he needs nitrogenized substances; the other dog requires carbohydrates.

Whether it is a question of a man or a dog, no two individuals have exactly the same needs. The idea that an ideal diet can be chosen just on the basis of the calories it contains is an illusion. There are no two human motors which are exactly alike.

The same diet will make one person put on weight whilst another will be quite unaffected by it. A question of temperament, one says. It is just this question of temperament which is at the root of the matter.

Each organism is drawn to the substances of which it has need, and this attraction is the basis of *gourmandise.*

A diabetic is greedy for water. Let him drink. This need for water corresponds to an urgent requirement of his organism. The diabetic has an excess of glucose in his blood and of acid derivatives which are poisoning him. He drinks water in order to dilute the poisons.

Watch some children at a meal. Some of them make a bee line for fat. Others won't touch it. Should one, on the pretext of discipline, restrain the first and force the second to eat the fat which they detest? No; it would be, from the physiological point of view, a waste of effort.

Each of these groups of children has need of different kinds of body-building materials. These needs are shown by the preference for one substance or another which is so often stigmatized as greed.

Children run and jump and play. They need the foods which serve as fuel for their muscles. Amongst these, the most valuable is sugar. Now children love sugar in its various forms, from the most elaborate pudding to the simple lump of sugar which they crunch. Should one refuse them these sweet things on the grounds that they are bad for their teeth? Yes, says the hide-bound theorist. No, says the physiologist, who knows that sugar is a dynamogenic food of the greatest value.

In general, children love butter and fruit. They will even eat unripe fruit too, because they crave for the vitamins which it contains.

Now let us leave the dog and the child. The latter is too often the victim of experiments in any case. We return to the adult, to the *gourmand* with his round tummy and his jolly, red face.

The *gourmand* arrives at your house for dinner. He sniffs appreciatively at the smell of cooking in the hall. You apologize but he stops you, for he is charmed. This delicious smell has stimulated all his internal secretions. You can be sure that he will do honour to your dinner. He will digest his food and assimilate it perfectly. Tomorrow you will hear that he has woken up with a mouth as fresh as if he had eaten nothing but a boiled egg and a plate of chicory cooked in water.

For a *gourmand* there is no need to produce complicated dishes with fancy names. Prepare for him raw materials of good quality. Transform them as little as possible and accompany them with suitable sauces and you will have produced a meal which is just right.

The *gourmand* is always happy and cheerful. He is always in a state of pleasant well-being. Not surprising, since what he has eaten has been assimilated and absorbed into his individual being. The *gourmand* is in harmony with the outside world. He is, in fact, a normal person.

The 'non-*gourmand*' is afraid of eating this and that as he will not be able to digest them. When he has finished eating he will be out of sorts. He is out of step with the world and, in fact, abnormal. That is why he is unhappy, embittered, pessimistic, disagreeable, and even dangerous for those around him.

How should one satisfy one's natural greed? To the extent to which it is not harmful to health. That is to say with art and moderation.

Art, to merit the title, must always be balanced if it is static, or rhythmic if it is in motion. Art, in my opinion, should never be tormented, agitated, a-rhythmic.

The *gourmand* should follow these precepts. His meals should be simple, very simple. One should not complicate things for the sake of originality. Don't imagine that it is as easy to create a new dish as to write a new symphony.

With the seven notes of the musical scale one can compose millions of different musical symphonies. With the far more numerous notes of the culinary scale one ought to be able to compose millions of culinary symphonies. Even if we include the every-day dishes, however, these are far less numerous than their musical counterparts. Why? Because music only touches the spirit, whilst cooking touches not merely the spirit but the whole of our physiological economy as well.

One can write music in a whole range of different keys. One can get used to chords which, yesterday, seemed complete discords.

But it is impossible, for the sake of originality, to salt a soup more than a certain amount. After a time our organism would suffer serious disturbances. Our physiology would refuse to adapt itself. Gastronomy is the only art which touches our organism in two realms so closely linked – in its psycho-physiological functioning.

The natural instinct which impels us to enjoy this salutary art is – and again I am forced to use the French word for want of a true English equivalent – *gourmandise*.

1976

PATIENCE GRAY

Edible Weeds

Edwardian Englishmen laughed at French governesses for picking wild chervil, dandelions and sorrel in spring for salads, for cutting nettle-heads for soup. The governesses ridiculed the Englishmen for their addiction to stewed rhubarb. Each person, through instinct, habit or prejudice, likes to pursue his or her own way to health.

I became interested in weeds on Naxos: everyone in Apollona, but more especially women and children, wandered about in February and March, before the spring declared itself, in search of weeds, picked before their flower-heads appeared. They called them by the portmanteau name *radíkia*, meaning plants with beneficial roots and leaves, but also specifically dandelions.

Many of these weeds belonged to the daisy and dandelion family. The most beneficent in this group are dandelions, *Taraxacum officinale*, and wild chicory, *Cichorium intybus*, but it includes yellow and purple goat's beard, the latter being wild salsify; wild endive, *Cichorium endivia*; hawkweed, hawksbeard and hawkbit; a daisy, *Bellis silvestris*, larger than the common one; the ox-eye daisy or marguerite; various kinds of sowthistle and a plant called *Urospermum picroides* resembling them (*picroides* meaning bitter, *picrá* in Greek). The more bitter the weeds, the better, as far as the Naxians were concerned. Milk thistles were also gathered, as was the blessed thistle. The field marigold, *Calendula arvensis*, was gathered whole when it first appeared, as was the corn marigold, *Chrysanthemum segetum*, and little plants of chamomile.

Their baskets also contained four umbelliferous plants – wild carrot, wild parsnip, wild fennel and wild chervil – and several crucifers – wild mustard, *Sinapis alba*, and allied white rocket, *Diplotaxis erucoides*, growing in cultivated fields, and also yellow rocket, *Eruca sativa*, growing in the wild. In the collection several mints appeared, particularly pennyroyal, *Menta pulegium*, as well as wild thymes and mountain savory, *Satureja montana*.

Most of these plants were gathered by cutting a section of the root, thus preserving the plant entire. Washed at the fountain, they were boiled and served with oil and lemon juice, the lemons picked from neighbouring groves.

During the Lenten fast they were eaten in quantity like vegetable *spaghettini*, but without the olive oil.

Filling my water jar at the spring, I had a daily opportunity to examine these weeds and ask advice, and began to gather them myself, but at first always offering them for inspection. At the time I was reading the landscape and its flora with as much attention as one gives to an absorbing book.

Mediterranean people value 'bitterness' in weeds, as once did all European peoples. On Naxos, on a restricted winter diet, everyone suffered from appalling pains in the liver region, deriving not only from monotonous diet but also from impure water and the terrible north wind. The Sculptor and I soon discovered the benefits conferred by weeds.

Chi vo far 'na bona zena   Who wants to eat a good supper
i magn'un erb' d'tut la mena   should eat a weed of every kind

This old Carrarese saying puts the matter in a nutshell, diversity being as important in weeds as it is in human beings.

I had my first weed lesson in Castelpoggio with Dirce. She used to pounce on a great variety of mountain plants, pull them out with a penknife, and thus abstract the crown of leaves with a piece of root. She stuffed them in a cloth and thrust them into the foraging sack. She called them all *radici* or *radicchi*, meaning roots.

These plants were much the same as those gathered by the Apollonians from the carrot and daisy families. They also included several kinds of sorrel; lady's smock, *Cardamine pratensis*; primrose, *Primula vulgaris*; foxglove but (NB) only the yellow kind; mountain cowslip; mountain orache, *Atriplex hortensis*; plantain and dock. Dirce also snatched at new shoots of wild clematis, wild hop, wild vine and wild asparagus.

At home she washed them all under the tap which she kept permanently running in the kitchen, as if it were the village fountain – piped water being a recent event. She boiled a cauldron of water on the fire, fuelled with Spanish chestnut faggots, boiled the weeds, drained them and ate them with olive oil and a few drops of wine vinegar, and hard-boiled eggs. She often shouted up the stairs with an offering of a dish of weeds, gladly accepted, both bitter and delicious.

Dirce said that during the war people ate the tuberous roots of mountain asphodel and the bulbs of the sea squill, *Urginea maritima*, belonging to the lily family. Speaking of bulbs, I mention here a cousin of the grape hyacinth. This is the tassel hyacinth, *Muscari comosum*, whose little bulbs are prised from the hard red earth in Apulia in March, called *pampasciune* in dialect and *cipollotto col fiocco* in Italian, a very welcome salad. The Naxians treat the corms of *Crocus cancellatus*, a pale lilac autumn-flowering crocus, in much the same way. (This should not be confused with the autumn crocus, *Colchicum autumnalis*, which is poisonous.)

At La Barozza I had a profitable weed lesson from a little girl of seven called Eugenia, who had an amazing weed vocabulary culled from the vineyard which her father worked. As she picked each plant, she said: 'This is for cooking' or 'This is for salad' (her plant categories).

The Tuscan vineyard weeds divide into two kinds, those that are boiled, *radici*, *radicchi*, which include most of the weeds already mentioned, plus wild leeks and wild garlic; corn poppy; wild clary, *Salvia sclarea*; comfrey, *Symphytum officinale*; young plants of borage; rampion, *Campanula rapunculoides*, which is a small campanula with fleshy white roots; sweet violet, *Viola odorata*; a white bulbous-flowered campion, *Silene inflata*; and alexanders, a celery-like plant, *Smyrnium olusatrum*.

Much of the medicinal value of these plants lies in the root, which is why they are picked with a stub of root; but only a stub, so that the plant is not destroyed but grows again.

The salad herbs, the other kind, include the flowers of borage, tasting of cucumber; rocket, *Eruca sativa* (which is also cultivated in gardens), and white wall rocket, *Diplotaxis erucoides*, and another little rocket, *Bunias erucago*, all three sharing the name *rucola* and all tasting of mustard. The leaves of the bladder campion when they first appear are also used as salad. So are the leaves and white roots of wild radish. Burnet is another salad plant, as are the small fresh leaves of centaury, hawkbits and hawkweeds, all with a bluish tinge. Fronds of wild fennel are picked for salad, and so is the buck's horn plantain, picked in its first youth; also wild lettuce, *Lactuca viminea* and *L. scariola*, and corn salad, *valerianella* in Italian. All these vineyard plants are painstakingly washed and scrutinized for fading leaves, before being incorporated into a delicious mixed salad, dressed with olive oil and wine vinegar.

The time to pick them is when they are crisp after a touch of frost. Once the flower-head appears the taste is lost, but in wet periods in May there is another crop. The leaves of this vineyard salad are small, various, perfumed and crisp. All these plants grow on the vertical slopes which separate the vine terraces, and in late May their flowers, scythed with the grass, become the fragrant hay fed to the cow whose main function is to manure the vines.

In Italy one is always coming across a portmanteau word which describes a wide variety of things. *Radicchio* and *radice*, like the Greek *radíki*, are portmanteau words for anything with a succulent root, edible leaves and bitter taste, and the plants they refer to provide a balm for the liver. *Erbe* and *erbucce* are all the delicate wild salad plants.

Knowledge of these and other plants was for centuries our common European heritage. The English, once familiar with these weeds and their specific virtues, as described in early herbals, are now showing a revived interest in this heritage.

The first treatise on medicinal plants was written by a Greek doctor, Cratevas, in the first century BC. This illuminated codex existed in Byzantium (Constantinople) until the seventeenth century and served as a model for subsequent treatises, but was then lost. Because of this, Dioscorides' *De Materia Medica*, written in the first century AD, has come to be regarded as the original study of plants. Christian monks, both Greek Orthodox and Roman Catholic, pursued these studies, raised the wild plants in their walled gardens, dried their roots and leaves, pounded them to powder, and produced unguents and specifics for many ills.

The monks' gardens or *herbularii* contained beds in which were separately grown rosemary, mint, sage, lilies, iris, rue, gladiolus, roses, fenugreek, fennel, cumin etc.

What is significant is the survival of this 'knowledge' in seasonal culinary practices, among Greeks, Italians, Catalans, in a tradition unsupported by literacy. The 'knowledge' is handed down, chiefly from mother to child, while stooping to gather the plants. (Fallow deer behave in the same way, the mother showing the fawn which plants to eat.)

The question now is – without Greek village ladies, Etruscan Dirce, and little girls like Eugenia, how are people to begin to recognize and identify plants? The answer is, I suppose, to consult good books on the subject, although this will be a slower and more uncertain method than those described above. One book to consult is Roger Phillips' *Wild Food*. In it you will find a warning. The subject – edible weeds – has aroused an interest just when its pursuit is threatened by the use of pesticides and weed-killers. One has now to acquire an acute awareness in any locality of the use of chemicals. In the Salento the user of these commodities hangs up a bottle or tin from a tree at the entrance to his terrain as a warning sign.

But there is another problem: in Britain, for example, certain wild plants are 'protected', and one must know which they are. Ignorance of the law can lead to heavy penalties.

So, quite apart from the ability to discern the edible plants, and awareness of their seasonal apparition, exact knowledge on two counts is required – the law and the application of pesticides.

It is unfortunate that many modern plant books, relying on colour photographs, ignore the nature of the roots of plants, often vital to the identification of edible weeds by amateurs. The entire plant is to be considered, not just its visible parts.

Nor are botanists particularly interested in edible properties of plants today, with a very lively exception in Geoffrey Grigson (*The Englishman's Flora*). His considered opinion of particular edible English weeds, even when prepared by a Queen of Cooks, is not always encouraging.

COOKING AND EATING WEEDS

The essence of a 'dish of weeds', whether cooked or served as a salad, lies in employing a variety of different plants. There are exceptions, of course. For instance, the poppy plants are sometimes cooked alone, as are wild asparagus, and the corms of the tassel hyacinth and *Crocus cancellatus*; and the Greeks cook the leaves and shoots of mallow, *Malva rotundifolia*, in spring to pacify the stomach and relieve it of winter ills. But the general approach, and the best one, is essentially that of Dirce at Castelpoggio. It is very similar to that of the goat in the hedge, who nibbles at a plant here and a plant there. The goat knows what will do it good. We can no longer say this about man and woman. So we have to fall back on botanical studies. Paul Schauenberg's *Guide des Plantes Médicinales* analyses the active principles of each plant and is well illustrated. A work of this kind is invaluable in indicating the method of drying plants and the preparation of infusions, and how the plants are used to mitigate common ills. But the real importance of weeds is that they help you to maintain good health.

Prospero's Feast

There is one feast I feel impelled to describe.

It is seldom that perfect hosts have the heart, the imagination to be also the perfect guests. Don Andrea Giovene and the lady Adeline arrived one summer afternoon at Spigolizzi, bearing in hand and covered with a cloth an enormous baking tin containing a *crostata*, a rustic cake baked in Ugento that morning, made with golden yeast pastry into which a good many eggs and some vanilla sugar had vanished, crowned with dense pear jam (*la perata*) and pastry cross-hatching. So gladly we sat down at the table under the vine to do it justice, with a delicious bottle of Ugentine muscat wine they had brought with them.

This visit heralded an invitation to lunch in two days' time. Precisely at 12.30 we were to find them on the outskirts of Ugento, a city older than Rome, but twice razed to the ground by the Saracens. The house where they were improbably staying belonged to the daughter of the tobacconist in the piazza whose husband manned the petrol pump. We could not imagine what form this feast would take; lunching out in Apulian villages is quite a risk.

We found Don Andrea dreaming in a deck chair on a small area of paving in front of a newly built concrete villa, its windows closed against the mid-day by metal roller blinds called 'saracens'. Waiting for us, he said he had been imagining what it would be like to be the owner of this villa, and in doing so, had succeeded in finding a genuine sense of satisfaction and achievement. In performing this imaginative feat, quite considerable for one whose past is intertwined with palaces, he had bridged the chasm which divides the old concept of peasant life from the concrete aspirations of their sons and daughters. As our neighbour said only the other day with a touch of irony: 'Now we are all *signori.*'

The villa was separated from others of its kind by a little garden of apple, peach and orange trees among which a few rows of dark-leaved summer chicory were growing, and round the corner we came upon Donna Adeline, a dish of roast red peppers in her hand, which, she lamented, though cooked in the local bread oven, had not been divested of their outer skins, nor seeded. So I sat down with her on a concrete parapet to do this, while Don Andrea and the Sculptor sauntered up the dusty August road to see how the feast was shaping. We followed at our leisure with the dish in hand, covered with a napkin.

Entered from the main street, what appeared to be a wine bar contained a beautiful little star-vaulted cell behind, which in days gone by had been a *trattoria.* It was now perfectly white and empty but for a few cobwebs and a trestle table and chairs set in one corner, from where one had a reassuring view through an open door of a small kitchen in whose ample hearth already a splendid olive wood fire was glowing. In Apulia the hidden things are the things that matter: cool vaulted rooms, the secret gardens behind high walls betrayed by the delirious scent of lemon flowers, the deep ravines.

Lunch began in the conventional summer southern way with spaghetti in a deep red tomato sauce, served with grated *pecorino*. 'It is right,' said Don Andrea, 'for the first course to be eaten in silence. This vaulted room reminds me of the rule of silence during meals in the Convent of the Lily when I was at school.' The next dish provoked a torrent of opinions – scorpion fish, to my delight, their rosy forms bathed in a rosy *sughetto* in which were traces of green celery and wafts of garlic. Donna Adeline proclaimed that the scorpion's head was the best part of the fish, and was shocked when I said 'Yes, I appreciate the cheek.' 'The cheek is nothing to the rest of the head,' she protested, as, tearing it apart with fork and fingers, she vigorously sucked the fragments. The Sculptor chivalrously passed his head across the table, Don Andrea firmly remarking that the only civilized way of eating fish was with a fork in one hand and a hunk of bread in the other.

Meanwhile the barman's wife was anxiously hovering about the table praying that everything was as it should be; and he was bending over the hearth and before long materialized an exquisitely bronzed offering of month-old lamb, cut from the fragile bones, perfumed with olive oil, thyme, rosemary, some drops of lemon juice, and expertly wound and impaled onto long hardwood spits. The roast peppers were served with this, an inspiration perhaps of Donna Adeline, and now dressed with black pepper, olive oil and garlic.

Perfection thus attained, to our amazement a dish of grilled red mullets followed, fished that morning, as were the *scorfani*, off San Giovanni, the one-time Messapian port of Ugento, now submerged.

Then came a salad containing leaves of *rucola*, cultivated rocket, rather piquant, with a lovely fresh goat's cheese from Gemini. Then a green melon, called *melone* or, in dialect, '*minne di monaca*', nun's tits, refreshing; and then came wisps of almond cakes which may have been called '*sospiri*', sighs, reflecting other sighs of profound satisfaction. Don Andrea, a Prospero conjuring wonders from the void, was perfectly light-hearted. He had enchanted the normally gloomy hearts of an Ugentine Caliban and his Rita. 'Ri-ta' he called in his voice pitched rather high, rolling the *r* through the doorway into the kitchen. Rita darted back into the cell, her cheeks flushing. We drank the golden muscat wine, Ugentine, to start with, and a dark red wine with the lamb and mullets. Four villages, besides the sea, had been ransacked at his bidding.

Should I have made an error in recalling, this could be corrected. I can imagine the feast described in detail in some huge book, beautifully bound for him by Donna Adeline, and filled with extracts from his journal, written in a superb calligraphic hand and decorated with drawings and jewelled letters.

But I *have* forgotten something. There was a fifth guest: the young director of the Ugento Museum, but he was speechless. A bell must have rung. We were lunching with a genius. I now realize that Don Andrea and Gertrude Stein have one thing in common. They both have written somebody else's autobiography. And there is nothing to prevent anyone from getting to know him through *The Book of Giuliano Sansevero*.

1986

CLAUDIA RODEN

Middle Eastern Food

My compilation of recipes is the joint creation of numerous Middle Easterners who, like me, are in exile, either forced and permanent, or voluntary and temporary. It is the fruit of nostalgic longing for, and delighted savouring of a food that was the constant joy of life in a world so different from the Western one. The Arab sayings, 'He who has a certain habit will have no peace from it,' and 'The dancer dies and does not forget the shaking of his shoulders,' apply to us.

The collection began fifteen years ago with a recipe for *ful medames*. I was a schoolgirl in Paris then. Every Sunday I was invited together with my brothers and a cousin to eat *ful medames* with some relatives. This meal became a ritual. Considered in Egypt to be a poor man's dish, in Paris the little brown beans became invested with all the glories and warmth of Cairo, our home town, and the embodiment of all that for which we were homesick.

Our hosts lived in a one-room flat, and were both working, so it was only possible for them to prepare the dish with tinned *ful*. Ceremoniously, we sprinkled the beans with olive oil, squeezed a little lemon over them, seasoned them with salt and pepper, and placed a hot hard-boiled egg in their midst. Delicious ecstasy! Silently, we ate the beans, whole and firm at first; then we squashed them with our forks and combined their floury texture and slightly dull, earthy taste with the acid tang of lemon, mellowed by the olive oil; finally, we crumbled the egg, matching its earthiness with that of the beans, its pale warm yellow with their dull brown.

Since that time, I and many relatives (Sephardic Jews), acquaintances and friends, exiled from our Middle Eastern homelands, have settled in various countries. We have kept in close touch by letter and occasional visits. Some of us have tried to re-create certain aspects of the way of life to which we were accustomed after centuries of integrated life in the Ottoman and Arab worlds, in particular the food, which meant so much in the Middle East and has come to mean even more in exile.

It has been, for me, a matter of great delight to acquire an extra recipe from some relative passing through London, a well-known ex-restaurateur from

Alexandria, or somebody's aunt in Buenos Aires – another treasure to pass on to the Middle Eastern community in Paris, Geneva or Milan.

Friday night dinners at my parents', and gatherings of friends at my own home have been opportunities to rejoice in our food and to summon the ghosts of the past.

Each dish has filled our house in turn with the smells of the *Muski*, the Cairo market, of the *corniche* in Alexandria, of Groppi's and the famous Hati Restaurant. Each dish has brought back memories of great and small occasions, of festivals, of the emotions of those times, and of the sayings invariably said. They have conjured up memories of street vendors, bakeries and pastry shops, and of the brilliant colours and sounds of the markets. Pickles and cheeses have re-created for us the atmosphere of the grocery shop round the corner, down to which a constant flow of baskets would be lowered from the windows above, descending with coins, and going up again with food. It is these smells, emotions, habits and traditions, attached to and inseparable from our dishes, a small part of our distinctive culture, that I have tried to convey with the food.

At first, on leaving Egypt, I imagined our food to be uniquely Egyptian. In Europe, I discovered that the Turks claimed most of our dishes, and that the Syrians, Lebanese and Persians claimed the rest, leaving us with only a few specialities, our 'national dishes'. Nearly all our food was common to other Middle Eastern countries, so to write about 'our food' was to write about Middle Eastern food generally. I have not been able to disentangle what is an Egyptian culinary tradition from a Turkish, Persian or Syrian one, and I have had to include various countries which I did not intend to at first, but which were necessary to make a complete and comprehensible picture of what was originally my 'family's food'. The countries which imposed themselves were, in a broad sense, the countries of the Middle East.

The Middle East is a broad and fluid term which today means different things to different people. Its more recent history and events, tragic, intricate and tumultuous, have made it, for all those who have any mild involvement with it, loaded with explosive emotion. I cannot attempt in this book of food to make any sort of political or geographical definition, since even the latter is tragically complex and unsettled.

The region embraces many different countries, races and religions. The people call themselves 'orientals', a term more often used in the West when referring to the Far East. The area is one of geographical, climatic, human and social contrasts. It has been the birthplace of our present civilization, and the battle-ground of most of the creeds, philosophies and religions which form the basis of those now occupying the minds of much of the world today.

Some parts of the Middle East are racially pure, such as those inhabited by Bedouin Arabs. Others, such as the Mediterranean coast, inhabited by people loosely termed 'Levantines', are extremely mixed in racial origin, nationality and religion, embodying the numerous human changes brought about by various empires, invasions, foreign settlers and traders. A name invented by my community for these people is 'Bazramites'.

With a few exceptions, the Arabic language is spoken throughout the region in its numerous and varied dialects. The religion is that of Islam, but each country until recently sheltered a large number of small communities of Christians and Jews, and various small sects and factions of these.

Here is my choice of countries included in this book: Syria, the Lebanon, Egypt, Iran, Turkey, Greece, Iraq, Saudi Arabia, the Yemen, the Sudan, Algeria, Tunisia, Morocco and Israel. Their cooking is inextricably linked.

Although the Balkan countries have adopted culinary traditions from their former Ottoman rulers, I have not included them, since they are now far removed from the Middle East, and they have not notably fed many dishes back to the common pool. I have dealt with Greece in as much as its tradition is almost identical with the Turkish one.

I have treated the food of the individual countries arbitrarily, giving preference and most careful scrutiny to all aspects of food belonging to my own personal background, but, I hope, doing justice to the food of other countries too. Iran, the Lebanon, Syria, Turkey and Morocco I found ready to pour out an abundant variety of splendid recipes, while other countries, possessing a poorer and more limited range, had only a few dishes to offer.

The early sources of my collection of recipes have been my family and my own community from Egypt; people who were either born in Egypt or who had lived, themselves and their forefathers, for centuries in various countries of the Middle East, and had come to settle in Egypt. Their culture and traditions ran parallel to, and were part of, wider national traditions.

To explore the food of the different countries was made easy for me by the fact that we were particularly spoilt in the very cosmopolitan atmosphere of Egypt, which contained communities of other Middle Eastern nationals. My own family has a Syrian and a Turkish branch, and many of my relatives have married into families coming from the Lebanon, North Africa and Iran. This enabled us to savour the best of many worlds.

I was extremely lucky in having the help of Turks, Syrians, Iranians, Lebanese, Saudi Arabians, Armenians, Israelis and North Africans, whom I met in London and with whom I spent long, rich and interesting hours, taking in their experience, watching them cook, sampling the dishes they prepared for me before trying them myself. All those who contributed recipes have a feeling for, and deep understanding of, food.

Most of these people explained in the minutest detail the washing and the handling of ingredients, the feel, the smell and the colour of the food – but usually omitted quantities, weights and cooking times. I learnt that to some 'leave it a minute' meant an hour, that 'five spoonfuls' was in order to make a round figure or because five was for them a lucky number, and that a pinch could be anything from an eighth of a teaspoon to a heaped tablespoon . . .

SOCIAL ASPECTS

The activities of cooking and eating reflect many subtly intricate facets of the Middle Eastern character and way of life. They are intensely social activities, while the dishes hold within them centuries of local culture, art and tradition.

Hospitality is a stringent duty all over the Middle East. 'If people are standing at the door of your house, don't shut it before them,' and 'Give the guest food to eat even though you yourself are starving,' are only two of a large number of sayings which serve to remind people of this duty, a legacy of nomadic tribal custom when hospitality was the first requirement for survival.

Sayings of Muhammad in the Quran, folk proverbs, religious, mystical and superstitious beliefs set up rules of social *savoir-vivre* to the minutest detail – sweetly tyrannical, immutable and indisputable rules of civility and manners – to dictate the social behaviour of people towards each other, and sometimes submerge and entangle them in social obligations.

The ultimate aim of civility and good manners is to please: to please one's guest or to please one's host. To this end one uses the rules strictly laid down by tradition: of welcome, generosity, affability, cheerfulness and consideration for others.

People entertain warmly and joyously. To persuade a friend to stay for lunch is a triumph and a precious honour. To entertain many together is to honour them all mutually. The amount of food offered is a compliment to the guest and an indication of his importance. Failure to offer food and drink shows a dislike of visitors and brings disrepute to the host.

It is equally an honour to be a guest. Besides the customary obligations of cordiality and welcome, there is the need for the warmth of personal contact and cheerful company, the desire to congregate in groups, and the wish to please. It is common when preparing food to allow for an extra helping in case an unexpected guest should arrive. Many of the old recipes for soups and stews carry a note at the end saying that one can add water if a guest should arrive.

When a meal is over there should always be a good portion of food left, otherwise one might think that someone has not been fully satisfied and could have eaten more.

The host should set before his guest all the food he has in the house, and apologize for its meagreness, uttering excuses such as: 'This is all the grocer had,' or 'I was just on my way down to the confectioner's,' or 'For the past two weeks I have been preparing for my niece's wedding and have not had time to make anything else.'

If a guest comes unexpectedly, the host must never ask why he has come, but receive him with a smiling face and a look of intense pleasure. After a ceremony of greetings, he should remark on the pleasure of seeing him and the honour of such a visit. The guest should never say right away why he has come, if there is a reason, but first inquire about the family, friends and affairs of his host. The latter must treat his guests as though he were their servant; to quarrel with them would be a disgrace. He must never argue with them about politics or religion, but should always acquiesce. He must never ask his guests if they would like food or drink, but provide these automatically, insisting that they have them and ignoring repeated refusals.

'The first duty of a host is cheerfulness' is a maxim strictly abided by. A host must amuse and entertain, provide light gossip, jokes, and, occasionally, riddles and a little satire. He may also offer a tour of the house and an inspection of new acquisitions.

A guest, in turn, must also play his role correctly. He should 'guard his voice, shorten his sight and beautify [praise] the food'. That is, although he must commend everything, exclaim in admiration and congratulate, he should not look about too much, nor inspect too closely. The Quran advises him to talk nicely and politely: 'Sow wheat, do not sow thorns; all the people will like you and love you.' 'Don't enter other people's houses, except with permission and good manners.' 'Beautify your tongue and you will obtain what you desire.'

A guest must at first refuse the food offered to him, but eventually give in on being urgently pressed. In particular, he must never refuse dishes which have already been sampled by others of the company, as this would put them in an uncomfortable position. If he comes invited, he must bring a present, and if this happens to be a box of confectionery, the host must open it immediately and offer him some.

The Quran advises that 'It is not right for a man to stay so long as to incommodate his host.' When a guest leaves, he must bless his host and he is under an obligation to speak well of him to others.

However, this beautifully laid-out pattern has its pitfalls. The wrong sort of admiration might be mistaken for envy, and give rise to a fear of the 'evil eye', of which it is said that 'half of humanity dies'. Folklore provides phrases to avoid this. The words 'five on your eye' are equivalent to the Western 'touch wood'. Blessings uttered towards various saints and the invocation of the name of God also act as a protection from evil. The person who is the object of admiration may protect himself by denouncing the reality of his good fortune and protesting that he has also been the victim of various misfortunes. However, a remark of admiration directed towards a personal possession may oblige the owner to offer it instantly and pressingly.

Cooks always cook to suit the taste of those who will eat the food. They need and expect approval. Often, dishes for the evening are lengthily discussed in the morning. Husbands express their wishes as to what they would like for dinner, and while they are eating, often remark on the success of the dish. However, a few husbands of my acquaintance believe that they must criticize something in a meal or complain that the dish requires a little more of one thing or another, thereby preventing their wives from becoming complacent.

Cooks are constantly coaxed and encouraged to surpass themselves and to perfect family favourites. Cooking ability is rated highly among female accomplishments. One Arab saying goes: 'A woman first holds her husband with a pretty face, then by his tummy and lastly with the help of a *sheb-sheb* [a wooden slipper].'

Cooking is often done in company. Mothers and daughters, sisters, cousins and friends love to talk about what they will serve their family for lunch or dinner, and they sit with or help each other to prepare delicacies which require time and skill. At all special occasions, such as family gatherings and national or religious holidays, the hostess can count on the help of many eager and generous relatives and friends, who come to help prepare the food, sometimes two or three days ahead. If they are unable to be present at the preparations, they will often send a plateful of their own particular speciality instead.

People always turn to food to mark important events. Weddings, circumcisions, religious festivals, new arrivals, in fact most occasions call for a particular dish or delicacy, or even a whole range of specialities. If these are lacking when it is customary to include them, it is a cause for offence and gossip. Criticism and disapproval are feared most by those who wish to impress and do the right or customary thing. This accounts for the fact that parties, though often extraordinarily lavish and varied, are also repetitive within each community. No table could be without stuffed vine leaves, *kahk*, *ma'amoul* or *baklava* and the usual range of delicacies. How fearful one is of the critical gaze of a guest searching for some speciality which is missing from the table!

*

It is said that there is a language of flowers. In the Middle East there exists a language of food. A code of etiquette for serving and presenting particular dishes expresses subtle social distinctions. Which piece, of what, and in what order, gives away the status of the person who is being served. There are rules of procedure according to social and family status and age. A dignitary or the head of the family is served the best helping first. A guest who comes seldom or who comes from afar is served before one who is a regular and familiar visitor to the house. A bride-to-be is served ceremoniously at the house of her husband-to-be. But when she is married, her status drops considerably at the table (as it does everywhere else), to rise again when she is expecting a baby. Then, she is often pampered and allowed to indulge in extravagant yearnings. If she then gives birth to a son, her status remains high.

A person of 'low extraction' who insists on sitting next to one of high birth or importance might be asked: 'What brought the sardine to the red mullet?' A proverb advises men to pay respect to status, and to give to each according to his station: 'Divide the meat and look at the faces.' And a saying describes this regard: 'When a wealthy man comes to a feast, the host tells some poor man to get up and give his place to the newcomer.'

In some parts of the Middle East where folklore is rich in beliefs about the evil eye, djinns and omens, some foods are believed to have magical powers.

Garlic is believed by some to ward off the evil eye and is sometimes hung at the front door of a house to protect its inhabitants. For its disinfectant qualities it is hung on a string around children's necks during epidemics. In some parts, people do not eat brains for fear of becoming as stupid as the animal; in others, they eat them to fortify their own brains and become more intelligent. Some do not eat the hearts of birds in case they might acquire their timidity.

Certain beliefs are uncommon and localized, and few people will have even heard of them. Others are widespread in all the countries and communities. One of these is that eating yellow things will result in laughter and happiness; another, that eating honey and sweet things will sweeten life and protect one from sadness and evil. Predictably, things coloured black, such as very black aubergines, are considered by some to be unlucky, while green foods encourage the repetition of happy and prosperous events.

In the past, some foods were believed to have aphrodisiac qualities. Sheikh Umar Ibn Muhammad al Nefzawi, in his now famous sixteenth-century book, *The Perfumed Garden*, recommends various foods as a cure for impotence or as powerful sexual stimulants. For the former, he recommends eating 'a stimulant pastry containing honey, ginger, pyrether, syrup of vinegar, hellebore, garlic, cinnamon, nutmeg, cardamoms, sparrows' tongues, Chinese cinnamon, long pepper, and other spices'; also 'nutmeg and incense mixed with honey'. Of foods which 'all learned men' acknowledge to have a positive effect in stimulating amorous desires are: an asparagus omelette, a fried-onion omelette, camel's milk mixed with honey, eggs boiled with myrrh, coarse cinnamon and pepper, eggs fried in butter, then immersed in honey and eaten with a little bread, and simply plain chick peas. He assures his readers that 'the efficacy of all these remedies is well known, and I have tested them'. Even today, a certain belief in the aphrodisiac powers of some foods still exists.

Cooking in the Middle East is deeply traditional and non-intellectual – an inherited art. It is not precise and sophisticated like Chinese cooking, nor is it experimental and progressive like American cooking today. Its virtues are loyalty and respect for custom and tradition, reflected in the unwavering attachment to the dishes of the past. Many have been cooked for centuries, from the time they were evolved, basically unchanged.

Yet each cook feels that within the boundaries of tradition she can improvise. She can pit her artfulness and wits, her sensuous feeling for the food, its texture and aroma, to create a unique and exquisite dish with the imprint of her own individual taste.

Of the people who have given me recipes, most added remarks such as: 'Personally, I like to add a little mint,' implying that this was their own innovation; or 'I always put double the usual amount of ground almonds,' meaning that they are extravagant; or 'I use dry breadcrumbs instead of soaked bread,' to show their ingenuity; or, with a touch of guilt, 'I use stock cubes instead of making a chicken stock because it is easier, but I find it very acceptable.' Somebody even devised a way of stuffing courgettes without actually doing so, by curling slices around a compact ball of meat and rice filling and securing them tightly with a toothpick.

Nevertheless, if I suggested to those same people a totally new taste or a totally new form or method for a dish, they were mildly outraged or laughed incredulously at the folly of such a suggestion.

A certain malleability and a capacity to absorb new cultures while still remaining true to themselves have enabled the people of the Middle East to adopt dishes brought back by the Moors from Spain, those introduced by the Crusaders, Greek dishes, North African dishes such as couscous and, more recently, French, Italian and even English dishes, and then to adapt them to suit local tastes.

Of the dishes created by the local way of life and general character are the large variety of *mezze*, served before a meal, or to accompany drinks at any time of the day. These reflect the passion that the Middle Eastern peoples have for leisure and the importance they attach to their peace of mind, the luxury of tranquil enjoyment which they call *keif*. It is for them a delight to sit at home on their balconies, in their courtyards, or at the café, slowly sipping drinks and savouring *mezze*.

The numerous stuffed *mahshi*, *börek*, *sanbusak* and pastries, all requiring artful handiwork, denote a local pride in craftsmanship and skill. The smaller they are the more esteemed, for it is more difficult and it takes longer. The traditional decoration of dishes down to the humblest sauce or soup with a dusting of red paprika or brown cumin and a sprinkling of chopped parsley is the result of a love of beauty and ornamentation, the same that has produced the luscious Islamic decorative arts. The sensuous blue and green patterns of the ceramics are echoed in the green chopped pistachios and pale chopped blanched almonds adorning cream puddings. The criss-cross wooden patterns of the balconies behind which the women used to hide haunt the lozenge shapes of *basbousa* and *baklava*. The colours of confectioneries, syrups and pickles are those of the brilliant dresses which appear at *mûlids* (festivals).

THE TRADITIONAL TABLE

Before proceeding to the table, guests are entertained in a different room, where they often sit on sofas at floor level. A maid comes round with a large copper basin and flask, pouring out water (sometimes lightly perfumed with rose or orange blossom) for the guests to wash their hands. A towel is passed round at the same time.

Dining tables are low and round – large metal trays resting on a type of stool, or on short, carved, folding wooden legs, sometimes inlaid with mother of pearl and tortoise-shell. The trays themselves are of copper, brass or silver, beaten and engraved, sometimes inlaid with silver or other metals. Thin threads of the metal are beaten into crevices with a little hammer, making traditional oriental decorative patterns and writings: words of blessing, charms against the evil eye and words in praise of Allah. Usually several tables are placed in the room, and the diners sit around them on cushions.

Several bowls containing a variety of dishes are placed on each table for guests to enjoy the pleasure of deciding which dish to start with, and with which delicacy to follow.

Before the meal is started, the word *Bismillah* (In the name of God!) is uttered by all.

In eating, a strict code of etiquette is observed. It is related that the Imam Hassan (son of Ali) listed twelve rules of etiquette to be observed.

The first four are *necessary*, namely: to know that God is the Provider; to be satisfied with what He has provided; to say 'In the name of God!' when beginning to eat and to say 'To God be thanks!' when you finish. The next four are *customary*, and it is well to observe them, though they are not required: to wash the hands before eating; to sit at the left of the table; to eat with three fingers; and to lick the fingers after eating. The last four are rules of particular politeness: to eat out of the dish that is immediately in front of you and out of your own side of the dish; to take small pieces; to chew the food well; and not to gaze at the others at the table with you. These twelve rules form the traditional basis for the table manners of the majority of the people.

Besides these rules, there are other, subtler points of *savoir-vivre*. It is tolerated to eat with five fingers when eating food of a not too solid consistency, such as couscous.

It is considered sociable and polite to detach choice morsels such as chicken hearts or livers, or fish roes, and to offer these to a neighbour.

If one feels satiated, one should nevertheless continue to nibble at a dish from which others are still eating, since if one person stops eating, everyone else may feel compelled to stop too, and the dish will be removed from the table.

One must lick one's fingers at the end of a meal only. To do so before would be a sign that one had finished.

One must always talk about pleasant and joyful things and never introduce a sad or bitter note into the conversation. One must be cheerful and entertaining, and remark on the perfection of dishes, saying, 'Your fingers are green!' if the hostess has prepared them or helped in their preparation; and 'May your table always be generous to all!' – a phrase entertaining the hope that one will be asked to eat there again soon.

Sometimes, in parts where women have not yet become emancipated, men only are invited. Islam looks upon women with suspicion. According to Muslim tradition, the Prophet Muhammad said: 'I have not left any calamity more hurtful to man than woman.' In some parts, women are believed to have more power to cast the evil eye, so they are served first, before their look of longing can have a harmful effect on the food.

If two people have eaten together, they are compelled to treat each other well, as the food contains a conditional curse. This is alluded to in the sayings: 'God and the food will repay him for it,' and 'Cursed, son of a cursed one, is he who eats food and deceives him who shared it with him.' Host and guest in particular are tied in a relationship governed by this conditional curse.

When the meal is finished, guests leave the table to go through the handwashing ceremony again and to partake of coffee or tea.

Similar rules to these are added to Western manners in homes where Western habits of eating have been adopted. Actions and words reveal an attachment to ancient tradition. At buffet dinner parties in our house, for example, the guests stood far away from the table and had to be urged and pressed to eat. Although the mechanics of the European table, the knife and fork, and the table napkin, had been adopted, the old, Middle Eastern manners and rules of *bienséance* remained.

To those of the Middle East who might misunderstand my motives and feel offended, as I believe some will, by my description of 'table manners', I would like to say that the manner of eating with the fingers is most delicate and at least as refined as any belonging to the culture of the West, and I have only respect for the elegance of these rules of *savoir-vivre*.

1968

ROBERT IRWIN

In the Caliph's Kitchen

Some people read cookery books in bed for pleasure – say, Elizabeth David's *French Provincial Cooking* or Claudia Roden's *A Book of Middle Eastern Food* – in preference to novels. It may indeed be true that a cook who writes well can achieve the same effects that a novelist strives after, but with greater economy. *Brideshead Revisited* was first published in 1945. In a preface added over a decade later, Waugh noted that it was written in a period of austerity, 'and in consequence the book is infused with a kind of gluttony, for food and wine, for the splendours of the recent past, and for rhetorical and ornamental language, which now with a full stomach I find distasteful'. For once, it is hard not to agree with Waugh. Readers seeking to flee in their imaginations from the horrors of post-war British austerity (rationing was not finally abolished until 1954) were probably better served by Elizabeth David's *A Book of Mediterranean Food* (1950), with its unaffected prose and wonderful John Minton illustrations.

However, it would be unwise to overdraw the contrast between cookery books and novels. Many novels have included recipes, and some cookery books should be covered as largely works of fiction. In an essay entitled 'Social Reality and Culinary Fiction: The perspective of cookbooks from Iran and Central Asia', Bert Fragner, a German Professor of Iranian Studies, remarks that there are 'many more fictional elements in cookbooks than is commonly supposed'. He draws attention to the unlikelihood that all the recipes in a given book have actually been tested by their compiler. He goes on to suggest that the inclusion of Western recipes in early-twentieth-century Persian cookery books was intended for show and discussion, rather than for cooking.

Fragner's is a fascinating contribution to *Culinary Cultures of the Middle East*, generally an extremely valuable collection of seventeen papers, presented mostly by academics who participated in a conference on Middle Eastern food at the School of Oriental and African Studies, London University, in 1992. The subjects covered included such matters as food production, the changing fortunes of rice, Jewish food, the breaking of the Ramadan fast, colours and smells in medieval Arab cooking, the role of food in the works of Naguib

Mahfouz and other novelists, and food as a regional marker of gender, race or class. In their introduction, Sami Zubaida and Richard Tapper not only distil some of the conclusions to be drawn from the chapters which follow, but they offer additional insights and references. Among other things, they draw attention to the modernization of cuisine under the regime of the mullahs in Iran, where the attempt to return to older and purer religious practices runs in tandem with a switch to modern Western eating habits and an undiscriminating enthusiasm for pizzerias, sandwich bars and freezer foods. Iran's culinary misfortune contrasts strongly with developments in modern Turkey, where, as Holly Chase shows in 'The *Meyhane* or McDonald's: Changes in eating habits and the evolution of fast food in Istanbul', the demand for fast food has actually restimulated the demand for such traditional Turkish dishes as kebabs, aubergines with yoghurt and tripe soup. A vaguely similar revival of traditional cuisine has been taking place in Mecca, as Mai Yamani shows in her paper on the subject.

One of the most persuasive fictions disseminated by Middle Eastern cookery books is the changelessness of its cuisine. Zubaida and Tapper take Roden's *A Book of Middle Eastern Food* gently to task for its overemphasis on culinary continuity in the region, commenting that our 'perceptions of the past as origins predispose us to an emphasis on similarity and continuity'. Linguistic slippage and the application of the same word to different dishes contribute to the illusion. For example, in *The Rock of Tanios*, Amin Maalouf's Goncourt Prize-winning novel set in the Lebanon in the early nineteenth century, the hero Tanios is nicknamed *Kishk* by the villagers. Maalouf's narrator explains that the word 'refers to a sort of thick, bitter soup whose basic ingredients are curdled milk and corn'. However, in *Culinary Cultures*, Françoise Aubaile-Sallenave shows how across the centuries and regions roughly the same word has been used to refer to a disconcerting variety of foods: in ancient Iran, *kashk* seems to mean barley bread, but in modern Iran it refers to dried yoghurt. Elsewhere the word or its cognates refer to a product made from fried butter-milk, a kind of cheese, a sweetmeat, a kind of stew, a mixture of cereals and meat, and so on. The diffusion of this word of Persian origin is one sign among others of the prestige of Persian culture and, more specifically, its cooking in the medieval Islamic world.

The Arabist David Waines, in his *In the Caliph's Kitchen: Mediaeval cooking for the modern gourmet* (1989), argued that under the Abbasids a sort of *nouvelle cuisine* was introduced. However, we really know so little about Umayyad cuisine that it is difficult to be sure how much of Abbasid cookery was really innovative. What is certain is that cooking was much discussed in eighth- and ninth-century Baghdad, and at the highest level. The phenomenon of the celebrity cook is not peculiar to modern times. In the Abbasid period, the authors of cookery books included the caliphs Ibrahim ibn al-Mahdi and al-Wathiq, and among the foodie pundits one finds poets of the first rank, such as Ibn al-Mu'tazz. Indeed, to judge from the surviving written sources, cookery was exclusively the province of the prince, the courtier and the intellectual. What we do not find is cookery books written by or for housewives.

It does not do to exaggerate the continuity of the Middle Eastern tradition, for while it is easy to spot continuities or alleged continuities, one has to be alert in order to spot cooking traditions which have ceased. Whole ranges of dishes and condiments have become extinct since Abbasid times. Tapper and Zubaida cite *murri* as an example of a vanished food. This condiment, prepared from rotted wheat or barley, was immensely popular in the early Middle Ages. At an Oxford Food Symposium some years ago, Charles Perry, a leading food writer, reported on his attempt to revive the dish. Bread, left to rot for weeks, acquired the appearance of 'a furry black kitten with pink patches'. Having scraped the black bits off and sifted them, Perry left them for a further week by which time the preparation smelt 'like a ripe salami' and looked 'loathsome'.

In the centuries immediately following the heyday of the Abbasid caliphate, there seems to have been a decline in the elaboration and extravagance of the dishes as well as in the status of those who wrote about them. However, most historians of food seem to be agreed that the rise of the Ottoman Turks, from the fourteenth century onwards, went hand in hand with a revival of standards in cookery which benefited the whole of the eastern Mediterranean region. There is little in *Culinary Cultures* to enthuse hellenophiles. Zubaida and Tapper criticize the inturned nature of a conference on Greek food held in Salonika in 1991. Fragner sees the Greeks and others as heirs to the Ottoman lifestyles and 'culinary empire'. Charles Perry, in 'The Taste for Layered Bread among the Nomadic Turks and the Central Asian Origins of Baklava', contests the notion put forward by Speros Vryonis, in *The Decline of Hellenism in Asia Minor and the Process of Islamization from the Eleventh through the Fifteenth Century* (1971), that the origins of baklava are to be sought in the Byzantine Empire.

The twentieth century has brought further changes. Even in the nineteenth century, Western dietetics and concern with healthy eating were having an impact on Arabic and Persian cookery books. This influence has led to the scrapping of a traditional system of dietetics based on a wholly spurious contract between what were classed as 'hot' and 'cold' foods, with, for example, beef, turkey and cabbage classified as 'cold', duck, lamb and carrots as 'hot'. Although the theory had no basis in any scientific reality, the greatest philosophic and scientific minds of the Middle Ages subscribed to it. Other aspects of the growing influence of Western cuisine on that of the Middle East have been a decline in the use of animal fats for cooking, an increase in the use of olive oil and of lemons, as well as the straightforward incorporation into Arabic recipe books of such dishes as *al-hisa' al-iskotlandi* (Scotch broth).

In 'The Revival of Traditional Cooking in Modern Arab Cookbooks', Peter Heine, another of the distinguished contributors to *Culinary Cultures*, notes the role of nationalism in the production of cookery books. He takes as his example a Kuwaiti book, whose compiler 'tried to establish a Kuwaiti cuisine and at the same time to give the impression that this cuisine is very old'. Just as every nation must have its own airline, so every nation must have its own recipe book. Anissa Helou's new book, *Lebanese Cuisine*, can be viewed as an example of the same phenomenon. So concerned is Helou to emphasize the distinctive nature of the Lebanese cuisine, that she eschews altogether the words 'Arab' and 'Arabian', preferring instead to stress the hypothetical contribution of the Phoenicians to the history of cooking. Helou is unenthusiastic about the notion put forward in Roden's *A Book of Middle Eastern Food* that there is such a thing as 'a collective cuisine' in the region, and as for the widely held opinion that Lebanese cooking has been strongly influenced to its advantage by the Ottoman Turks, she suggests instead that the influence may have been the other way round. Helou's book is no mere utilitarian manual, but a wistful evocation of feasts and picnics held in an easygoing, Levantine environment which all but came to an end when the civil war broke out in 1975. Books on food are well suited to carry this sort of nostalgic burden, and it was Proust who noted the powers of taste and smell to bear 'the vast structure of recollection'. *Lebanese Cuisine*, written by an author based in London, is a book of exile, and in this respect it can be compared to recent (and very good) Persian cookery books written by Najmieh Batmanglij and Margaret Shaida, in which exiles evoke the *dolce vita* of Iran before the rise of the mullahs and in which they seek to perpetuate older Persian values. Theoretical issues apart, *Lebanese Cuisine* is an attractively produced book, and those recipes which I have tested are excellent and will become part of my permanent repertoire.

Madame Guinaudeau's classic *Traditional Moroccan Cooking*, first published in French in 1958, combines recipes with ethnographic observation and an evocation of the sights and sounds of old Fez. The book appears to be aimed at an unusual readership. The prospective readers seem to be French expatriates, resident in Fez, for Guinaudeau offers guidance to the precise sources in the city where her ingredients are to be found. Thus for camel meat one goes to Souk el-Khemis, the Thursday market. After the camel has been slaughtered, its meat 'finishes upon the butcher's stall cut up in unappetizing violet coloured pieces . . . The white and sickly fat from the hump, cut out in thick petals, decorates the stall and will be bought to make *khli* (preserved meat) of mutton, beef or camel.' These readers will have plenty of time on their hands, for the recommended dishes commonly take four to five hours to prepare, and plenty of friends, for the quantities given are sufficient to feed ten, twelve or twenty people. When it comes to the necessary *batterie de cuisine*, Guinaudeau is uncompromising in her demands. Thus to prepare *greeouch*, one requires not only a pastry board and rolling pin, but also a *gssa* and a *mqla*. Her friendly readers are adventurous eaters, for the book includes recipes for *majoun* (a hashish cake) and snail soup (a medicinal appetizer), as well as a ringing endorsement for the eating of sheep's eyes. 'You insert a finger delicately in the socket; a quick turn of the nail and the orb will fall out. Extricate it and eat well seasoned with salt and cumin.' (Those who are averse to this last recommendation may take comfort from the strictures of the Ayatollah Khomeini, who listed the eyes and nasal secretions of animals among proscribed foods.)

Guinaudeau makes clear the distinctive nature of the Moroccan cooking in which spiced meat is central. This contrasts strongly with, for example, Lebanese cooking where vegetables and fruit have more prominence. *Traditional Moroccan Cooking*, which has a preface by the novelist and short-story writer Ahmed Sefrioui, is a thoroughly literary affair. Its author, determined to capture in words the vision of a traditional community threatened with change and even obliteration, vividly evokes the gestures employed in the making of bread or the offering of tea, chronicles the effect of the changing seasons on the fruit and vegetable markets, and paints verbal pictures of the dishes to be cooked. This being so, one wonders again about the real identity of her readers. If they were already resident in Fez, what need for all this gastronomic ekphrasis?

1994

ELIAS CANETTI

Choosing a Loaf

In the evenings, after dark, I went to that part of the Djema el Fna where the women sold bread. They squatted on the ground in a long line, their faces so thoroughly veiled that you saw only their eyes. Each had a basket in front of her covered with a cloth, and on the cloth a number of flat, round loaves were laid out for sale. I walked very slowly down the line, looking at the women and their loaves. They were mature women for the most part, in shape not unlike the loaves. The smell of the loaves was in my nostrils, and simultaneously I caught the look of their dark eyes. Not one of the women missed me; they all saw me, a foreigner come to buy bread, but this I was careful not to do, wanting to walk right to the end of the row and needing a pretext for doing so.

Occasionally there was a young woman. The loaves looked too round for her, as if she had had nothing to do with their making. The young women's eyes were different too. None of the women, young or old, was long inactive. From time to time each would pick up a loaf of bread in her right hand, toss it a little way into the air, catch it again, tilt it to and fro a few times as if weighing it, give it a couple of audible pats, and then, these caresses completed, put it back on top of the other loaves. In this way the loaf itself, its freshness and weight and smell, as it were, offered themselves for sale. There was something naked and alluring about those loaves; the busy hands of women who were otherwise shrouded completely except for their eyes communicated it to them. 'Here, this I can give you of myself; take it in your hand, it comes from mine.'

There were men going past with bold looks in their eyes, and when one saw something that caught his fancy he stopped and accepted a loaf in his right hand. He tossed it a little way into the air, caught it again, tilted it to and fro a few times as if his hand had been a pair of scales, gave the loaf a couple of audible pats, and then, if he found it too light or misliked it for some other reason, put it back on top of the others. But sometimes he kept it, and you sensed the loaf's pride and the way it gave off a special smell. Slipping his left hand inside his robe, the man pulled out a tiny coin, barely visible beside the great shape of the loaf of bread, and tossed it to the woman. The loaf then disappeared under his robe – it was impossible to tell where it was any more – and the man went away.

1978

REAY TANNAHILL

Imperial Rome

LIQUAMEN AND SILPHIUM

If Classical recipes are uninformative about texture, so they also are about taste, not only because of their reticence on quantities but also because they include ingredients that are either unfamiliar today or difficult to reproduce with any guarantee of exactitude. Even so, it is safe to say that in imperial times the Romans had very little enthusiasm for natural, unadulterated flavours.

One of the commonest and strongest seasonings was *liquamen* (or *garum*), a clear, golden, fermented fish sauce with a distinctively salty flavour. A keeping sauce, it was popular enough to be commercially produced; the best brews came from Pompeii, Leptis Magna and Antipolis (Antibes).

Of the several recipes for *liquamen*, the following seems to have been standard. 'It is best to take large or small sprats or, failing them, anchovies or horse-mackerel or mackerel, make a mixture of all and put into a baking trough. Take 2 pints of salt to the peck of fish and mix well to have the fish impregnated with salt. Leave it for one night, and then put it in an earthenware vessel which you place open in the sun for two or three months [eighteen months for large fish], stirring with a stick at intervals, then take it up, cover it with a lid and store away. Some people add old wine, 2 pints to 1 pint of fish.'* If the sauce were made from especially fine fish, or from something like shrimps, the result was gastronomically superior (and correspondingly high in price).

There was a quick-brew version that could be made at home. 'Take brine and test its strength by throwing an egg into it to try if it floats; if it sinks the brine

---

* As an example of the imponderables that make it difficult to assess and impossible to reproduce the dishes of the ancient world, *liquamen* is a good example. The final flavour would depend not only on the quality of the fish but, at least partly, on the quality of the salt – sprats, anchovies and mackerel being oily fish that go rancid very quickly. If, as seems likely, Roman salt had its ration of impurities, chemical decomposition may well have begun before the salt reached the centre of the fish – which would give the end product a character almost impossible to reconstruct with modern materials.

does not contain enough salt. Put the fish into the brine in a new earthenware pot, add oregano, put it on a good fire until it boils . . . Let it cool and strain it two or three times, until it is clear.' This was no more than a salty fish stock, a poor substitute for the real thing.

The nearest modern equivalents to *liquamen* are probably the fermented fish sauces known in Thailand as *nam pla*, in Vietnam as *nuoc mam*, in the Philippines as *patis*, and in Cambodia as *tuk trey*. Ten million gallons a year are said to have been consumed in the 1950s – the last period for which statistics are available – in what was then French Indo-China.

The scene at Eastern ports today may not differ greatly from that at the great *liquamen* factories of antiquity. A chain of labourers passes baskets of fish up from the boats to a foreman on shore, who levels the fish out in great wooden vats partially open to the air, alternating layers of fish with layers of salt until the vat is full. After a few days the liquid rendered from the fish is drained off from below and tipped back in on top of the heap, a process that has to be repeated several times over the course of the following days. Finally a wicker lid is placed on the vat and weighted down, and the brew is left to ferment and mature for several months, thickening slightly by a slow process of evaporation before the liquid is drained off and bottled.

Nutritionally, the resultant sauce is very valuable; as long as it is supplemented with vitamins, a few spoonfuls a day are said to provide almost a full quota of the nutrients required by the human body.

Nam pla tastes more of salt than fish, and a light soy sauce is usually recommended as the modern cook's alternative, but *liquamen* is generally believed to have been fishy as well as salty; the brine from salted anchovies, with a little anchovy creamed into it, might be the best option for anyone experimenting with Roman recipes. Other European fermented fish products – such as Norwegian *rakørret* (which tastes like strong cheese), Swedish *surströmming* and the *pissalat* of Provence – are no real substitute, since the Romans used the strained-off liquor rather than the fish (in which they are followed by the majority of South-East Asians), while Europeans prefer to eat the fish and ignore the liquor.

Liquamen may have been an acquired taste, but it was so commonly used that its absence from a dish must have been more noticeable than its presence.

Not quite as ubiquitous as *liquamen* but no less necessary to the Roman kitchen was the herb silphium, which came from the former Greek colony of Cyrene (Cyrenaica) in North Africa. Cyrene's economy was unhealthily dependent on two exports. 'I will *not* sail back to the place from which we were carried away,' complained one character in an Antiphanes comedy, 'for I want to say goodbye to all – horses, silphium, chariots, silphium stalks, steeplechasers, silphium leaves, fevers and silphium juice!'

Something happened to silphium, however – possibly there were crop failures as a result of overproduction – because it disappeared from the market in the middle of the first century AD, and no one today is entirely sure which plant it was. As a substitute, Rome began to import Persian asafoetida, the brown resinous juice of one of the giant fennels, a substance with the evil, penetrating smell of rotting garlic.

Asafoetida was expensive, especially when a money-hungry government found it worth taxing, as happened in Alexandria in the second century AD. Apicius even gave a way of stretching it by keeping it in a jar of pine nuts to which it would communicate its savour (just as a vanilla pod flavours a jar of sugar). When a recipe needed silphium, a few of the pine nuts could be used instead.

Despite the smell, a microscopic drop of asafoetida does give an indefinably pleasant taste to fish dishes, and it is much used (under the name of *hing*) in Indian vegetarian cookery. It is also worth noting that among the ingredients of that long-lived modern favourite, Worcestershire sauce, there are very small quantities of both asafoetida and anchovy essence . . .

THE FLAVOUR OF FOOD

The fact that no one even knows what Roman food was *intended* to taste like has never acted as a bar to speculation. There are two schools of thought. The first is revolted by an Apician recipe that recommends saucing cold chicken with dill, mint, dates, vinegar, *liquamen*, oil, mustard, asafoetida and boiled-down grape juice, forgetting that some of the ingredients of a modern *Salade à la Geisha*, if set down in the same random and unquantified fashion, would sound even less appetizing – crab, tomato ketchup, grapefruit, eggs, skimmed milk cheese, prawns, sunflower oil . . .*

The second, more sophisticated view is that the ingredients listed in Roman recipes, if judiciously balanced, could produce a very acceptable result. But from this perfectly tenable† position, apologists often go on to imply that the food actually served on Roman tables in Classical times would be acceptable

---

* With apologies to Michel Guérard's *Cuisine Minceur*, pp. 133 and 200.
† Within limits. There remain fundamental problems about the quality of Roman raw materials, not only in the case of salt and *liquamen*. How fatty was Roman pork compared with today's? How aromatic (or how musty) were the old, semi-wild spices, sun-dried and carried on camel-back and on months'-long voyages in foul-smelling, leaky ships? And so on.

today, which is not the same thing at all. 'Balance' and 'acceptability' are matters of taste and conditioning, and who is to say what a modern cook's taste has in common with that of a chef in a Roman villa?

Despite all this, it is possible to make at least a few deductions from the atmosphere of the recipes, and to integrate them with what is known about Roman life and attitudes of mind.

The very size of the city had an influence on the cuisine. In Sumer, Egypt and Greece even the greatest centres of population were relatively small, still intimately linked with the countryside that continued to provide most of their perishable foodstuffs. But imperial Rome expanded until it covered an area about quarter the size of modern Paris. The countryside receded. Transport was slow. 'Fresh' foods had to be stockpiled in warehouses. There was no refrigeration.

For the rich, these problems were not insurmountable. Indeed, there was no great emphasis in the cookery manuals on the dried and salted foods that might have been expected to figure largely on the winter menu, and although smoked meats were there it seems to have been less of necessity than because the Romans enjoyed their taste and texture. The rich had their own methods of dealing with seasonal food shortages. They had *piscinae*, or fishponds, in which fresh or salt water fish were kept alive until needed for the table, and aviaries in which thrushes were reared on millet, crushed figs and wheat flour. Fieldfares, counted as the finest of the thrush family, were even raised commercially. It was also possible, within limits, to control the timing of fresh supplies by setting slaves to tasks that could be slowed down or speeded up as the situation required – feeding snails on milk until they were too fat to slither back into their shells, stuffing dormice with nuts until they were plump enough to satisfy even the most demanding chef, clipping pigeons' wings or breaking their legs to immobilize them, and then fattening them for the table on chewed bread. (There is nothing new about the battery hen.) And the Roman fondness for fish was matched by the all-the-year-round availability of at least some of the multitude of kinds that swam in Mediterranean waters.

Even so, slow transport meant that the cook must often have been faced with the problem of having to disguise rancidity. The fishy/salty flavour of *liquamen* would certainly be useful in masking the milder fishiness of meat and poultry that had begun to go off. It would be valuable, too, for dressing up commonplace foods like eggs when, of necessity, they had to stand in for oysters or sea urchins, as well as for livening up wilted vegetables from the master's country estate. And the sometimes hard, dry flesh of exotics like the peacock undoubtedly needed improving; it was characteristic of the strongly competitive Romans, if by no means unique to them, that what was expensive or rare had to be good, by definition – even if the cook had a hard time making it so.

Spices fulfilled the same function as *liquamen*, especially in the rare (by Roman standards) cases where *liquamen* might have been too much of a good thing. Indian pepper was so important that it was numbered among the five 'essential luxuries' on which the whole foreign trade of the empire was said to be based. The others were Chinese silk, African ivory, German amber and Arabian incense.

Of the five, pepper came nearest to being a true essential, not because spices were vital to Roman *haute cuisine* but, on the contrary, because they transformed the food of everyday life. Lucullus, dining alone and presented by his cook with a plain supper, might reprimand the man with, 'What, did you not know, then, that today Lucullus dines with Lucullus?' but in other households a line seems to have been drawn between family eating and social dining.

Whatever the impression conveyed by Roman recipe books (and Roman gossips), the simplicity of the Roman breakfast (*jentaculum*) and lunch (*prandium*) suggests that even the rich retained memories of their rustic origins. Breakfast was bread with a few olives or raisins, lunch something quick and easy – leftovers, perhaps some cold meat or eggs. The main meal (*cena*) may have been little more extravagant except in households where it was necessary to give a multitude of slaves something to do.

Far more than company food, plain food like grain-pastes, beans and bread *needed* spices. A strong sauce, even in small amounts, has the ability to transform disproportionate quantities of starchy food. The most intense of the world's repertoire of sauces – the soy mixtures of China, the curries of India, the chilli pastes of Mexico – developed basically as seasonings for bulky carbohydrates, which both absorb and dilute them. Only when the rich enter on the scene, the people who can afford to have meat or fish every day, are sauces like these eaten with flesh foods, which dilute them scarcely at all; so the whole essence of the cuisine is changed. This may have happened in the case of Rome, a plain, rural society transfigured by the vision of its legislators and the success of its legions.

The theory that most of the Roman aristocracy suffered from lead poisoning (which contributed to the decline of the Roman Empire) emphasizes the impression of Roman food given by literary sources and suggests that city Romans, at least, may have had a need, as well as a desire, for strong flavours.

The people of Rome absorbed lead from the water that ran through their pipes, from cups and cooking pots, from cosmetics such as the white lead women used as face powder, and from their wine. To improve the rougher Roman wines, a sweet grape syrup was often added that had been boiled down in lead-lined pots; during the process, it became strongly contaminated. When the poet Martial drank five pints of wine at a sitting, therefore, he consumed, even allowing for the Romans' habit of watering their wine, not only the alcoholic equivalent of well over a bottle of whisky but something over fifty milligrams of lead.*

Among the symptoms of lead poisoning, many of which fit the Roman situation with impressive exactitude, are loss of appetite and a metallic taste in the mouth. It may be supposed that chronic sufferers would go to some lengths to find dishes that would stimulate their appetites and kill the taste of lead.

But whatever the truth about the flavour of Roman food, it was a fitting irony that the barbarians who materialized outside the gates of the city at the beginning of the fifth century AD should have demanded as tribute not only land, subsidies and military titles for their chiefs – but 3,000 pounds of pepper.

1973

---

* The lead concentration of the syrup (before blending with wine) has been estimated at between 240 and 1,000 milligrams per litre.

F. T. MARINETTI

The Manifesto of Futurist Cooking

On 28 December 1930 there appeared in the *Gazzetta del Popolo* in Turin

THE MANIFESTO OF FUTURIST COOKING

Italian Futurism, father of numerous Futurisms and avant-gardeisms abroad, will not remain a prisoner of those worldwide victories secured 'in twenty years of great artistic and political battles frequently consecrated in blood', as Benito Mussolini put it. Italian Futurism will face unpopularity again with a programme for the total renewal of food and cooking.

Of all artistic and literary movements Futurism is the only one whose essence is reckless audacity. Twentieth-century painting and twentieth-century literature are in reality two very moderate and practical Futurisms of the right. Attached to tradition, dependent on each other, they prudently only essay the new.

Against pasta

Futurism has been defined by the philosophers as '*mysticism in action*', by Benedetto Croce as '*anti-historicism*', by Graça Aranha as '*liberation from aesthetic terror*'. We call it '*the renewal of Italian pride*', a formula for '*original art-life*', '*the religion of speed*', '*mankind straining with all his might towards synthesis*', '*spiritual hygiene*', '*a method of infallible creation*', '*the geometric splendour of speed*', '*the aesthetics of the machine*'.

Against practicality we Futurists therefore disdain the example and admonition of tradition in order to invent at any cost something *new* which everyone considers crazy.

While recognizing that badly or crudely nourished men have achieved great things in the past, we affirm this truth: men think dream and act according to what they eat and drink.

Let us consult on this matter our lips, tongue, palate, taste buds, glandular secretions and probe with genius into gastric chemistry.

We Futurists feel that for the male the voluptuousness of love is an abysmal excavator hollowing him out from top to bottom, whereas for the female it works horizontally and fan-wise. The voluptuousness of the palate, however, is for both men and women always an upward movement through the human body. We also feel that we must stop the Italian male from becoming a solid leaden block of blind and opaque density. Instead he should harmonize more and more with the Italian female, a swift spiralling transparency of passion, tenderness, light, will, vitality, heroic constancy. Let us make our Italian bodies agile, ready for the featherweight aluminium trains which will replace the present heavy ones of wood iron steel.

Convinced that in the probable future conflagration those who are most agile, most ready for action, will win, we Futurists have injected agility into world literature with words-in-liberty and simultaneity. We have generated surprises with illogical syntheses and dramas of inanimate objects that have purged the theatre of boredom. Having enlarged sculptural possibility with anti-realism, having created geometric architectonic splendour without decorativism and made cinematography and photography abstract, we will now establish the way of eating best suited to an ever more high speed, airborne life.

Above all we believe necessary:

a) The abolition of pastasciutta, an absurd Italian gastronomic religion.

It may be that a diet of cod, roast beef and steamed pudding is beneficial to the English, cold cuts and cheese to the Dutch and sauerkraut, smoked [salt] pork and sausage to the Germans, but pasta is not beneficial to the Italians. For example it is completely hostile to the vivacious spirit and passionate, generous, intuitive soul of the Neapolitans. If these people have been heroic fighters, inspired artists, awe-inspiring orators, shrewd lawyers, tenacious farmers it was in spite of their voluminous daily plate of pasta. When they eat it they develop that typical ironic and sentimental scepticism which can often cut short their enthusiasm.

A highly intelligent Neapolitan Professor, Signorelli, writes: 'In contrast to bread and rice, pasta is a food which is swallowed, not masticated. Such starchy food should mainly be digested in the mouth by the saliva but in this case the task of transformation is carried out by the pancreas and the liver. This leads to an interrupted equilibrium in these organs. From such disturbances derive lassitude, pessimism, nostalgic inactivity and neutralism.'

An invitation to chemistry

Pastasciutta, 40 per cent less nutritious than meat, fish or pulses, ties today's Italians with its tangled threads to Penelope's slow looms and to somnolent old sailing-ships in search of wind. Why let its massive heaviness interfere with the immense network of short long waves which Italian genius has thrown across oceans and continents? Why let it block the path of those landscapes of colour form sound which circumnavigate the world thanks to radio and television? The defenders of pasta are shackled by its ball and chain like convicted lifers or carry its ruins in their stomachs like archaeologists. And remember too that the abolition of pasta will free Italy from expensive foreign grain and promote the Italian rice industry.

b) The abolition of volume and weight in the conception and evaluation of food.

c) The abolition of traditional mixtures in favour of experimentation with new, apparently absurd mixtures, following the advice of Jarro Maincave and other Futurist cooks.

d) The abolition of everyday mediocrity from the pleasures of the palate.

We invite chemistry immediately to take on the task of providing the body with its necessary calories through equivalent nutrients provided free by the State, in powder or pills, albumoid compounds, synthetic fats and vitamins. This way we will achieve a real lowering of the cost of living and of salaries, with a relative reduction in working hours. Today only one workman is needed for two thousand kilowatts. Soon machines will constitute an obedient proletariat of iron, steel, aluminium at the service of men who are almost totally relieved of manual work. With work reduced to two or three hours, the other hours can be perfected and ennobled through study, the arts, and the anticipation of perfect meals.

In all social classes meals will be less frequent but perfect in their daily provision of equivalent nutrients.

The perfect meal requires:

1) Originality and harmony in the table setting (crystal, china, décor) extending to the flavours and colours of the foods.

2) Absolute originality in the food.

'Sculpted meat'

Example: to prepare *Alaskan Salmon in the rays of the sun with Mars sauce*, take a good Alaskan salmon, slice it and put the slices under the grill with pepper, salt and high-quality oil until golden. Then add halved tomatoes previously cooked under the grill with parsley and garlic.

Just before serving place on top of the slices some anchovy fillets interlaced in a chequerboard pattern. On every slice a wheel of lemon with capers. The sauce will be composed of anchovies, hard-boiled egg yolks, basil, olive oil and a little glass of Italian Aurum liqueur, all passed through a sieve. (Formula by Bulgheroni, head chef at the Penna d'Oca.)

Example: to prepare the *Woodcock Mount Rosa with Venus sauce*, take a good woodcock, clean it, cover its stomach with slices of prosciutto and fat bacon, put it in a casserole with butter, salt, pepper and juniper berries and cook in a very hot oven for 15 minutes, basting it with cognac. Remove from the pan and place immediately on a large square slice of bread soaked in rum and cognac, and cover it with puff pastry. Then put it back into the oven until the pastry is well cooked. Serve it with this sauce: half a glass of marsala and white wine, four tablespoons of bilberries and some finely-chopped orange peel, boiled together for 10 minutes. Put the sauce in the sauce boat and serve it very hot. (Formula by Bulgheroni, head chef at the Penna d'Oca.)

3) The invention of appetizing food sculptures, whose original harmony of form and colour feeds the eyes and excites the imagination before it tempts the lips.

Example: the *Sculpted meat* created by the Futurist painter Fillìa, a symbolic interpretation of all the varied landscapes of Italy, is composed of a large cylindrical rissole of minced veal stuffed with eleven different kinds of cooked green vegetables and roasted. This cylinder, standing upright in the centre of the plate, is crowned by a layer of honey and supported at the base by a ring of sausages resting on three golden spheres of chicken.

Equator + North Pole

Example: the edible food sculpture *Equator + North Pole* created by the Futurist painter Enrico Prampolini is composed of an equatorial sea of poached egg yolks seasoned like oysters with pepper, salt and lemon. In the centre emerges a cone of firmly whipped egg white full of orange segments looking like juicy sections of the sun. The peak of the cone is strewn with pieces of black truffle cut in the form of black aeroplanes conquering the zenith.

These flavourful, colourful, perfumed and tactile food sculptures will form perfect simultaneous meals.

4) The abolition of the knife and fork for eating food sculptures, which can give prelabial tactile pleasure.

5) The use of the art of perfumes to enhance tasting.

Every dish must be preceded by a perfume which will be driven from the table with the help of electric fans.

6) The use of music limited to the intervals between courses so as not to distract the sensitivity of the tongue and palate but to help annul the last taste enjoyed by re-establishing gustatory virginity.

7) The abolition of speech-making and politics at the table.

8) The use in prescribed doses of poetry and music as surprise ingredients to accentuate the flavours of a given dish with their sensual intensity.

9) The rapid presentation, between courses, under the eyes and nostrils of the guests, of some dishes they will eat and others they will not, to increase their curiosity, surprise and imagination.

10) The creation of simultaneous and changing canapés which contain ten, twenty flavours to be tasted in a few seconds. In Futurist cooking these canapés have by analogy the same amplifying function that images have in literature. A given taste of something can sum up an entire area of life, the history of an amorous passion or an entire voyage to the Far East.

11) A battery of scientific instruments in the kitchen: *ozonizers* to give liquids and foods the perfume of ozone, *ultra-violet ray lamps* (since many foods when irradiated with ultra-violet rays acquire active properties, become more assimilable, preventing rickets in young children, etc.), *electrolysers* to decompose juices and extracts, etc. in such a way as to obtain from a known product a new product with new properties, *colloidal mills* to pulverize flours, dried fruits, drugs, etc.; *atmospheric and vacuum stills, centrifugal autoclaves, dialysers*. The use of these appliances will have to be scientific, avoiding the typical error of cooking foods under steam pressure, which provokes the destruction of active substances (vitamins etc.) because of the high temperatures. *Chemical indicators* will take into account the acidity and alkalinity of the

sauces and serve to correct possible errors: too little salt, too much vinegar, too much pepper or too much sugar.

1989

LESLEY BLANCH

Grand Food, Good Food and Grub

Grand food is not always good, nor is good food necessarily grand, while grub, so-called, the sausage and mash, jellied ell, shepherd's pie or pork pie plenty as once found in pubs, remains to me, at any rate, *hors* category – simply delicious. Grub (I do not know the etymology of the word) need not be a derogatory term unless applied to such horrors as technicolour pastries oozing imitation cream, or frozen fish fingers sloshed with ketchup. Once upon a time, really fresh fish used to be everywhere about our sea-girt isle. FRYING TONIGHT was chalked up outside the lowlier establishments and customers took away a packet wrapped in newspaper, hot, crisp, rather greasy and very good. It has been superseded in most places by more pretentious take-away stuff, just as traditional pub food has given place to pizzas or plates of pasta: the result, perhaps, of packaged Mediterranean holidays.

To define the exact category into which the different dishes fall is tricky. Often, they overlap, or are borderline cases, one being elevated by the manner in which it is prepared, while another is degraded. A rack of lamb with mint sauce is, to my mind, grand food: yet Alexandre Dumas' *gigot de sept heures* is probably considered far more grand, by its reputation, if not its complication. A *soufflé aux oeufs mollets* sounds grand. Yet it is, in fact, only soft-boiled eggs popped into a soufflé at the crucial moment. What puts it into a top category is knowing how and when to get the eggs into the soufflé. Legerdemain as well as ingredients count here.

A pudding of undisputed grandeur and pomposity is the Byculla Soufflé, invented by the Byculla Club of Bombay. It was the sort of thing Simla hostesses aspired to when out to dazzle; there may still be some very old ladies who can recall its multi-coloured layers of *mousse*, green Chartreuse, yellow Bénédictine and crimson Maraschino. That is grandeur – though not necessarily goodness.

Flamboyance of that order would not be found at the tables of such acknowledged epicures as the Rothschild dynasty *en bloc*, or at the table of that prince of bankers and epicures, the late Pierre David Weill. In that exclusive coterie of top French chefs – those who *choose* their employers rather than being chosen by them – Monsieur David Weill ranked above almost every other *fine fourchette* (literally, 'a delicate fork'), which somehow promises a more appreciative approach that our 'good trencherman'.

This specialized world of aesthetic gastronomy, which in France does still exist, though diminished, was encouraged during the presidency of Monsieur Giscard d'Estaing, another *fine fourchette* who had the Élysée humming with chefs, or *toques* as they are known, after the high pleated caps of their profession. ('*C'est à table qu'on gouverne*', as Bossuet remarked.) These *toques*, or *gros bonnets* as they are also called, are pundits, who stand no nonsense from any dilettante employer. There must be no nerve-racking sudden change of menus planned some days ahead. They, like those who can afford to pay them, and the feasts they concoct, live in a very rarefied atmosphere.

My life in Paris and New York sometimes gave me glimpses of this world when I dined with Pierre David Weill or *chez* Élie de Rothschild. However, once inside the latter's historic house in the seventh arrondissement (a quarter where, between the embassies and other historic houses, the thickest concentration of chefs is found), the Baronne's extraordinary collection of pictures, furniture and bibelots once belonging to Queen Marie-Antoinette quite distracted me from my plate. But while below stairs the chef and his *marmitons* were conjuring up masterpieces, a lively and critical interest was maintained upstairs. A dish which I took to be perfection, the Baron Élie might pronounce as middling.

There can be no family with more great dishes named after them than the Rothschilds, and their initiation into the subtleties of gourmandise, begun early, is always developed by their close association with the great chefs they employ. I remember the Baron Élie told me he was brought up, like his brothers and cousins, to take the art of cooking seriously. As a schoolboy, his weekly half-day holidays were largely spent in the kitchens learning the rudiments of gastronomy from the chef. Tuition began at the beginning – how to boil an egg, and so on, to higher flights.

The disciplines of the *haute cuisine* did not quench the boy's enthusiasm, nor did the rigid niceties of wine tasting, of forming the palate, as imposed by the butler. There is a story, perhaps apocryphal and attributed, I think, to Alan Pryce-Jones, which I beg leave to quote. It goes something like this: on entering a Rothschild nursery to fetch his little son who was partying there, he observed one of the children fidgeting to get down. 'Not till you have finished your Château Lafite,' said Nanny.

*

In Paris I sometimes dined with the Windsors, another house where the finer shades of gastronomy were perfectly expressed. The menus the Duchess composed were never banal; she boldly mixed simple and sophisticated food, thus tickling the most jaded palate. Countrified dishes and local fare such as a *cassoulet*, or a *navarin printanier* were found at her beautiful table, where she might mix rustic pottery with a service of vermeil. Subtle oriental sauces, Mexican black-eyed peas or the homely spud baked in its jacket were enjoyed there, as well as the classic French cuisine at its finest. The Duchess's knowledge was held in high respect by the critical circle of Paris chefs. 'She was the perfect *patron*' was their verdict. The Duke, who sometimes disturbed his chefs' Olympian calm by asking for a sandwich at some unlikely hour, used to speak fervently of typical English food, York ham, crumpets or Gentleman's Relish and once told me he had retained some aged servitor solely for the way in which he cooked the Duke's breakfast bacon.

I suppose I shall now receive spiteful letters from some of the Duke's detractors: but as the saying goes, I speak as I find, and I remember many delightful times with the Windsors, enjoying both their company and their table.

I have not written of Indian food here, nor of my travels in that fabled land. The fiery cuisine caused me suffering too strong for any recollection in tranquillity. I do remember, however, an occasion when our car drew up before a wayside gas station which advertised Snacks. The proprietor rushed out and, thrusting a smiling turbanned head in at the window, enquired 'Memsahib, stopping for a snake?' And at that moment, in the molten heat, my mouth still blistered from the last curry, I could have relished a nice cool slice of cobra.

The most dismal meal I ever faced – grub at its lowest denomination – was on a Red Indian reservation set high on a desolate, wind-bitten *mesa* or table-land on the Arizona and Nevada border. These were Hopi Indians, a tribe not quite so dramatic or terrifying as the Sioux or Comanches, the kind with whom I was familiar through a lifelong passion for Westerns – still, Redskins.

The Hopi were aloof, if not hostile to the outside world of palefaces; they were not the more gregarious lot who paraded and performed their war dances for the annual tourist jamboree at Flagstaff. Only the good offices of a Mexican friend who was *persona grata* among these Hopi, had secured my invitation, so I set off in a ferment of ethnological enthusiasm. The long rough drive was a trial for both my small car and myself, while the case of whisky I had been advised would be an acceptable gift shifted ominously in the boot as we bucketed about the rock-strewn track – I was to stay the night on the reservation, and the further I drove into the remote distances the less I liked the idea.

On reaching the *mesa*-top, all was desolation: a huddle of shacks and lean-to sheds, a dipper well, with a decrepit mule tethered to it, and a bricked-up structure, once the school-house, I learned later, which had been imposed by the US government and soon rejected. In the shelter of a rock ledge, a flint-faced gaffer was carving one of those sinister Katchina doll-figures now regarded as museum pieces. There was no other sign of life. Where were the tepees – the braves, the mustangs? A vicious wind raged round and tumbleweed shifted to and fro aimlessly. It was high time for a whisky.

Presently a bundled-up group of beady-eyed matrons waddled towards me – squaws – the real thing, and a monosyllabic lot; but at last I understood that an important festival was about to begin, something to do with invoking the rain gods, though perhaps I got it wrong for a heavy drizzle was now falling before it had been invoked. The squaws led me to a deep pit and I climbed down a shaky ladder to where, in the middle of the pit, a large fire smoked uncomfortably as the rain hissed down. Circling the fire were a number of men – the braves at last! Impassively, they were performing a curious ritual dance, hopping, capering and grunting rhythmically. Some wore blue jeans: all were hung with strips of coloured cloth, and little bells, thus bearing a fatal resemblance to Morris dancers.

The ceremony was still going on some hours later when the squaws summoned me to the surface, pantomiming a meal. A real Red Indian meal? Strips of dried buffalo? Some aromatic stew of deer meat? But it was not to be. With a generous hospitality they could ill afford, the Hopi had sent one of their younger men to the nearest village store many miles away, for the sort of thing the pale-faces ate. *He* knew. *He* had been a corporal in the US army and his purchases were now spread before me in triumph. 'Convenience foods' in all their ghastly variety. Beefburgers, hamburgers, cheeseburgers and Mother's Bake deep-freeze apple pie. All were frozen rock hard . . . Several hours were now spent thawing them over a fitful fire, or, in desperation, burying them among the embers. It was nightfall when at last I could start on a few chips of Mother's Bake pie. The rest of the company had long since devoured some kind of delicious-looking corn mush which, although hot, was not for me, the pale-face. So much for grub, Hopi or supermarket style.

When I returned to Hollywood, where my husband and I were then living, an affluent society was in full fling all around. I have often been asked since what the film stars ate, what sort of parties they gave and so on. The stars' first consideration was inevitably their weight, and their usual menu grills, salads and fat-free milk. Poor souls. The big studios, MGM, Warner Bros or Universal provided cafeterias where I often ate during a later, happy time when I was working for George Cukor at MGM. In these cafeterias everyone from star to technician could be found though some stars preferred to eat – or drink – in their dressing rooms. Alcohol was not obtainable at the cafeterias. But the most hallucinatory salads abounded, cottage cheese with pieces of lettuce, banana, and a cherry or two imprisoned in green jelly. These and other equally odd combinations were named after various stars. Thus an order would ring out for 'Elizabeth Taylor on rye', or 'Gary Cooper sunny side up with pecan pie'. Enormous almost raw Texan steaks were popular – macho food for macho men. Yet, curiously, puddings seemed to lose all control, weight-wise, and were baroque structures, jumbo sundaes and milk shakes.

In their sumptuous houses at Bel Air or Beverly Hills, the inner circle of success, top stars, directors, producers and agents entertained each other lavishly, usually on Saturday nights, when there was no brooding shadow of a five-a.m. studio call to which the stars were liable, since it often required three or four hours of being made up, dressed and prepared for the camera by eight a.m. Sometimes there were Sunday lunches round the pool when the host worked hard at a smoking barbecue, and occasionally wore a chef's cap. Dinners in this society were luxurious, conventional, and very good. The living was high – the best of everything along with the latest styles of interior decorating. Cooks were usually Europeans, French for preference, or at any rate were cooks of some style, like the butlers, who were prized especially if British.

After dinner, the pattern was generally the same. Replete and sunk in voluptuously padded armchairs we sipped our coffee and liqueurs and waited while the walls – invariably hung at that time with French Impressionists (genuine, if not always Grade A) – slowly folded back giving place to a large screen which treated us to the newest preview, or maybe some Golden Oldie starring our hostess in her prime. There was always a lot of ribald comment and chaff, besides chilling silences. This was an audience of critical professionals. Yet there was something cosy, an almost family atmosphere in the Hollywood I knew in the 'fifties. Those were the last years before television took over; the Hollywood of directors such as John Ford, George Cukor and David Selznick, and stars such as Marlon Brando, Marilyn Monroe, Gary Cooper, Charles Boyer and John Wayne, with high-powered agents such as Charlie Feldman and Swifty Lazar who manoeuvred them. Kirk Douglas was on the way up, and the young Paul Newman was being tipped for a big future. Kate Hepburn, who lived in a bungalow at the end of George Cukor's garden, always refused to attend his dinners (the best of all, sparked by his outrageous, extravagant wit and sophisticated taste). But Miss Hepburn abhorred dressing up as much as social life – though she sometimes sneaked up to the kitchens, a shadowy figure in blue jeans, to pick over the delicacies, unrebuked by cook or host.

But before I take leave of Hollywood, where good food was *de rigueur*, if not in the grandest category, I am reminded of one of the most perfect dinners I have ever known, in Hollywood or elsewhere. Cole Porter was the host, and Fred Astaire was the only other guest beside my husband and myself. The menu? Caviare, followed by pheasant and a soufflé Grand Marnier. Grand food, in the grandest company. And if in this chapter I have appeared to be name-dropping, what else can I do? Were I to write: 'Dinner with C.P. and F.A.', even such food would lose some of its lustre.

I had better get back to nameless company and grub – the best sort – which is, essentially, ever my choice, to be sought with the zeal of a truffle hunter. As I have remarked earlier, this is traditional English food and for all my life of travel, of pilaffs, kebabs and fricassees, I love best suet pud., bangers and toad-in-the-hole . . . When I return occasionally to London, and sight one of those small chalet-like green structures, the cab-man's shelter (unique, I believe, to London streets), I stand transfixed, sniffing the heady wafts of boiled beef and cabbage or Irish stew and dumplings simmering within, hot and plentiful, awaiting the fortunate taxi-man and his appetite.

Yet even as I assert my preference for grub, I am contradicted by a faraway memory. Some un-nameable exotic aroma rises round me. It overcomes the homely wafts of cabbage, for it is the cuisine of Byzantium I am remembering. I have written of this elsewhere but to recall such historic grandeur seems fitting here.

Long ago I was staying in a country house at Rhinebeck up the Hudson River. Each night I tasted food which aroused my curiosity to fever pitch. Such food was unlike anything I had ever eaten – and far more exquisite. Although the ingredients were recognizable, there was some subtle opulence, some exoticism which baffled me. It was a cuisine of immense intricacy, yet bold: Asiatic, rather than Arab, I thought. It was certainly *haute cuisine*, yet mysteriously spiced and treated. 'Ah! that is Vassili's secret,' said my hostess.

Vassili was her old chef and had been with the Obolenskys since they fled from Russia during the revolution. He had begun as one of the hundreds of *marmitons* at the Winter Palace, and also served in the kitchens of the Grand Duke Vladimir's palace. The Romanoff Court maintained certain archaic rituals which were handed down like certain culinary traditions, an almost unbroken line stemming originally from the Byzantine court of Constantinople.

They had reached Russia along with the first roses and that double-headed eagle, symbol of Byzantine sovereignty which was adopted by Russia, when the Paleologi princess Zöe journeyed north to become the Tsarina Sophia, wife of Ivan III. Thus even the faintest echoes of Byzantine grandeur must take pride of place over any other cuisine, in these pages.

1989

JONATHAN MEADES

Meat on Canvas (1)

Jesus Christ is the food that is most often represented in western art. Calling Him the Lamb doesn't make the Eucharist any the less cannibalistic. It's a *man's* body and blood that Christians eat. This elemental meat is shown us at many stages of its development: The first is when it's a babe, when it is indeed lamb, or veal or sucking pig. There follow childhood, miracles, feasts, trials, calumnies, betrayals. The greatest image though is when it's dead, when it's a casualty that has died for our plates, when it's a bull that has undergone the physical change that makes it beef, when it's a pig that has undergone the change that makes it pork. Calvary was an abattoir. The last stage is when it is bread and wine – or, in the case of the artotyrites, bread and cheese – when, anyway, it is no longer recognizable as the creature save by faith in transsubstantiation.

Now, with other meats, more literal meats, the central and most potent image in that progress is missing. Painting that shows the killing of animals for human consumption is not a genre – there is not a word for it: slaughterscape, still death, conversion piece . . . None of these is currency. And hunting scenes are not primarily concerned with the death of the prey, let alone with its evisceration and preparation for the market. Of course there are films like Georges Franju's *Le Sang des Bêtes* which show the horror of abattoirs, but their concern and effect is to hit the senses rather than to preach. They are not works of vegan propaganda. Jesus's death is crucial to the Christian mystery, to its morbidity and pathos. It must not be forgotten. The death of calves and of pigs shrieking as they try to keep their foothold is simply not part of the tradition of alimentary art. And that tradition has other laws, other proscriptions which are adhered to as much by the photographer as by the painter. The link between beast and stew is bridged by a neat ellipsis.

Take a bull. Call him Hamlet, not after the Dane from the problem family, but after his dad who was Dublin District Milk Board's most prolific sire, an Aberdeen Angus with 75,000 offspring. That Hamlet died in 1977 and was made into dog meat. Our Hamlet is destined for human consumption, not for bovine generation and canine delight. His nativity will not be recorded – we don't want to be reminded of the vulnerability and cuteness of future meat. And no one will snap the moment when he is about to be led into a windowless building and he glances a pair of eyes through the slats of a cattle truck and recognizes them as those of his father who was forced to give him life so he'd have an early death. No, not that sort of stuff. No, what suits next is the triumphal pastoral. This is where Hamlet, full grown and in the flush of early manhood – which is the only manhood he'll get – is found in a field with a famous chef. The weather is great. There are lots of variables: the landscape may be fell or fen; there can be trees – anything but species like the stone pine or the cypress which are suggestive of parched rather than of lush ground; houses are OK so long as they're yeoman vernacular or grand, and farm buildings have got to be old ones – no metal sheds no matter how gleamy they may be, no silage towers. Cars are Range Rover, not greedy farmer Volvos and Mercs parked in front of rancho bungalows. There can be a farmer provided he's got outdoorsy clothes. The chef is got up for the country too, and of course what he's doing is inspecting his raw materials on the hoof the way an agent of murder meets his victim before he puts out a contract. He's claiming Hamlet's life with a gingerly made pat to the flank. The next time we see Hamlet he has shrunk, he has changed shape and colour, he has stopped being a quadruped. The chef has put on new clothes, white for absolution – but anyway, it wasn't him, *he* didn't give Hamlet the old volt jolt, did he? The sun's gone in too. These suns you see were brought along and lugged in by the photographer's assistant. No landscape – everything's tempered metal now, blades and flame. Chef is making his first incision, he's a surgeon and an artist. And we only know that these lumps of amputee used to fit together to make Hamlet because we are told so.

Often we won't see Hamlet in the field; often the story begins posthumously, with no reference to the life save in terms of the sort of pasture where it was

led, maybe. And absolutely no reference to the death. Often Hamlet, who of course won't have a name – you don't give names to dark red cushions with wax spilled on them – often he'll be in a state of very quick metamorphosis, bumping through a serial Hell of mallets and blades and hot boxes and drownings.

To a point, food art – whatever the medium – is an expiation of our bad feelings about what we eat. The more noble the beast the deeper our atonement – you don't get photos of famous chefs patting potatoes, you do get photos of big time vignerons with their hands round bunches of grapes. In the leguminous, fructuous hierarchy the grape is a lord; the potato is a serf. Also, spuds aren't sexy: Bacchanalia have no use for these roots. And even if Bacchanalia had been a common genre when potatoes came to Europe they'd still have had no use for them. Grapes are different. They are forever shown in conjunction with breasts, they are a synecdoche of breasts, they are metaphorical promises of the mother's milk, vinous analogues of lactic splendour etc.

We could go on linking the gustatory to the sacramental. But though we recognize the symbolism and understand the iconography of representations of food because of Christianity's ubiquity and its impingement on our minds, we live in an age when overtly religious art is not much made. Nevertheless we can't avoid seeing its shadow cast over the secular and the utile and the fancifully decorative. But it is no more than a shadow that we see. Our increased secularity has coincided with, has perhaps even occasioned the end of the painted still life of food. And the photography that is now abundantly practised hasn't the weight of association of the painting it vainly tries to replace. It means nothing outside itself.

Loss of meaning is manifest in the death of ritual – no one says grace any more. Ritual is not a cosmetic. It is a means of transportation to sublimity and awe. Without it the multiplicity of responses to food vanishes. Food is reduced to fuel. I believe the current preoccupation with effortfully gimmicky photographs of food is an attempt to regain some sort of meaning, to invest food with a new set of non-nutritional properties. The properties I'm talking about are banally temporal ones – they're concerned with status, social placement and so on. Food has become chic, it's an OK subject. The food photography in the glossy magazines and the colour supplements and the specialist magazines is ineffably vulgar and manages to disassociate posh eating from the notions of glut and excess: it invariably shows food that is cooked to be photographed. The tyranny of the visual over the gustatory suits the English very well: the English suffer, as we all know, a collectively defective palate and a sense of embarrassment about eating well. If food can be made to look so nice, why, then it can be counted a decorative art, and to taste it must be a quasi-

aesthetic experience, quite as intellectually demanding and emotionally trying
as an interior by John Fowler or a design by Cecil Beaton.

As a result of the efforts of the food photographers who see themselves as
the heirs to Arcimboldi and Miró and god knows which minor Nip print-
makers chefs have submitted to the dictates of art direction. They make food
which is to be looked at. It is *not* sustaining. They talk about presentation, *all
the time*, believe me, they do. High cooking is not something you eat and are
thankful for, it is not celebratory of nature's fecundity. It is like a disposable and
expensive accoutrement, a prop to what we must call a lifestyle. A Rolex Oyster
that you swallow.

1986

Meat on Canvas (2)

When Claude Chabrol's film *Le Boucher* opened in this country one critic, presumably Francophobe, certainly ignorant, commented that the director sig-
nalled the titular character's capacity for evil by having him finish off his soup
by pouring a glass of wine into it and drinking the resultant broth straight from
the bowl. The facts of the matter are, of course, that Chabrol is a native of
Périgord where this practice is commonplace and that it signals no more than
the start of the meal proper – soup being considered literally hors d'œuvres.
Moreover, this practice is known as *faire chabrot* or, more rarely, *faire chabrol*:
Chabrol enjoys his little jokes and here is one on his name, no more, no less.
The lesson is clear – unless we wish to present ourselves as dunces we should
beware of ascribing particular meanings to the representation of food and
drink in cultures that we don't understand. The idea of universality is at best
dubious and in matters of the table quite inapposite; and it is especially
difficult (and presumptuous) for the British to apply their standards to other
countries for there are few other countries in which food and drink are so
peripheral to the general culture: only tea, beer, beef and fish and chips have
held anything approaching a central position in these islands in this century
and despite the evidence of gastronomic magazines they probably maintain
their paramountcy. Maybe they've been joined by burgers; maybe roast beef is
on the wane in the collective conscious as it is on the dining table – but I doubt
it, the collective conscious is a tenacious beast. It clings on to ideas even when
they are based in folk myth rather than actuality, perhaps *because* they are based

in folk myth which is set firm in the recent past and is thus easier to cope with than the fluid, elusive present. It is, *pace* L. P. Hartley and that silly film, the *present* which is a foreign country, not the past which is well mapped. The English attitude to food in different parts of the past can be discerned in the work of various painters. The attitude that was till recently prevalent (and, as I say, perhaps still is) was of Protestant distaste, of mistrust of culinary art, of the appreciation of that only half-accurately entitled phenomenon called 'good plain cooking', of self-congratulatory frugality, of xenophobia, of guarded and rare admission of the 'slap-up' treat, of – and this is fundamental – embarrassment. The meagreness of all this is amply evident in the work of a social realist such as Harold Gilman. Now, admittedly Gilman was a socialist herbivore (he lived part of his life at Letchworth during the years when that town was 'dry') and admittedly he was not a rich man, but his implicit association of anything that is edible or potable with tedium and drabness is above and beyond what might be occasioned by the circumstances of a life such as his. What I mean is that Gilman's art unwittingly distils the archetypical British attitudes I just mentioned. His lonely figures, victims of circumscribed lives led in dreary rooms, sit rueing the hand that chance has dealt them off the bottom of the pack and gaping at brown teapots and chipped mugs, or stoking themselves – they eat with no delight, they eat as though they begrudge the time taken over the whole sullying process. Gilman was not merely an illustrator but in his paintings, and those of the British realist tradition, food is no more than a prop, an indication of class status, an objective correlative. I can think of no British painter, realist or otherwise, who has a) described the essence, the quiddity of food or b) has done anything transcendent with it as subject matter; and it's not just painting, there is little in British art of any sort which treats gastronomy seriously. The gluttonscapes of a film such as *Tom Jones* certainly don't; the pretentious restaurant as location is simply invertedly Gilmanesque; the tripe and cowheel stuff in *Walter Greenwood* is local colour. Another Lancastrian, Anthony Burgess, is however unencumbered by our national dread of the stomach and tongue: that he is a Catholic and an expatriate no doubt have much to do with it – in his 1966 novel *Tremor of Intent* the sensual equation between eating and making love is properly made, that's to say it is made in earnest and without sniggering. Perhaps no one but a Catholic, or a product of Catholicism (which is probably the same) can do this. The Eucharist is ritual cannibalism, food and wine are sacred . . . it is no coincidence that Protestant countries are the ones that eat badly. Look at a painting by Gilman's contemporary, Picasso. *Blind Man's Meal* (1903, 'blue period') is an explicit title which does not begin to hint at the rawness and potency of the composition it's attached to. It is, certainly, socially acute in that

it is graphically demonstrative of the wretchedness that accrues from blind-
ness, indigence and malnourishment – but so is, say, *Hamlet* a socially acute
play: the important point is that Picasso's painting goes beyond the socially and
economically illustrative into a realm of pain and awe and sanctity. It is about
very primitive things. It is stripped down. It concerns itself with elemental
senses – touch, sight, taste – by its concentration on lack and absence. Its
depictions of hunger and thirst say more about the importance of nourishment than any number of groaning tables. The painting possesses a beady
candour and unsentimental pathos. Now, it may not be 'fair' to invoke such a
master as Picasso, especially not the Picasso of that epoch when he was at the
height of his powers. But I am citing him not because he was a supremely
gifted maker of paintings but because he was an exemplar of an artistic
tradition – I'm talking here about subject and attitude to subject – which
mirrors the centrality that food and the table have in the cultures which
nurture that tradition. (No doubt the critic who mistook Chabrol's jest for an
essay in character-delineation would reckon the blind man a bit of a no-good
because he has no knife, no fork and clearly eats bread without buttering it: that
would be another misreading.) The line to which *Blind Man's Meal* and *The Frugal
Repast* and Picasso's numerous kindred works of the first half-decade of this
century belong is one that treats food with reverence and humility, as something hard-earned, as something whose source is in the earth and in creatures.
The link between what is on the plate and that food's fructuous life or its days
on the hoof, that link is always there. Just as there is a willingness on the part
of many southern European artists to treat food 'head on', so are they bereft
of the squeamishness which informs both the Protestant kitchen and
northern foodscapes. The truth is that many still lives are still deaths – the
pheasant that flew into a firing squad, the salmon that got a spike through its
lower lip, the thigh of the bull whose last sight of daylight was outside an
abattoir; *nature mort* is the apter term, it isn't euphemistic, it isn't trying to hide
something. What the English locution hides, because it occludes the matter of
its subjects' demise, is the fact that food wasn't always food. The pheasant was
a rather stupid bird leading a blameless life in that wood or this, the salmon was
a lovely tyro dolphin, leaping and glinting like pearl, and the bull was something
to avoid, a bellowing danger. You can bet they never guessed the fate that
would befall them. A still life of yet to be cooked stuff mediates between field
and table, between river and stove; it captures a moment in the transforma-
tional process called cooking, the process that makes bull beef. The contrary
pole to that of squeamishness is the sadistic carnagescape of an artist such as
François Bonvin who clearly revelled in the suffering inflicted on animals on
the point of being animals no more and becoming food; this man loved blood,

or at least he loved to paint it. We don't need to go so far as he did. But the southern tradition is salutary when it's more moderate: it joins man to the world by reminding him that he is, like it or not, part of a great and organic system. What he eats, what he lives on, actually comes from somewhere. The English paradox is that we have for years eaten poorly while taking food for granted. This self-congratulatory defeatism is, thankfully, on the wane. But it won't have had its day till food attains a central position in the collective conscious, a position which will be confirmed when unacknowledged legislators of one kind and another start coming to terms with food as a subject worthy for serious art – n.b. *serious*.

1987

HSIANG JU LIN AND TSUIFENG LIN

Chinese Gastronomy

If something is not right, this is due to carelessness, and it is the cook's fault. If something is good, say why, and when it is bad, pick out its faults. If one does not keep the cook in line, he becomes insolent. Before the food comes, send word down that the food tomorrow must be better.

YUAN MEI

THE COOK AS GASTRONOME

The Chinese cuisine is a world in itself. We have attempted the difficult task of showing what it is like. We have tried to show by example and explanation where the artist, the peasant, the food snob and the gourmet made their contributions, and so made it a thing of many parts. Its qualities are not readily summed up by generalizations: they are learnt one by one.

Why do we eat? In order to pursue the flavour of things. The word *gastronomy* now suggests a sensual indulgence, but the roots of the word mean *stomach* and *rule* – rules for the stomach. The art of eating has always been a disciplined habit. To eat well requires a sense of fitness (taste) and an adventurous spirit. Like good explorers, we must know when we have found something, then return to it, charting the approaches, so that it will be known to others. In this joyous adventure each person could travel alone, but the best team is made up of the gastronome and his cook. We have noted elsewhere in this book that the cuisine did not come into its own until the critics became articulate. They found fault with the food. They developed ideas and harassed their cooks. The gastronomes contributed their sense of form to the cuisine. Their prompting made the cooks masters of flavour and texture.

We had to learn how to eat before we could learn how to cook, and for this reason we have treated the arts of eating and cooking as a single subject, each supporting the other. We have emphasized the perfectly definite taste, texture and look of each dish, the joint creation of cook and gourmet, in order that the subtle judgments of the intelligent cook may be brought into play.

CHARACTER OF THE CUISINE

Chinese cuisine is known to some only by its curiosities, but it actually differs from Western cuisine in a number of fundamental aspects. Its peculiar character comes from the realization that cooking is a form of artifice. This attitude accounts for its triumphs, its faults and its sophistications. Because of the trickery involved, the psychology of eating is different. The criteria of excellence in cuisine are somewhat different and are discussed as a lesson in Chinese. The pursuit of flavour has resulted more often in the blending of flavours, sometimes successful, often mismatched. Chinese cuisine is uniquely distinguished by textural variation, which has also led to the use of parts. And it is one of the few cuisines in which some kinds of fat are treated as delicacies.

Cooking is a form of artifice, because the taste of food is both good and bad. Good taste cannot be achieved unless one knows precisely what is bad about each ingredient, and proceeds to correct it. The curious, omnivorous cook knows that the taste of raw fruit is quite delicious and cannot be improved upon. Raw fish is insipid, raw chicken metallic, raw beef is palatable but for the rank flavour of blood. It is pointless to talk about the natural taste of these things, as many people like to do. We take it to mean the characteristic flavour of each thing, which is mainly in the fat and in the juices. This is brought out by artifice and appreciated as the *hsien* and *hsiang*, the flavour and aroma. They are to food what soul is to man. Cooking is essentially the capturing of these qualities, gastronomy the appreciation of them. *Hsien* and *hsiang* are not associated with any form of cooking. Here is the pivotal point where Chinese cuisine swings away from the others and takes off on its own. Note that Western pastry-making is a departure from the natural form and perhaps the 'natural taste' of food. The *pâtissier* works only with butter, eggs, flour and sugar. But because he does not feel compelled to preserve the natural form, and present the flavour of each ingredient individually, he is often able to evolve something better. The palate can then perceive the taste of the ingredients interlocked in his inventions. The Chinese cook has done the same for food in general. (But Chinese sweet pastry is deplorably heavy and monotonous, often made up of glutinous rice, fat pork and sweet bean paste.) One discerns the *hsien* and *hsiang* of each ingredient in dishes of novel texture and appearance, these qualities having been brought out by artifice.

Criteria of Excellence

The unique qualities of the cuisine are contained in some almost untranslatable words. The words *hsien*, *hsiang*, *nung* and *yu-er-pu-ni* are the criteria of excellence in flavour. 'Flavours must be rich and robust, never oily, or they must be delicate and fresh without being too thin. A flavour which is *nung* means that the essences are concentrated and the scum has been removed. Those who like greasy food might just as well dine on lard. When some dish is *hsien*, its true flavour is present. Not the least particle of error can be tolerated or you will have missed the mark' (Yuan Mei).

Hsien (鮮) Sweet natural flavour. *Usage*: to describe the delicate taste of fat pork, or the taste of butter; the taste of fresh fish, bamboo and prawns (shrimps). It may be simulated by a combination of seasonings, principally sugar. In an exceptional case, the *hsien* of fish is simulated by a mixture of seasonings and pork (Mock Fish.)

Hsiang (香) Characteristic fragrance; aroma. *Usage*: applied to those dishes which can give pleasure by their smell as well as their taste; characteristic fragrance of chicken fat, of roasted meats, of mushrooms, of sautéed onions, etc. *Hsiang* is almost impossible to duplicate by artifice, for it depends mainly on the oils present in each ingredient.

Nung (濃) Rich, heady, concentrated. *Usage*: in contrast to *hsien*, which must always appear natural and effortless, dishes which are *nung* are strongly flavoured with meat essences or spices. Applied to richly aromatic food (Glazed Duck); to Cream Stock; composed of three kinds of meat. *Nung* is not always used in a complimentary sense: it may mean too rich, like overripe cheese.

Yu-er-pu-ni (油 而 不 膩) To taste of fat without being oily. *Usage*: applicable to the yolks of preserved eggs, to roe, to properly cooked belly pork. Compare the taste of these: caviare, cold fresh unsalted (sweet) butter or avocado. This phrase occurs frequently because of the importance of solid fat in the cuisine. Always used as a compliment.

The two following words describe texture. They are interesting because cooks try to achieve *tsuei* and *nun* textures with foods that do not naturally have them.

Tsuei (脆) Crisp, crunchy. A texture often brought out or concocted. *Usage*: applicable to dipped and sautéed snails, tripe, squid, Dipped Snails, Blanched Kidneys, prawns (Rule for Prawns) and Fish Balls; pork crackling, roasted skin of fowl (Peking Duck).

Nun (嫩) Soft and tender; non-fibrous. A somewhat resilient texture brought out by skilful cooking, to be distinguished from another word *ruan* (軟) meaning soft and loose-textured. *Usage*: applied to texture of a perfect soft-boiled egg, Velvet Chicken, texture of *quenelles de brochet*.

These words are by no means sufficient to describe the range of flavours and textures, but they are most important and interesting words which have provoked a lot of thought. They embody qualities aimed at in cooking. The most famous dishes of Chinese cuisine combine several of these qualities. The skin of Peking duck is fragrant, crisp and rich without being oily (*hsiang, tsuei, yu-er-pu-ni*). Fish balls are at once fresh, crisp and tender (*hsien, tsuei* and *nun*). The combination of these qualities in a single dish suggests the complexity of classic Chinese cuisine. Note how no one quality contradicts any other.

Blending of Flavours

Plain flavours. The plain flavour appears simple because all the seasonings blended into it are undetectable. Cooks are satisfied when people appreciate the 'natural' fragrance and taste of the food, unaware of the seasoning that has gone into it. They keep perfectly quiet about the amount of art that went into bringing out the 'natural' taste. The fragrance and taste (*hsiang, hsien*) of many foods are brought out by the use of supporting ingredients which should merge into a single flavour. It was once suggested that bamboo be sautéed with marbled pork to extract its *hsien* juices, and then the pork be discarded before serving. This is an extreme case to illustrate the importance of undetected seasoning.

Once supporting ingredients have done their job, they should be removed from view. If wine or vinegar is added, it can be evaporated away. If ginger and spring onions (scallions) are included, it is better to remove them before serving the dish. Light soy sauce should be used when seasoning prawns (shrimps) or vegetables. Sugar must not be detected in grains, nor should salt, unless it is served in a separate dish. Things are served either with or without sauce. Make it very obvious which you are doing.

Complementary flavours. Chinese cooking has been called 'the marriage of flavours'. This is very apt, for the individual ingredients should preserve their identity while complementing each other. Unlike the subtle alterations of flavour discussed above, the second type of blending depends on showing up the flavours of individual ingredients by contrasting them with similar or totally different ingredients. The delicate taste of bird's nest is matched with very finely chopped winter melon (blending of similar flavours) or with minced ham (matching of contrasting flavours). This is comparable to matching several shades of white to each other, or contrasting black with white. The combination of cheese with other ingredients in French cooking comes closest to this idea of mutual support.

Variation of Texture

The refinement of the cuisine is most obvious in its control of texture. Classic cuisine stresses the creation of crisp or tender textures, demanding of the cook a certain virtuosity. Fundamentally, textural variation is an effort to improve upon nature. For example, every piece of meat is encased in invisible membranes, with sinewy connections and silky ligaments. Even after all these substances have been cleared away, the texture of meat remains a problem. The beginner knows well that it is difficult to keep meat tender while cooking it. Any error will make the meat fibrous and dry and all the tricks used in cooking it have the common aim of keeping it tender.

Variation of texture runs like a minor theme throughout the whole of Chinese gastronomy. At the most sophisticated tables it became an end in itself. It led to the search for texture-foods, things that have interesting textures but no taste. Today, there is no banquet without bird's nest or shark's fins, both texture-foods. These ingredients brought on yet another development in the cuisine. The cook was confronted with the problem of creating flavours for things which had no flavour in themselves. In Chinese cooking at its most sophisticated, substances with texture but no flavour were wedded to stocks of great flavour but no substance.

Use of Parts

The search for new flavours and textures led naturally to the use of parts. This was carried to an extreme. People distinguished between the cheeks of the fish, its soft underbelly, the jelly-like tissue at the base of the dorsal fins. Country-style cooking was by necessity a cooking of parts, quite aside from the art of eating. The inherent textural variation of innards is interesting to gourmets. Chinese tongues and teeth are perhaps rather unusual. Many people can split a watermelon seed, extract the meat and carry on a rapid conversation at the same time, pausing only to expel the shell. Others, with a little practice, are able to tie one or two knots in a cherry stem with tongue and teeth. The Chinese tongue is a sensitive thing. So the grainy quality of liver, the unctuous intestine, the fibrous gizzard, the spongy maw and crunchy tripe all stand apart from each other, to be appreciated as delicacies, each with its unique texture.

The use of parts is also favoured by the cook, who knows that the white meat of chicken is done earlier than the dark, and that the wings must be stewed, the legs fried, the skin roasted or fried, the breast meat sautéed or minced. Each part must be cooked differently to bring out the best, and by separating the parts one can bring out the best in each.

Use of Fat

Fat is a delicacy. Despite the term *yu-er-pu-ni* (to taste of fat without being oily), which belongs to gastronomy more than to common taste, all oil is considered good. Pork fat can be made to soak up juices, chicken and duck fat to flavour vegetables. Sesame oil is used to suppress the fishy taste of seafood, to fry sweets and to flavour food. Sesame, peanut and vegetable oils are used in vegetarian cooking. The flavour of meat and fish is in the fat. Hence, the cooking of fat as such has developed in step with the techniques for cooking meat. The use of fat is particularly appreciated when the main substance is rice or wheat. The lean food of peasants was enriched by fat. 'The fat in meat, fish, ducks and chicken must be kept in the meat and not allowed to run out, else the flavour is all in the juices' (Yuan Mei).

KITCHEN ARTS

A number of methods for producing those particular tastes and textures we have just discussed are summarized [elsewhere in the book]. These are nothing but tricks of the cuisine, but without them the most patient and energetic cook would be misdirecting his efforts towards achieving the best. On the other hand, if he only knew these techniques but had no taste, the result would be equally sad. The application of each of these methods is limited to certain kinds of ingredients, as indicated [elsewhere in the book]. It would be unwise to use some of these rather drastic procedures on unspecified ingredients . . .

1969

PERMISSIONS
ACKNOWLEDGEMENTS

The editor and publishers gratefully acknowledge permission to use copyright material in this book as follows:

Nelson Algren: to University of Iowa Press for an extract from *America Eats* (1992)

Colman Andrews: to Lowenstein Associates Inc. on behalf of the author for an extract from *Everything on the Table* (Bantam). Copyright © 1992

Edward Behr: to Grove/Atlantic Inc. for extracts from *The Artful Eater*. Copyright © 1992 by Edward Behr

Ludwig Bemelmans: to David R. Godine Publishers Inc. for extracts from *La Bonne Table*. Copyright © 1964 by Madeleine Bemelmans and Barbara Bemelmans

Lesley Blanch: to The Peters, Fraser & Dunlop Group Ltd for extracts from *From Wilder Shores* (John Murray, 1989)

Keith Botsford: to Newspaper Publishing Plc for 'Something So Deliciously Corrupt About Them' from the *Independent* (25 February 1995)

Elias Canetti: to Marion Boyars Publishers Ltd for an extract from *The Voices of Marrakesh*, translated by J. A. Underwood (Marion Boyars, 1978). Copyright © 1967, 1982 by Elias Canetti

Robert Farrar Capon: to the author for an extract from *The Supper of the Lamb* (Pocket Books, 1970)

Samuel Chamberlain: to David R. Godine Publishers Inc. for an extract from *Clementine in the Kitchen*. Copyright © 1988 by Nercisse Chamberlain and Stephanie Chamberlain

Quentin Crewe and John Brunton: to Aitken & Stone Ltd for an extract from *Foods from France* (Ebury Press, 1993). Copyright © 1993 by Quentin Crewe and John Brunton

Elizabeth David: to the Estate of Elizabeth David for extracts from *An Omelette and a Glass of Wine* (Penguin, 1986)

Edouard de Pomiane: to Faber & Faber Ltd for an extract from *Cooling with Pomiane* (Serif, 1993)

Norman Douglas: to The Society of Authors as the literary representative of the Estate of Norman Douglas for extracts from *Venus in the Kitchen* (William Heinemann, 1952)

M. F. K. Fisher: to Alfred A. Knopf Inc. for extracts from *As They Were* (Vintage Books, 1983). Copyright © 1982 by M. F. K. Fisher

Patience Gray: to Prospect Books for extracts from *Honey from a Weed*. Copyright text © 1986 by Patience Gray and copyright illustrations © 1986 by Corinna Sargood

Jane Grigson: to David Higham Associates Ltd for an extract from *Food with the Famous* (Grub Street, 1979). Copyright © 1979 by Jane Grigson

Dorothy Hartley: to Sheil Land Associates Ltd for an extract from *Food in England* (Macdonald, 1954). Copyright © 1954 by Dorothy Hartley

Robert Irwin: to the author and *The Times Literary Supplement* for 'In the Caliph's Kitchen' (23 September 1994). Copyright © Robert Irwin/*Times Literary Supplement*, 1994

Barbara Kafka: to the author for 'Tempest in a Samovar' from *Antaeus*, Spring 1992. Copyright © 1992 by Barbara Kafka

Hsiang Ju Lin and Tsuifeng Lin: to The K. S. Giniger Company Inc. for an extract from *The Art of Chinese Cuisine* (originally published as *Chinese Gastronomy* by Charles E. Tuttle Company, Boston and Tokyo. Copyright © 1969 by The K. S. Giniger Company Inc., New York

Harold McGee: to HarperCollins Ltd for extracts from *The Curious Cook* (HarperCollins, 1992). Copyright © 1990 by Harold McGee

Fay Maschler: to the author for 'Sole Food' from *Punch* (11 October 1978)

Jonathan Meades: to The Peters, Fraser & Dunlop Group Ltd for extracts from *Peter Knows What Dick Likes* (Grafton Books, 1989). Copyright © 1989 by Jonathan Meades

Sidney W. Mintz: to Viking Penguin, a division of Penguin Books USA Inc. for an extract from *Sweetness and Power*. Copyright © 1985 by Sidney W. Mintz

Richard Olney: to Penguin Books Ltd for an extract from *Simple French Food* (1983). Copyright © 1974 by Richard Olney

George Orwell: to A. M. Heath and Company Ltd and Harcourt Brace & Company for extracts from *Down and Out in Paris and London* (Penguin, 1940). Copyright © by The Estate of the late Sonia Brownell Orwell and Martin Secker & Warburg Ltd

S. J. Perelman: to Harold Ober Associates for an extract from *The Most of S. J. Perelman* (Mandarin, 1992). Copyright © 1944 by S. J. Perelman. Copyright renewed 1972 by S. J. Perelman

Charles Perry: to the author for 'Medieval Near Eastern Rotted Condiments' from *In Taste: Proceedings of the Oxford Symposium of Food and Cookery* (1987), published by Prospect Books (1988)

Claudia Roden: to David Higham Associates Ltd for extracts from *A New Book of Middle Eastern Food* (Viking, 1985). Copyright © 1968, 1985 by Claudia Roden

Raymond Sokolov: to *Natural History* for 'One Man's Meat is Another Person (October 1975) and 'High Torte' (November 1976). Copyright © 1975, 1976 by American Museum of Natural History.

Jeffrey Steingarten: to the author for 'Jeffrey Steingarten goes on a year long quest for the primal bread . . . ' (*Vogue*, November 1990)

Reay Tannahill: to Penguin Books Ltd for extracts from *Food in History* (1988). Copyright © 1973, 1988 by Reay Tannahill

Calvin Trillin: to Lescher & Lescher Ltd, Authors Representatives, for an extract from *Third Helpings* (Penguin, 1984). Copyright © 1983 by Calvin Trillin

James Villas: to the author and his agent, Robin Straus Agency Inc. for extracts from *Villas at Table: A Passion for Food and Drink* (Harper & Row, 1988). Copyright © 1988 by James Villas

Margaret Visser: to Grove/Atlantic Inc. and HarperCollins (Canada) Publishers Ltd for an extract from *The Rituals of Dinner: The Origins, Evolution, Eccentricities, and Meaning of Table Manners* (Grove Weidenfeld/HarperCollins, 1991). Copyright © 1991 by Margaret Visser

Joseph Wechsberg: to John Hawkins & Associates Inc. for extracts from *Blue Trout and Black Truffles* (Victor Gollancz, 1953). Copyright © 1953 by Joseph Wechsberg and extracts from *Dining at the Pavilion* (Weidenfeld & Nicolson, 1963). Copyright © 1976 by Joseph Wechsberg

Every effort has been made to contact all copyright holders. The publishers would be grateful to be notified of any additions that should be incorporated in the next edition of this volume.

INDEX